DREAM SAGA

Volume 2

by
Megumi
Tachikawa

TOKYOPOP®

HAMBURG // LONDON // LOS ANGELES // TOKYO

Dream Saga Vol. 2
Created by Megumi Tachikawa

Translation - Emi Onishiu
English Adaptation - Solina Wong
Associate Editor - Hope Donovan
Retouch and Lettering - Junemoon Studio
Production Artist - Vicente Rivera, Jr.
Cover Design - Anna Kernbaum

Editor - Julie Taylor
Digital Imaging Manager - Chris Buford
Pre-Press Manager - Antonio DePietro
Production Managers - Jennifer Miller and Mutsumi Miyazaki
Art Director - Matt Alford
Managing Editor - Jill Freshney
VP of Production - Ron Klamert
President and C.O.O. - John Parker
Publisher and C.E.O. - Stuart Levy

A  Manga

TOKYOPOP Inc.
5900 Wilshire Blvd. Suite 2000
Los Angeles, CA 90036

E-mail: info@TOKYOPOP.com
Come visit us online at www.TOKYOPOP.com

ISBN: 1-59182-775-2

First TOKYOPOP printing: October 2004
10 9 8 7 6 5 4 3 2 1
Printed in the USA

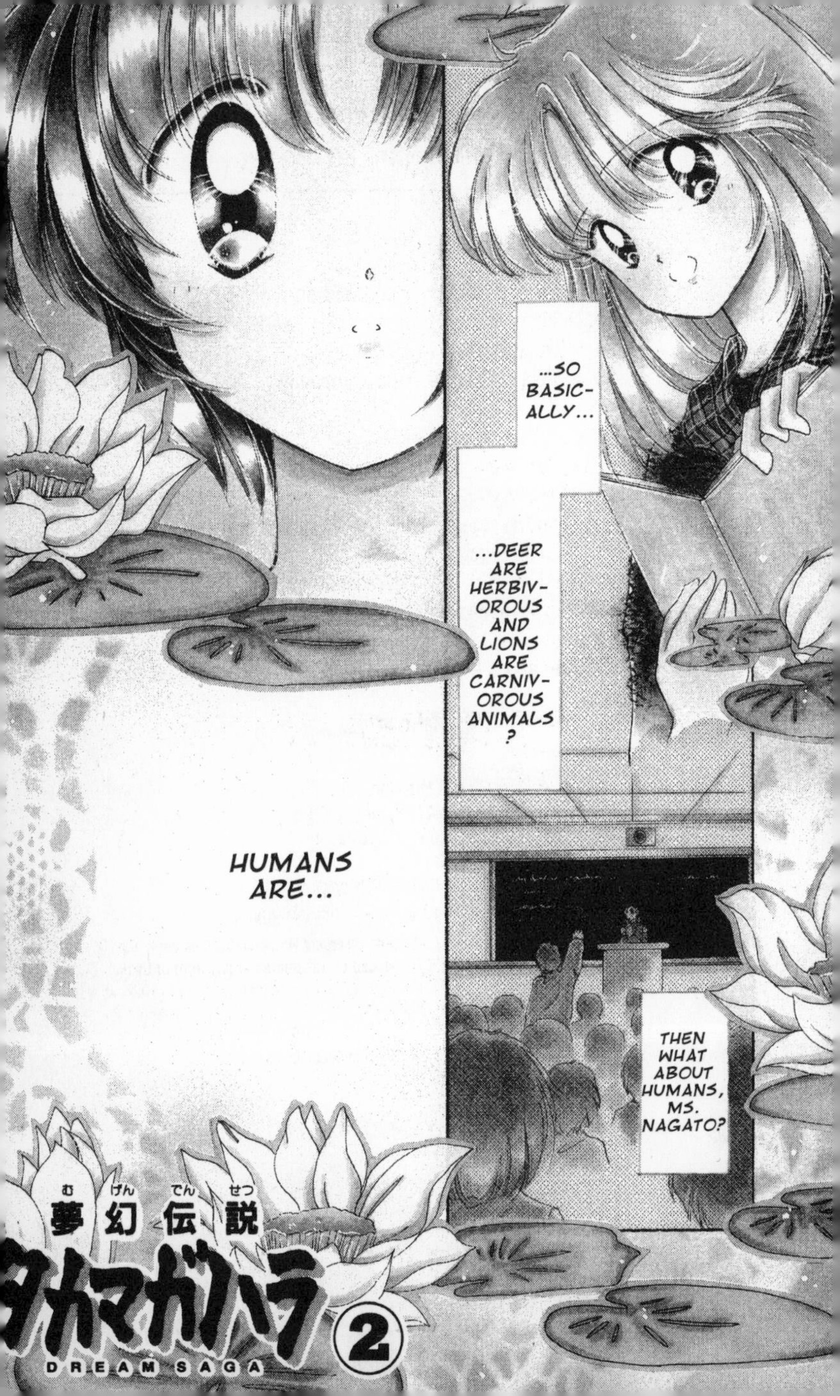
...SO BASICALLY...
...DEER ARE HERBIVOROUS AND LIONS ARE CARNIVOROUS ANIMALS?
THEN WHAT ABOUT HUMANS, MS. NAGATO?
HUMANS ARE...
夢幻伝説
2
DREAM SAGA

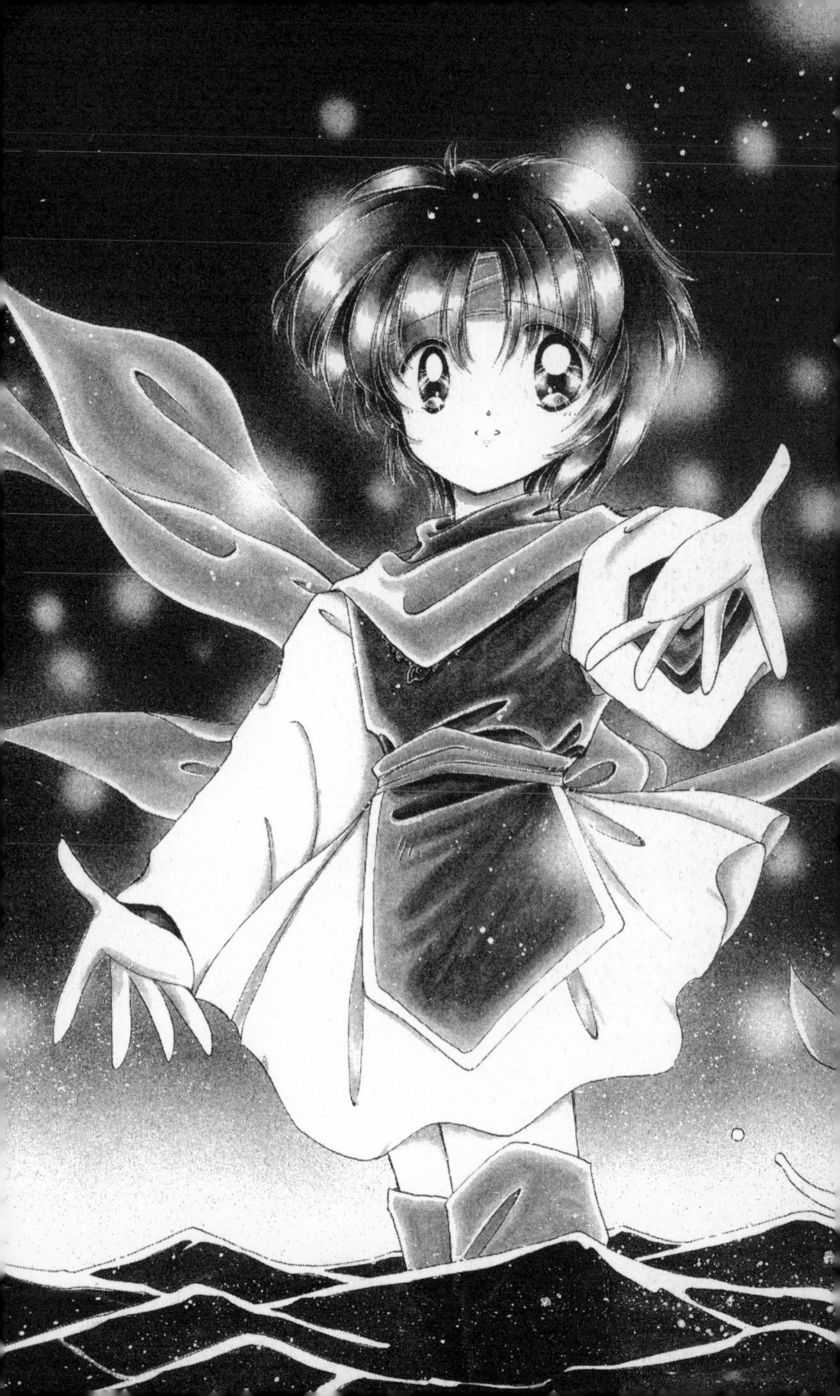

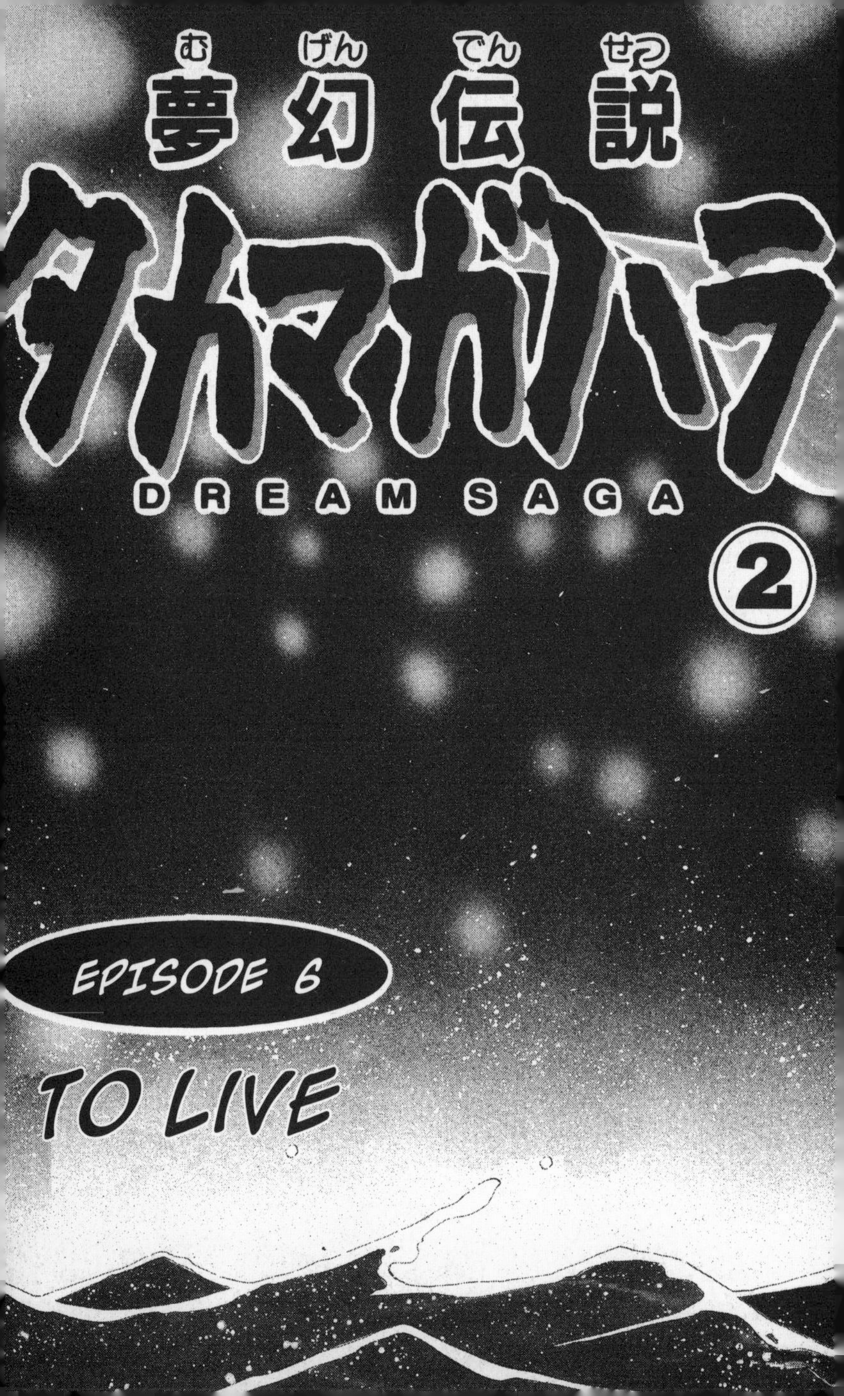

むげんでんせつ
夢幻伝説
タカマガハラ
DREAM SAGA
2
EPISODE 6
TO LIVE

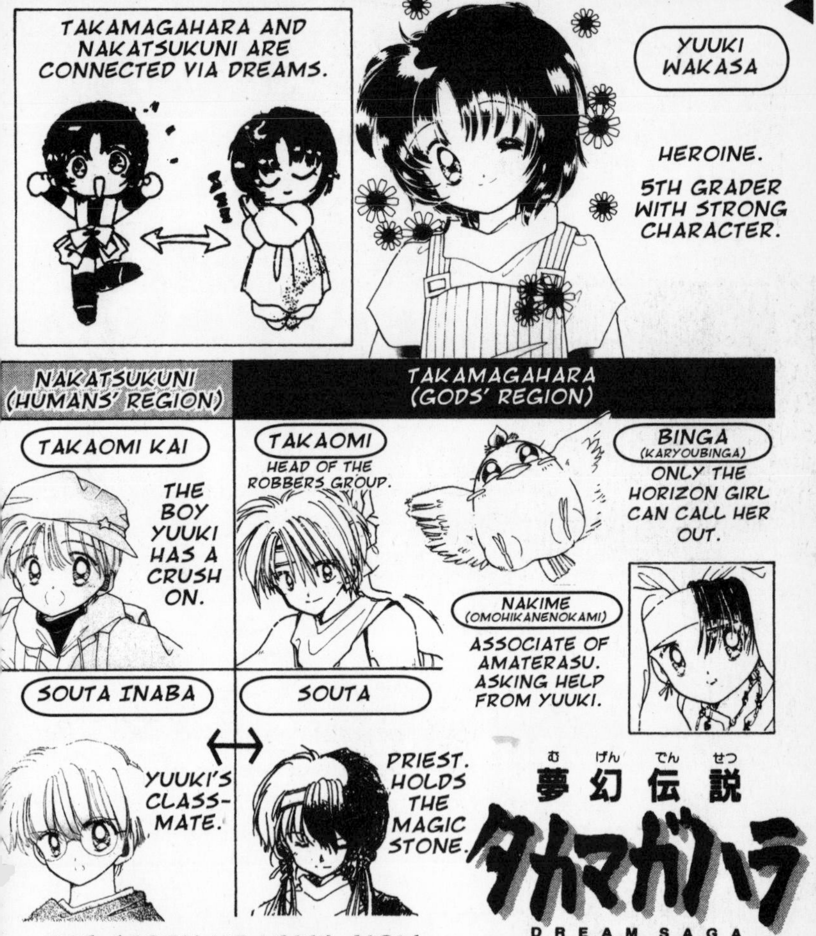
YUUKI WAKASA
HEROINE.
5TH GRADER WITH STRONG CHARACTER.
TAKAMAGAHARA AND NAKATSUKUNI ARE CONNECTED VIA DREAMS.
TAKAMAGAHARA (GODS' REGION)
NAKATSUKUNI (HUMANS' REGION)
BINGA (KARYOUBINGA)
ONLY THE HORIZON GIRL CAN CALL HER OUT.
TAKAOMI
HEAD OF THE ROBBERS GROUP.
TAKAOMI KAI
THE BOY YUUKI HAS A CRUSH ON.
NAKIME (OMOHIKANENOKAMI)
ASSOCIATE OF AMATERASU. ASKING HELP FROM YUUKI.
SOUTA
PRIEST. HOLDS THE MAGIC STONE.
SOUTA INABA
YUUKI'S CLASS-MATE.
夢幻伝説
タカマガハラ
DREAM SAGA

THE STORY UP UNTIL NOW:
A STONE FELL FROM THE SKY AND WAS GIVEN TO YUUKI. THEN A WOMAN IN A MIRROR TOLD YUUKI, "FIND THE FOUR AMATSUKAMI WHO HOLD THE MAGIC STONES AND SAVE AMATERASU." TAKAMAGAHARA (THE SPIRITUAL WORLD) AND NAKATSUKUNI (THE HUMAN WORLD) ARE CONNECTED THROUGH DREAMS. THE SUN WILL DISAPPEAR FROM BOTH WORLDS UNLESS THE LEGENDARY HORIZON GIRL, YUUKI, SAVES AMATERASU. YUUKI MEETS HER CLASSMATE SOUTA IN TAKAMAGAHARA AND TRAVELS WITH BINGA, SOUTA, AND TAKAOMI TO FIND THE OTHER PEOPLE WHO POSSESS THE MAGIC STONES. YUUKI SOON RUNS INTO A POACHER. THE TENSION MOUNTS WHEN SOMEONE ATTACKS TAKAOMI!

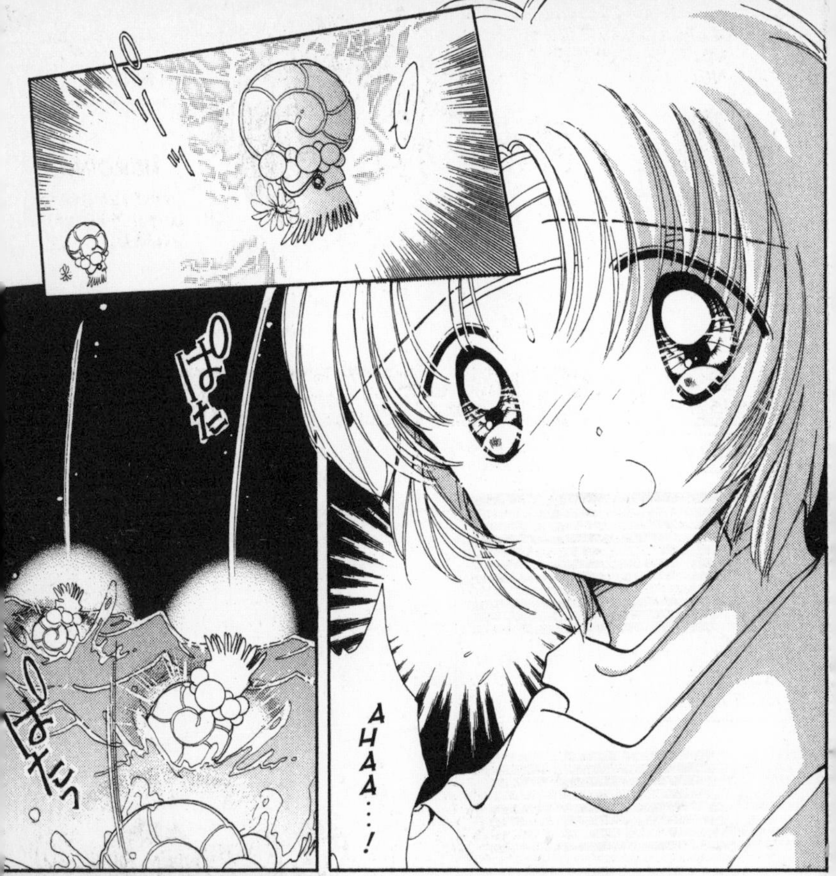
パーーッ
!
AHAAA...!
ぽた
ぽたっ

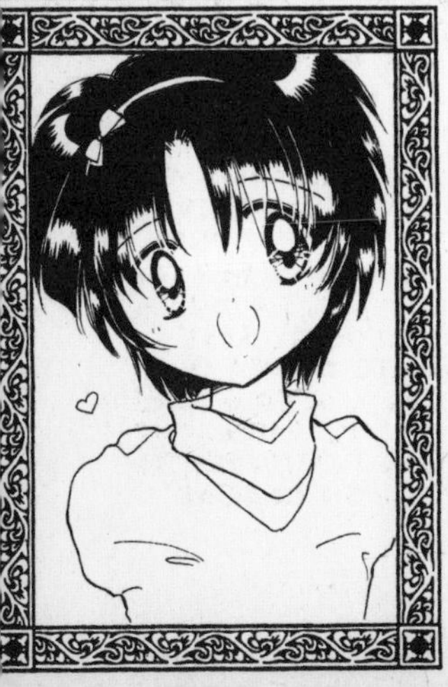

Hello! Megumi Tachikawa here.

Welcome to Dream Saga, Vol. 2. It seems like the stor is getting overpopulated with boys, but please be patien more girls will come out shortly. As always, I would like to answer questions I received from you asking about what is going on with my life. I hope you will all enjoy it. Enjoy the adventure with Yuuki in the Takamagahara.

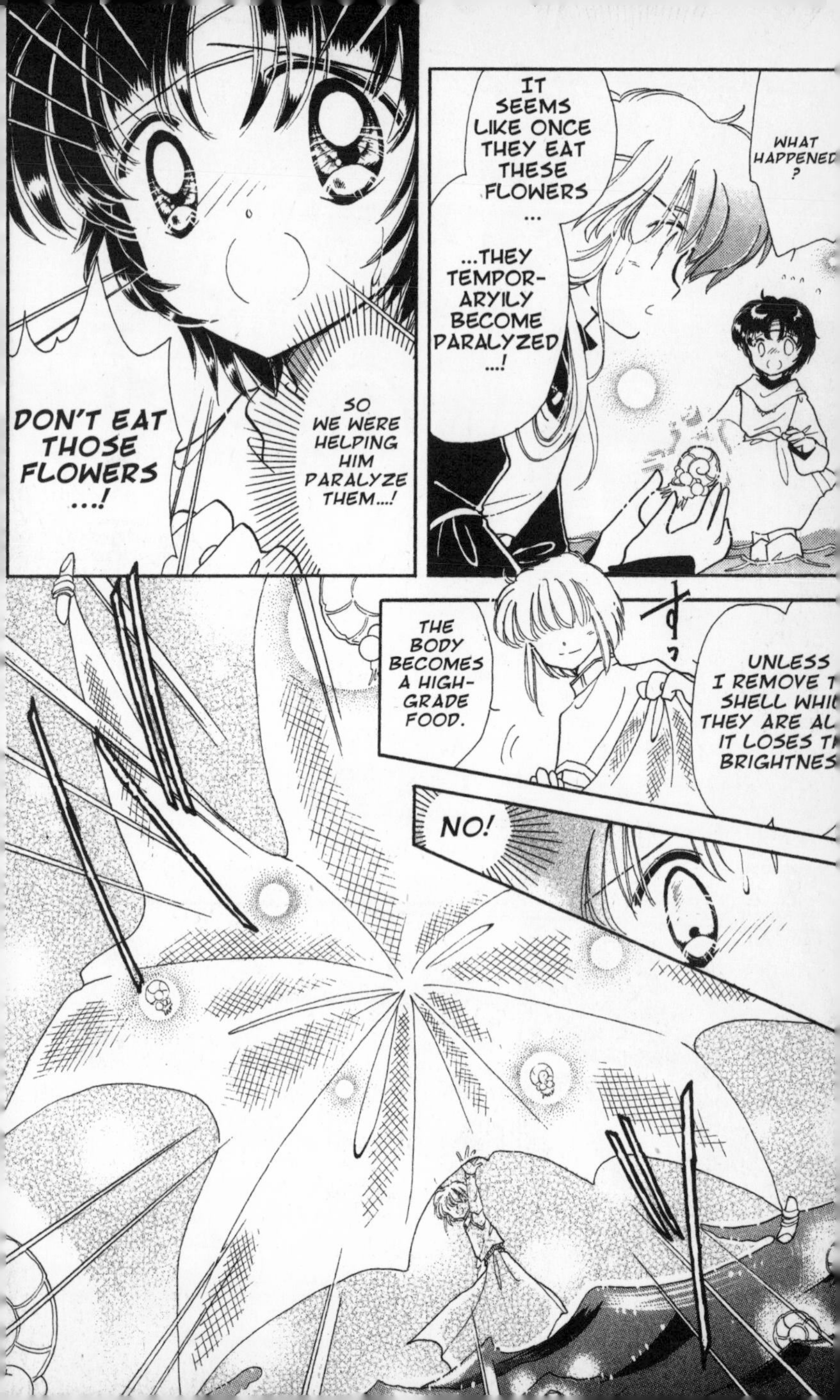
WHAT HAPPENED ?
IT SEEMS LIKE ONCE THEY EAT THESE FLOWERS ...
...THEY TEMPORARYILY BECOME PARALYZED ...!
SO WE WERE HELPING HIM PARALYZE THEM...!
DON'T EAT THOSE FLOWERS ...!
UNLESS I REMOVE T SHELL WHIC THEY ARE AL IT LOSES TH BRIGHTNES
すっ
THE BODY BECOMES A HIGH-GRADE FOOD.
NO!

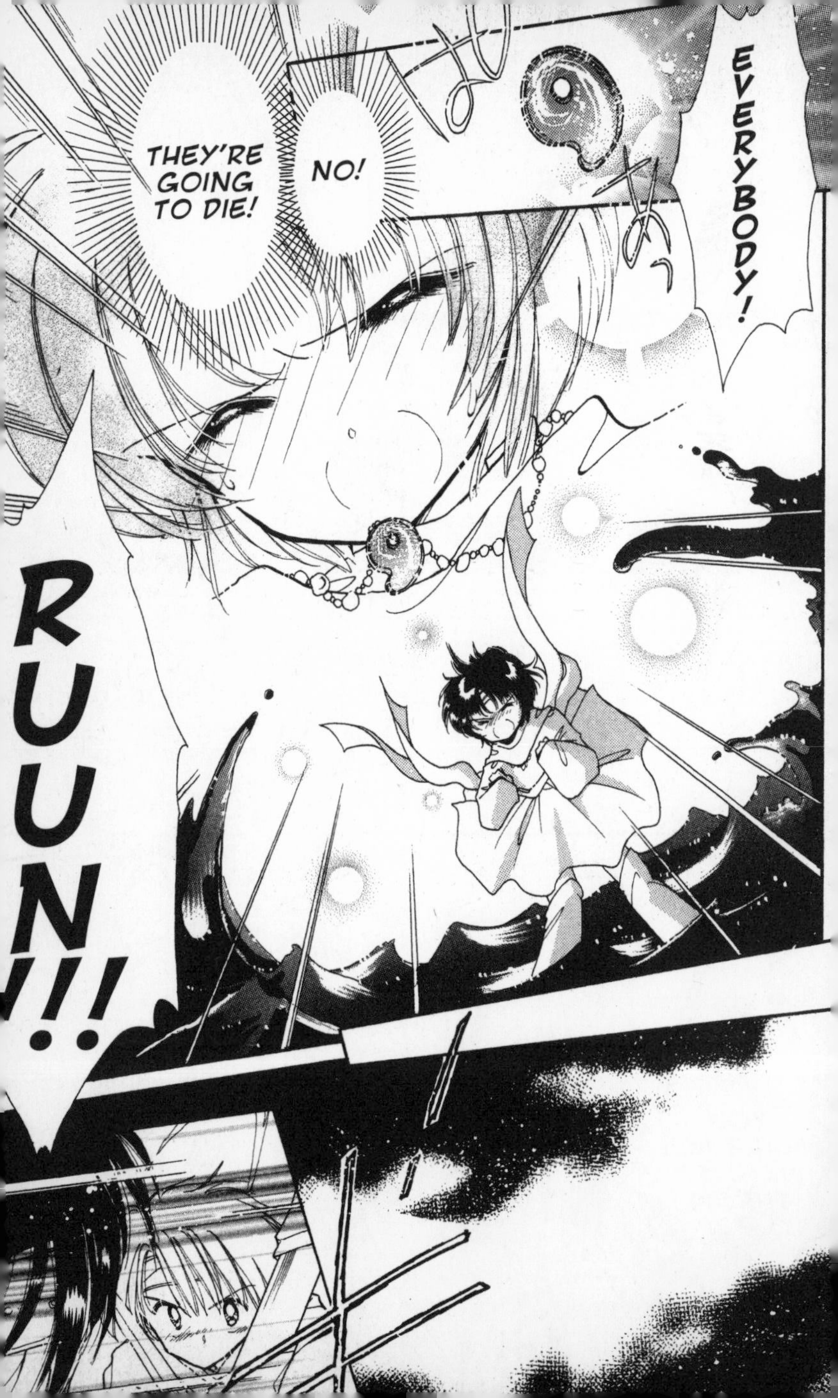
EVERYBODY!
NO!
THEY'RE GOING TO DIE!
RUUN!!

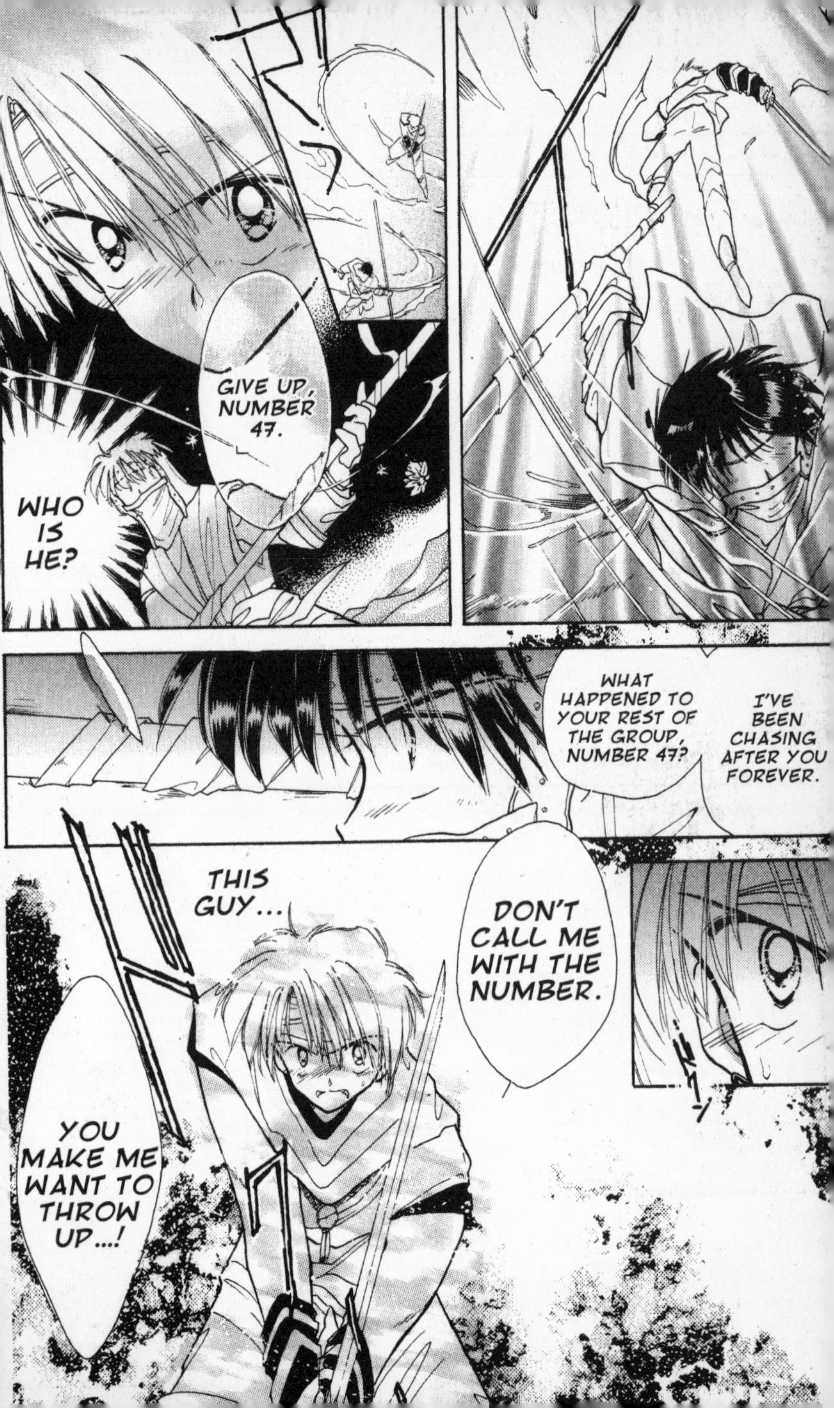
GIVE UP, NUMBER 47.
WHO IS HE?
I'VE BEEN CHASING AFTER YOU FOREVER.
WHAT HAPPENED TO YOUR REST OF THE GROUP, NUMBER 47?
DON'T CALL ME WITH THE NUMBER.
THIS GUY...
YOU MAKE ME WANT TO THROW UP...!

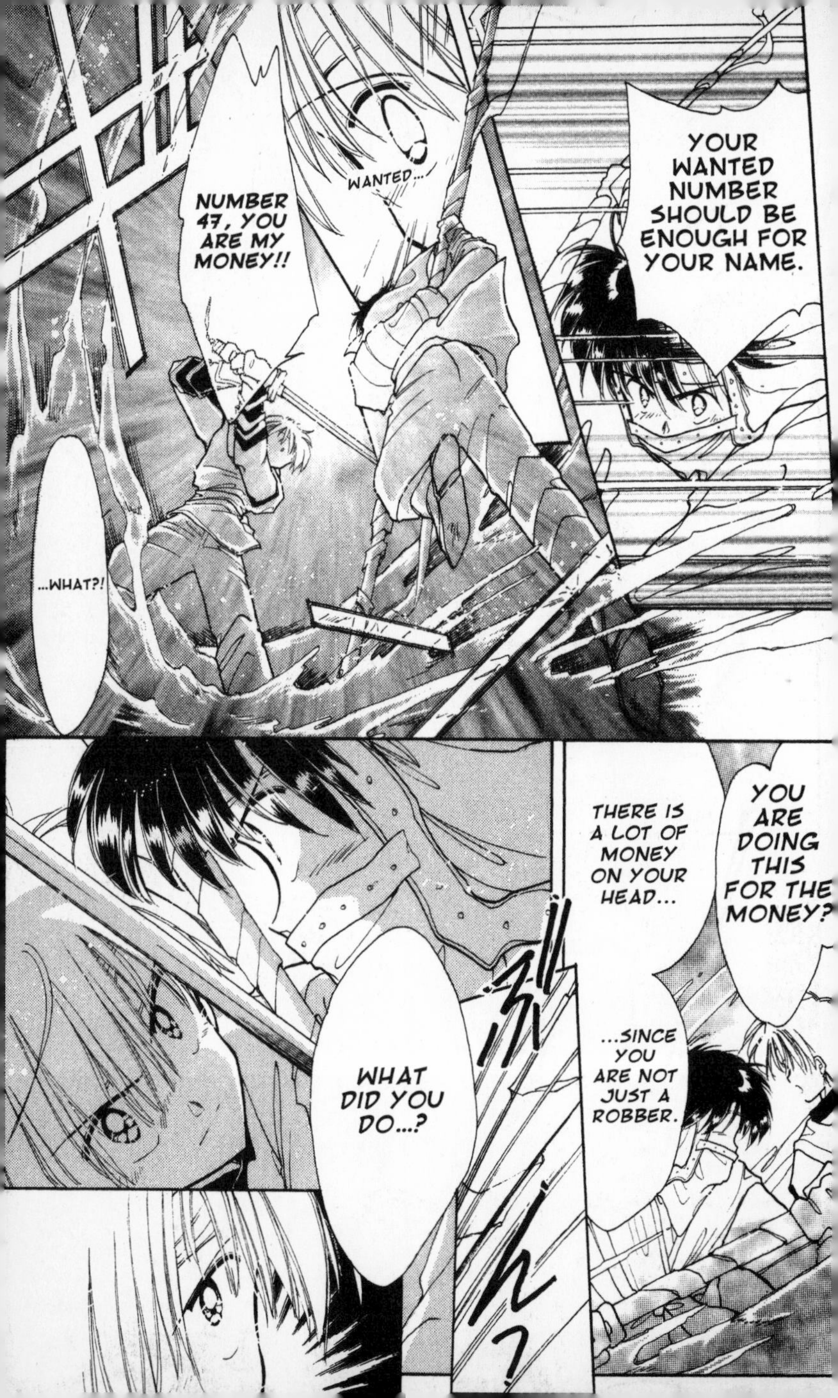

YOUR WANTED NUMBER SHOULD BE ENOUGH FOR YOUR NAME.
WANTED...
NUMBER 47, YOU ARE MY MONEY!!
...WHAT?!
YOU ARE DOING THIS FOR THE MONEY?
THERE IS A LOT OF MONEY ON YOUR HEAD...
...SINCE YOU ARE NOT JUST A ROBBER.
WHAT DID YOU DO...?

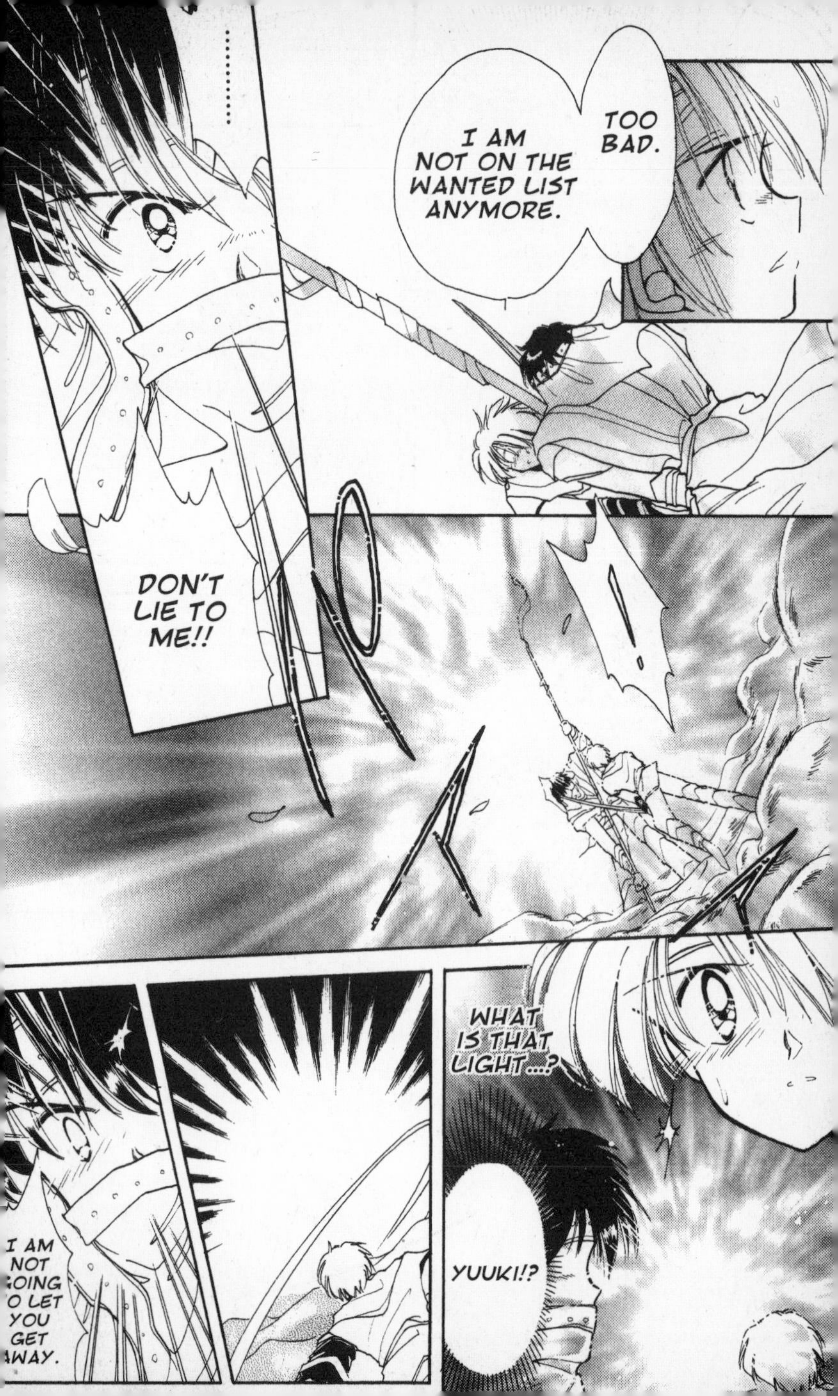
TOO BAD.
I AM NOT ON THE WANTED LIST ANYMORE.
......
DON'T LIE TO ME!!
!
WHAT IS THAT LIGHT...?
YUUKI!?
I AM NOT GOING TO LET YOU GET AWAY.

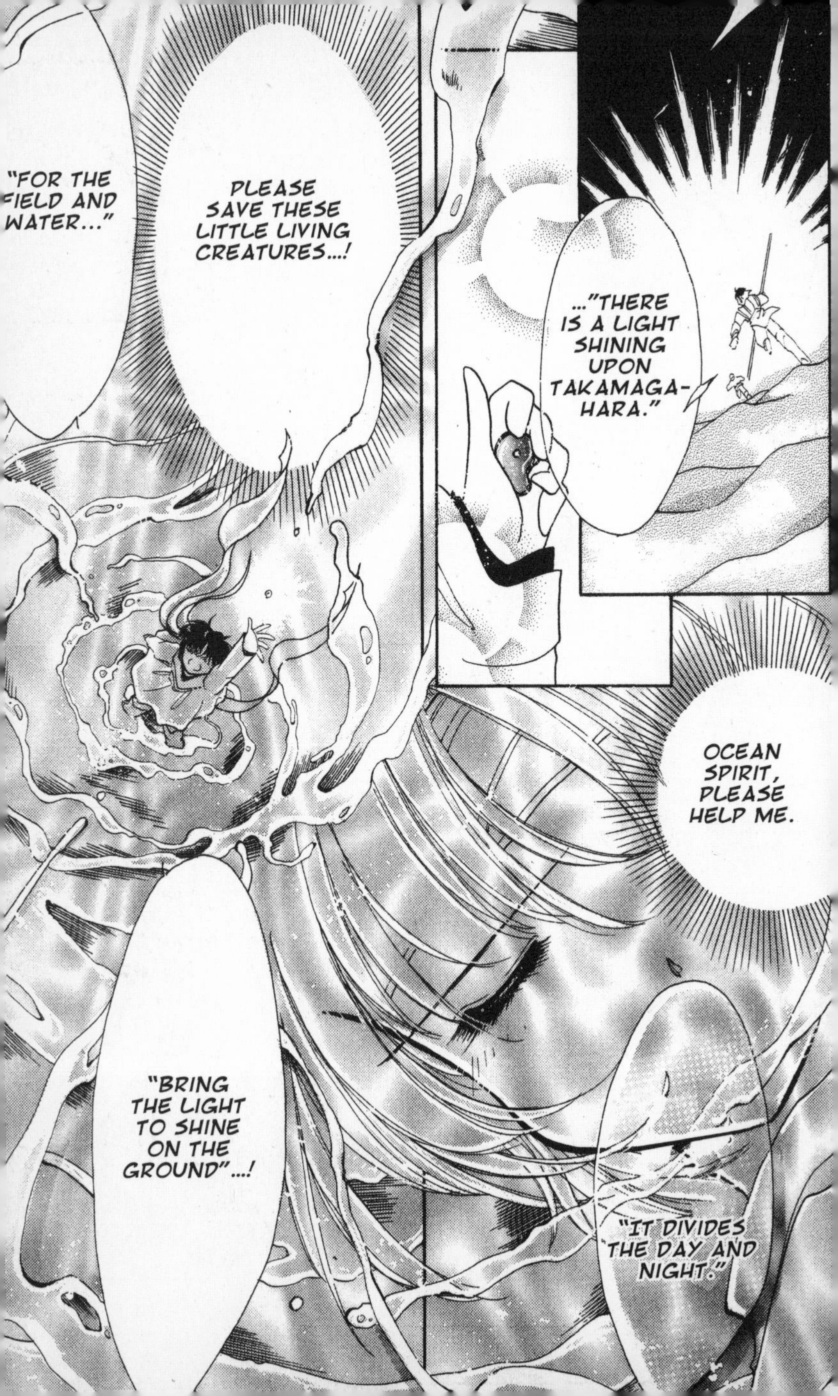
..."THERE IS A LIGHT SHINING UPON TAKAMAGA-HARA."
PLEASE SAVE THESE LITTLE LIVING CREATURES...!
"FOR THE FIELD AND WATER..."
OCEAN SPIRIT, PLEASE HELP ME.
"IT DIVIDES THE DAY AND NIGHT."
"BRING THE LIGHT TO SHINE ON THE GROUND"...!

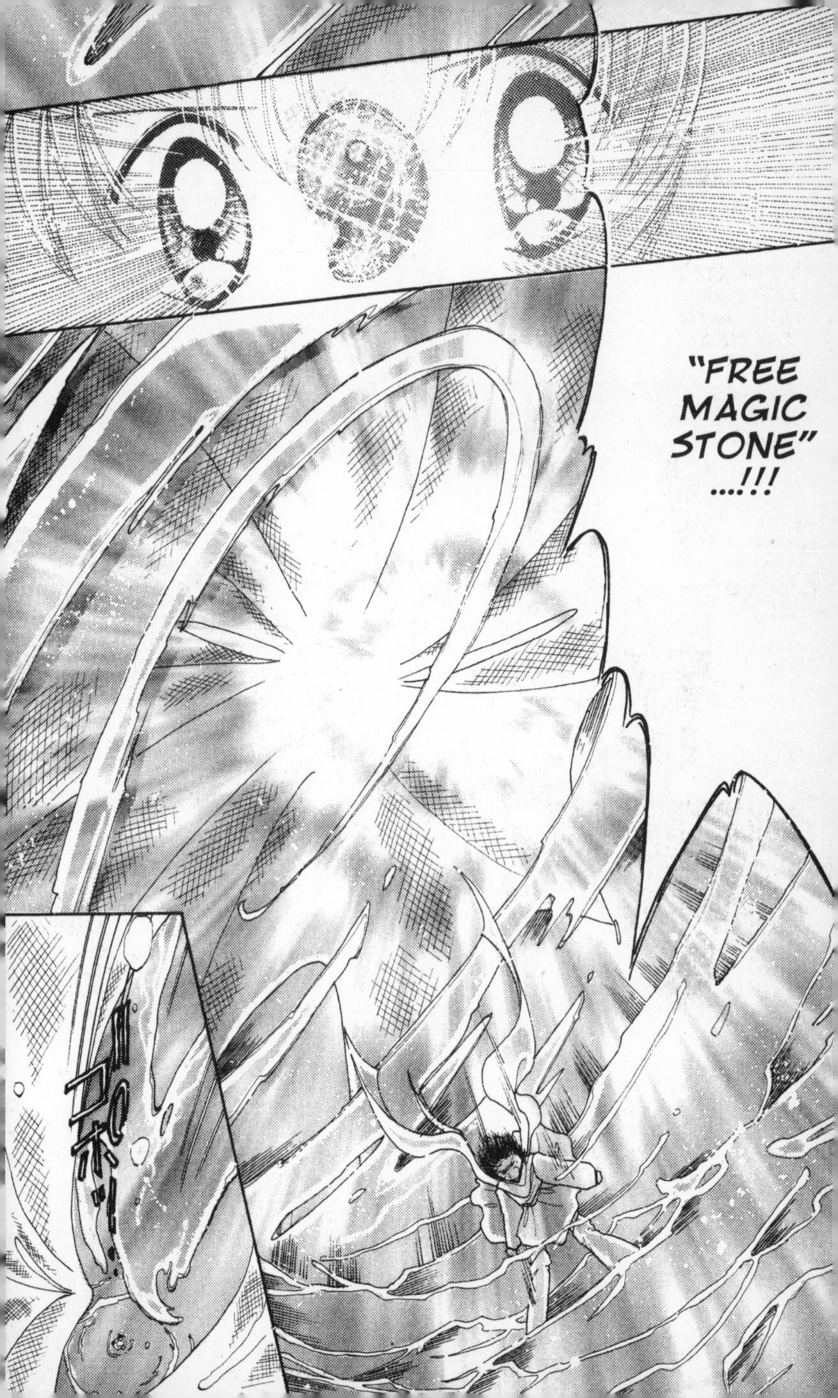
"FREE MAGIC STONE" ...!!!
ゴポー…

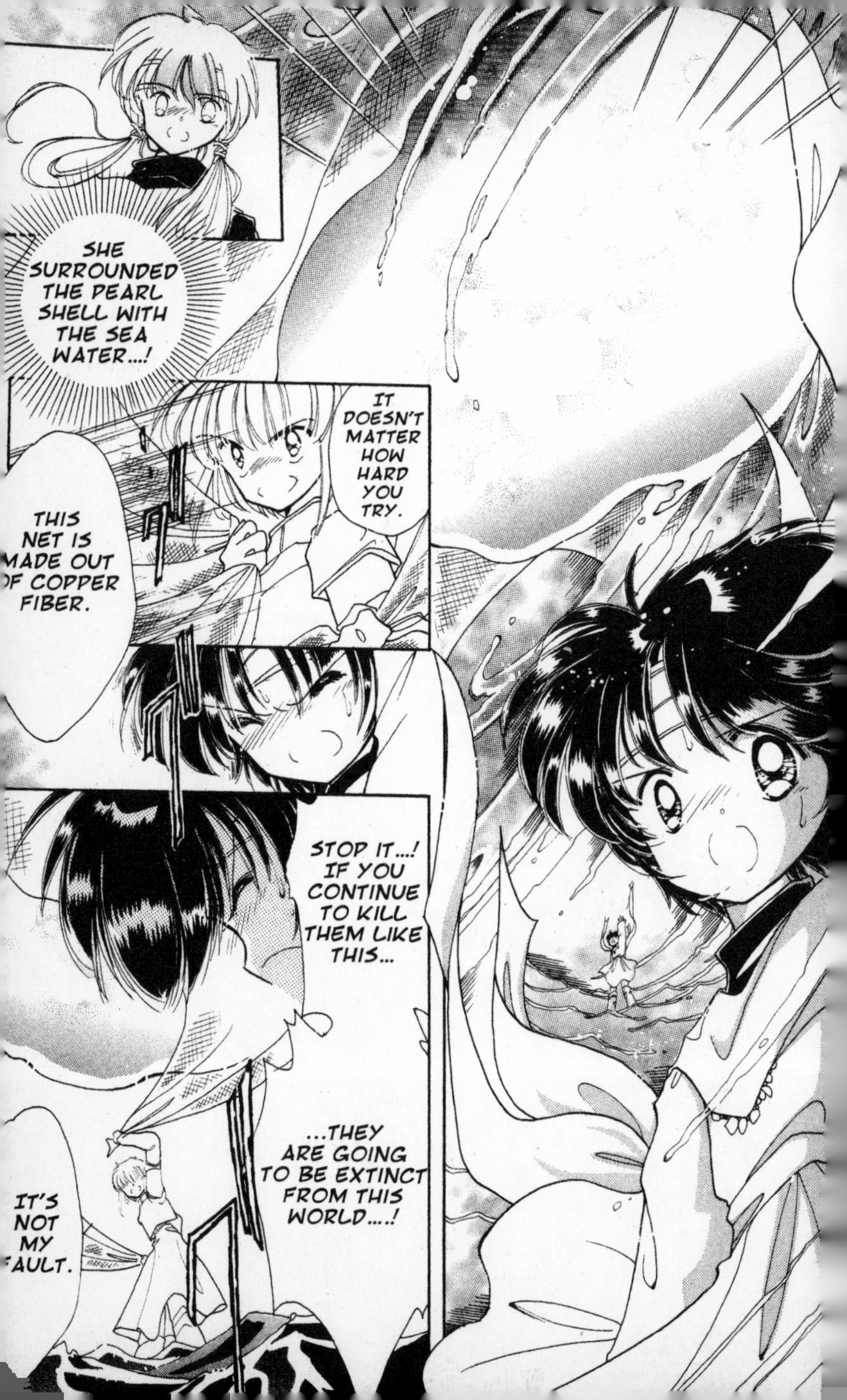
SHE SURROUNDED THE PEARL SHELL WITH THE SEA WATER...!
IT DOESN'T MATTER HOW HARD YOU TRY.
THIS NET IS MADE OUT OF COPPER FIBER.
STOP IT...! IF YOU CONTINUE TO KILL THEM LIKE THIS...
...THEY ARE GOING TO BE EXTINCT FROM THIS WORLD....!
IT'S NOT MY FAULT.

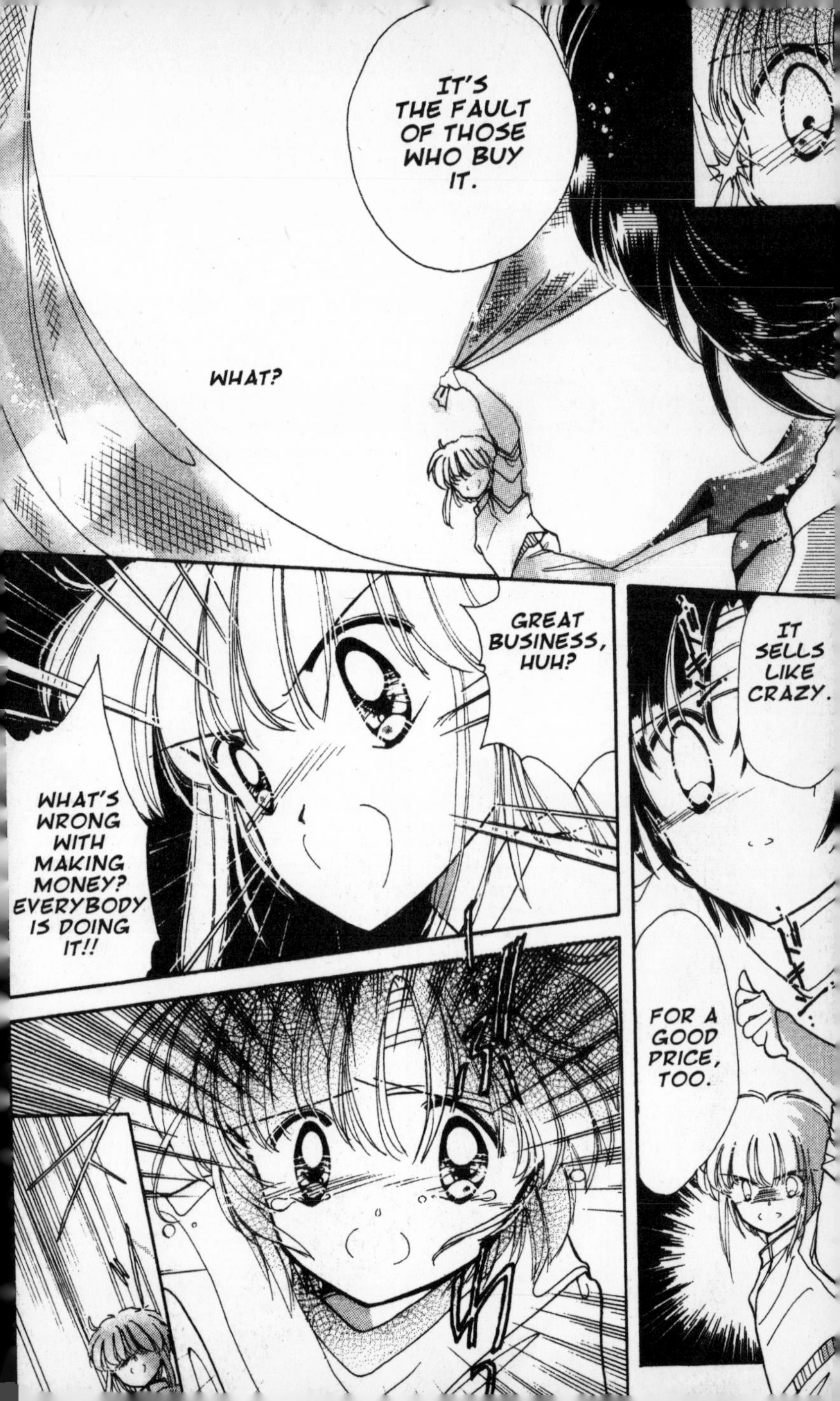
IT'S THE FAULT OF THOSE WHO BUY IT.
WHAT?
IT SELLS LIKE CRAZY.
FOR A GOOD PRICE, TOO.
GREAT BUSINESS, HUH?
WHAT'S WRONG WITH MAKING MONEY? EVERYBODY IS DOING IT!!

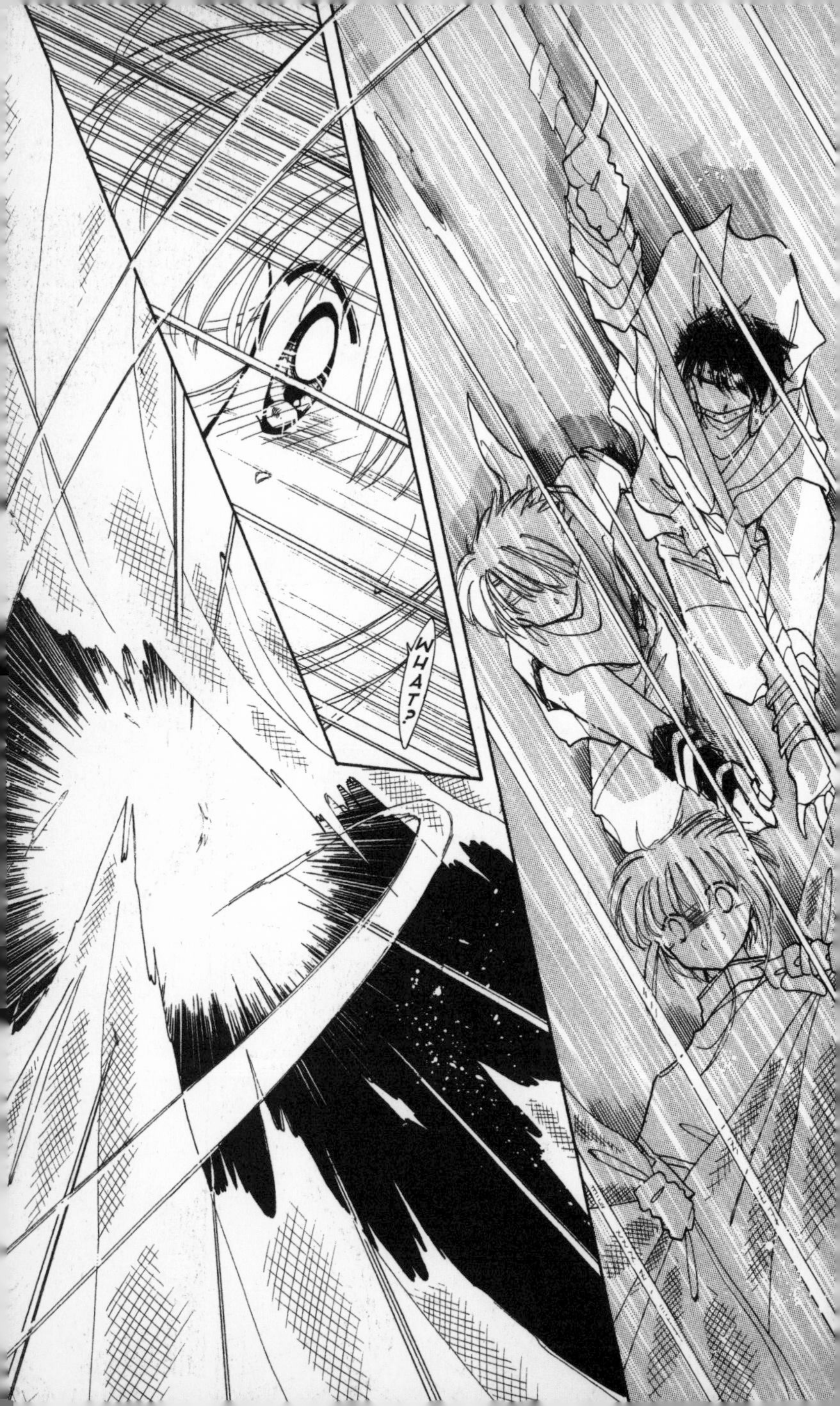
WHAT?

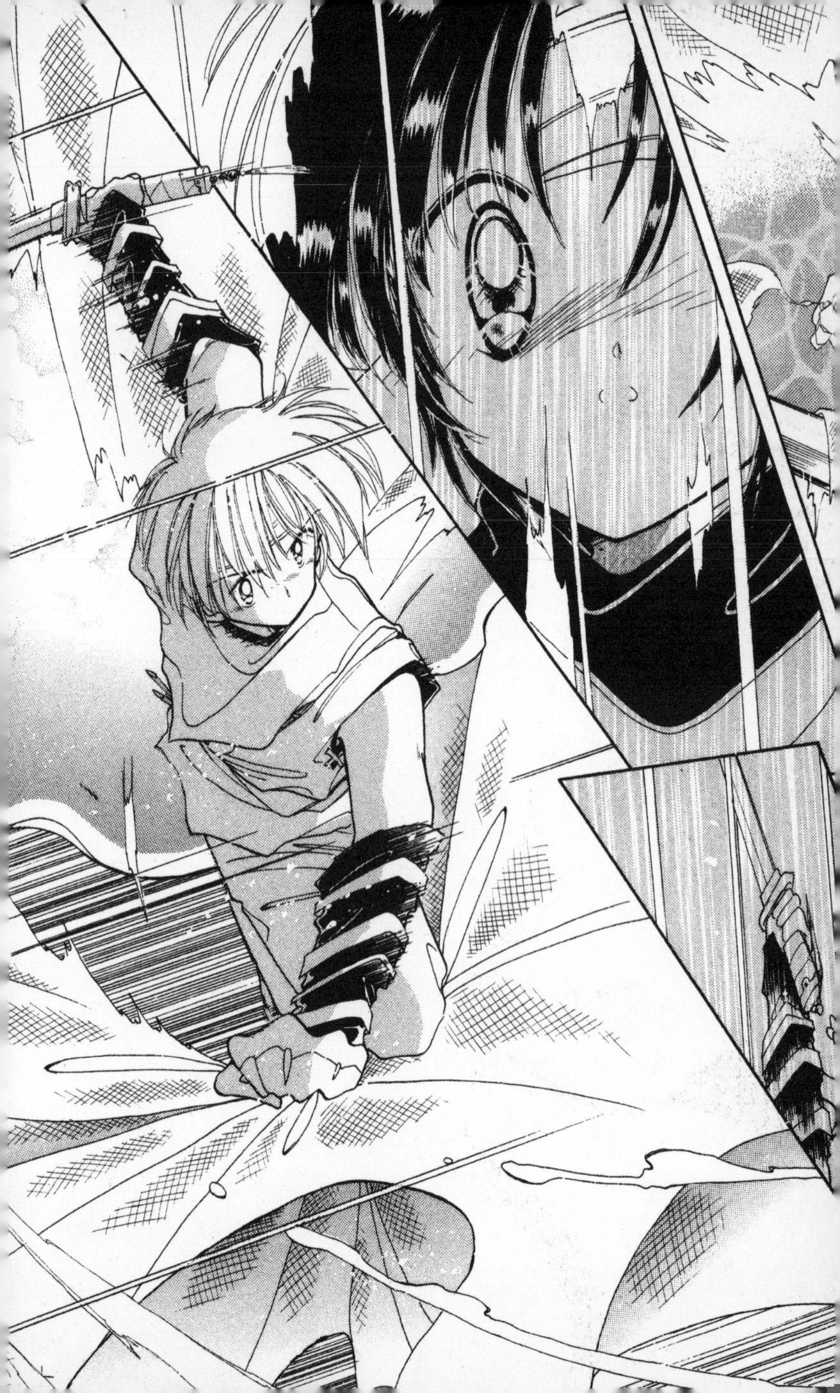

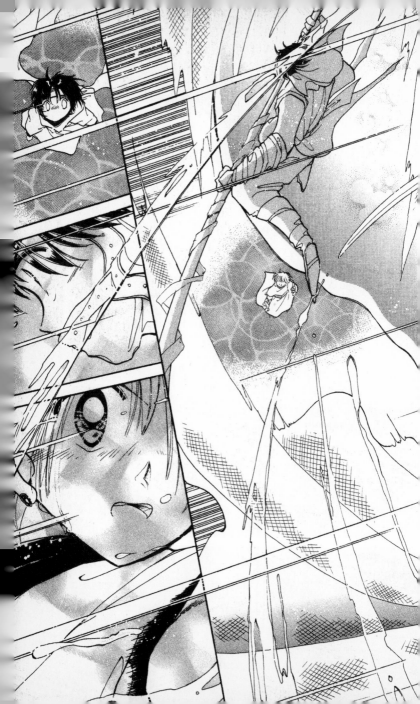

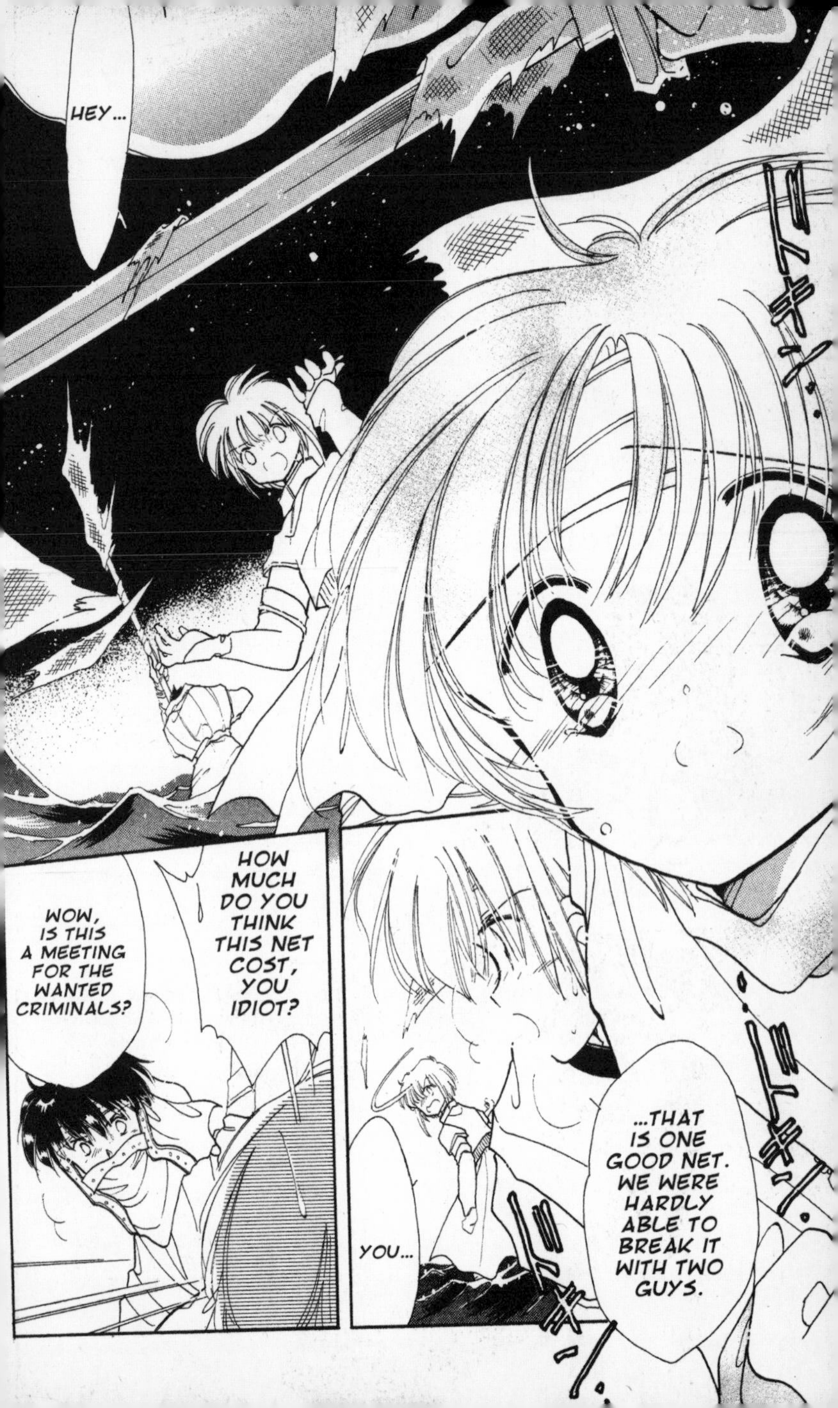
HEY...
...THAT IS ONE GOOD NET. WE WERE HARDLY ABLE TO BREAK IT WITH TWO GUYS.
YOU...
HOW MUCH DO YOU THINK THIS NET COST, YOU IDIOT?
WOW, IS THIS A MEETING FOR THE WANTED CRIMINALS?

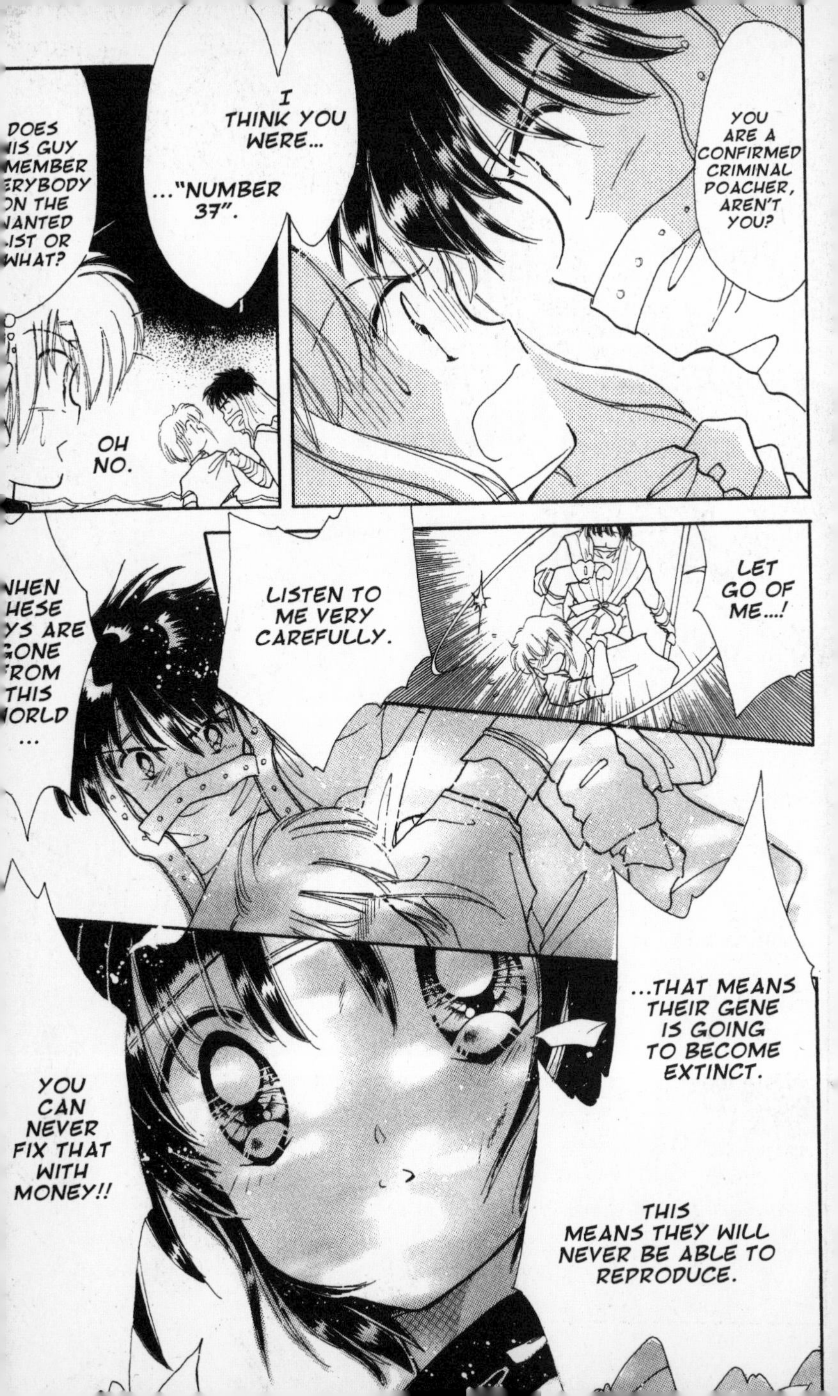
YOU ARE A CONFIRMED CRIMINAL POACHER, AREN'T YOU?
I THINK YOU WERE... ..."NUMBER 37".
DOES IS GUY MEMBER ERYBODY ON THE ANTED IST OR WHAT?
OH NO.
LET GO OF ME...!
LISTEN TO ME VERY CAREFULLY.
HEN HESE YS ARE GONE FROM THIS ORLD ...
...THAT MEANS THEIR GENE IS GOING TO BECOME EXTINCT.
THIS MEANS THEY WILL NEVER BE ABLE TO REPRODUCE.
YOU CAN NEVER FIX THAT WITH MONEY!!

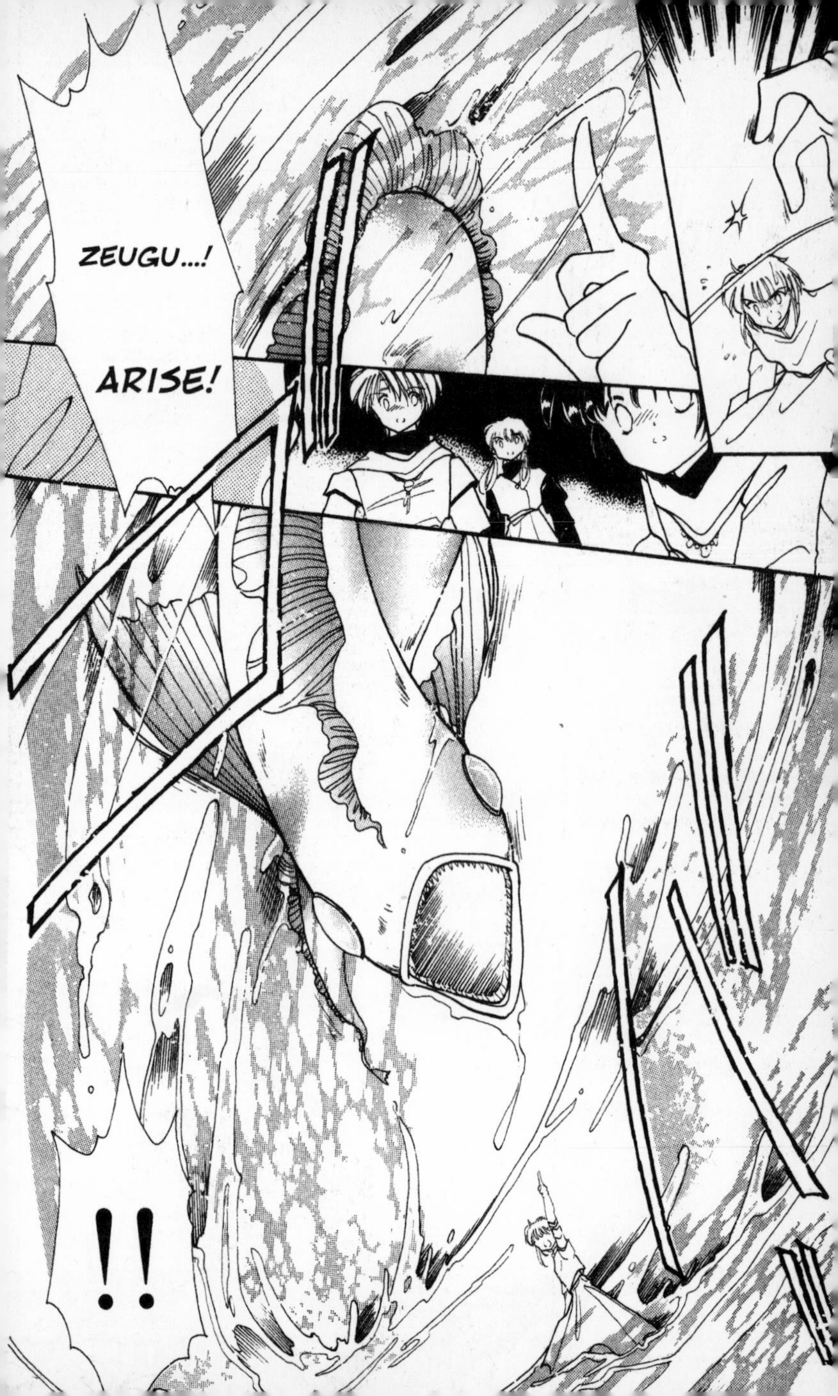
ZEUGU...!
ARISE!
!!

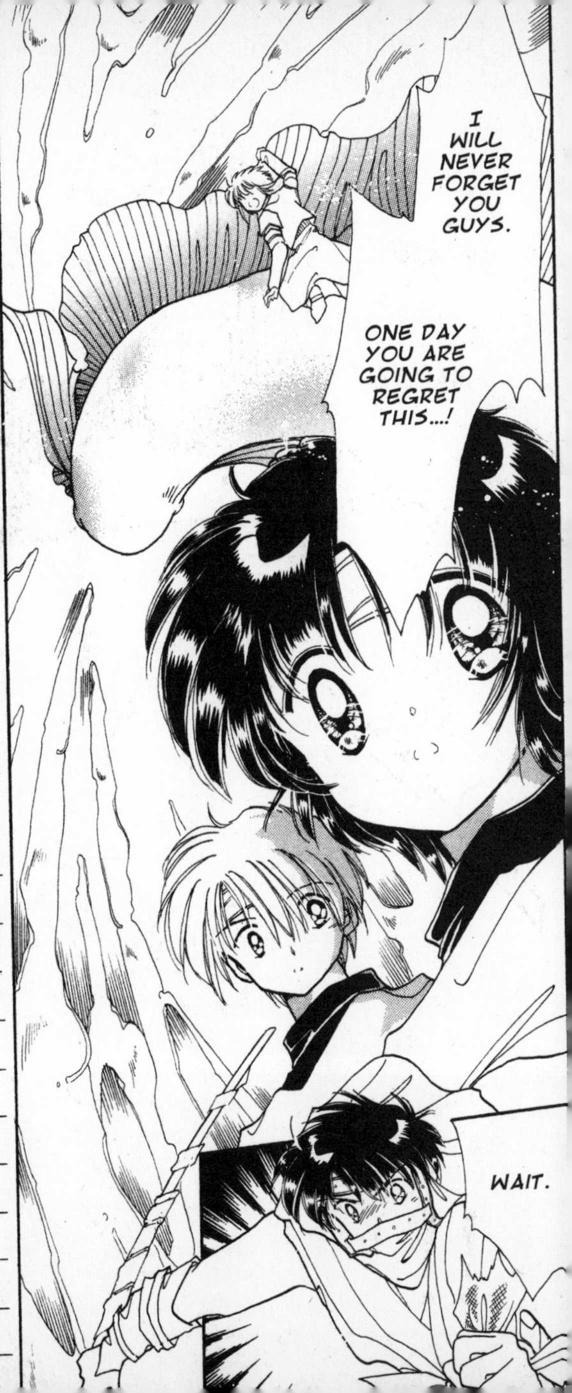
I WILL NEVER FORGET YOU GUYS.
ONE DAY YOU ARE GOING TO REGRET THIS...!
WAIT.

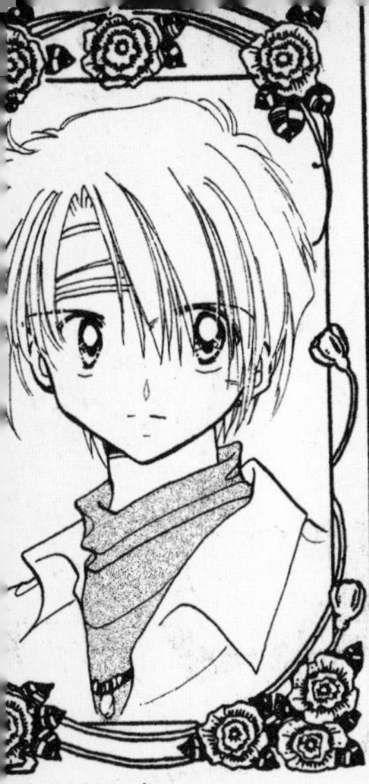

Takaomi

Born on the 15th of July

Blood type: A

When he first met Yuuki, he was the head of a group of robbers. He doesn't have the greatest personality, but don't hold that against him. He is currently 15 years old. He loves sleeping, eating (especially chicken...) and hitting on girls. Ummm.

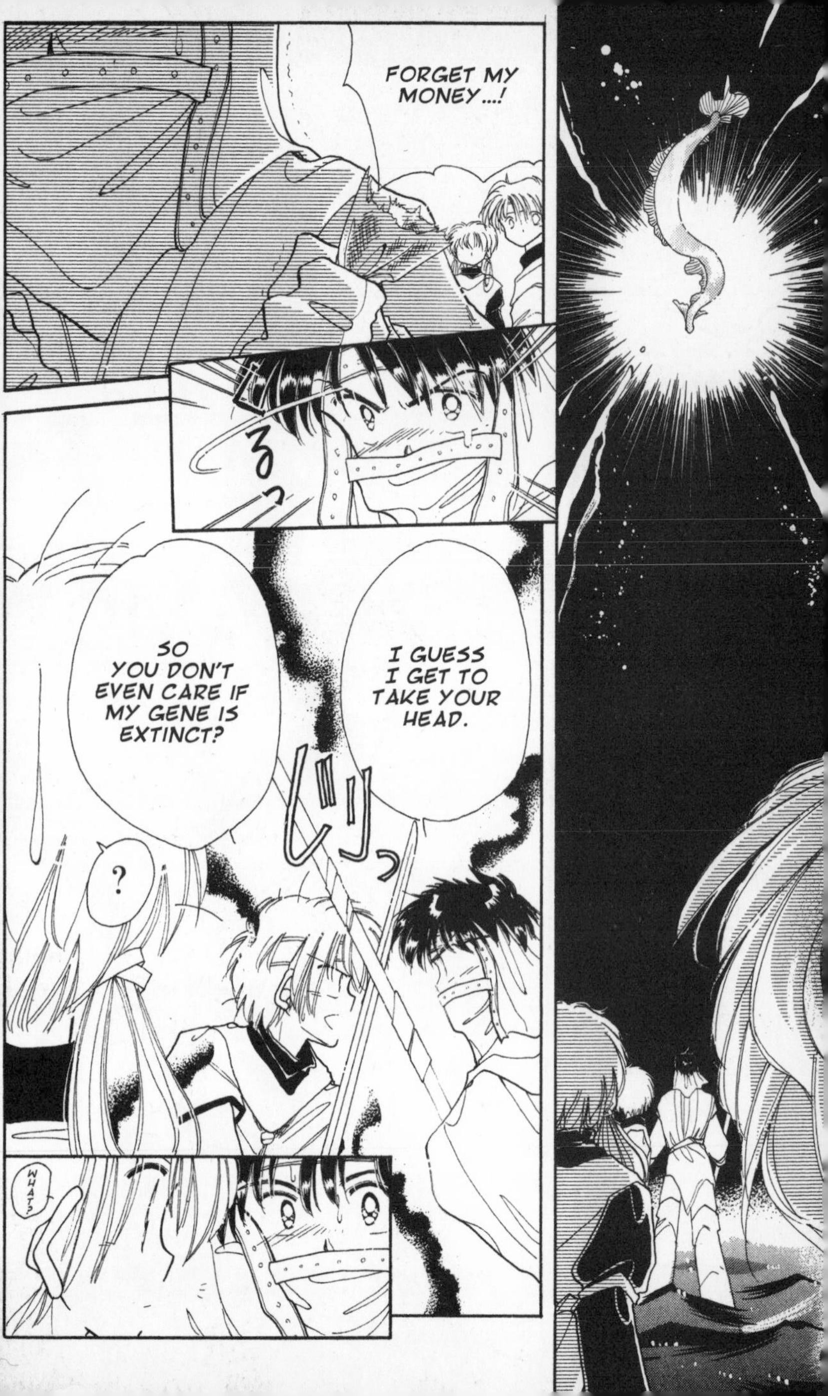
FORGET MY MONEY...!
I GUESS I GET TO TAKE YOUR HEAD.
SO YOU DON'T EVEN CARE IF MY GENE IS EXTINCT?
じりっ
?
WHAT?

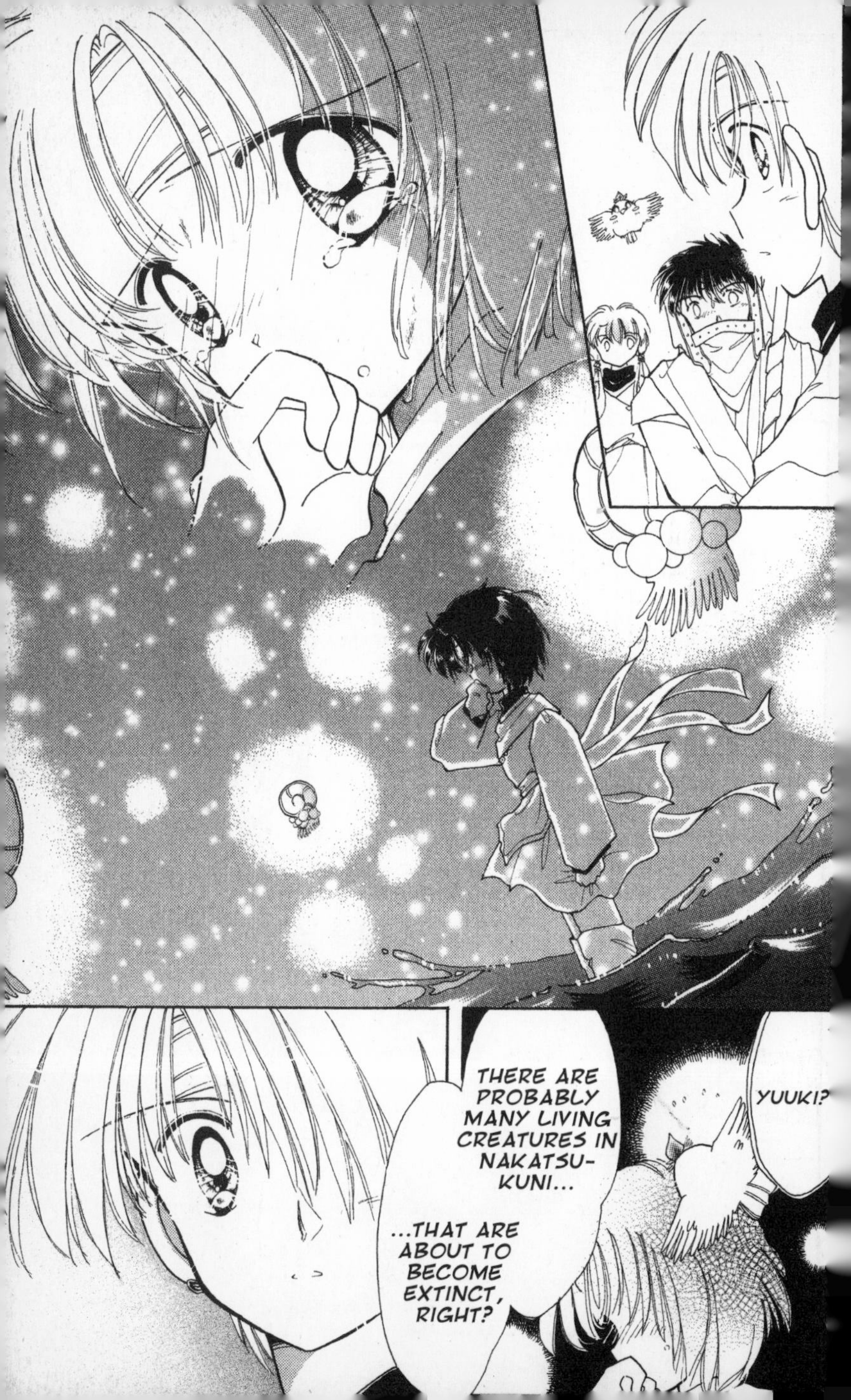
YUUKI?
THERE ARE PROBABLY MANY LIVING CREATURES IN NAKATSU-KUNI...
...THAT ARE ABOUT TO BECOME EXTINCT, RIGHT?

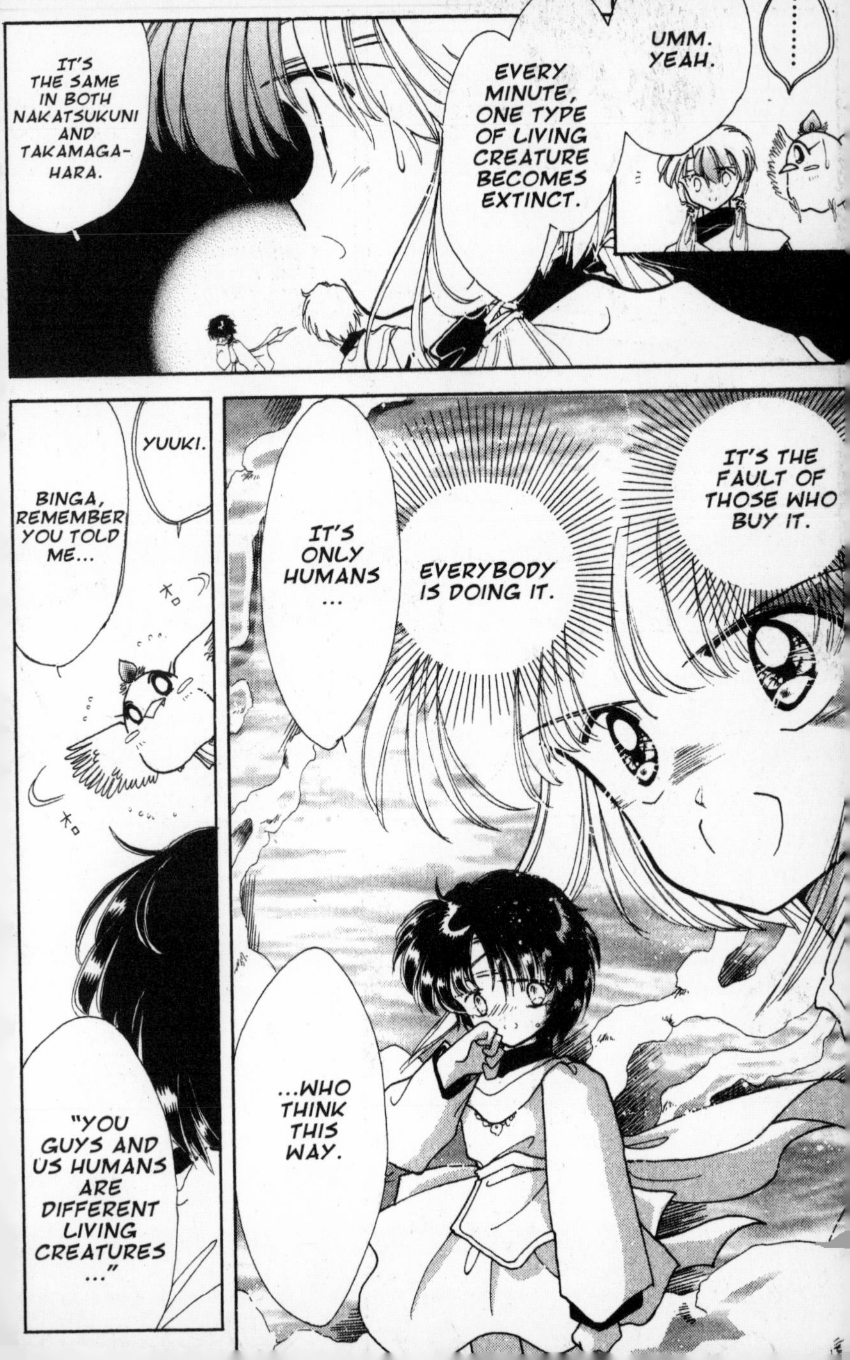
......
UMM. YEAH.
EVERY MINUTE, ONE TYPE OF LIVING CREATURE BECOMES EXTINCT.
IT'S THE SAME IN BOTH NAKATSUKUNI AND TAKAMAGA-HARA.
IT'S THE FAULT OF THOSE WHO BUY IT.
EVERYBODY IS DOING IT.
IT'S ONLY HUMANS ...
...WHO THINK THIS WAY.
YUUKI.
BINGA, REMEMBER YOU TOLD ME...
"YOU GUYS AND US HUMANS ARE DIFFERENT LIVING CREATURES ..."

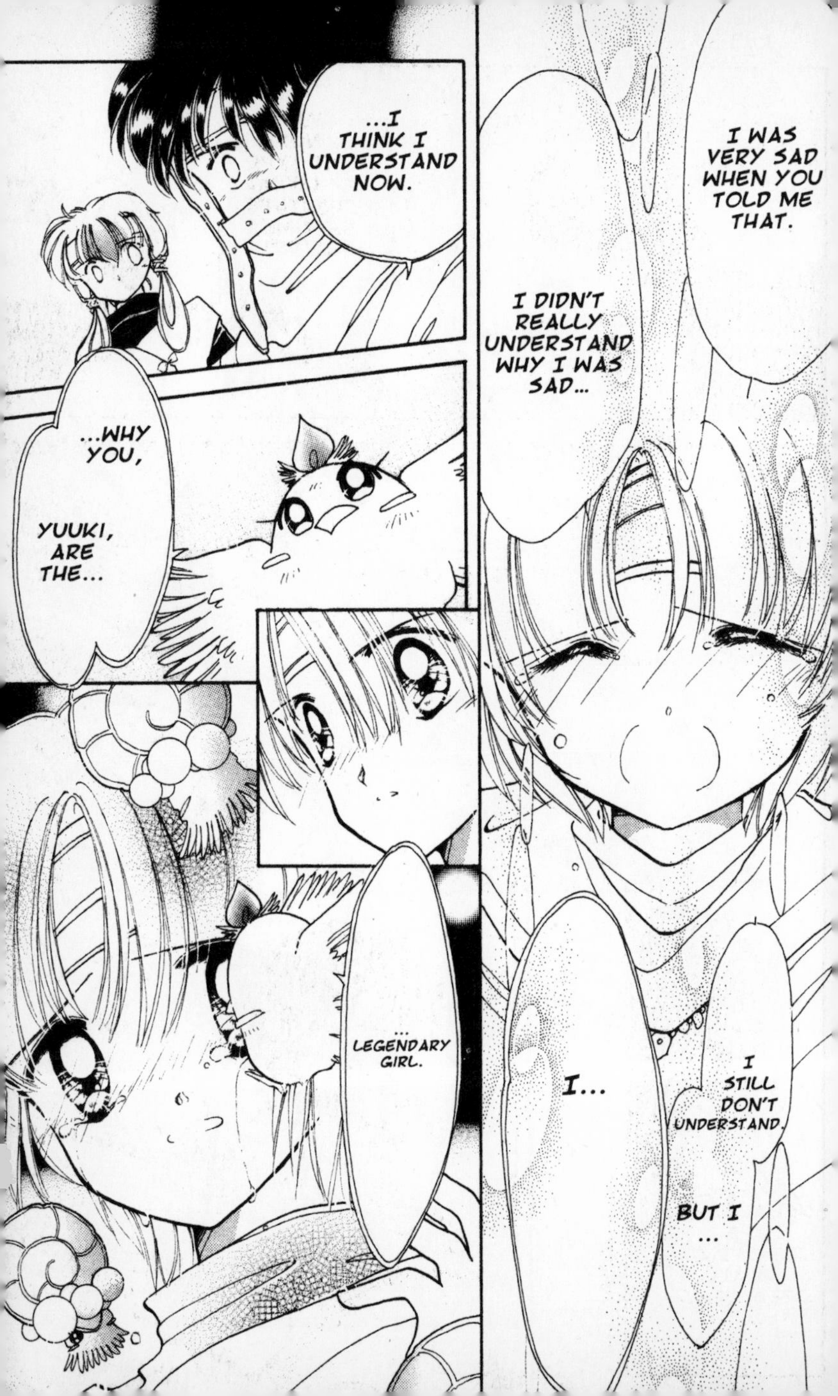
I WAS VERY SAD WHEN YOU TOLD ME THAT.
I DIDN'T REALLY UNDERSTAND WHY I WAS SAD...
I STILL DON'T UNDERSTAND.
BUT I ...
I...
...I THINK I UNDERSTAND NOW.
...WHY YOU,
YUUKI, ARE THE...
... LEGENDARY GIRL.

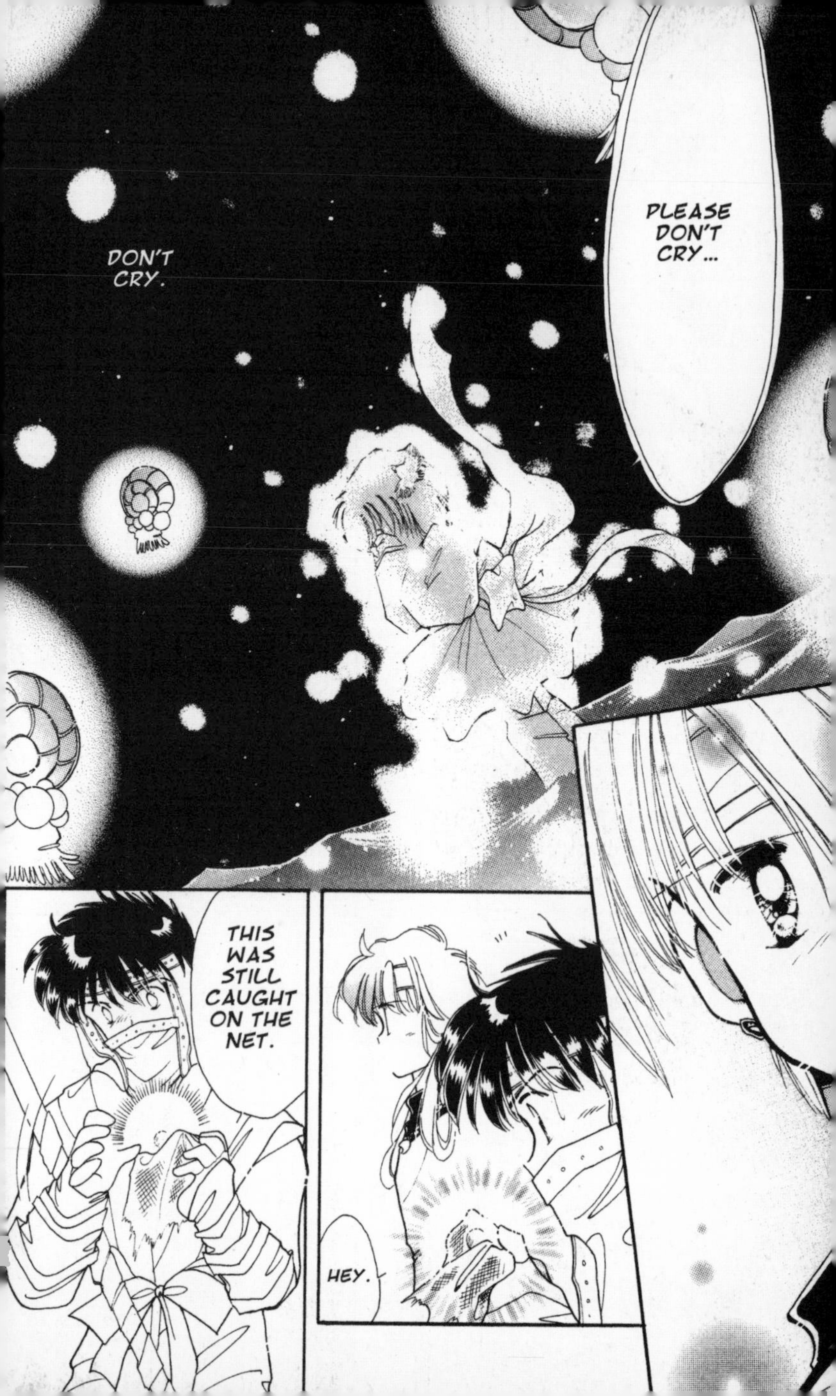
PLEASE DON'T CRY...
DON'T CRY.
HEY.
THIS WAS STILL CAUGHT ON THE NET.

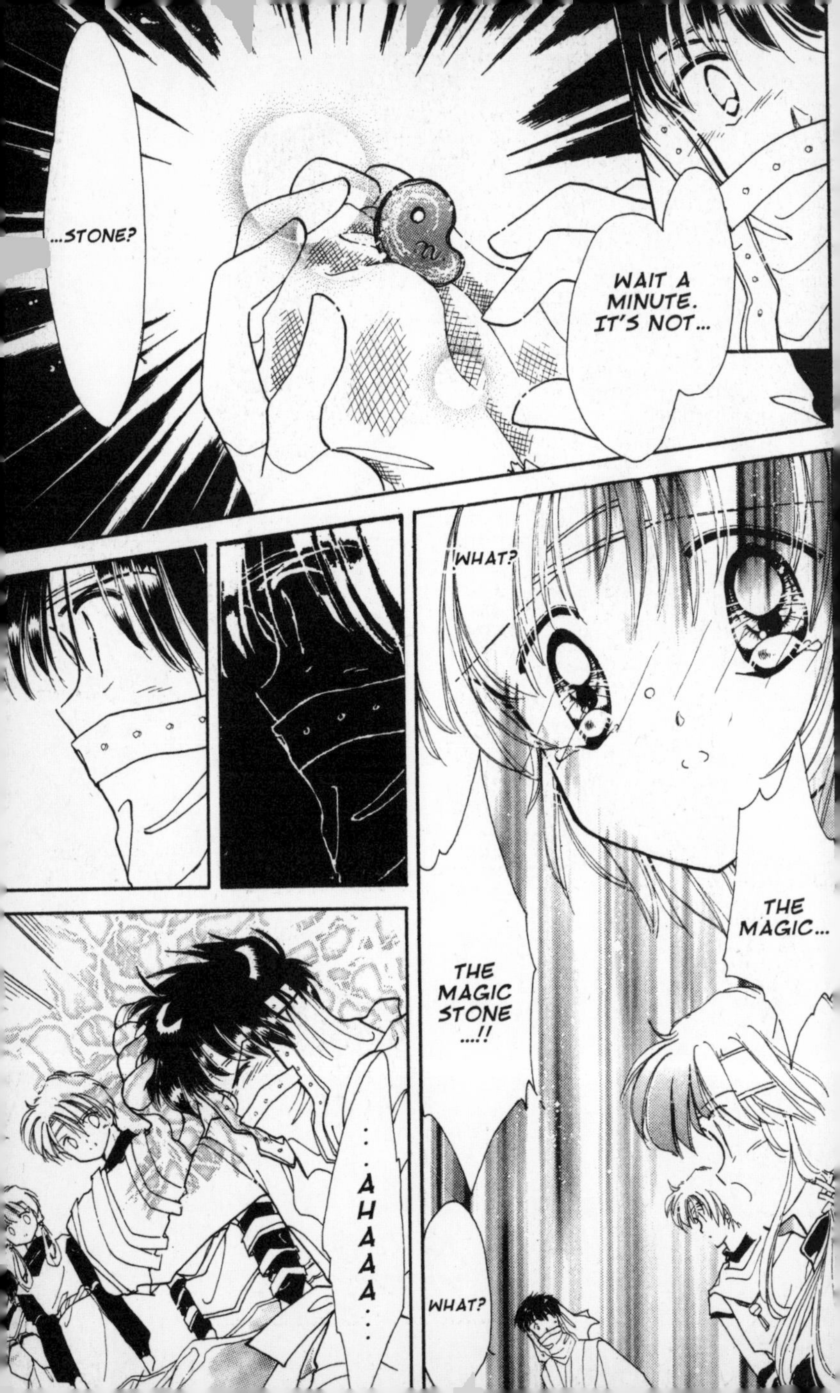
WAIT A MINUTE. IT'S NOT...
...STONE?
WHAT?
THE MAGIC...
THE MAGIC STONE ....!!
WHAT?
...AHAAAA...

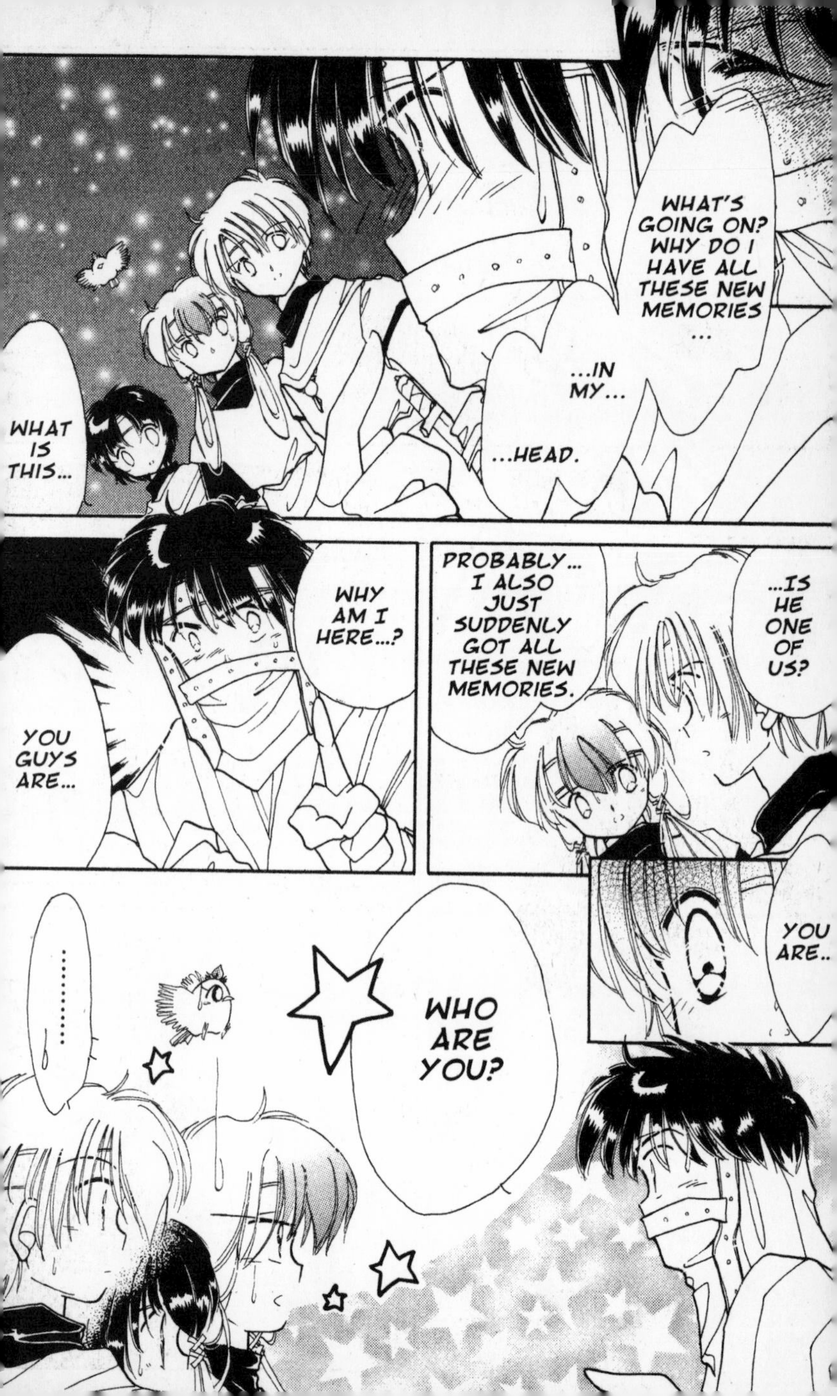
WHAT'S GOING ON? WHY DO I HAVE ALL THESE NEW MEMORIES ...
...IN MY...
...HEAD.
WHAT IS THIS...
...IS HE ONE OF US?
PROBABLY... I ALSO JUST SUDDENLY GOT ALL THESE NEW MEMORIES.
WHY AM I HERE...?
YOU GUYS ARE...
YOU ARE..
WHO ARE YOU?
....

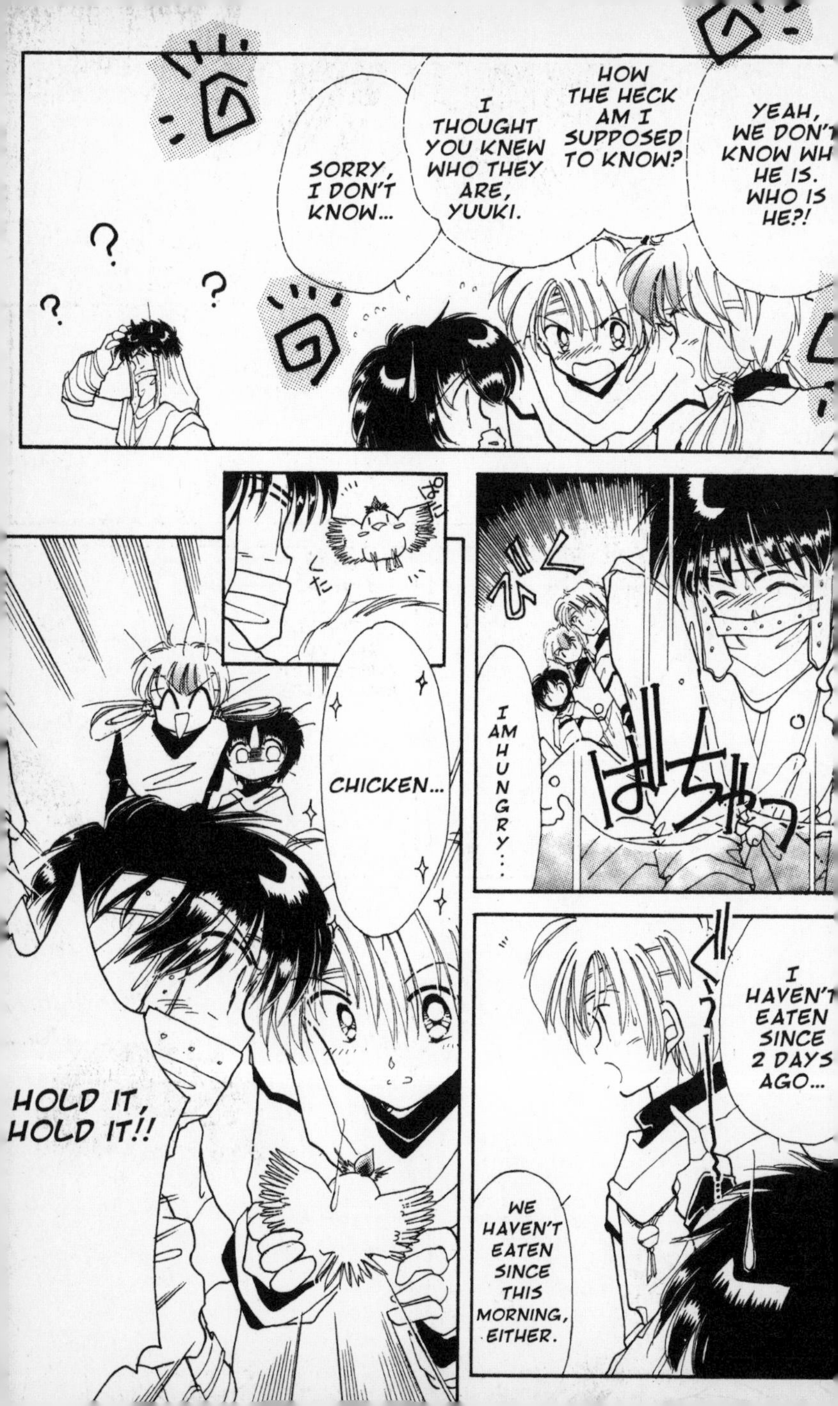
YEAH, WE DON'T KNOW WH HE IS. WHO IS HE?!
HOW THE HECK AM I SUPPOSED TO KNOW?
I THOUGHT YOU KNEW WHO THEY ARE, YUUKI.
SORRY, I DON'T KNOW...
ぱちゃっ
I AM HUNGRY...
I HAVEN'T EATEN SINCE 2 DAYS AGO...
WE HAVEN'T EATEN SINCE THIS MORNING, EITHER.
CHICKEN...
HOLD IT, HOLD IT!!

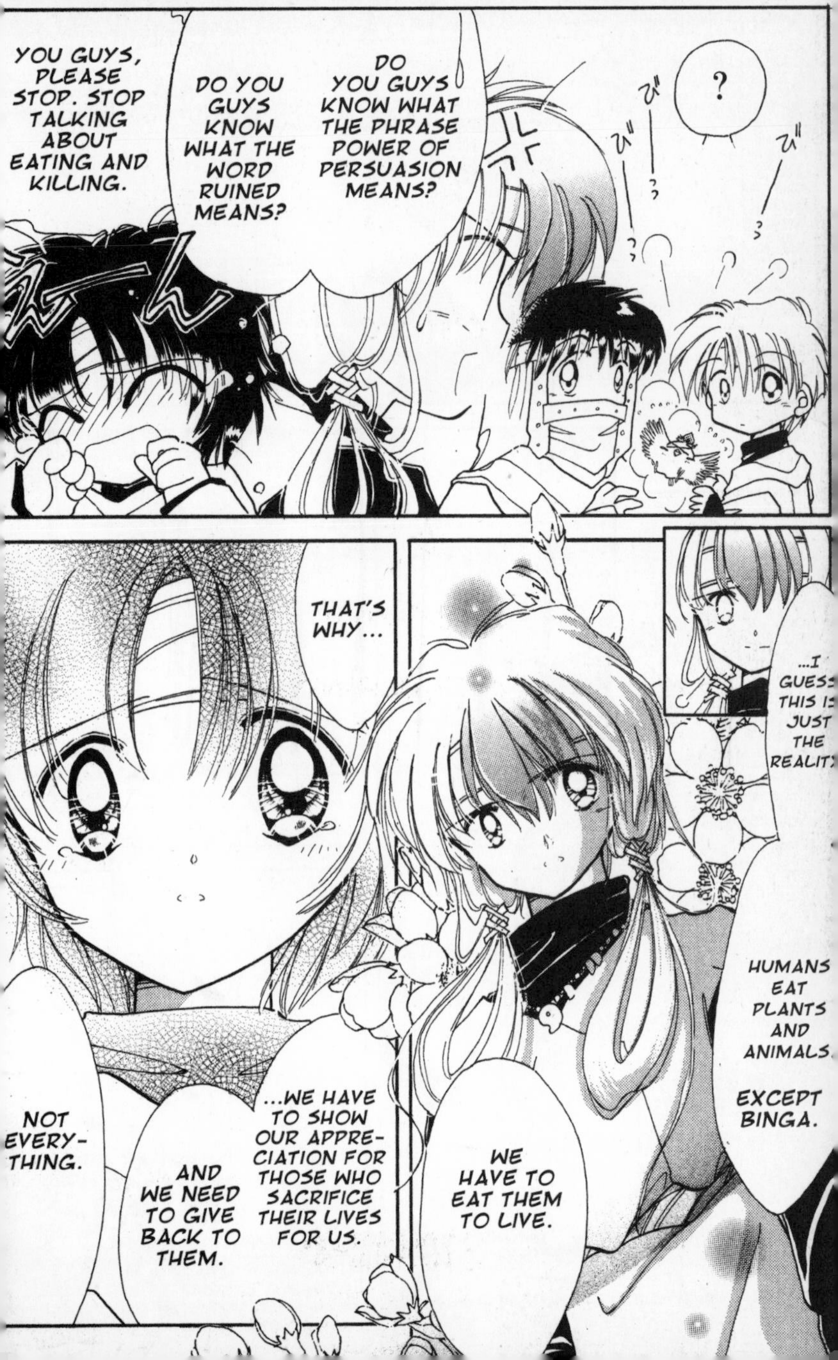
?
びー
DO YOU GUYS KNOW WHAT THE PHRASE POWER OF PERSUASION MEANS?
DO YOU GUYS KNOW WHAT THE WORD RUINED MEANS?
YOU GUYS, PLEASE STOP. STOP TALKING ABOUT EATING AND KILLING.
...I GUESS THIS IS JUST THE REALITY
HUMANS EAT PLANTS AND ANIMALS.
EXCEPT BINGA.
WE HAVE TO EAT THEM TO LIVE.
THAT'S WHY...
...WE HAVE TO SHOW OUR APPRECIATION FOR THOSE WHO SACRIFICE THEIR LIVES FOR US.
AND WE NEED TO GIVE BACK TO THEM.
NOT EVERYTHING.

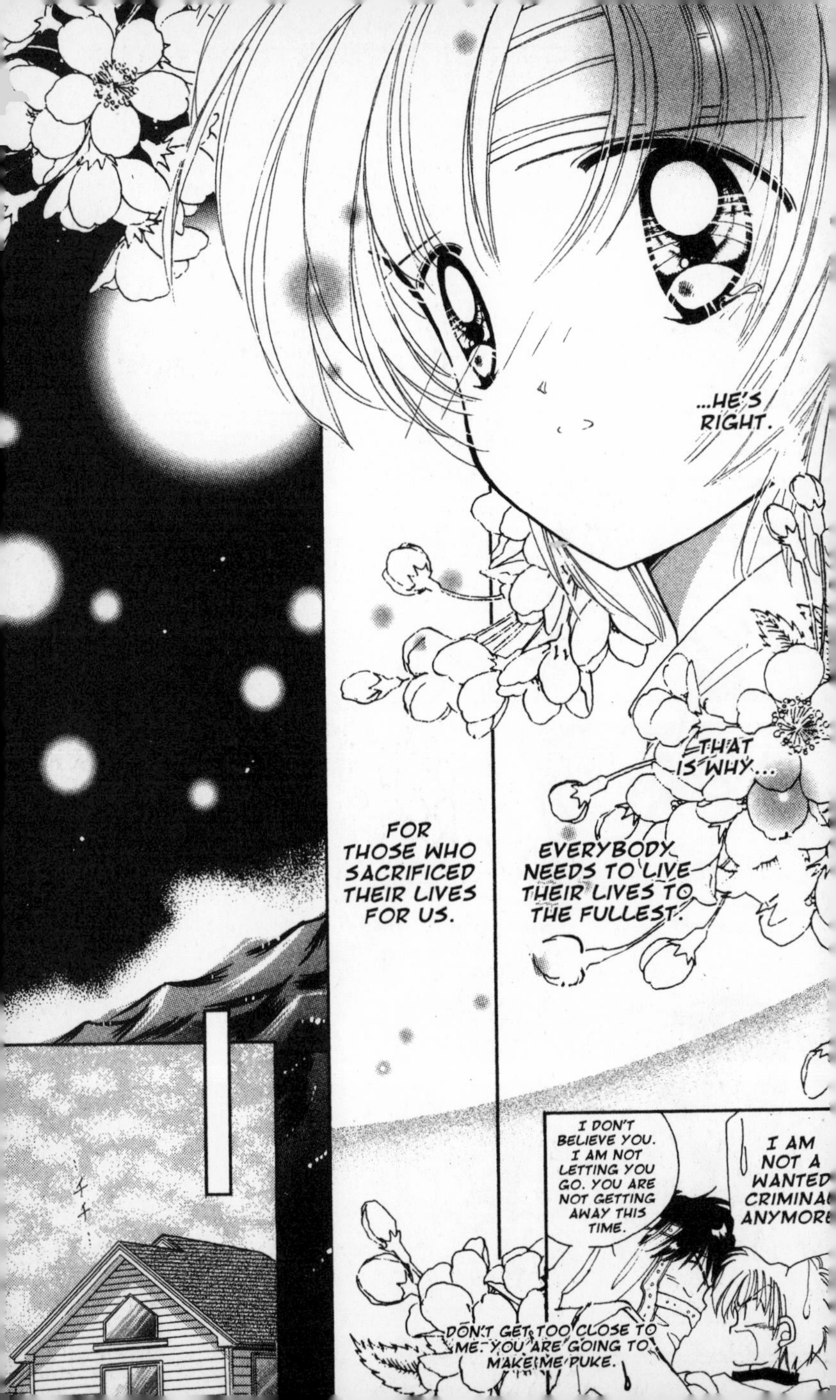
...HE'S RIGHT.
THAT IS WHY...
EVERYBODY NEEDS TO LIVE THEIR LIVES TO THE FULLEST.
FOR THOSE WHO SACRIFICED THEIR LIVES FOR US.
I AM NOT A WANTED CRIMINA ANYMORE
I DON'T BELIEVE YOU. I AM NOT LETTING YOU GO. YOU ARE NOT GETTING AWAY THIS TIME.
DON'T GET TOO CLOSE TO ME. YOU ARE GOING TO MAKE ME PUKE.
チチ…

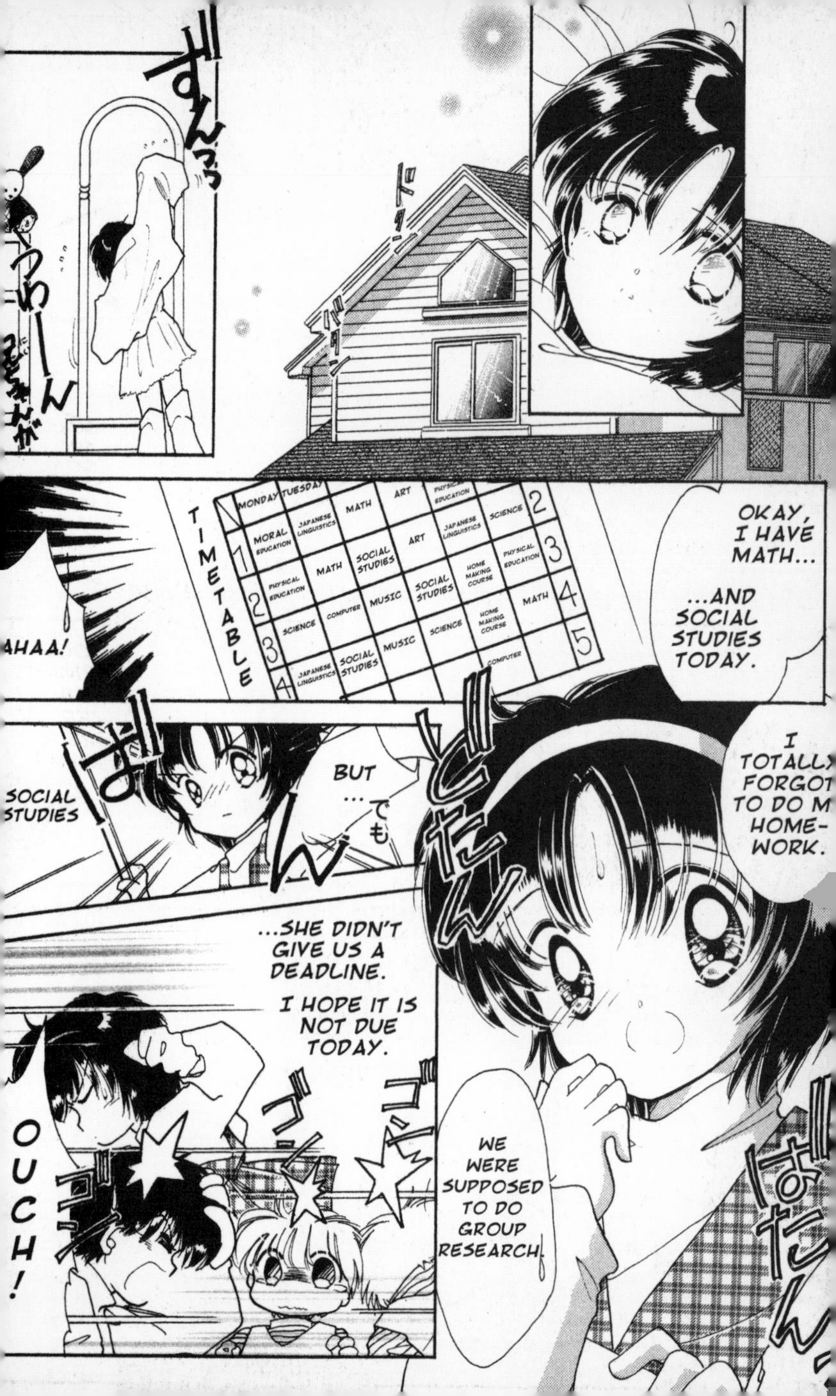

ドタ
バタン
TIMETABLE
MONDAY TUESDAY
MORAL EDUCATION
JAPANESE LINGUISTICS
MATH
ART
PHYSICAL EDUCATION
SOCIAL STUDIES
JAPANESE LINGUISTICS
SCIENCE
HOME MAKING COURSE
COMPUTER
MUSIC
OKAY, I HAVE MATH...
...AND SOCIAL STUDIES TODAY.
AHAA!
I TOTALLY FORGOT TO DO M HOME-WORK.
WE WERE SUPPOSED TO DO GROUP RESEARCH.
SOCIAL STUDIES
BUT ... でも
...SHE DIDN'T GIVE US A DEADLINE.
I HOPE IT IS NOT DUE TODAY.
OUCH!

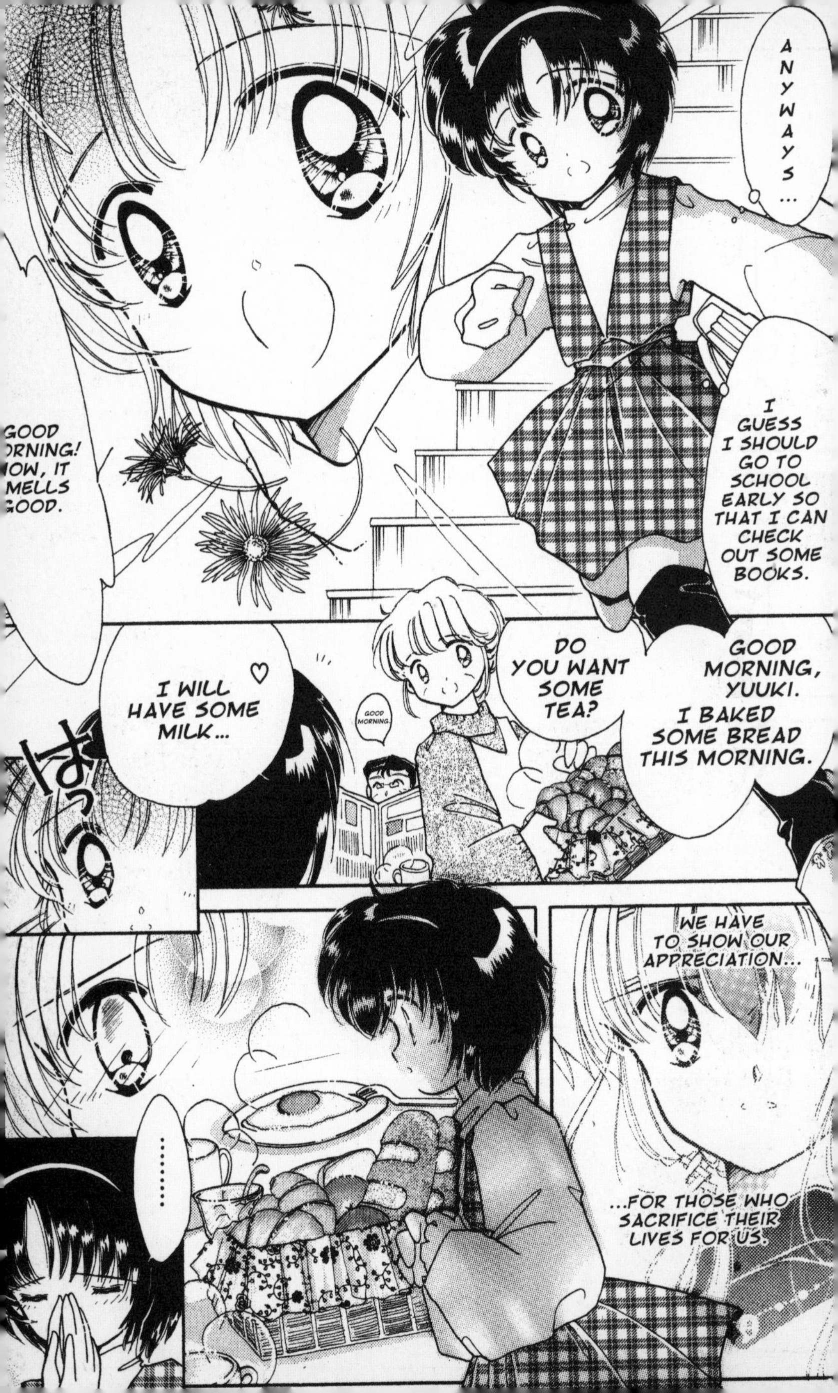
ANYWAYS...
I GUESS I SHOULD GO TO SCHOOL EARLY SO THAT I CAN CHECK OUT SOME BOOKS.
GOOD RNING! OW, IT MELLS GOOD.
GOOD MORNING, YUUKI. I BAKED SOME BREAD THIS MORNING.
DO YOU WANT SOME TEA?
GOOD MORNING.
I WILL HAVE SOME MILK... ♡
はっ
WE HAVE TO SHOW OUR APPRECIATION...
...FOR THOSE WHO SACRIFICE THEIR LIVES FOR US.
......

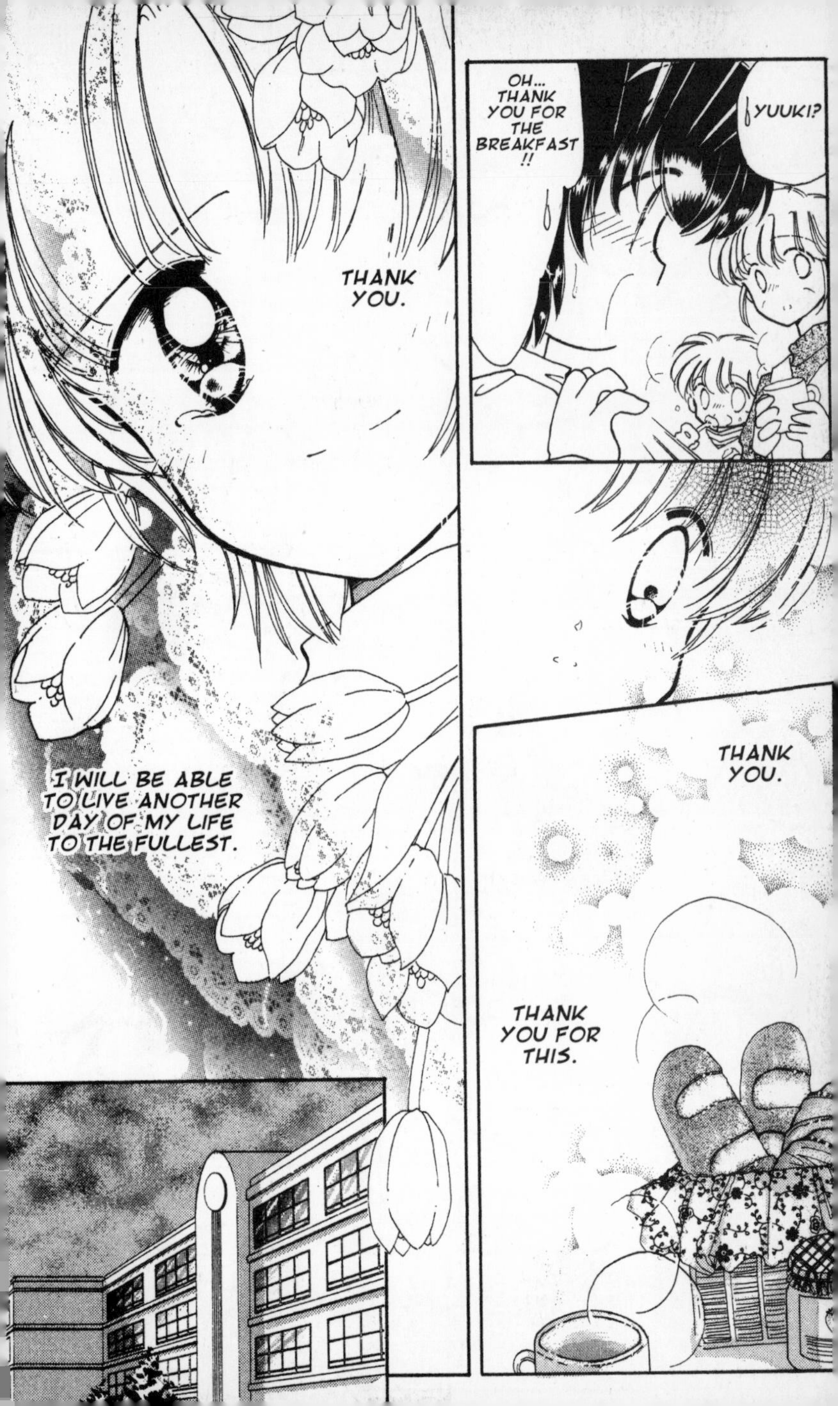
YUUKI?
OH... THANK YOU FOR THE BREAKFAST!!
THANK YOU.
THANK YOU FOR THIS.
THANK YOU.
I WILL BE ABLE TO LIVE ANOTHER DAY OF MY LIFE TO THE FULLEST.

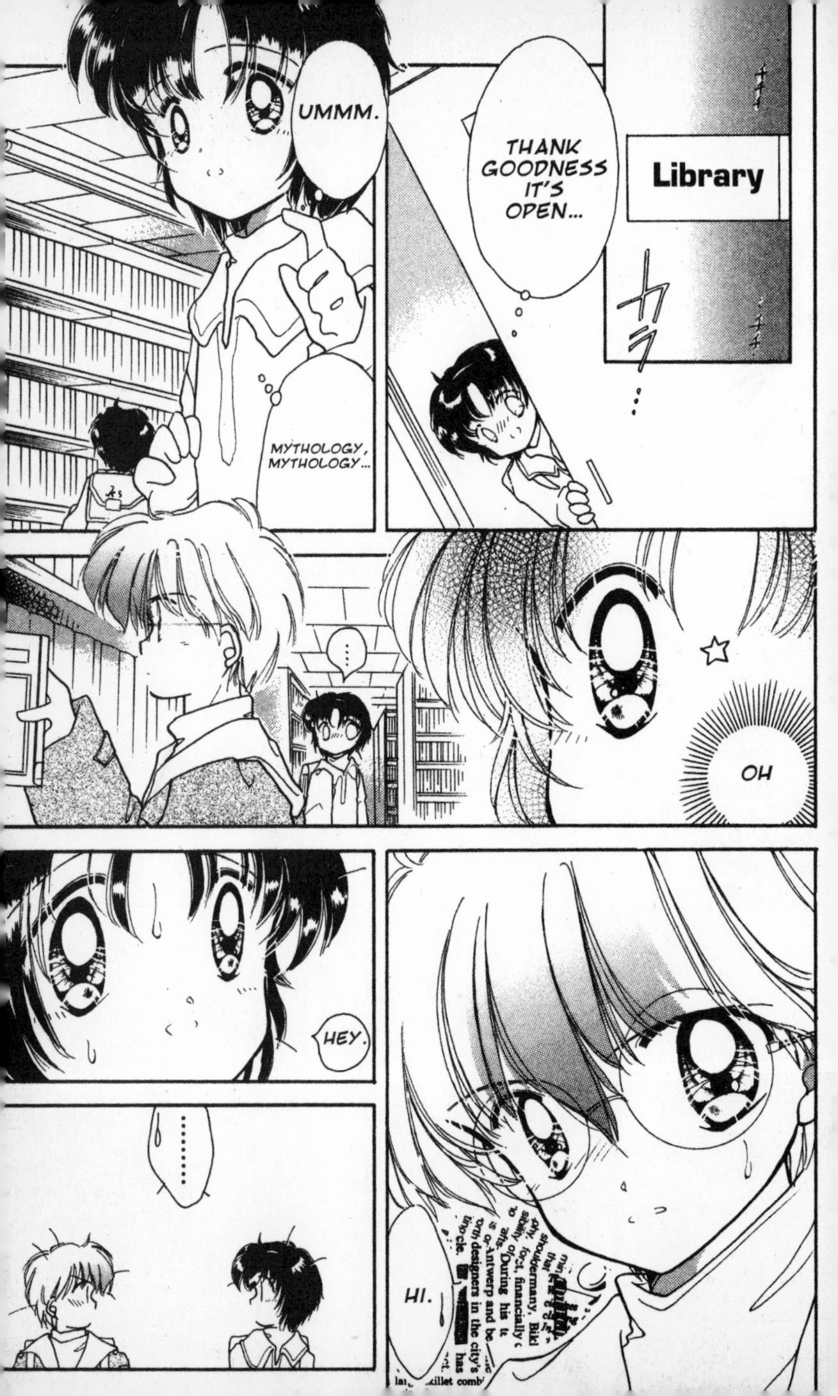
Library
カラ
THANK GOODNESS IT'S OPEN...
UMMM.
MYTHOLOGY, MYTHOLOGY...
OH
...
HI.
HEY.
....

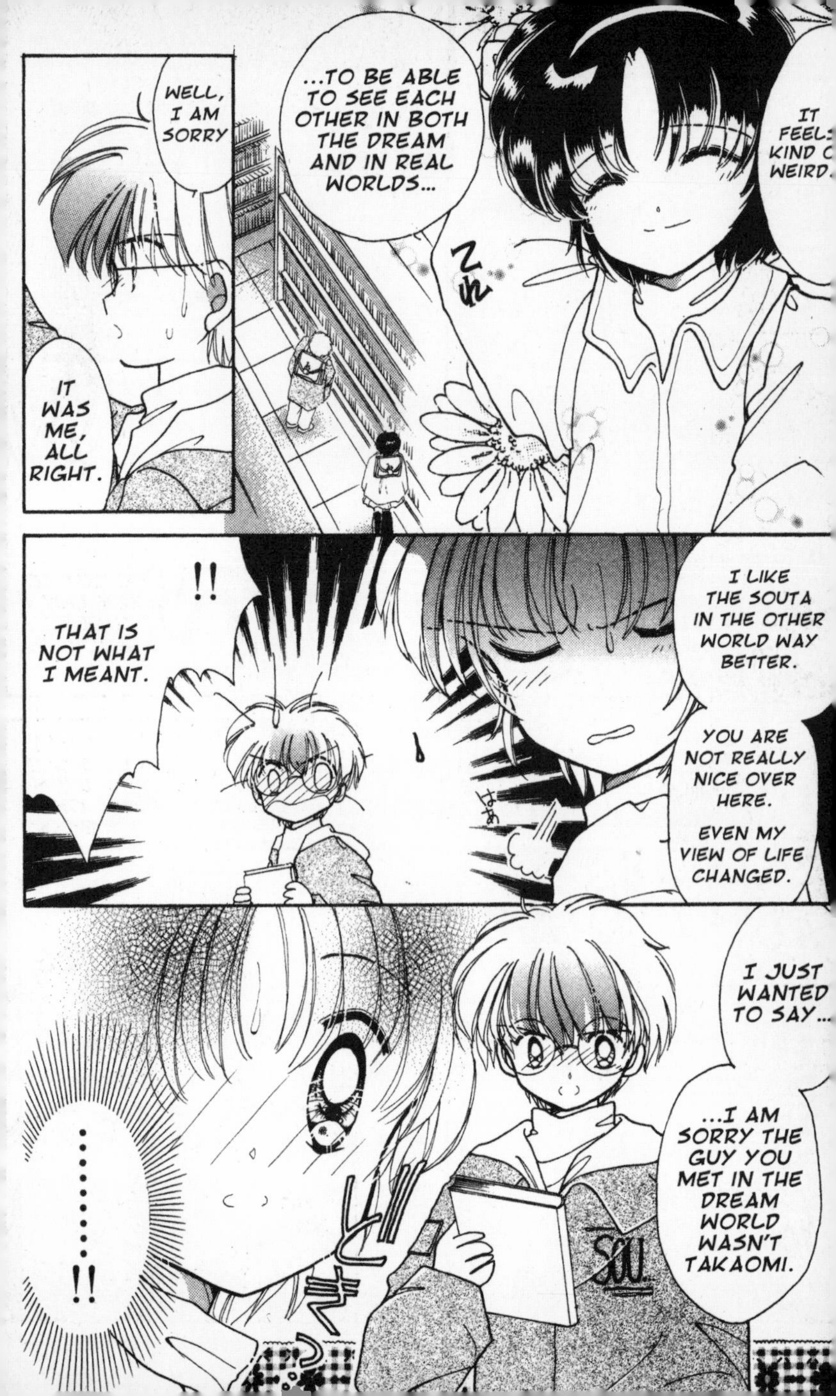
IT FEELS KIND OF WEIRD.
...TO BE ABLE TO SEE EACH OTHER IN BOTH THE DREAM AND IN REAL WORLDS...
てれ
WELL, I AM SORRY
IT WAS ME, ALL RIGHT.
I LIKE THE SOUTA IN THE OTHER WORLD WAY BETTER.
YOU ARE NOT REALLY NICE OVER HERE.
EVEN MY VIEW OF LIFE CHANGED.
はぁ
!!
THAT IS NOT WHAT I MEANT.
I JUST WANTED TO SAY...
...I AM SORRY THE GUY YOU MET IN THE DREAM WORLD WASN'T TAKAOMI.
SOU...
どきっ
......!!

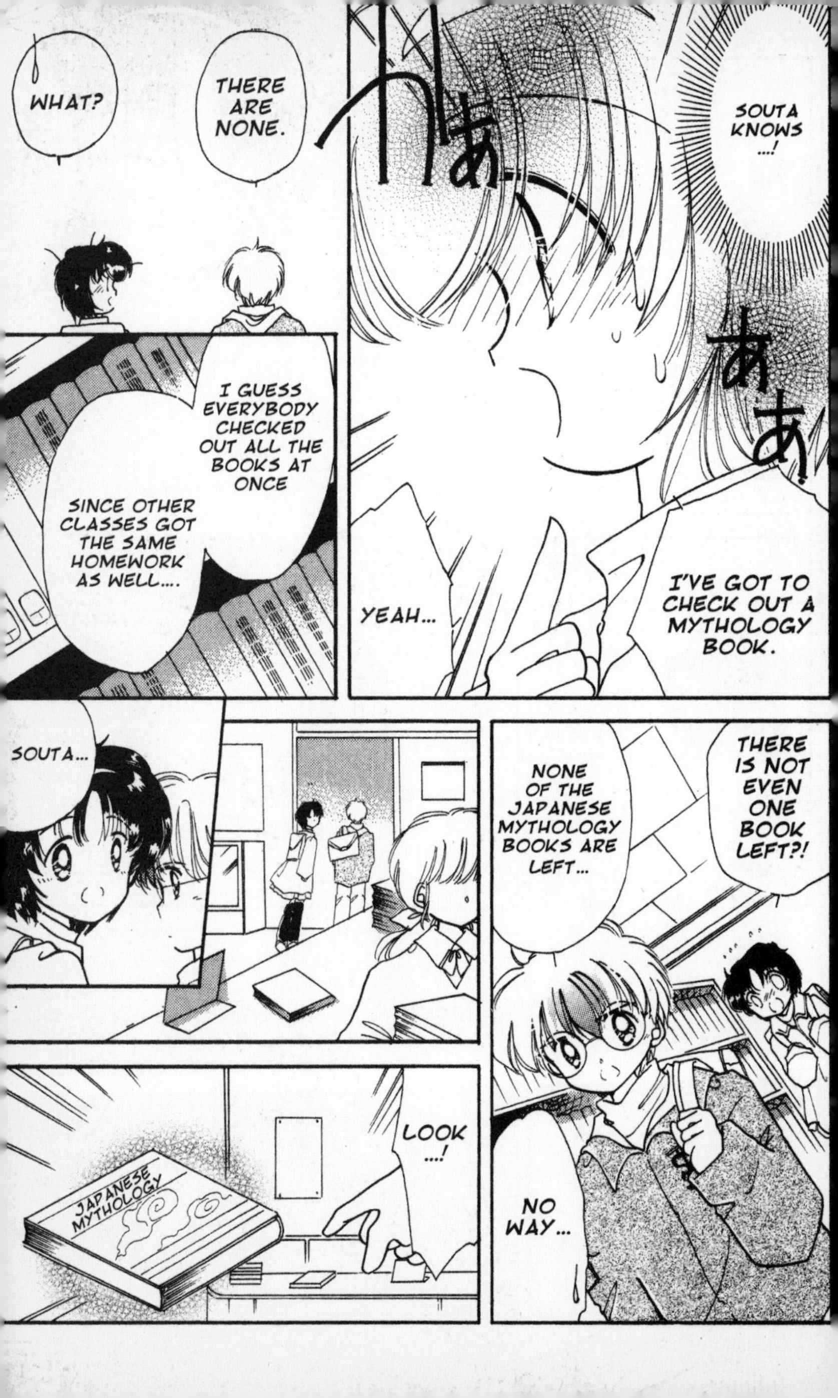

SOUTA KNOWS ...!
わあ
ああ
I'VE GOT TO CHECK OUT A MYTHOLOGY BOOK.
YEAH...
THERE ARE NONE.
WHAT?
I GUESS EVERYBODY CHECKED OUT ALL THE BOOKS AT ONCE
SINCE OTHER CLASSES GOT THE SAME HOMEWORK AS WELL....
THERE IS NOT EVEN ONE BOOK LEFT?!
NONE OF THE JAPANESE MYTHOLOGY BOOKS ARE LEFT...
NO WAY...
SOUTA...
LOOK ....!
JAPANESE MYTHOLOGY

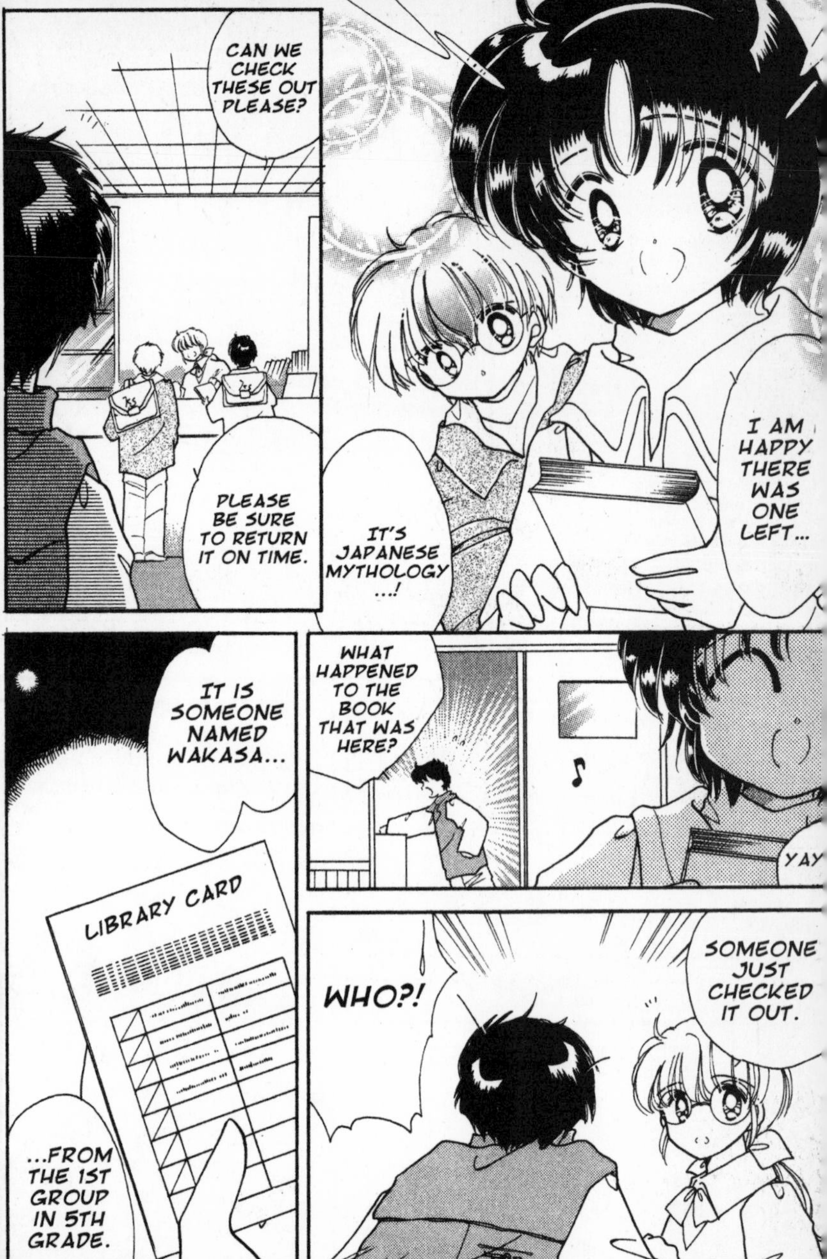
I AM HAPPY THERE WAS ONE LEFT...
IT'S JAPANESE MYTHOLOGY ...!
CAN WE CHECK THESE OUT PLEASE?
PLEASE BE SURE TO RETURN IT ON TIME.
YAY
WHAT HAPPENED TO THE BOOK THAT WAS HERE?
SOMEONE JUST CHECKED IT OUT.
WHO?!
IT IS SOMEONE NAMED WAKASA...
LIBRARY CARD
...FROM THE 1ST GROUP IN 5TH GRADE.

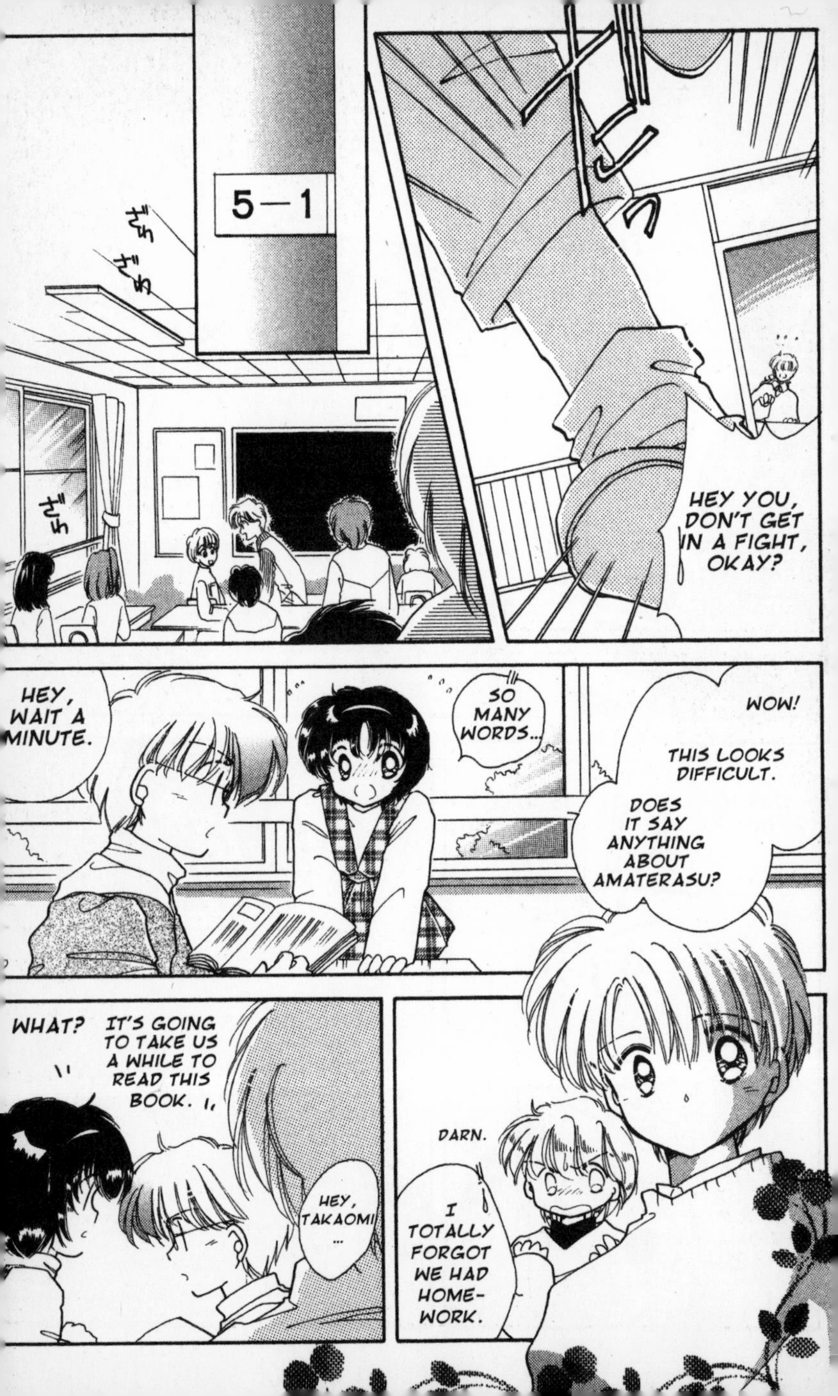
HEY YOU, DON'T GET IN A FIGHT, OKAY?
5—1
ざわ ざわ
ざわ
WOW!
THIS LOOKS DIFFICULT.
DOES IT SAY ANYTHING ABOUT AMATERASU?
SO MANY WORDS...
HEY, WAIT A MINUTE.
DARN.
I TOTALLY FORGOT WE HAD HOME-WORK.
HEY, TAKAOMI...
WHAT?
IT'S GOING TO TAKE US A WHILE TO READ THIS BOOK.

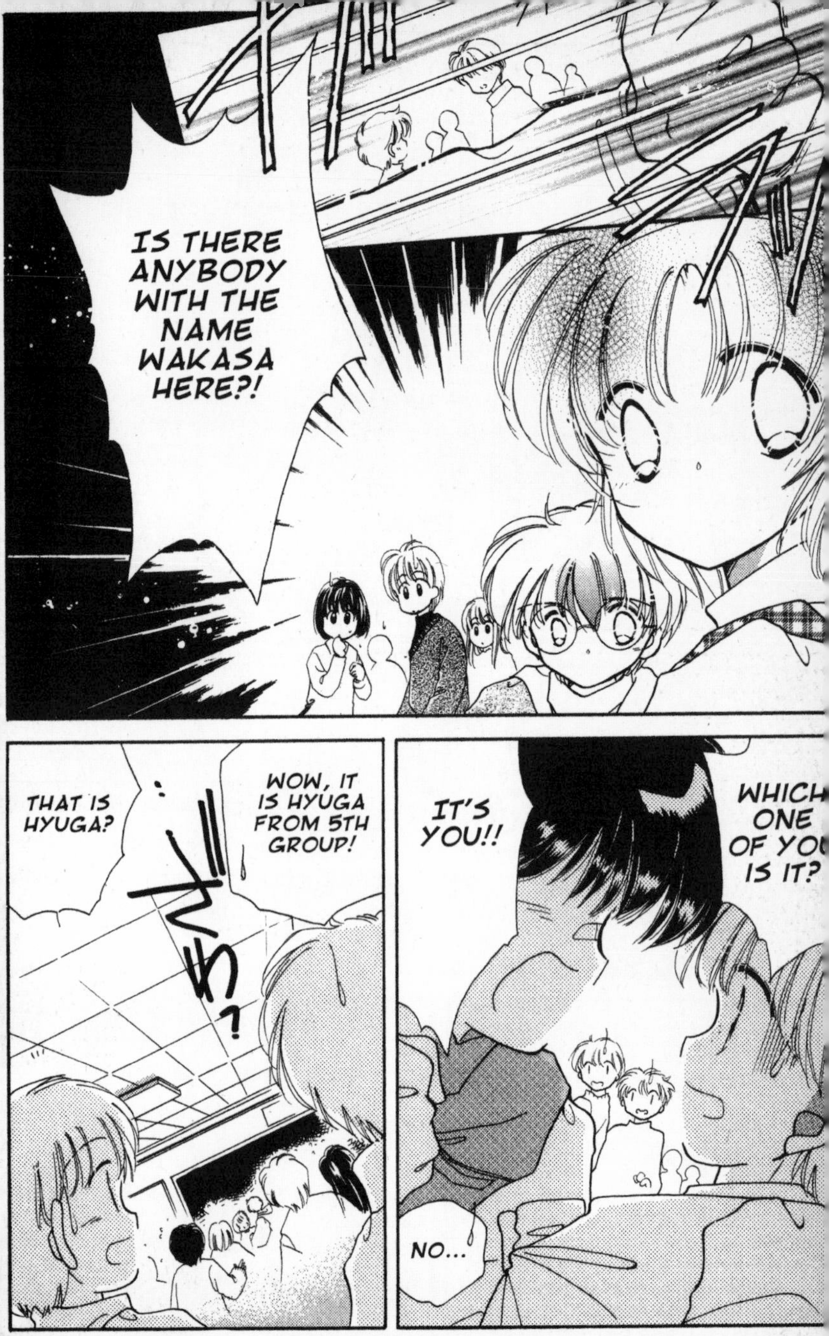
IS THERE ANYBODY WITH THE NAME WAKASA HERE?!
WHICH ONE OF YOU IS IT?
IT'S YOU!!
NO...
WOW, IT IS HYUGA FROM 5TH GROUP!
THAT IS HYUGA?

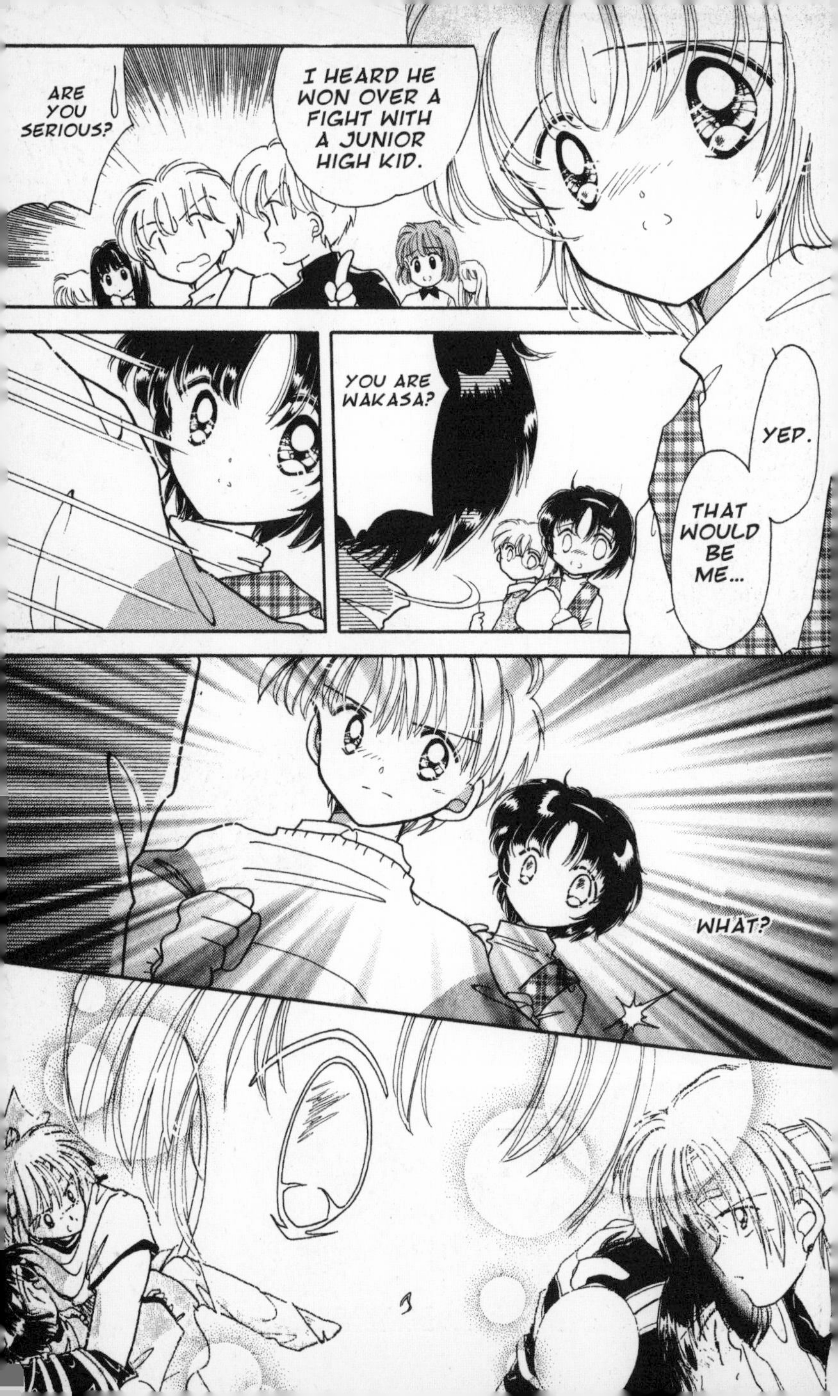

I HEARD HE WON OVER A FIGHT WITH A JUNIOR HIGH KID.
ARE YOU SERIOUS?
YOU ARE WAKASA?
YEP.
THAT WOULD BE ME...
WHAT?

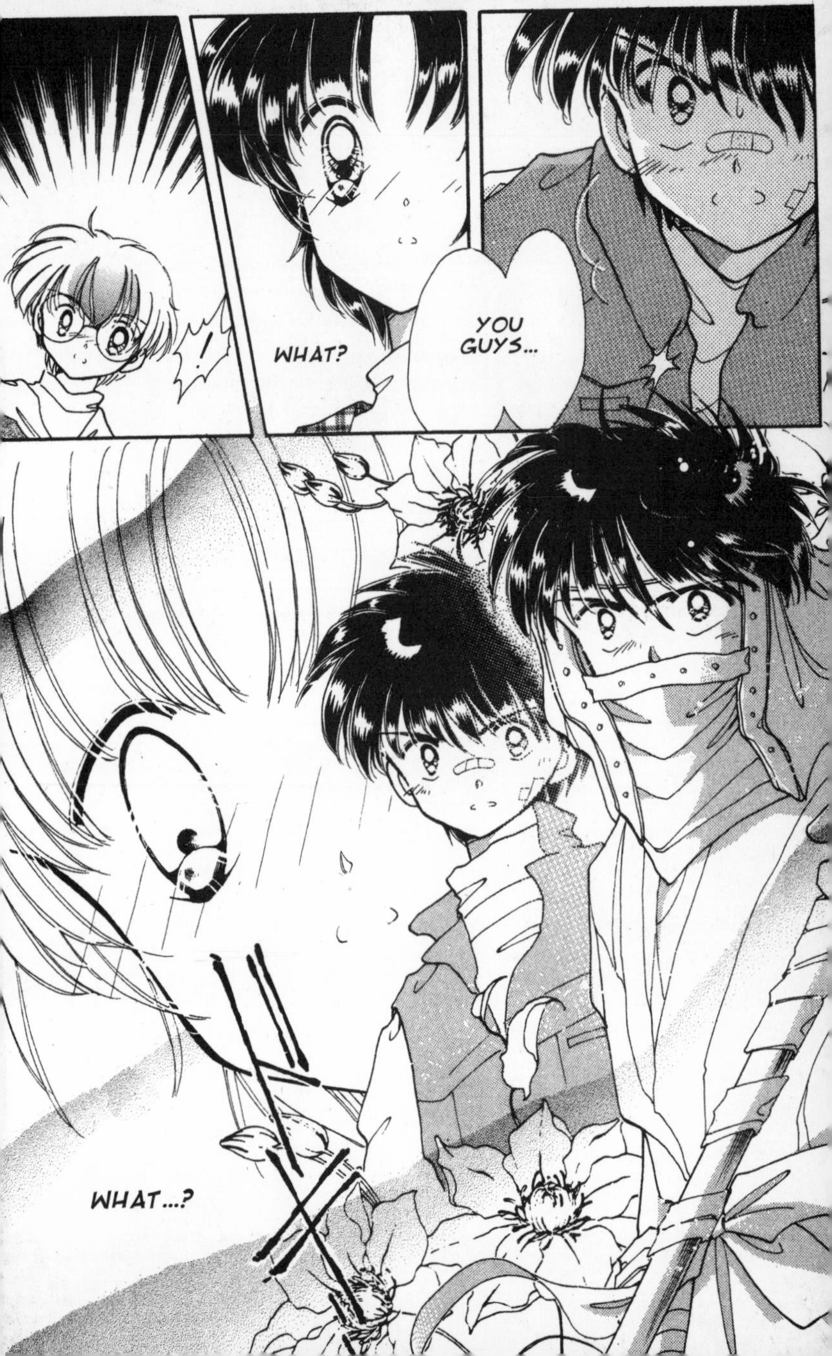
YOU GUYS...
WHAT?
!
WHAT...?

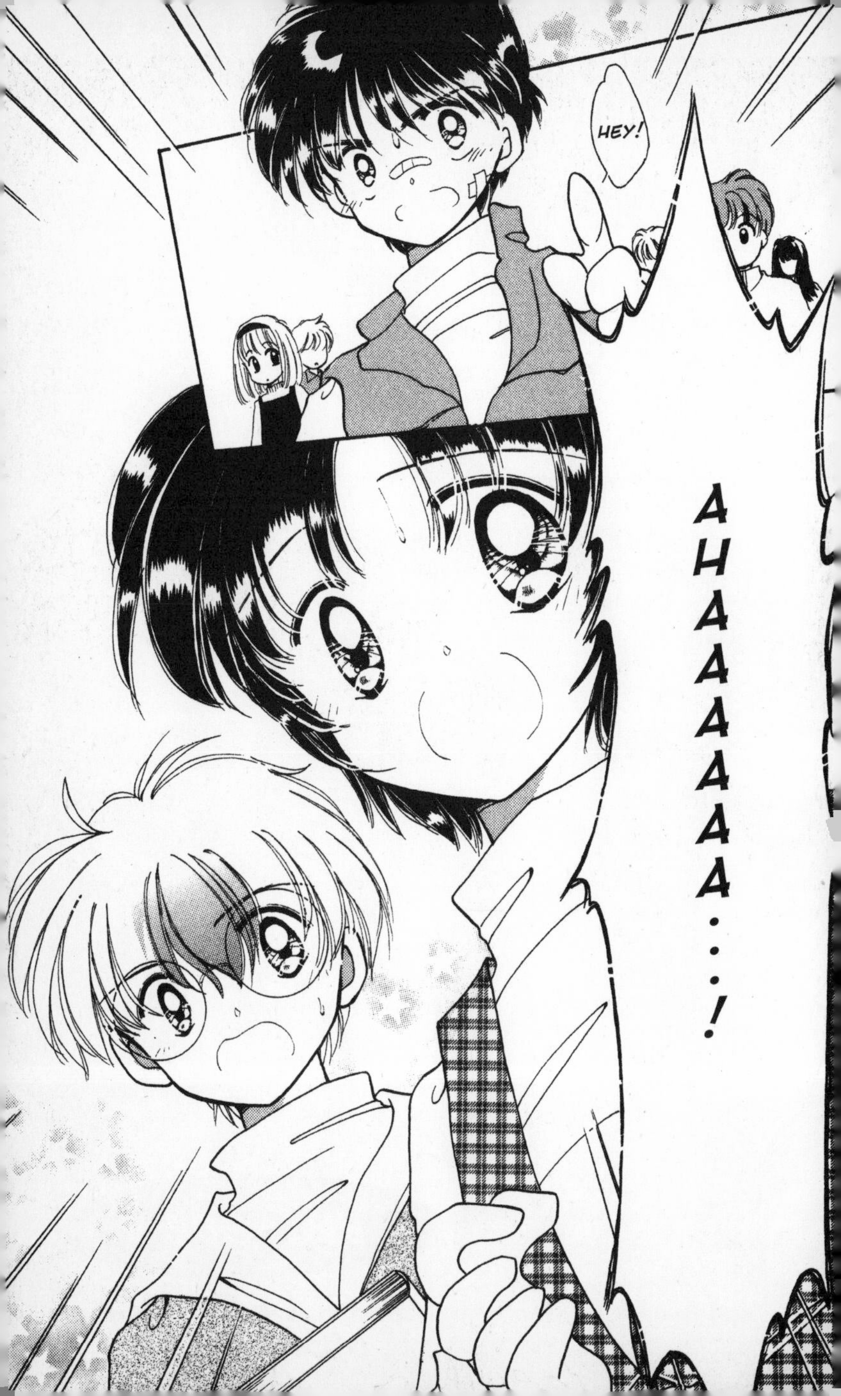
HEY!
AHAAAAAA...!

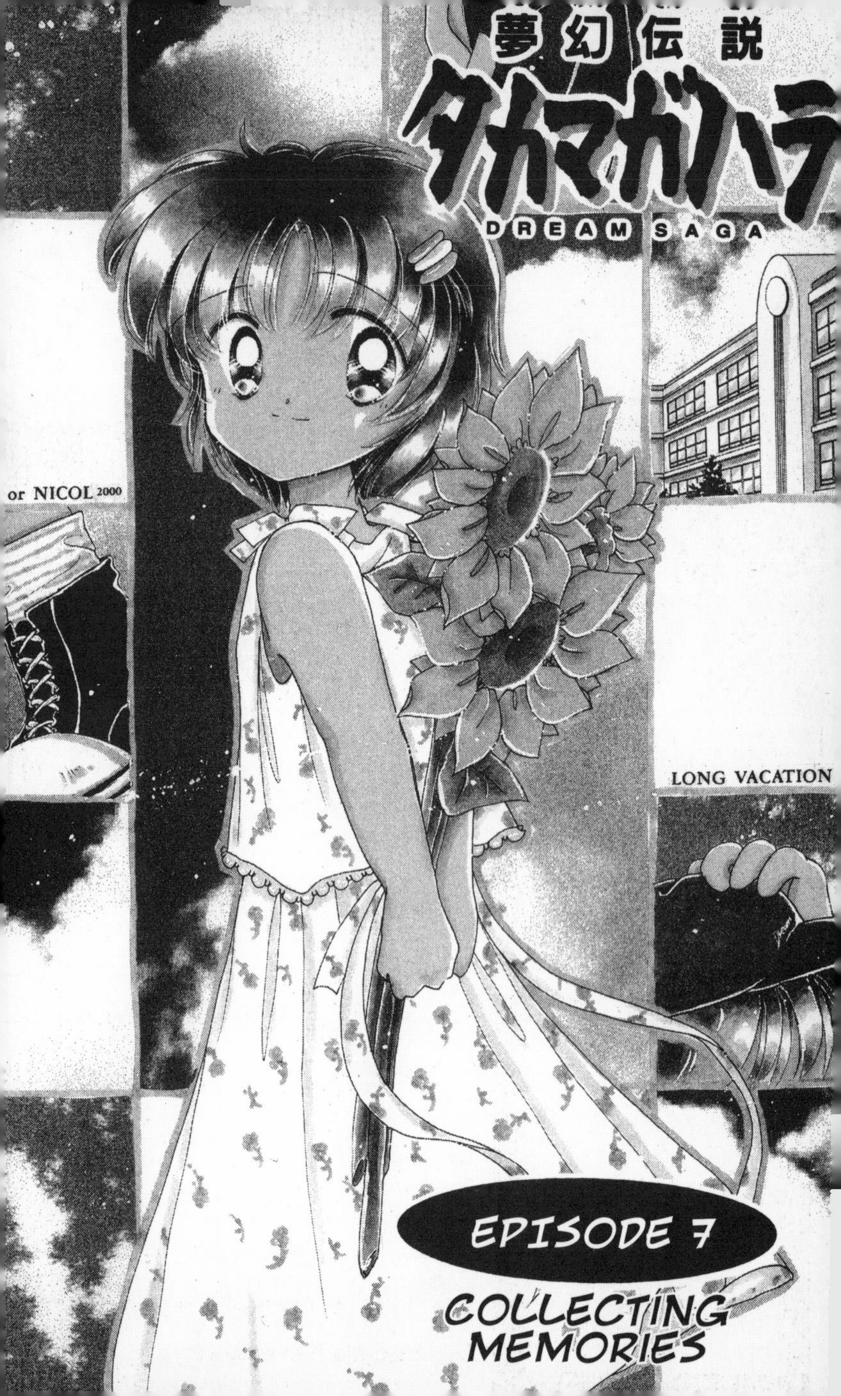

夢幻伝説
タカマガハラ
DREAM SAGA
or NICOL 2000
LONG VACATION
EPISODE 7
COLLECTING MEMORIES

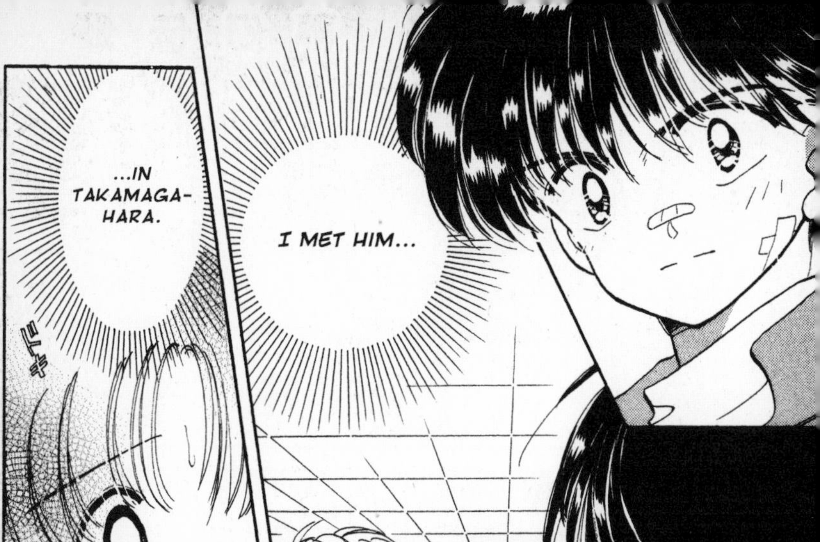
I MET HIM...
...IN TAKAMAGA-HARA.
UMMM ...

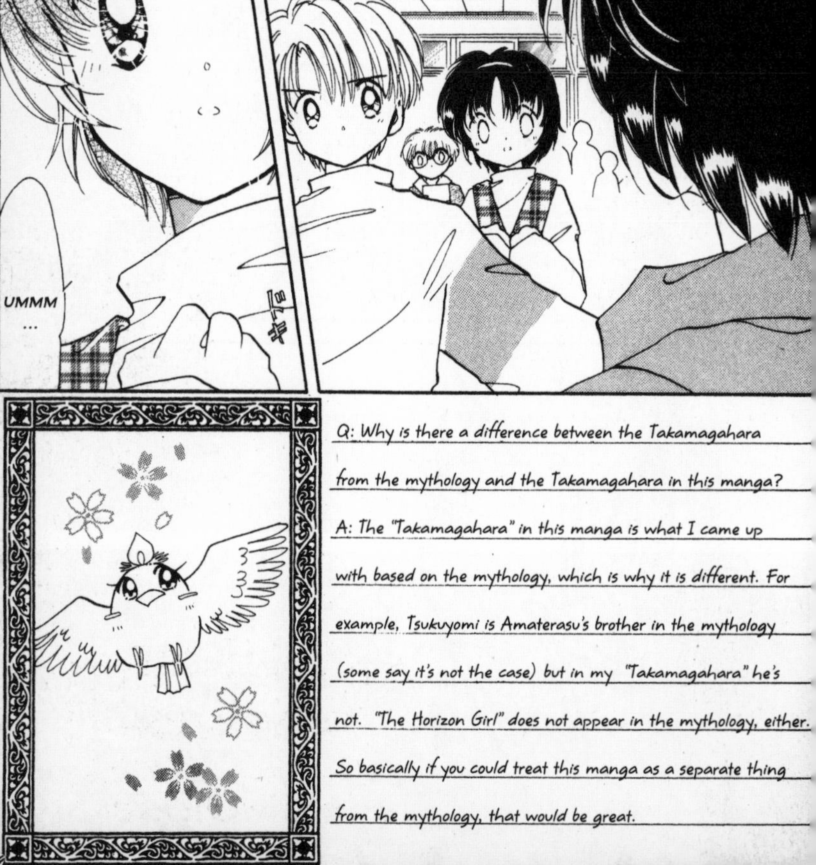

Q: Why is there a difference between the Takamagahara from the mythology and the Takamagahara in this manga?

A: The "Takamagahara" in this manga is what I came up with based on the mythology, which is why it is different. For example, Tsukuyomi is Amaterasu's brother in the mythology (some say it's not the case) but in my "Takamagahara" he's not. "The Horizon Girl" does not appear in the mythology, either. So basically if you could treat this manga as a separate thing from the mythology, that would be great.

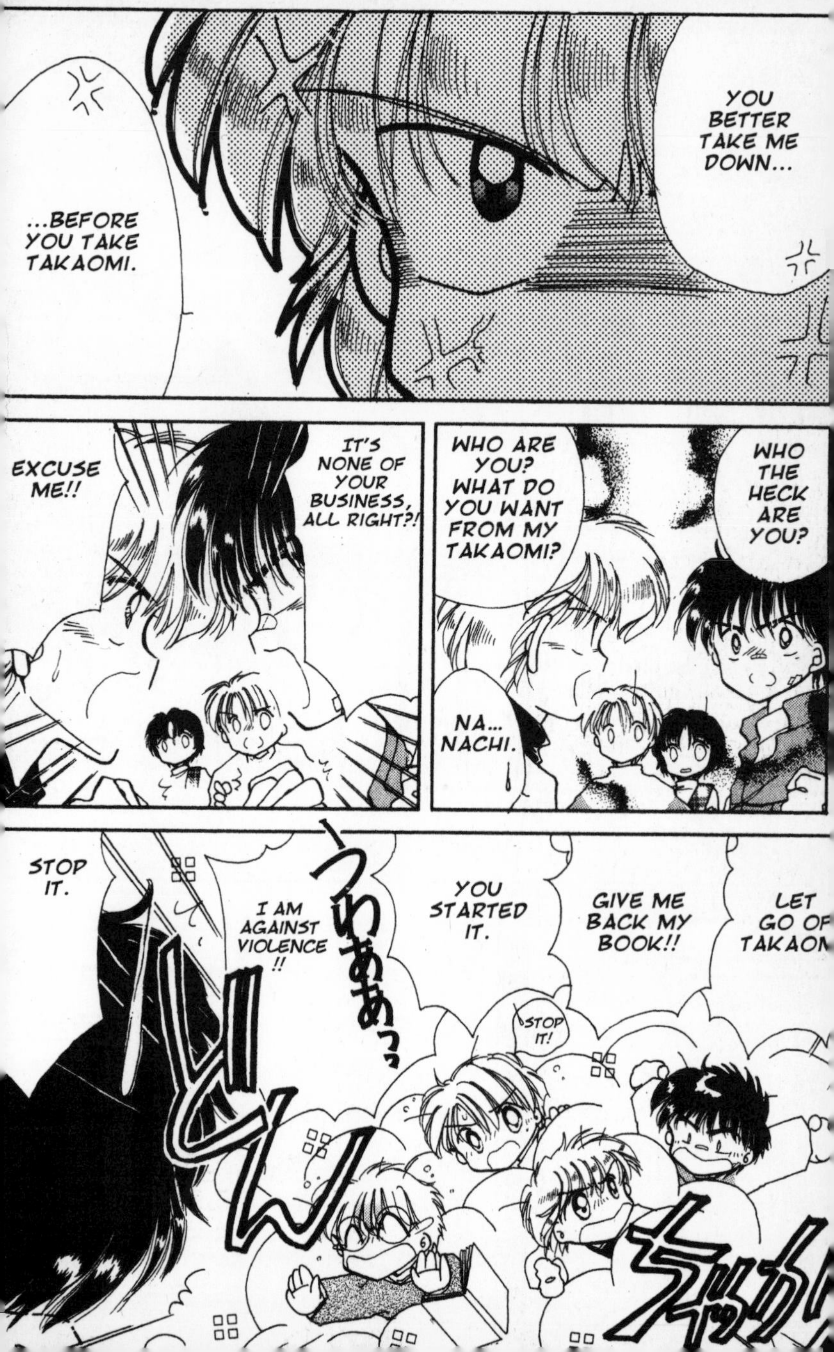
YOU BETTER TAKE ME DOWN...
...BEFORE YOU TAKE TAKAOMI.
WHO THE HECK ARE YOU?
WHO ARE YOU? WHAT DO YOU WANT FROM MY TAKAOMI?
NA... NACHI.
IT'S NONE OF YOUR BUSINESS, ALL RIGHT?!
EXCUSE ME!!
LET GO OF TAKAOM
GIVE ME BACK MY BOOK!!
YOU STARTED IT.
うわああっっ
STOP IT!
I AM AGAINST VIOLENCE!!
どん
STOP IT.

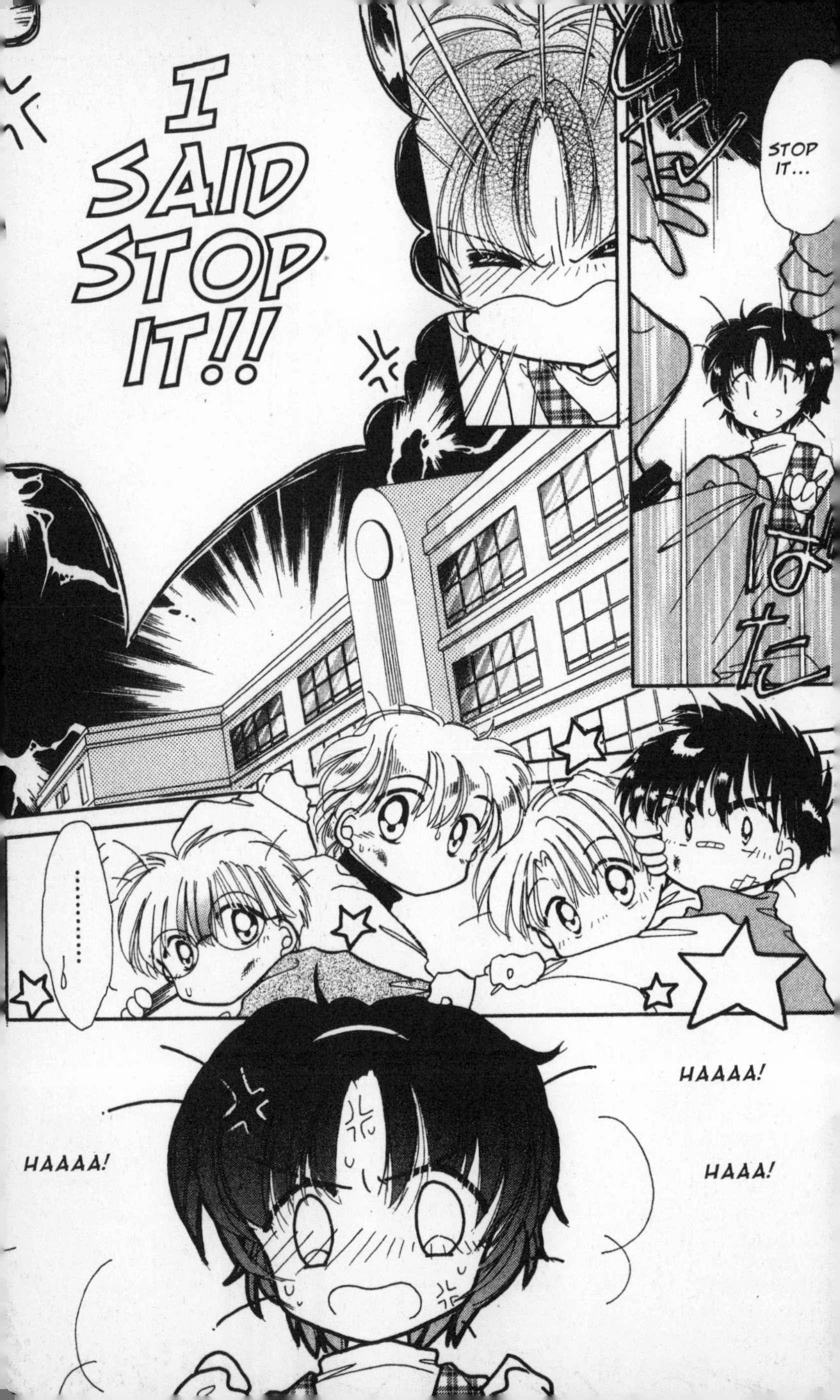
STOP IT...
はた
I SAID STOP IT!!
......
HAAAA!
HAAA!
HAAAA!

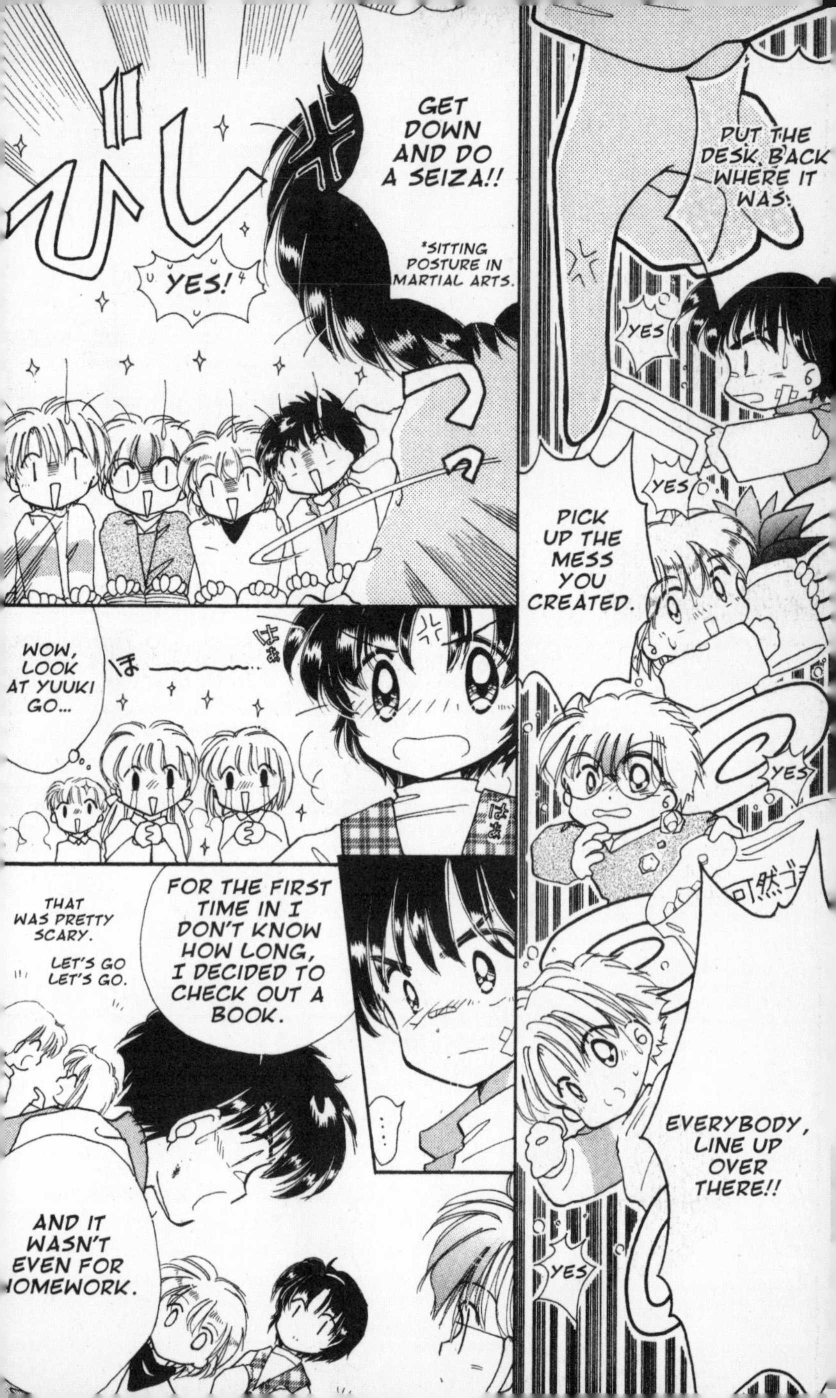
PUT THE DESK BACK WHERE IT WAS.
YES
YES
PICK UP THE MESS YOU CREATED.
YES
EVERYBODY, LINE UP OVER THERE!!
YES
ひし
GET DOWN AND DO A SEIZA!!
*SITTING POSTURE IN MARTIAL ARTS.
YES!
はぁ
ほ ――
WOW, LOOK AT YUUKI GO...
はぁ
....
FOR THE FIRST TIME IN I DON'T KNOW HOW LONG, I DECIDED TO CHECK OUT A BOOK.
THAT WAS PRETTY SCARY.
LET'S GO LET'S GO.
AND IT WASN'T EVEN FOR HOMEWORK.

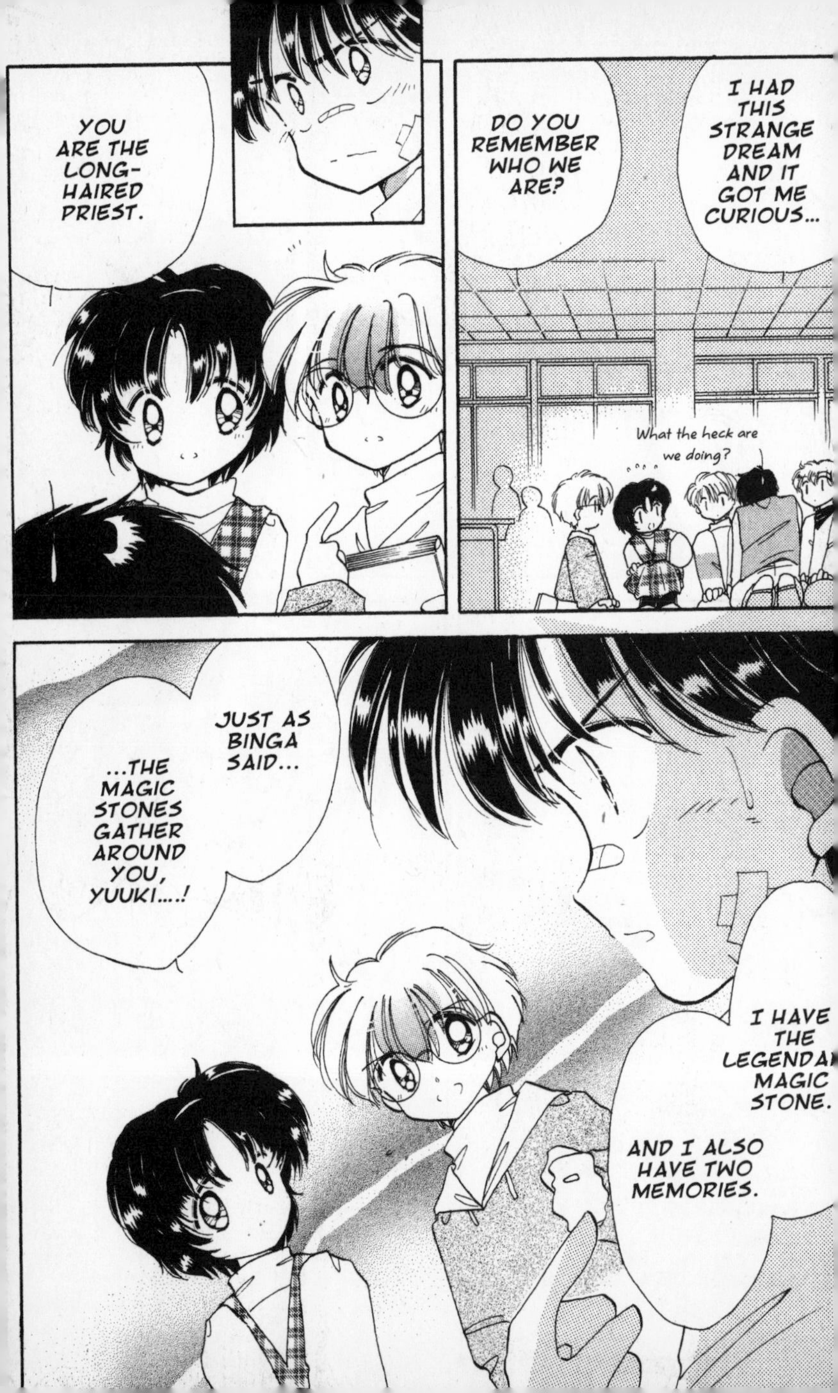
I HAD THIS STRANGE DREAM AND IT GOT ME CURIOUS...
DO YOU REMEMBER WHO WE ARE?
What the heck are we doing?
YOU ARE THE LONG-HAIRED PRIEST.
I HAVE THE LEGENDA MAGIC STONE.
AND I ALSO HAVE TWO MEMORIES.
JUST AS BINGA SAID...
...THE MAGIC STONES GATHER AROUND YOU, YUUKI....!

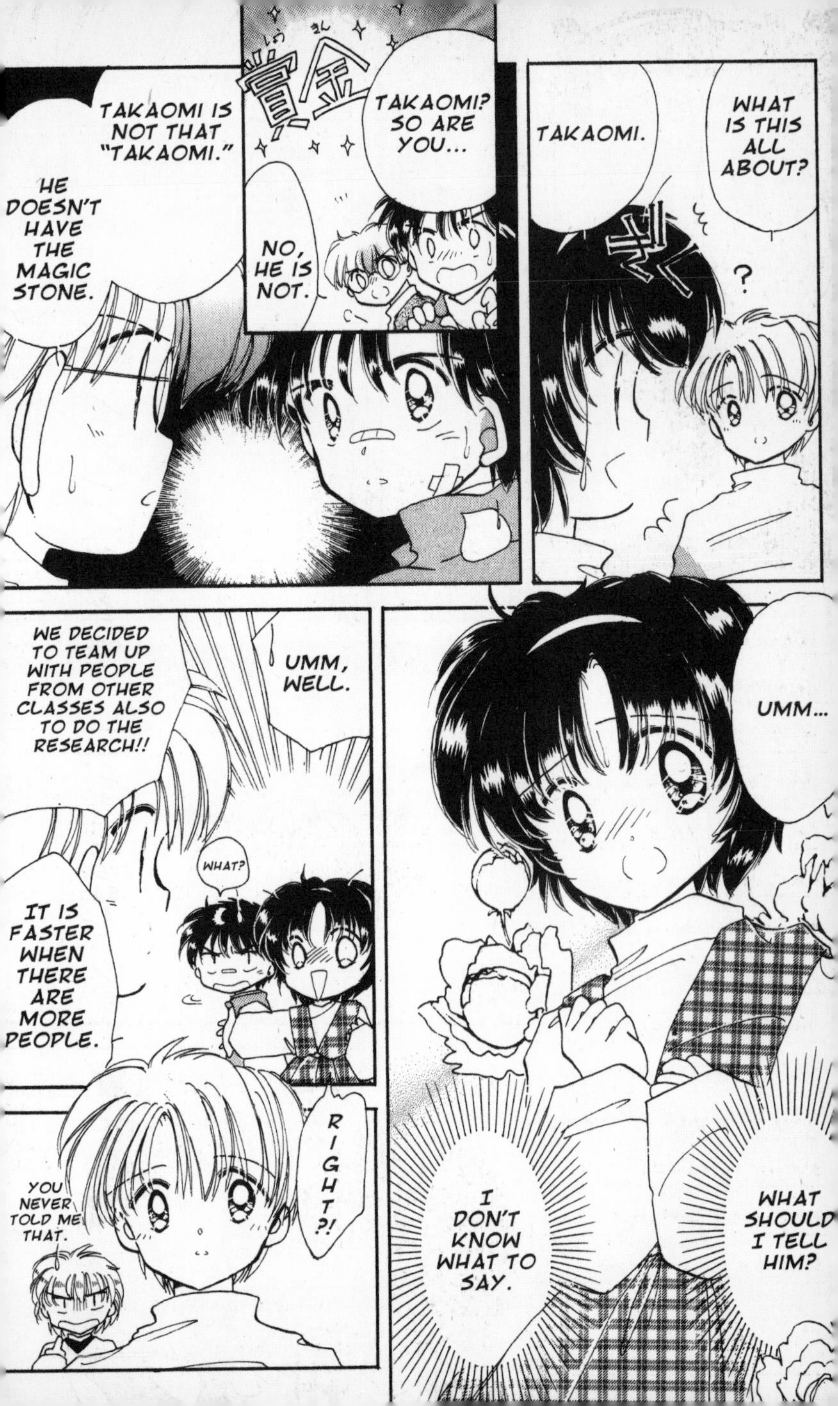
WHAT IS THIS ALL ABOUT?
TAKAOMI.
賞金
TAKAOMI? SO ARE YOU...
NO, HE IS NOT.
TAKAOMI IS NOT THAT "TAKAOMI."
HE DOESN'T HAVE THE MAGIC STONE.
UMM...
WHAT SHOULD I TELL HIM?
I DON'T KNOW WHAT TO SAY.
UMM, WELL.
WE DECIDED TO TEAM UP WITH PEOPLE FROM OTHER CLASSES ALSO TO DO THE RESEARCH!!
WHAT?
IT IS FASTER WHEN THERE ARE MORE PEOPLE.
RIGHT?!
YOU NEVER TOLD ME THAT.

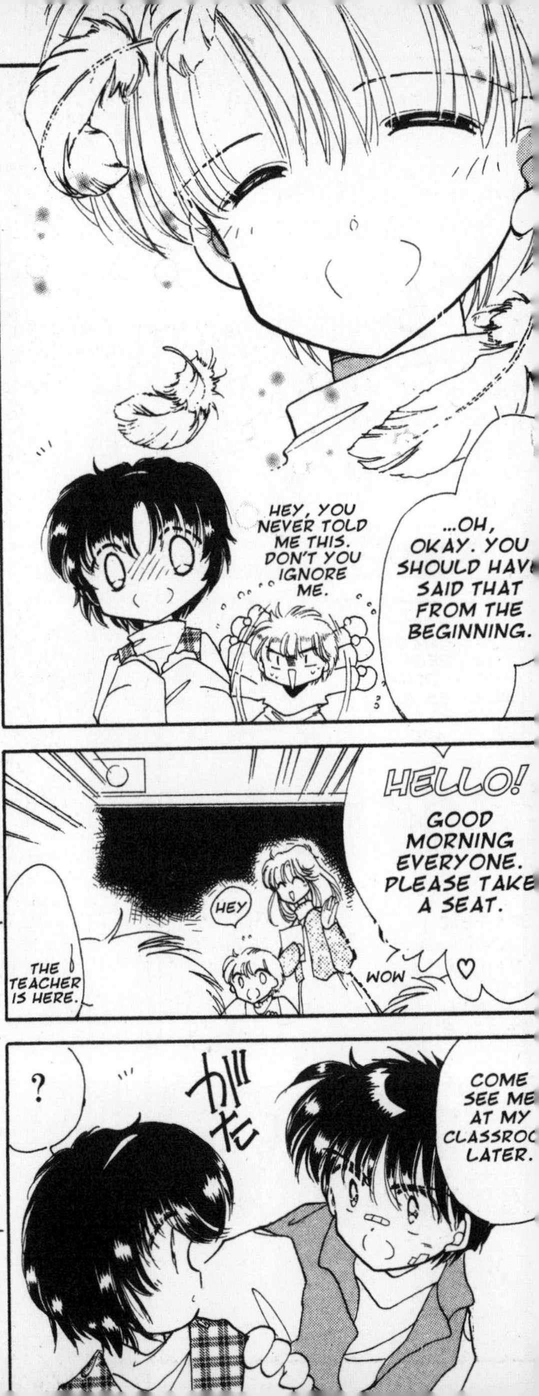
...OH, OKAY. YOU SHOULD HAV SAID THAT FROM THE BEGINNING.
HEY, YOU NEVER TOLD ME THIS. DON'T YOU IGNORE ME.
HELLO! GOOD MORNING EVERYONE. PLEASE TAKE A SEAT.
WOW
HEY
THE TEACHER IS HERE.
COME SEE ME AT MY CLASSROO LATER.
?

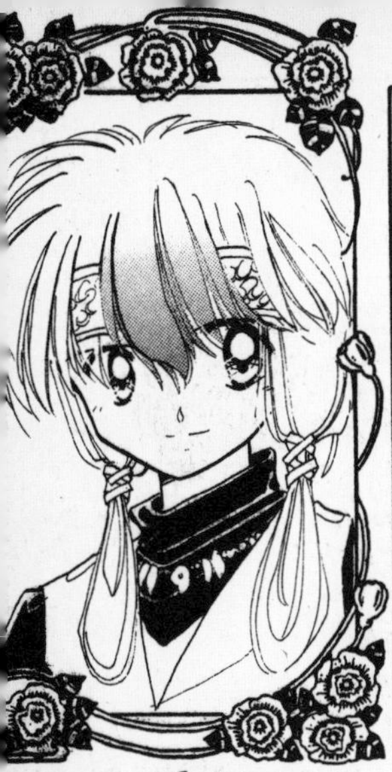

Souta

Born on February 21st.

Blood type: A

He is a priest and a psychic. Just like the Souta in Nakatsukuni, he is a very smart guy who studies hard. He has been doing research for a long period of time about the "the end of the legend." He is currently 14 years old. He doesn't like ghosts. Some are starting to suspect that he may have a crush on Yuuki... but it is a secret for now.

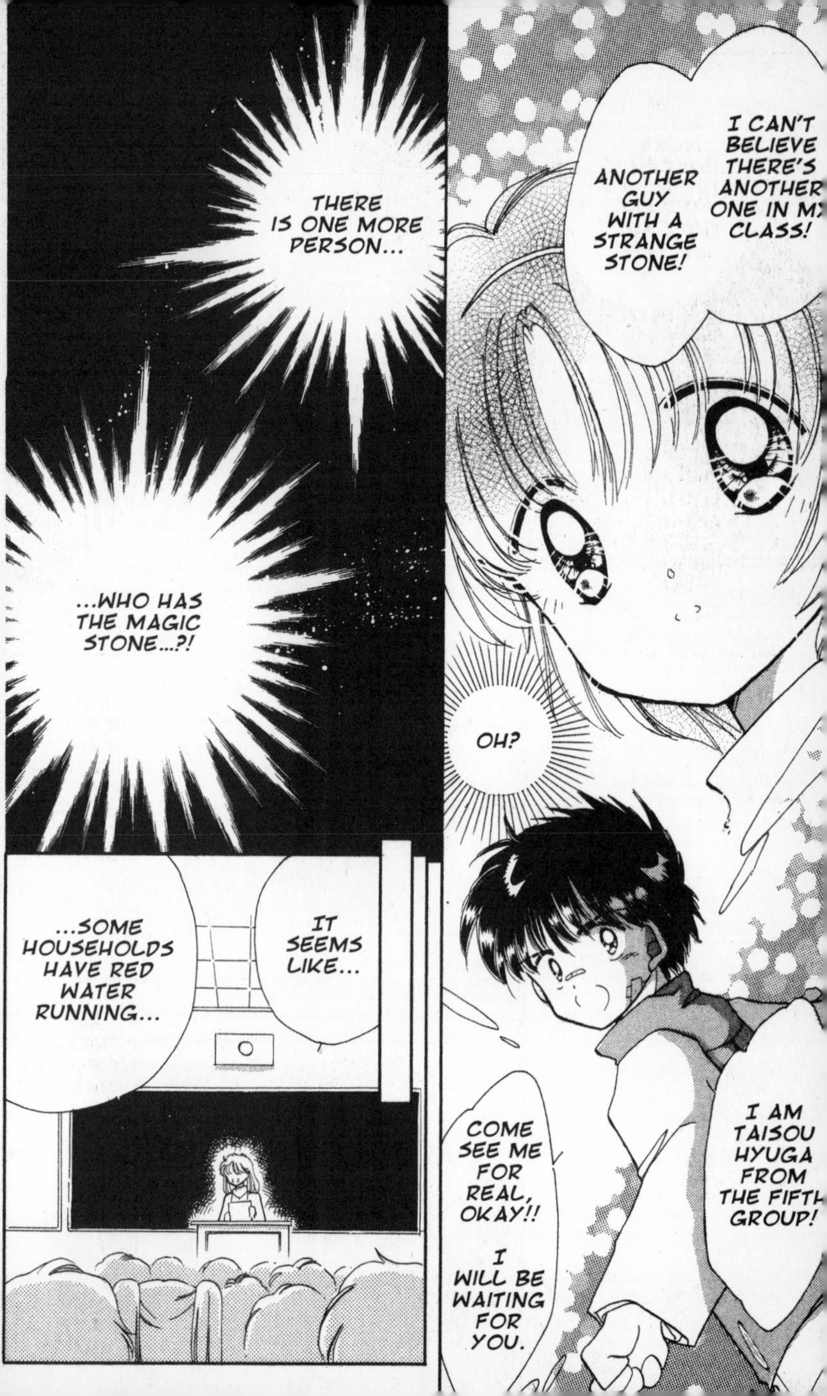
I CAN'T BELIEVE THERE'S ANOTHER ONE IN MY CLASS!
ANOTHER GUY WITH A STRANGE STONE!
OH?
I AM TAISOU HYUGA FROM THE FIFTH GROUP!
COME SEE ME FOR REAL, OKAY!!
I WILL BE WAITING FOR YOU.
THERE IS ONE MORE PERSON...
...WHO HAS THE MAGIC STONE...?!
IT SEEMS LIKE...
...SOME HOUSEHOLDS HAVE RED WATER RUNNING...

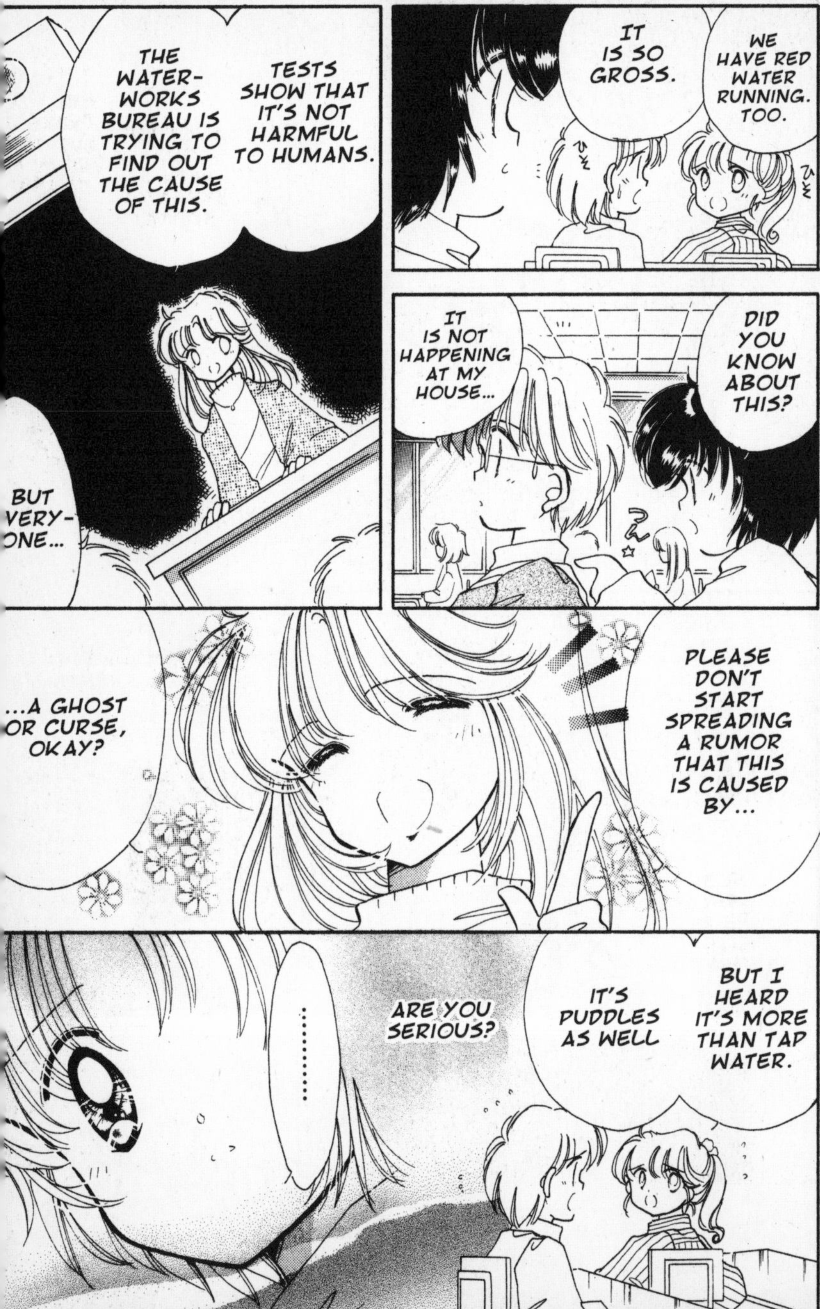
WE HAVE RED WATER RUNNING. TOO.
IT IS SO GROSS.
DID YOU KNOW ABOUT THIS?
IT IS NOT HAPPENING AT MY HOUSE...
TESTS SHOW THAT IT'S NOT HARMFUL TO HUMANS.
THE WATER-WORKS BUREAU IS TRYING TO FIND OUT THE CAUSE OF THIS.
BUT VERY-ONE...
PLEASE DON'T START SPREADING A RUMOR THAT THIS IS CAUSED BY...
...A GHOST OR CURSE, OKAY?
BUT I HEARD IT'S MORE THAN TAP WATER.
IT'S PUDDLES AS WELL
ARE YOU SERIOUS?
....

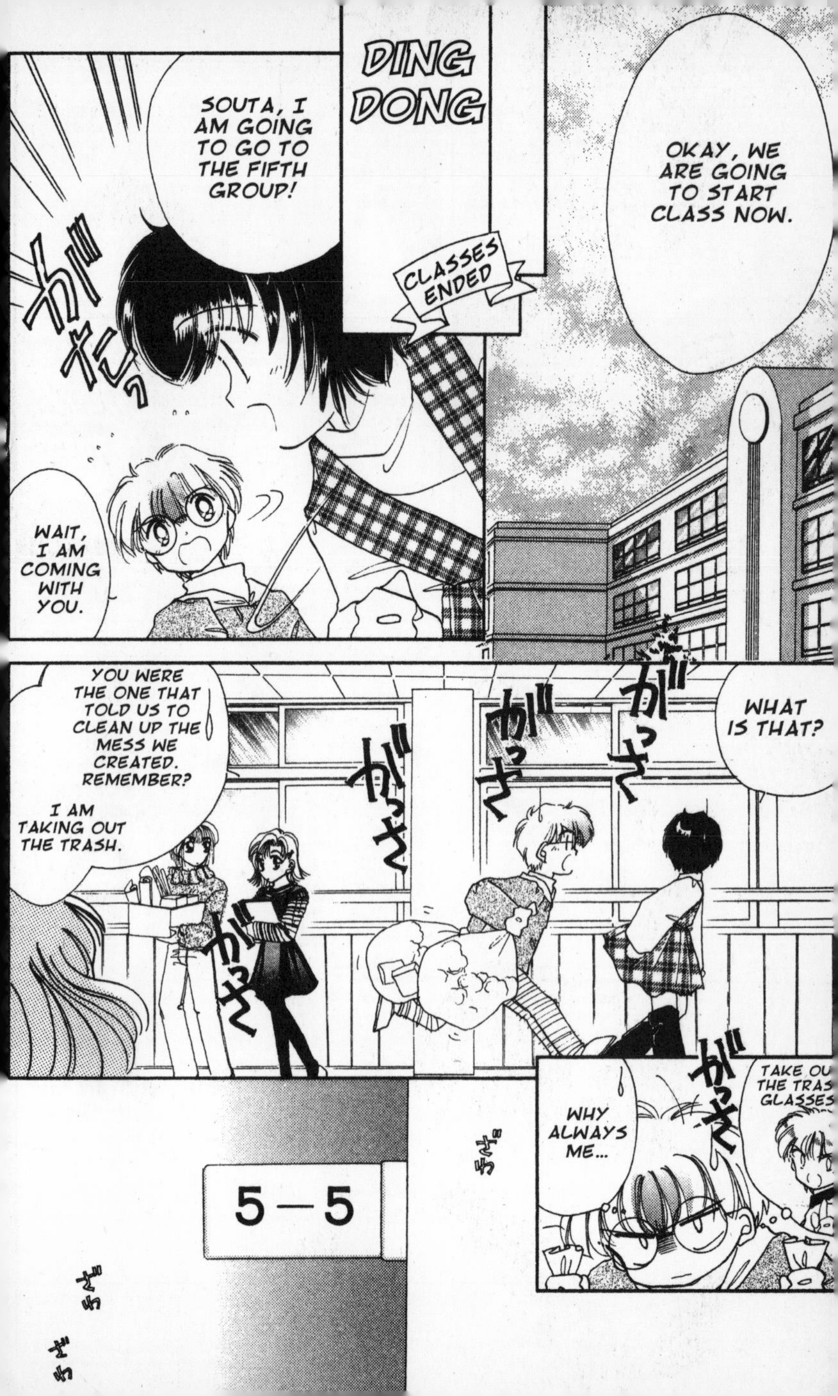
OKAY, WE ARE GOING TO START CLASS NOW.
DING DONG
CLASSES ENDED
SOUTA, I AM GOING TO GO TO THE FIFTH GROUP!
WAIT, I AM COMING WITH YOU.
WHAT IS THAT?
がっさ
がっさ
がっさ
YOU WERE THE ONE THAT TOLD US TO CLEAN UP THE MESS WE CREATED. REMEMBER?
I AM TAKING OUT THE TRASH.
がっさ
TAKE OU THE TRAS GLASSES
がっさ
WHY ALWAYS ME...
ざわ
5—5
ざわ
ざわ

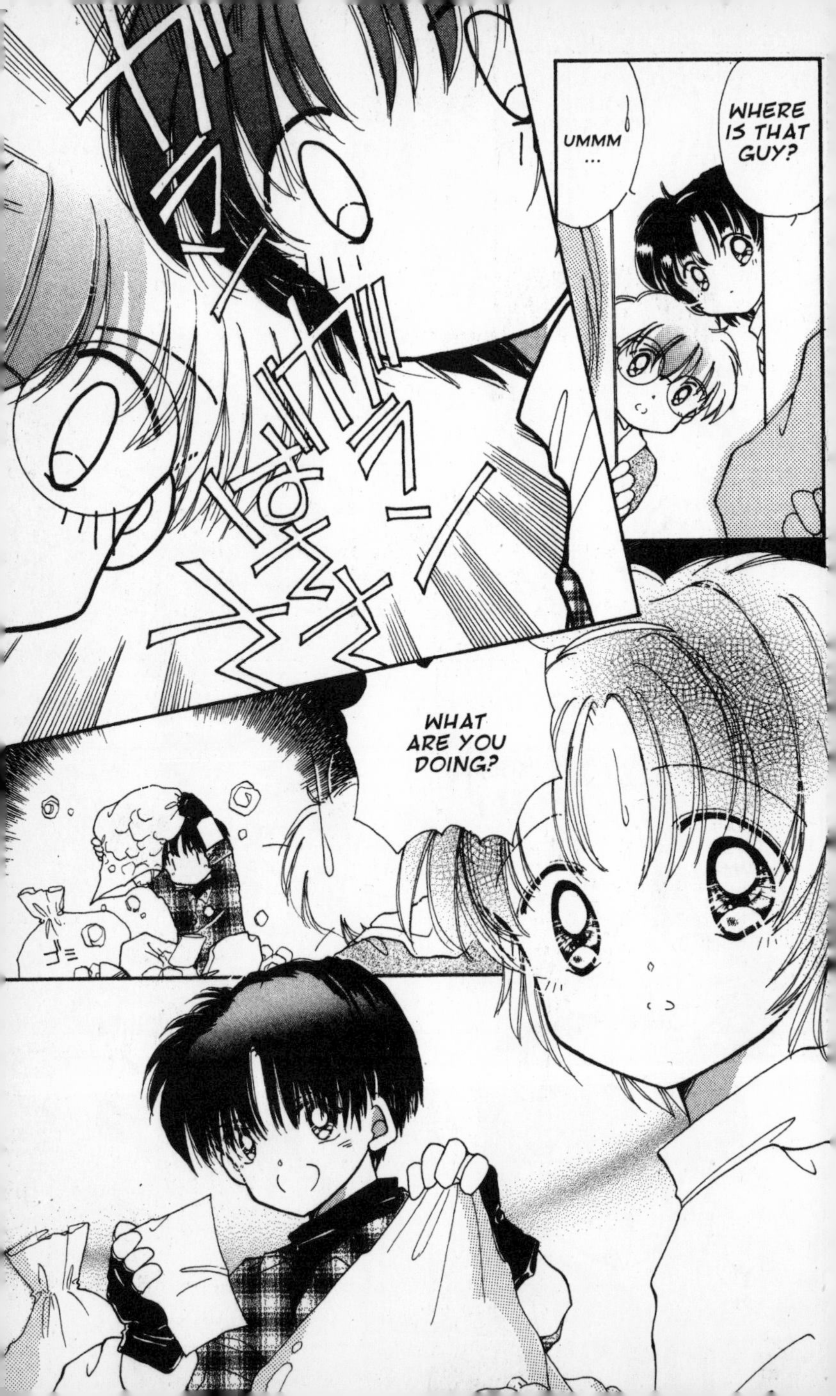
WHERE IS THAT GUY?
UMMM ...
WHAT ARE YOU DOING?
ゴミ

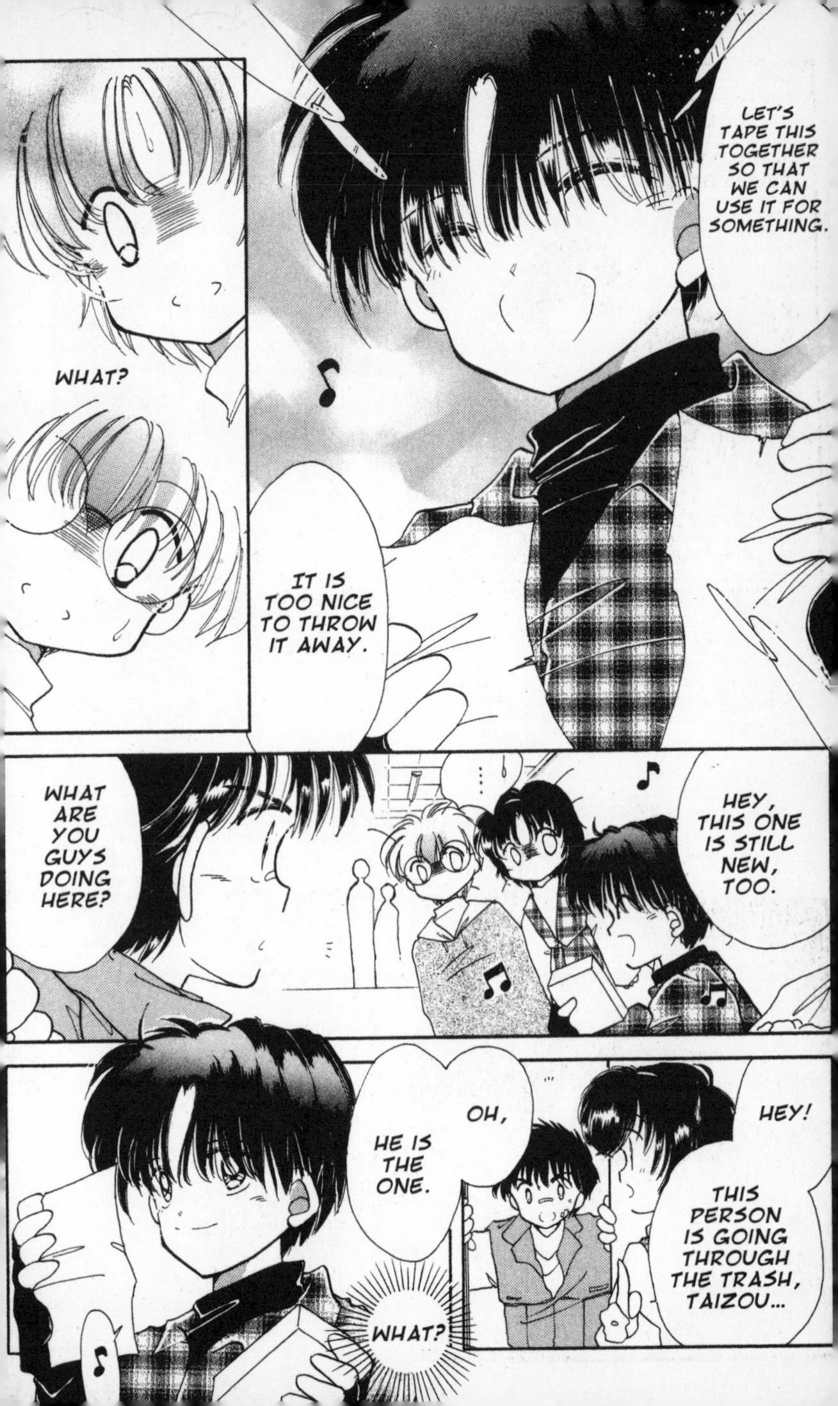
LET'S TAPE THIS TOGETHER SO THAT WE CAN USE IT FOR SOMETHING.
IT IS TOO NICE TO THROW IT AWAY.
WHAT?
HEY, THIS ONE IS STILL NEW, TOO.
WHAT ARE YOU GUYS DOING HERE?
HEY!
THIS PERSON IS GOING THROUGH THE TRASH, TAIZOU...
OH,
HE IS THE ONE.
WHAT?

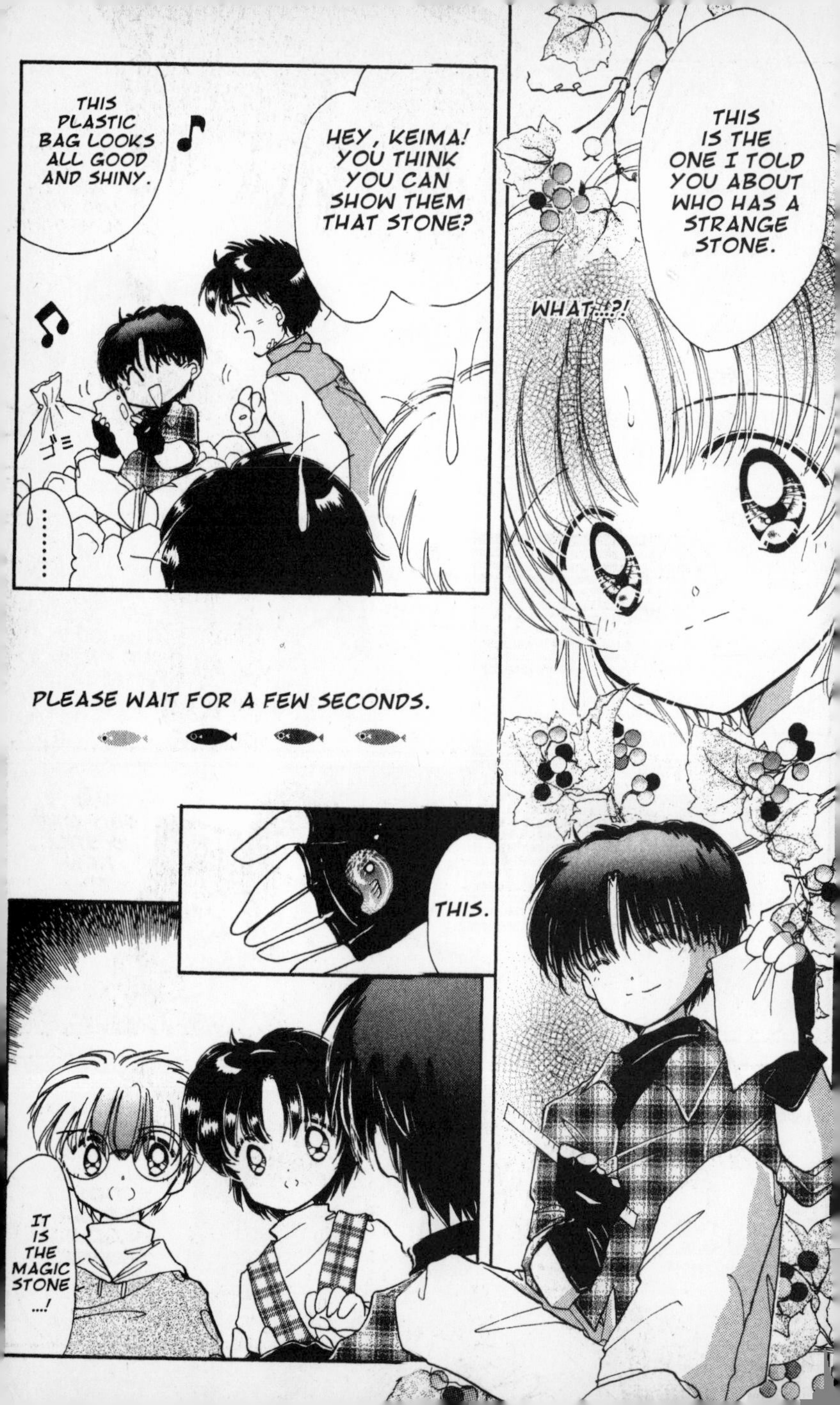

THIS IS THE ONE I TOLD YOU ABOUT WHO HAS A STRANGE STONE.
WHAT...?!
HEY, KEIMA! YOU THINK YOU CAN SHOW THEM THAT STONE?
THIS PLASTIC BAG LOOKS ALL GOOD AND SHINY.
ゴミ
......
PLEASE WAIT FOR A FEW SECONDS.
THIS.
IT IS THE MAGIC STONE...!

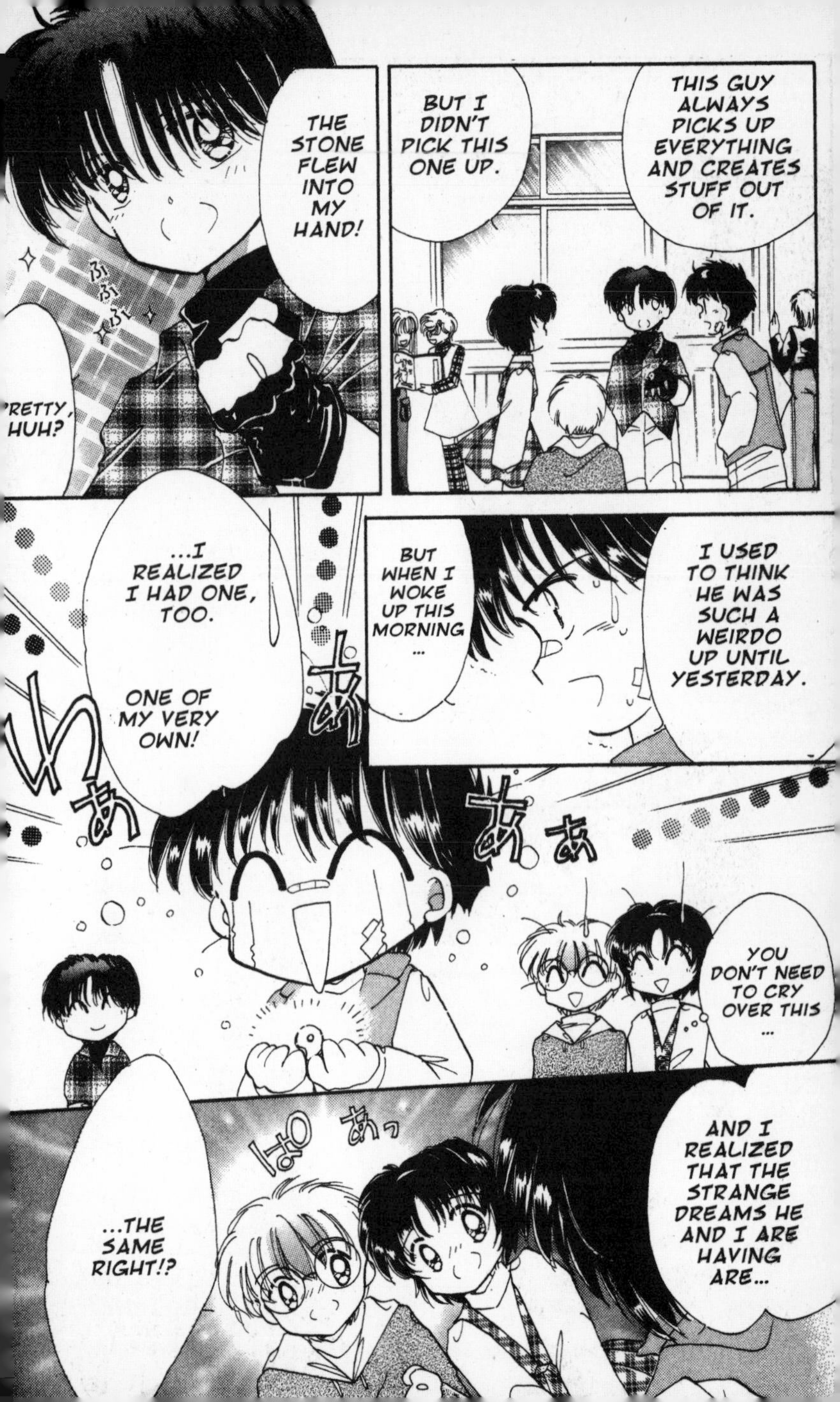
THIS GUY ALWAYS PICKS UP EVERYTHING AND CREATES STUFF OUT OF IT.
BUT I DIDN'T PICK THIS ONE UP.
THE STONE FLEW INTO MY HAND!
ふふふ
'RETTY, HUH?
I USED TO THINK HE WAS SUCH A WEIRDO UP UNTIL YESTERDAY.
BUT WHEN I WOKE UP THIS MORNING...
...I REALIZED I HAD ONE, TOO.
ONE OF MY VERY OWN!
わあああ
YOU DON'T NEED TO CRY OVER THIS...
AND I REALIZED THAT THE STRANGE DREAMS HE AND I ARE HAVING ARE...
あっ
はっ
...THE SAME RIGHT!?

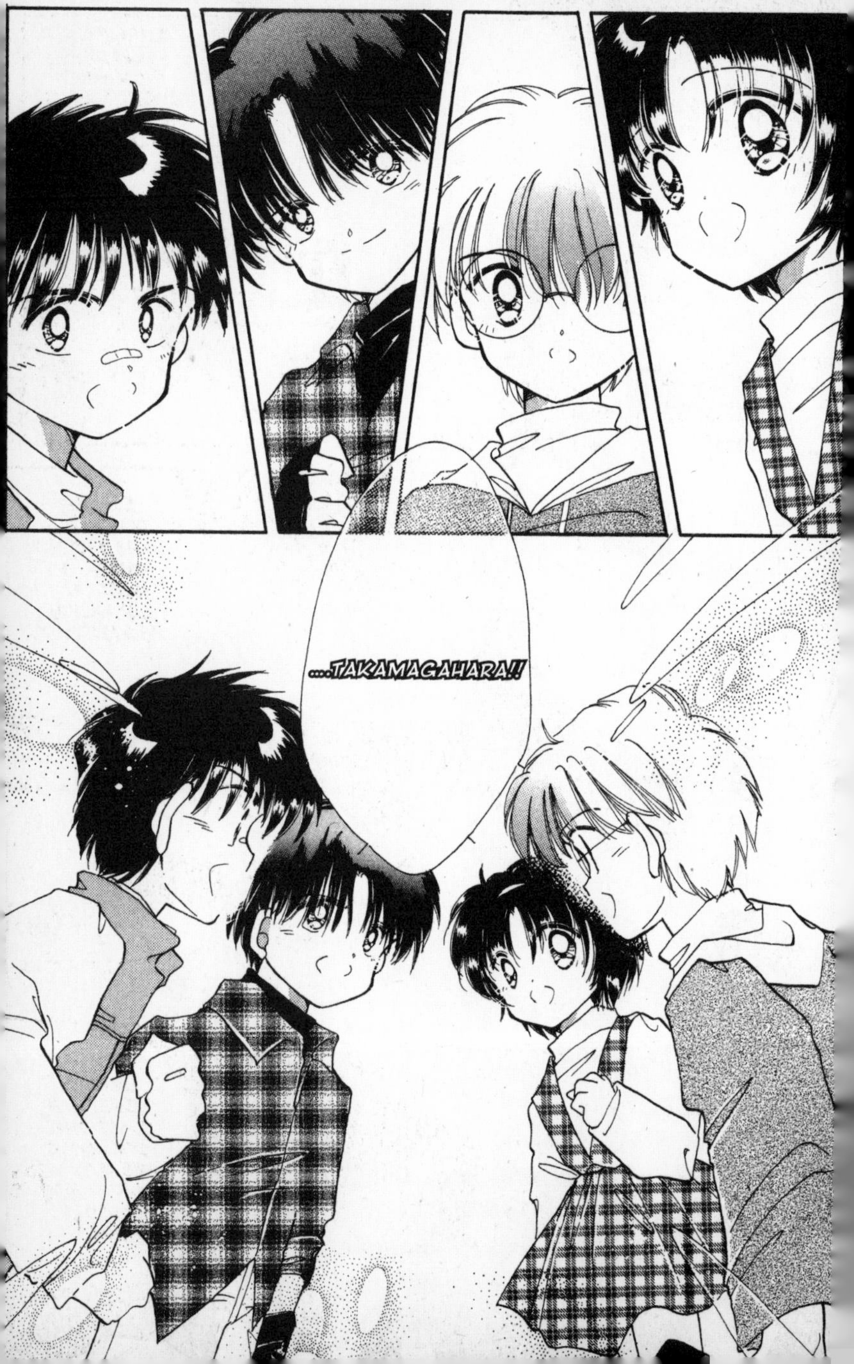
...TAKAMAGAHARA!!

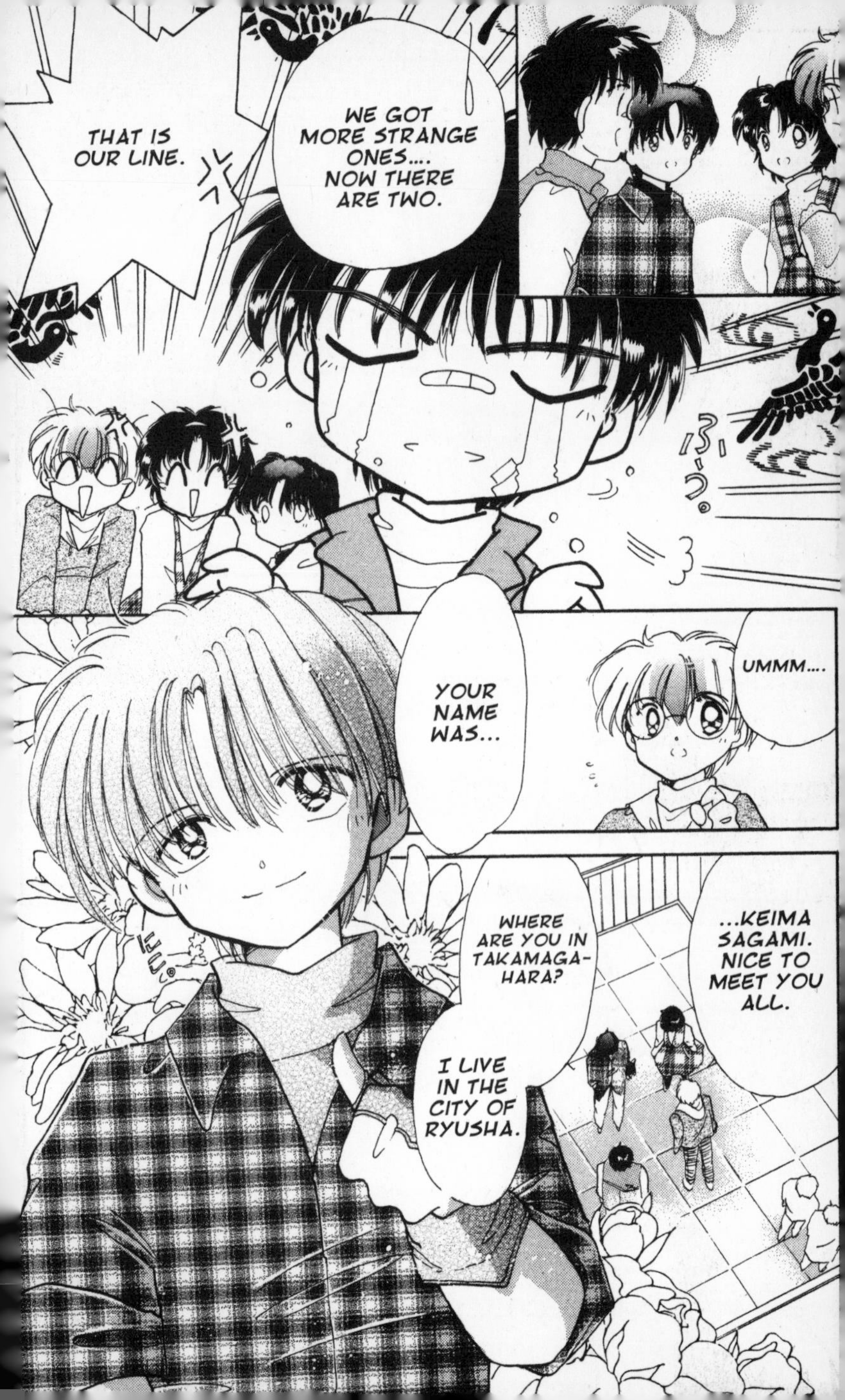
WE GOT MORE STRANGE ONES.... NOW THERE ARE TWO.
THAT IS OUR LINE.
UMMM....
YOUR NAME WAS...
...KEIMA SAGAMI. NICE TO MEET YOU ALL.
WHERE ARE YOU IN TAKAMAGA-HARA?
I LIVE IN THE CITY OF RYUSHA.

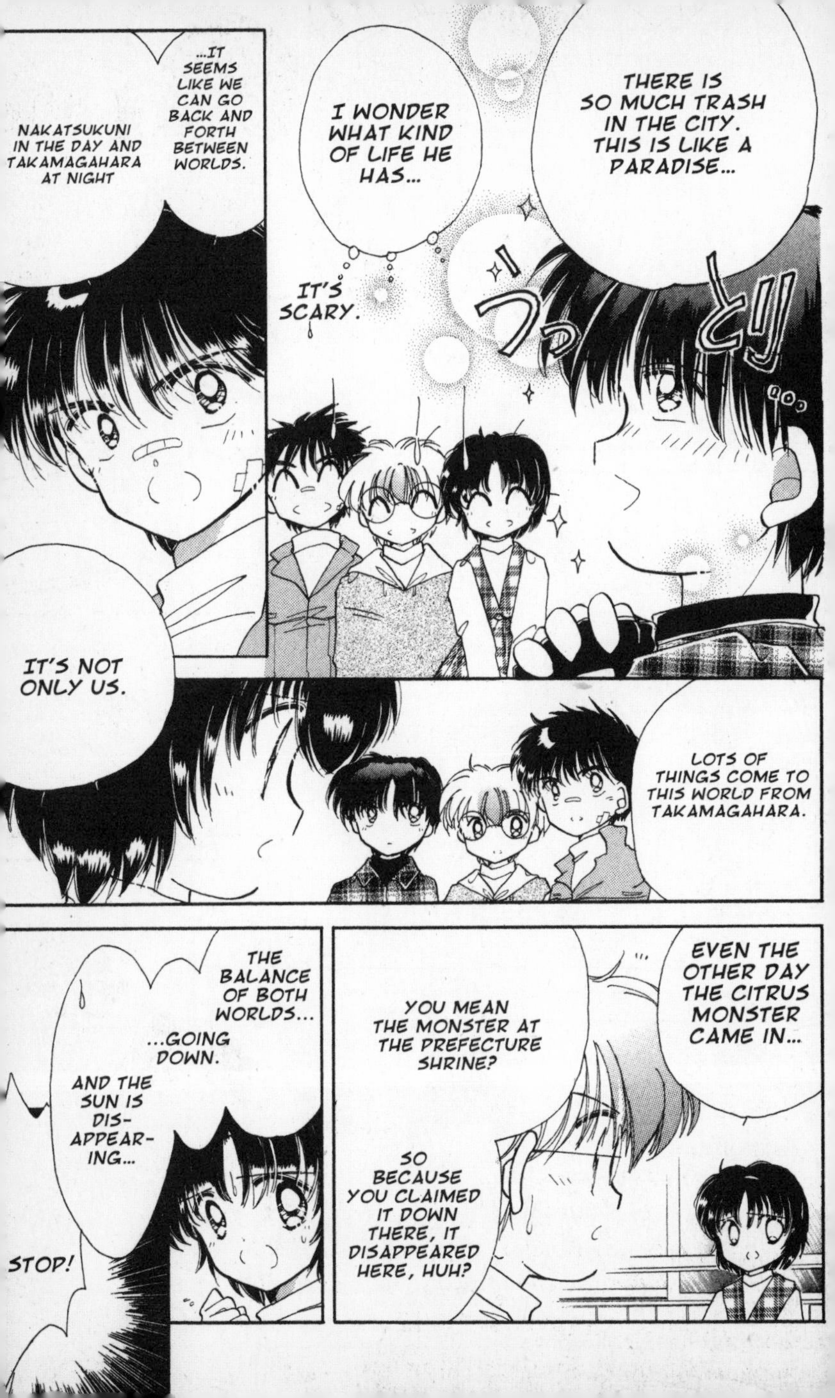
THERE IS SO MUCH TRASH IN THE CITY. THIS IS LIKE A PARADISE...
うっとり
I WONDER WHAT KIND OF LIFE HE HAS...
IT'S SCARY.
...IT SEEMS LIKE WE CAN GO BACK AND FORTH BETWEEN WORLDS.
NAKATSUKUNI IN THE DAY AND TAKAMAGAHARA AT NIGHT
LOTS OF THINGS COME TO THIS WORLD FROM TAKAMAGAHARA.
IT'S NOT ONLY US.
EVEN THE OTHER DAY THE CITRUS MONSTER CAME IN...
YOU MEAN THE MONSTER AT THE PREFECTURE SHRINE?
SO BECAUSE YOU CLAIMED IT DOWN THERE, IT DISAPPEARED HERE, HUH?
THE BALANCE OF BOTH WORLDS...
...GOING DOWN.
AND THE SUN IS DIS-APPEAR-ING...
STOP!

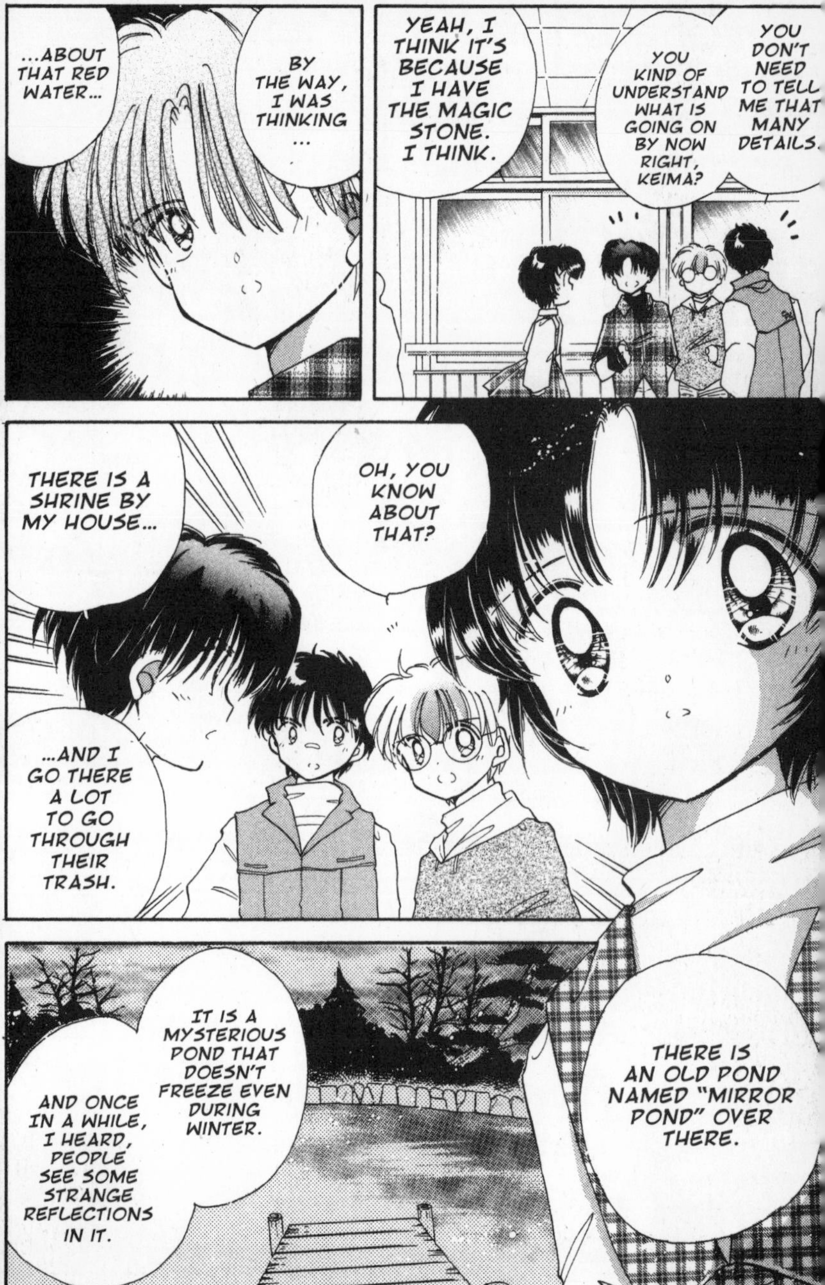
YOU DON'T NEED TO TELL ME THAT MANY DETAILS.
YOU KIND OF UNDERSTAND WHAT IS GOING ON BY NOW RIGHT, KEIMA?
YEAH, I THINK IT'S BECAUSE I HAVE THE MAGIC STONE. I THINK.
BY THE WAY, I WAS THINKING...
...ABOUT THAT RED WATER...
OH, YOU KNOW ABOUT THAT?
THERE IS A SHRINE BY MY HOUSE...
...AND I GO THERE A LOT TO GO THROUGH THEIR TRASH.
THERE IS AN OLD POND NAMED "MIRROR POND" OVER THERE.
IT IS A MYSTERIOUS POND THAT DOESN'T FREEZE EVEN DURING WINTER.
AND ONCE IN A WHILE, I HEARD, PEOPLE SEE SOME STRANGE REFLECTIONS IN IT.

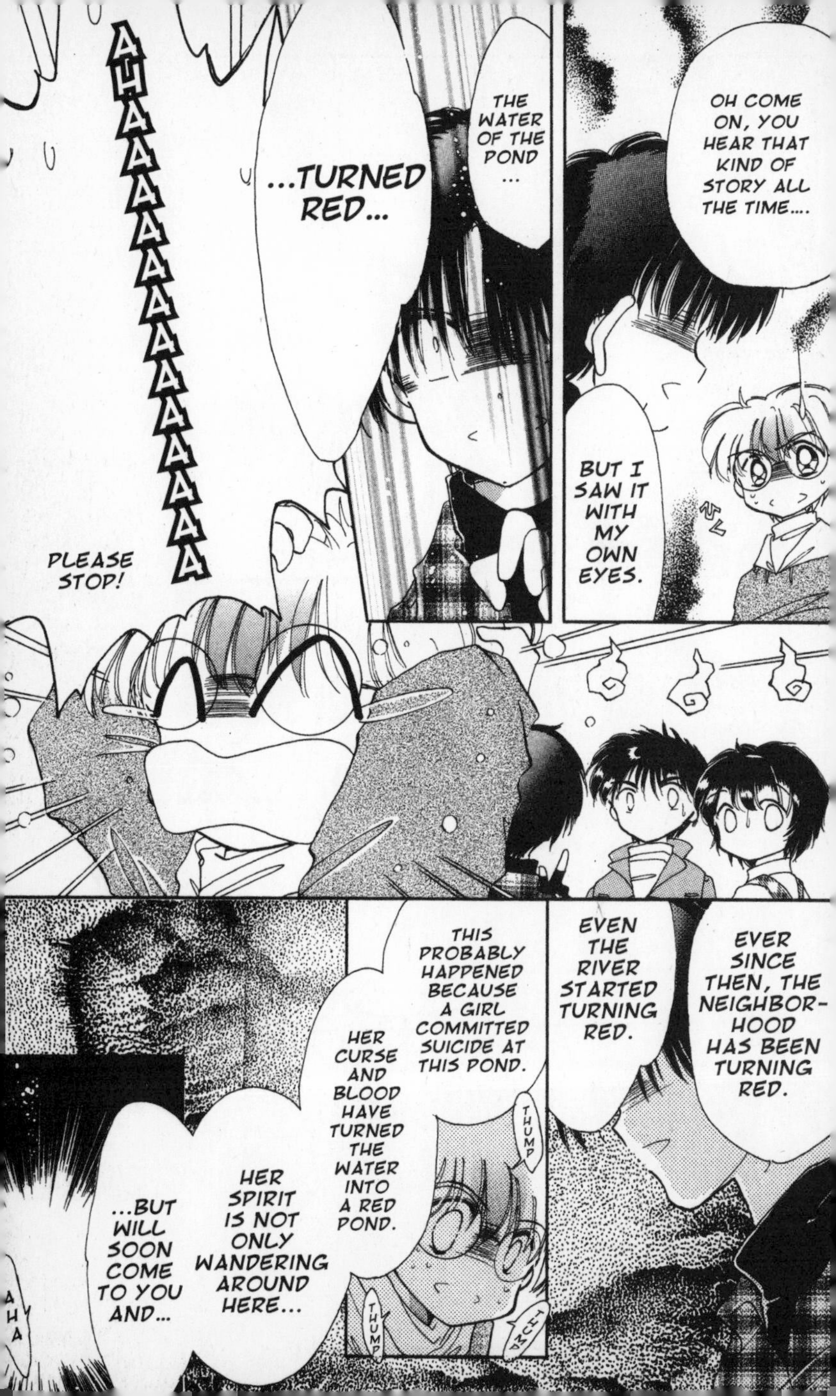
OH COME ON, YOU HEAR THAT KIND OF STORY ALL THE TIME....
BUT I SAW IT WITH MY OWN EYES.
THE WATER OF THE POND ...
...TURNED RED...
AHAAAAAAAAAAAAAAA
PLEASE STOP!
EVER SINCE THEN, THE NEIGHBOR-HOOD HAS BEEN TURNING RED.
EVEN THE RIVER STARTED TURNING RED.
THIS PROBABLY HAPPENED BECAUSE A GIRL COMMITTED SUICIDE AT THIS POND.
HER CURSE AND BLOOD HAVE TURNED THE WATER INTO A RED POND.
THUMP
THUMP
THUMP
HER SPIRIT IS NOT ONLY WANDERING AROUND HERE...
...BUT WILL SOON COME TO YOU AND...
AHA

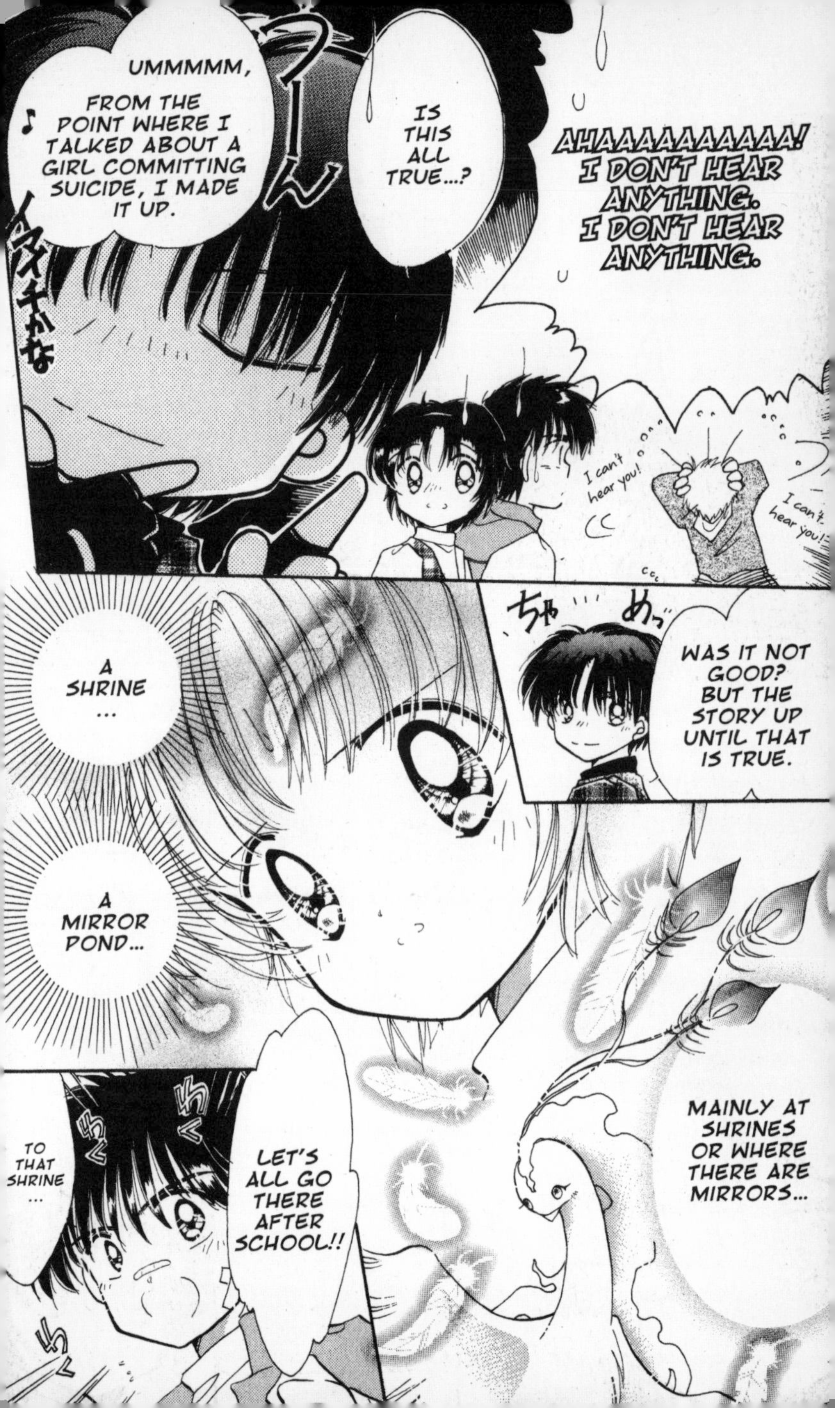

AHAAAAAAAAAA! I DON'T HEAR ANYTHING. I DON'T HEAR ANYTHING.
IS THIS ALL TRUE...?
UMMMMM, FROM THE POINT WHERE I TALKED ABOUT A GIRL COMMITTING SUICIDE, I MADE IT UP.
I can't hear you!
I can't hear you!
ちゃ めっ
WAS IT NOT GOOD? BUT THE STORY UP UNTIL THAT IS TRUE.
A SHRINE ...
A MIRROR POND...
MAINLY AT SHRINES OR WHERE THERE ARE MIRRORS...
LET'S ALL GO THERE AFTER SCHOOL!!
TO THAT SHRINE ...

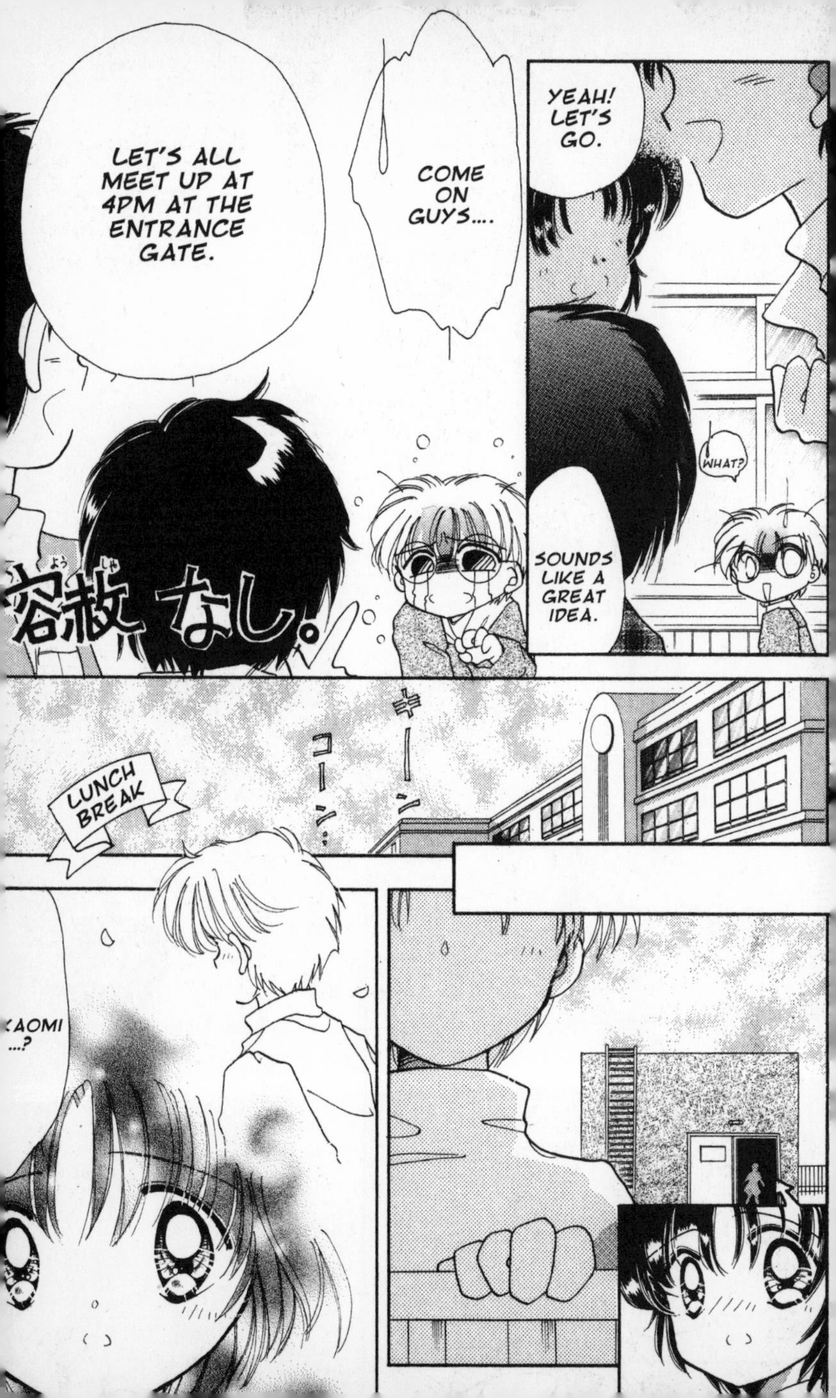
YEAH! LET'S GO.
SOUNDS LIKE A GREAT IDEA.
WHAT?
LET'S ALL MEET UP AT 4PM AT THE ENTRANCE GATE.
COME ON GUYS....
容赦なし。
キーンコーン…
LUNCH BREAK
AOMI ...?

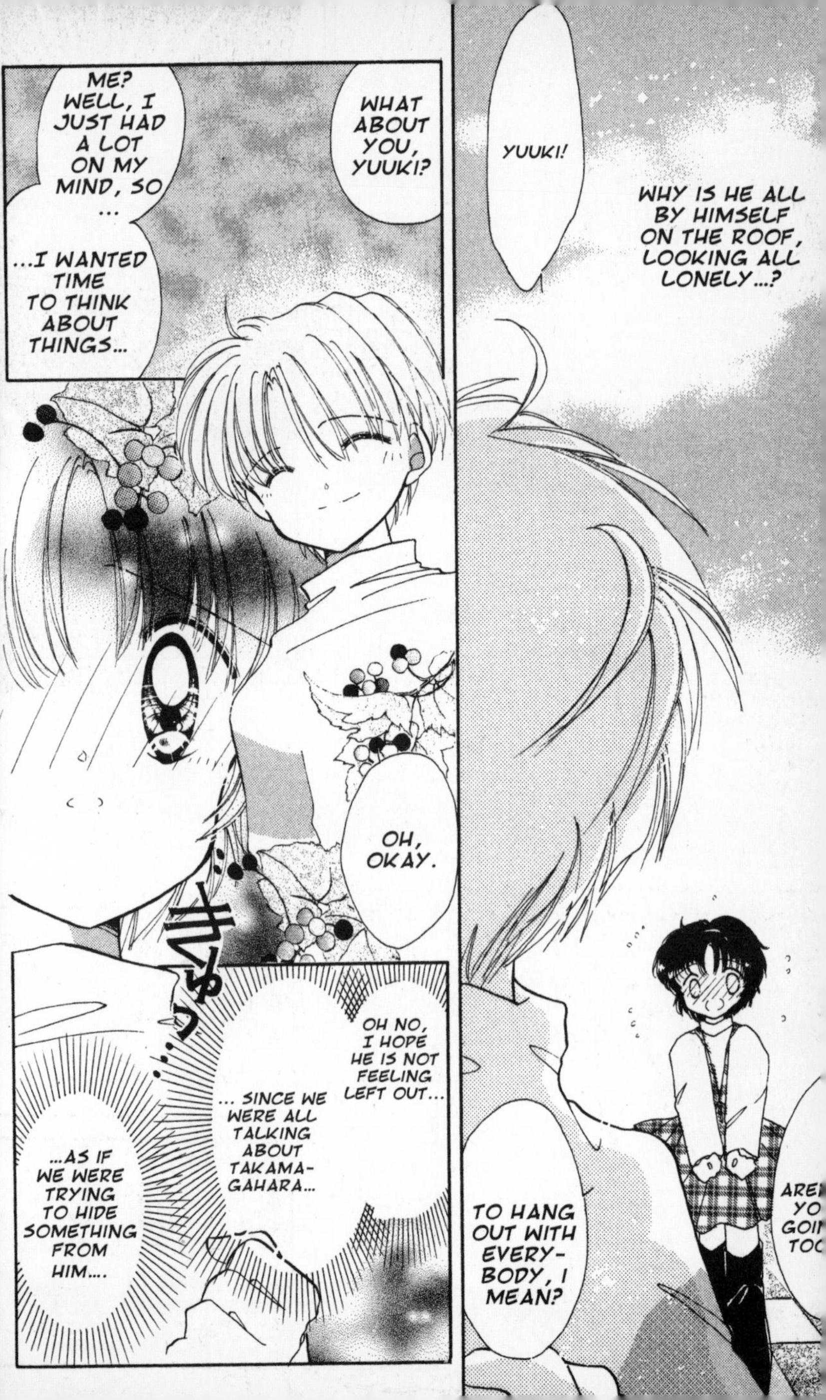
YUUKI!
WHY IS HE ALL BY HIMSELF ON THE ROOF, LOOKING ALL LONELY...?
ARE YO GOI TO
TO HANG OUT WITH EVERY-BODY, I MEAN?
WHAT ABOUT YOU, YUUKI?
ME? WELL, I JUST HAD A LOT ON MY MIND, SO ...
...I WANTED TIME TO THINK ABOUT THINGS...
OH, OKAY.
きゅっ...
OH NO, I HOPE HE IS NOT FEELING LEFT OUT...
... SINCE WE WERE ALL TALKING ABOUT TAKAMA-GAHARA...
...AS IF WE WERE TRYING TO HIDE SOMETHING FROM HIM....

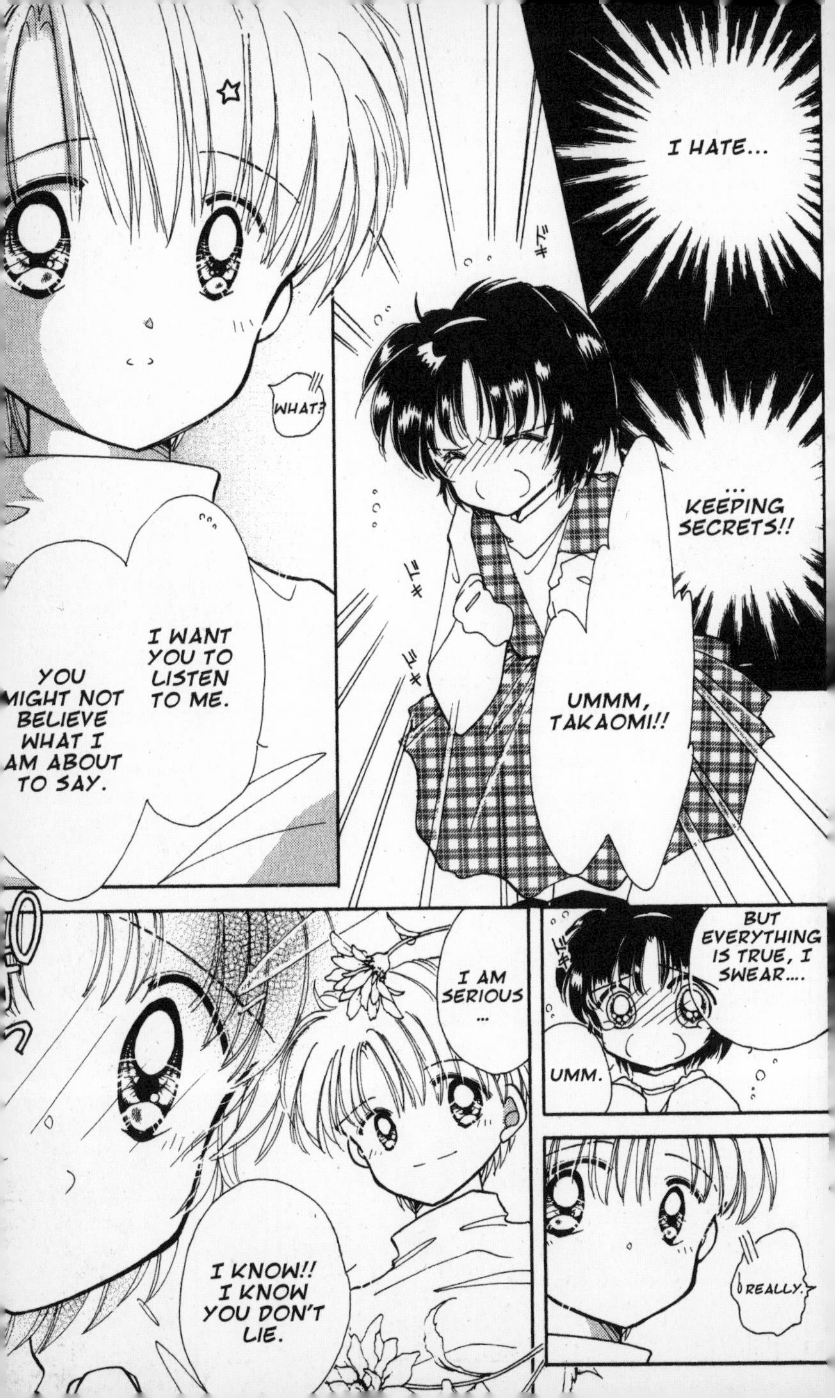
I HATE...
ドキ
... KEEPING SECRETS!!
ドキ
ドキ
UMMM, TAKAOMI!!
WHAT?
I WANT YOU TO LISTEN TO ME.
YOU MIGHT NOT BELIEVE WHAT I AM ABOUT TO SAY.
BUT EVERYTHING IS TRUE, I SWEAR....
UMM.
REALLY.?
I AM SERIOUS ...
I KNOW!! I KNOW YOU DON'T LIE.

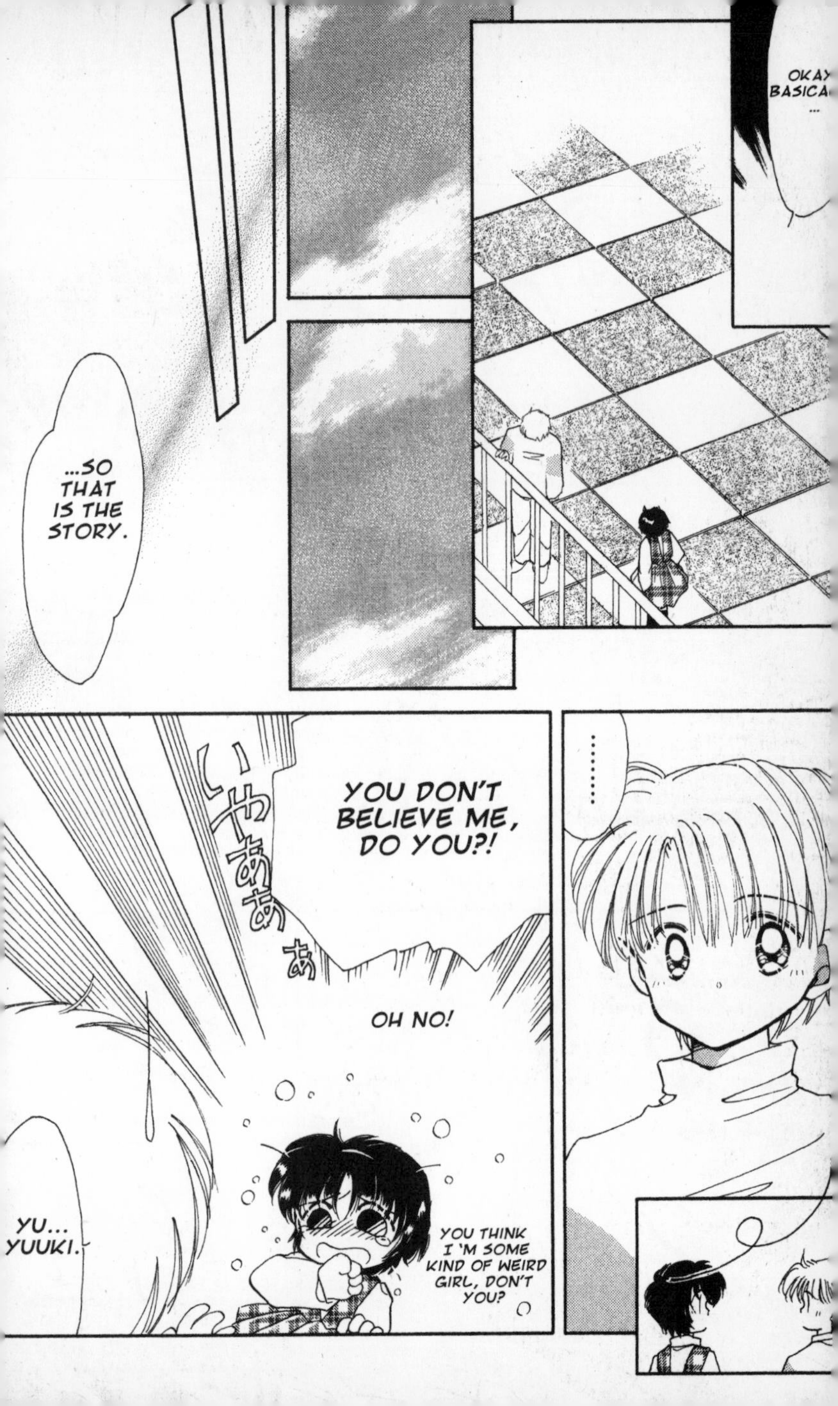

OKAY BASICA...
...SO THAT IS THE STORY.
......
いやあああ
YOU DON'T BELIEVE ME, DO YOU?!
OH NO!
YOU THINK I 'M SOME KIND OF WEIRD GIRL, DON'T YOU?
YU... YUUKI.

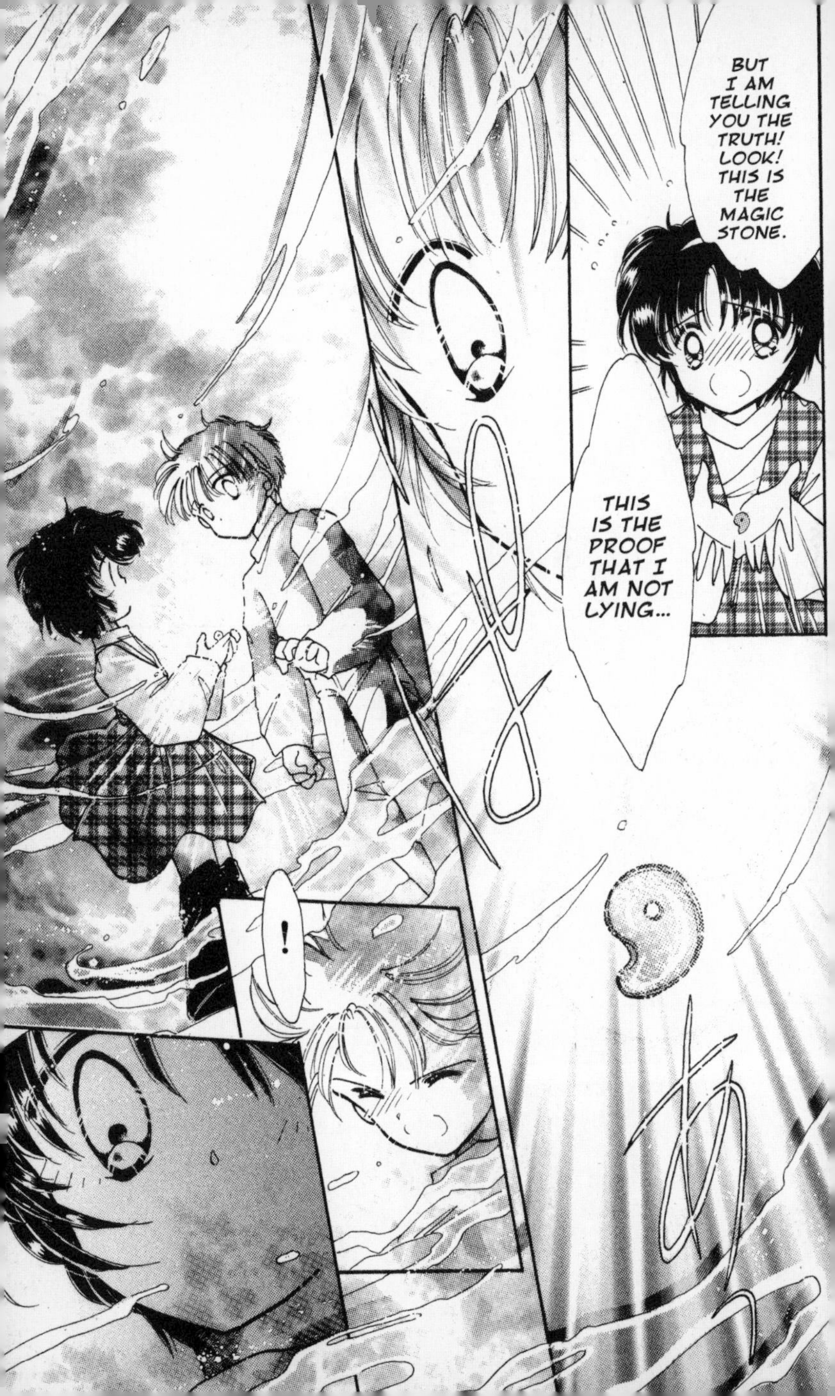
BUT I AM TELLING YOU THE TRUTH! LOOK! THIS IS THE MAGIC STONE.
THIS IS THE PROOF THAT I AM NOT LYING...
!

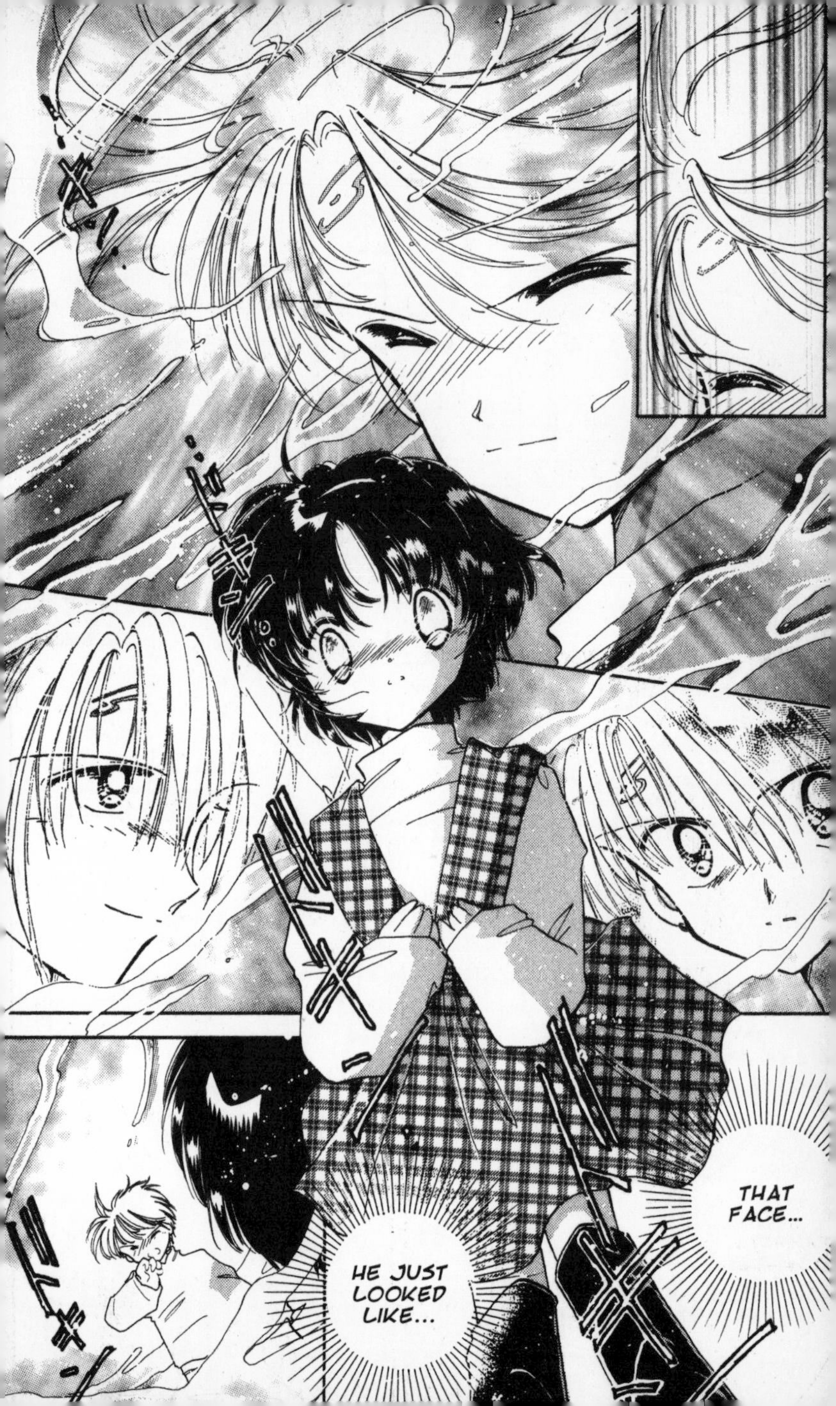
THAT FACE...
HE JUST LOOKED LIKE...

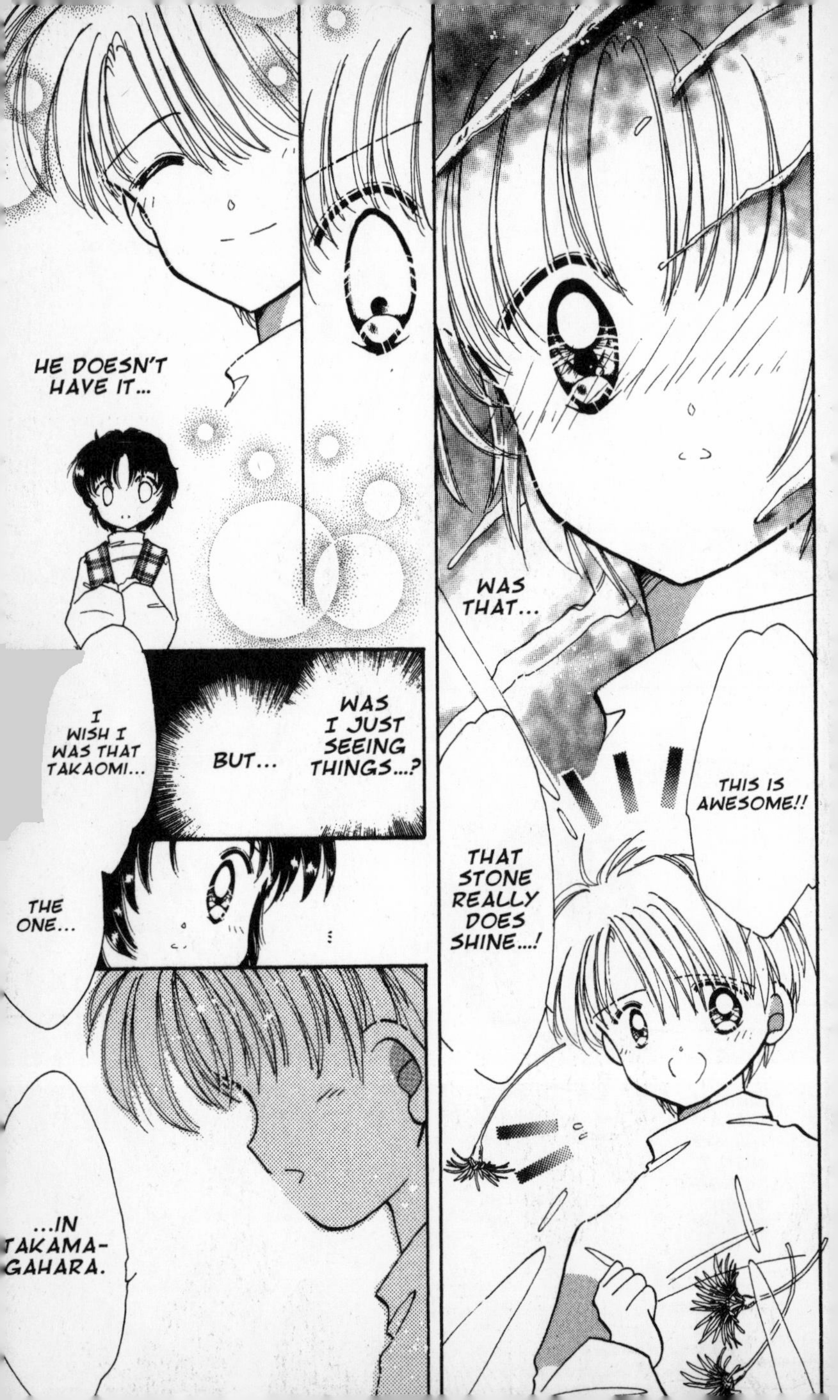
WAS THAT...
THIS IS AWESOME!!
THAT STONE REALLY DOES SHINE...!
HE DOESN'T HAVE IT...
WAS I JUST SEEING THINGS...?
BUT...
I WISH I WAS THAT TAKAOMI...
THE ONE...
...IN TAKAMA-GAHARA.

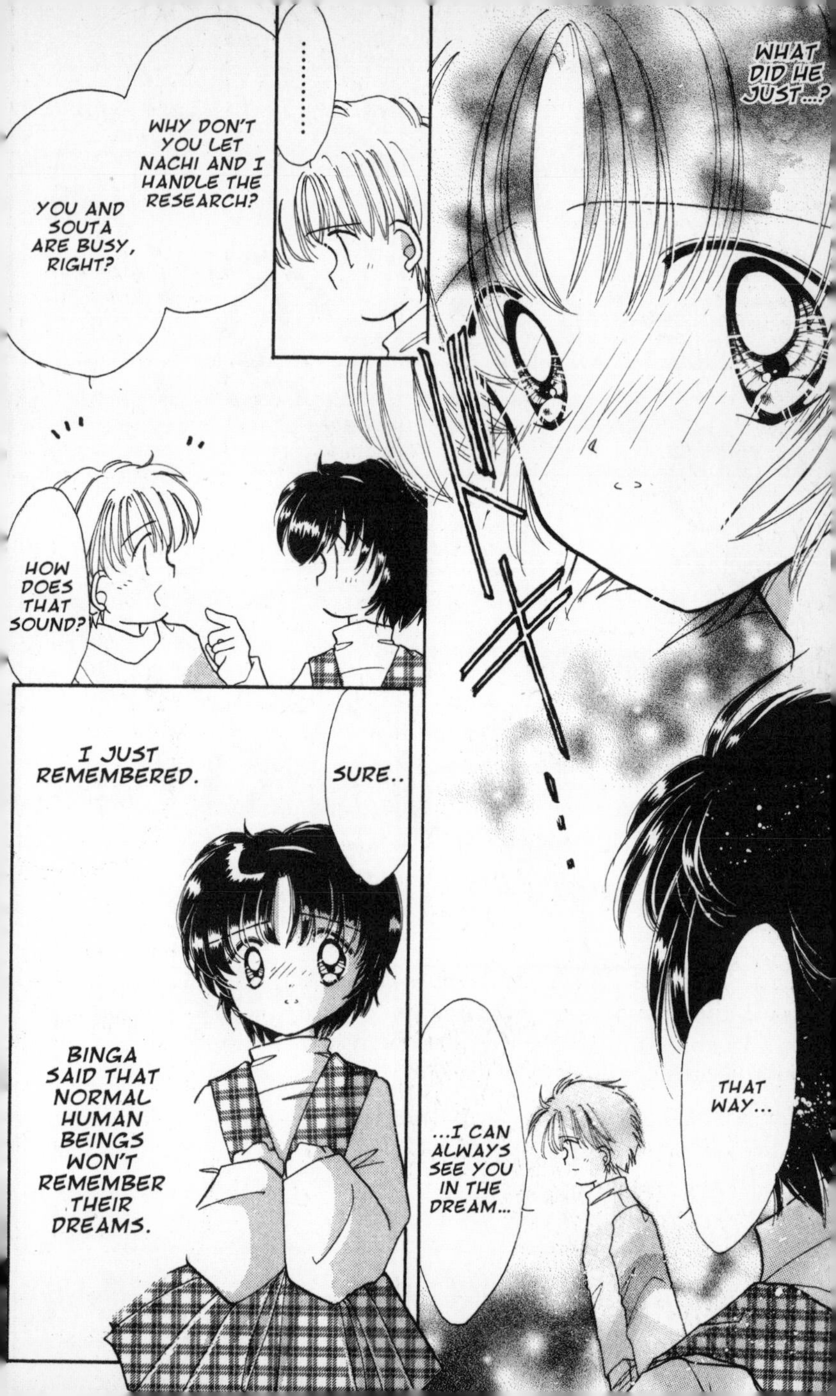
WHAT DID HE JUST...?
THAT WAY...
...I CAN ALWAYS SEE YOU IN THE DREAM...
......
WHY DON'T YOU LET NACHI AND I HANDLE THE RESEARCH?
YOU AND SOUTA ARE BUSY, RIGHT?
HOW DOES THAT SOUND?
SURE..
I JUST REMEMBERED.
BINGA SAID THAT NORMAL HUMAN BEINGS WON'T REMEMBER THEIR DREAMS.

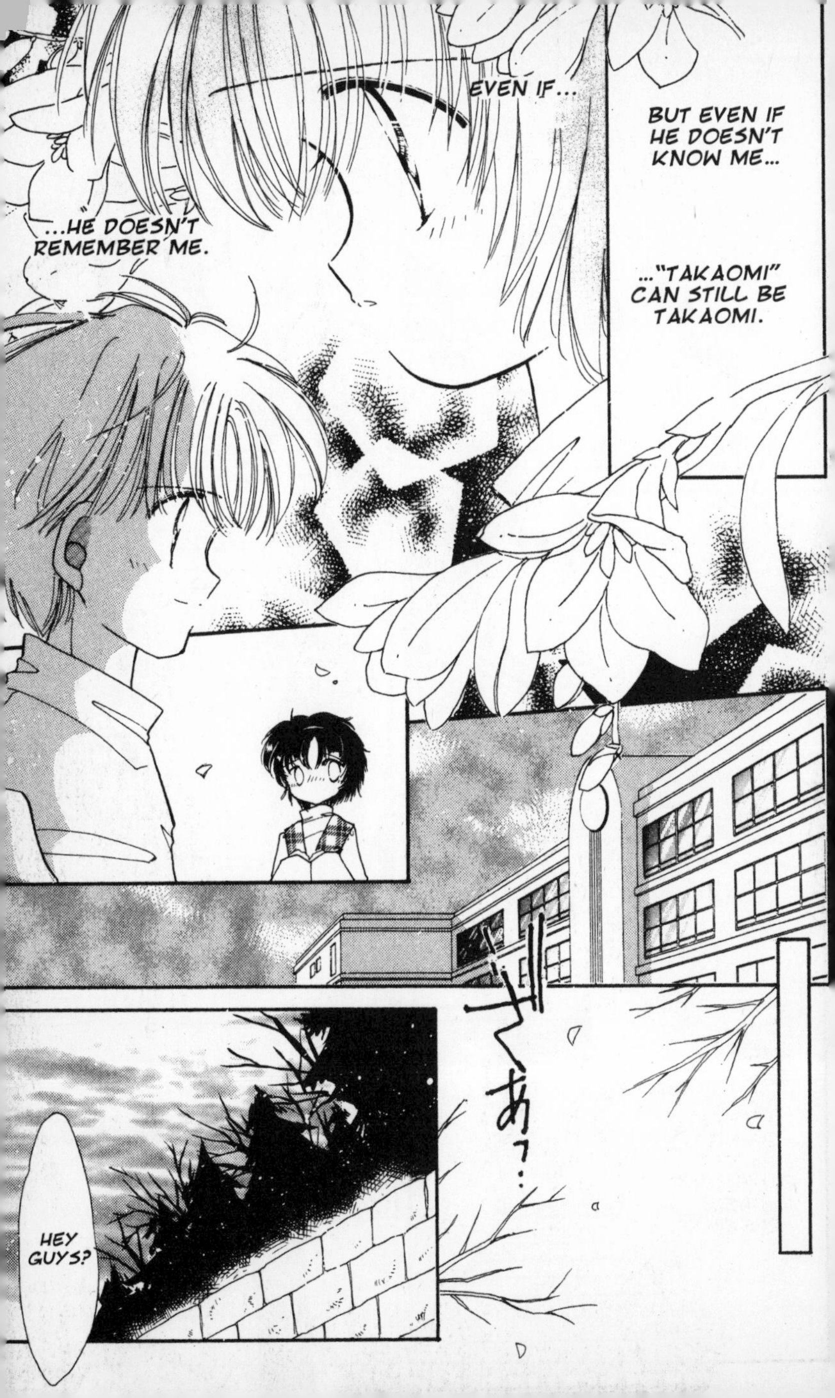

BUT EVEN IF HE DOESN'T KNOW ME...
..."TAKAOMI" CAN STILL BE TAKAOMI.
EVEN IF...
...HE DOESN'T REMEMBER ME.
ざあっ…
HEY GUYS?

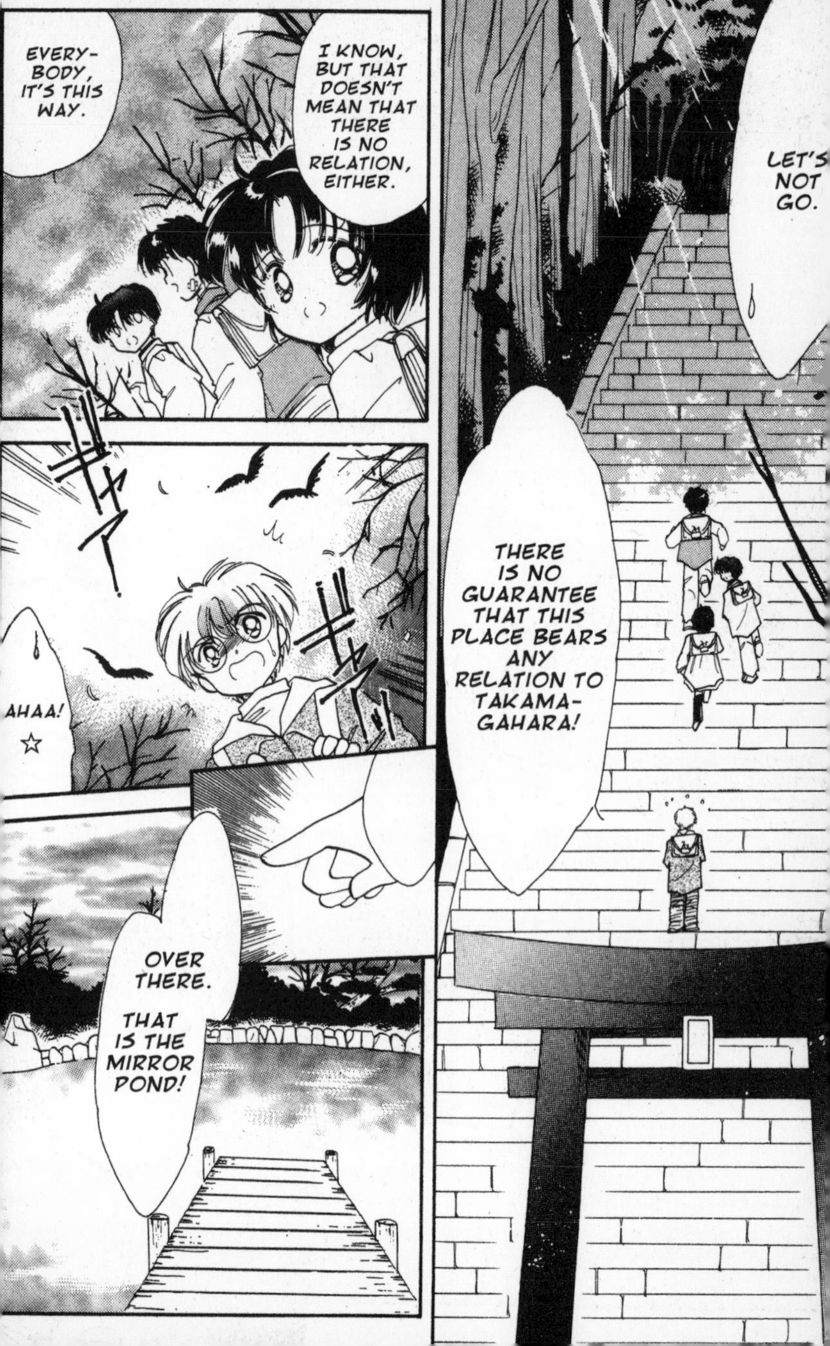

LET'S NOT GO.
THERE IS NO GUARANTEE THAT THIS PLACE BEARS ANY RELATION TO TAKAMA-GAHARA!
I KNOW, BUT THAT DOESN'T MEAN THAT THERE IS NO RELATION, EITHER.
EVERY-BODY, IT'S THIS WAY.
AHAA! ☆
OVER THERE.
THAT IS THE MIRROR POND!

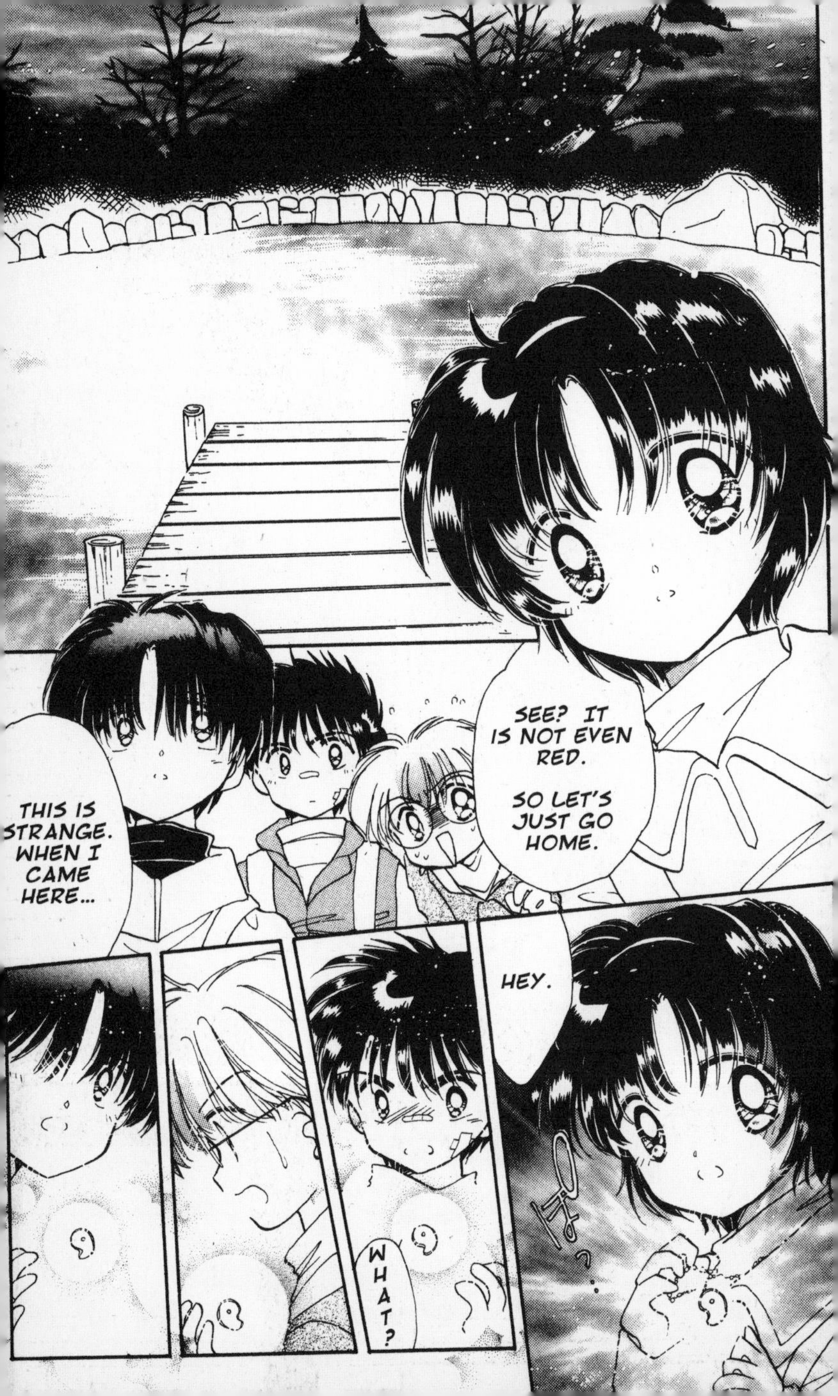

SEE? IT IS NOT EVEN RED.
SO LET'S JUST GO HOME.
THIS IS STRANGE. WHEN I CAME HERE...
HEY.
WHAT?

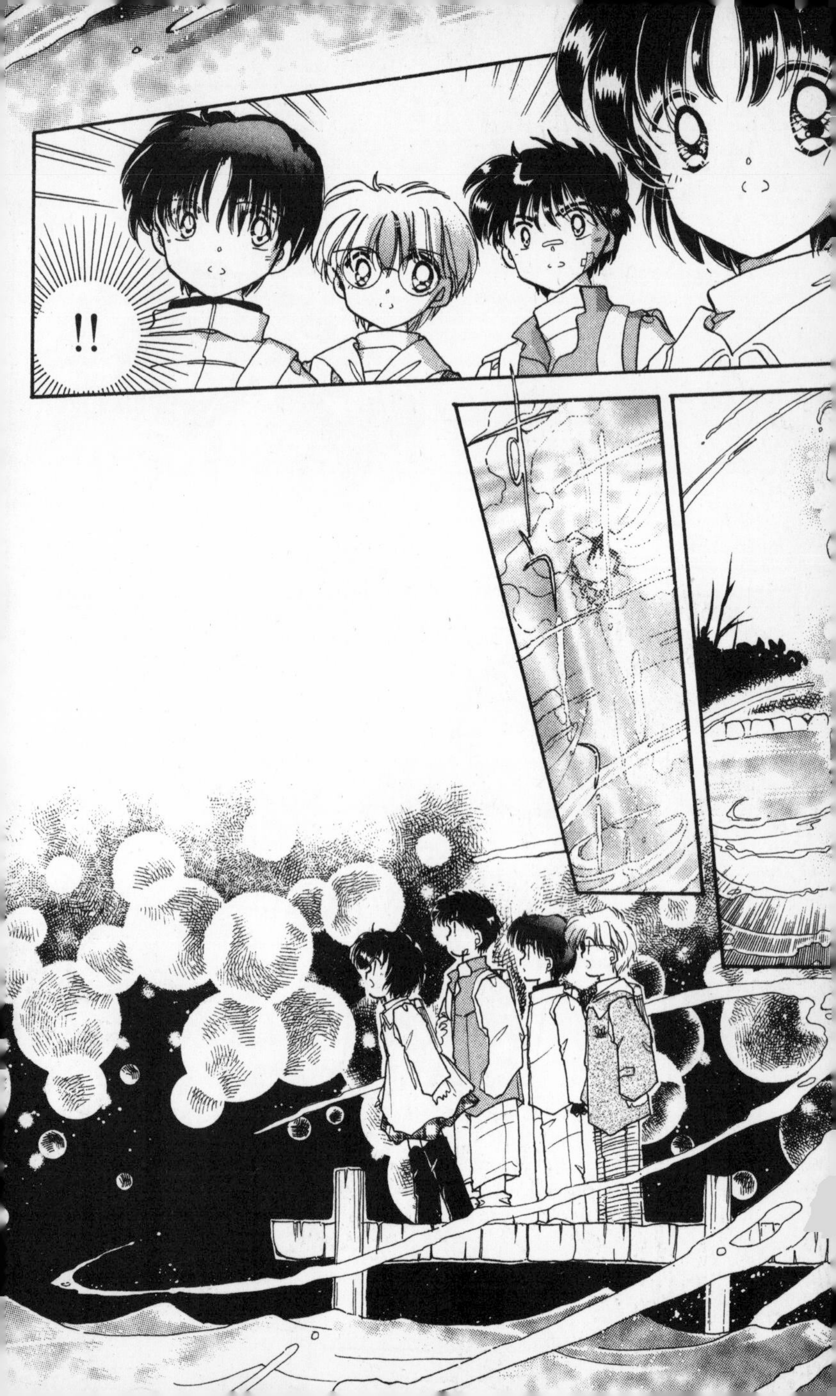
!!

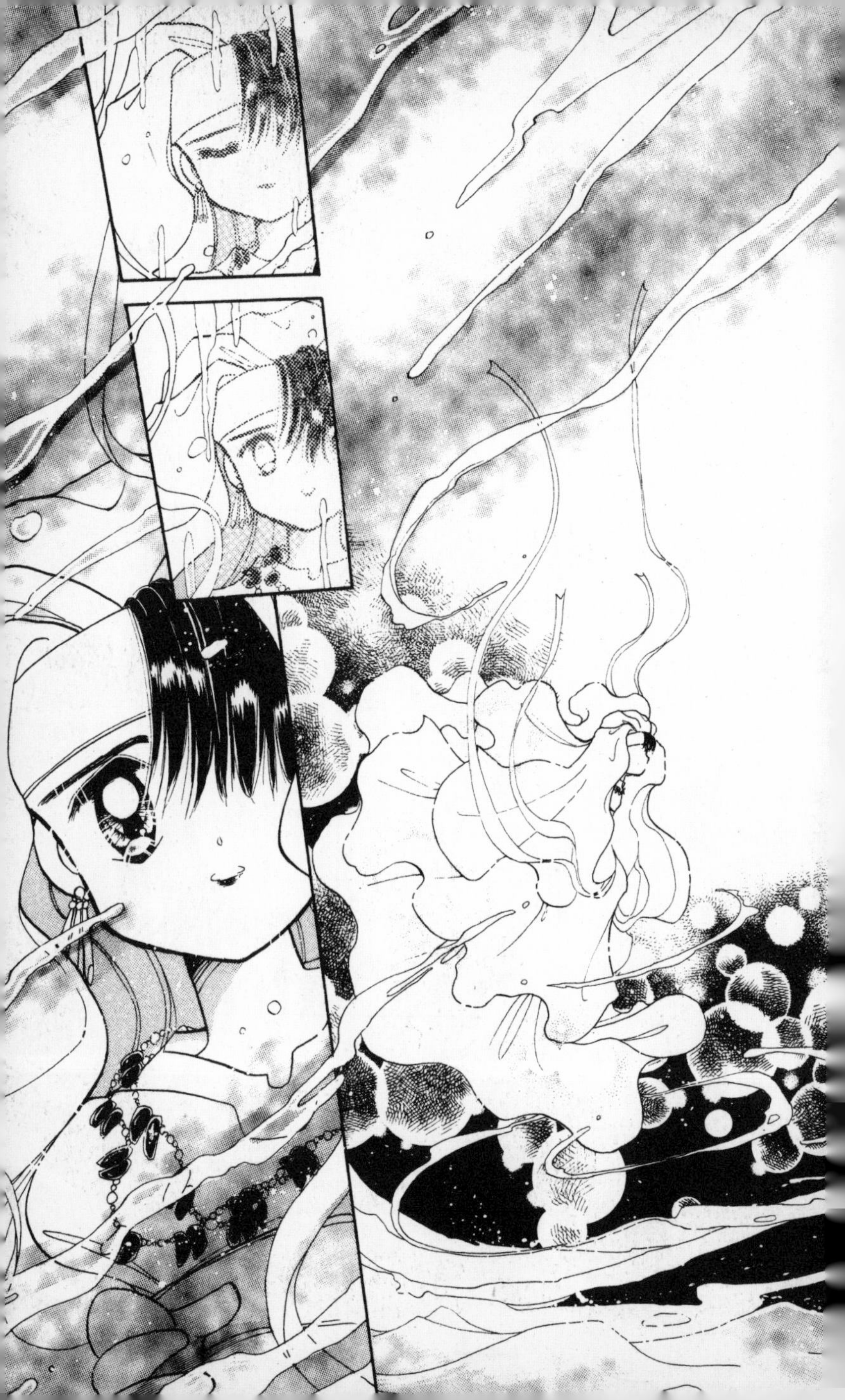

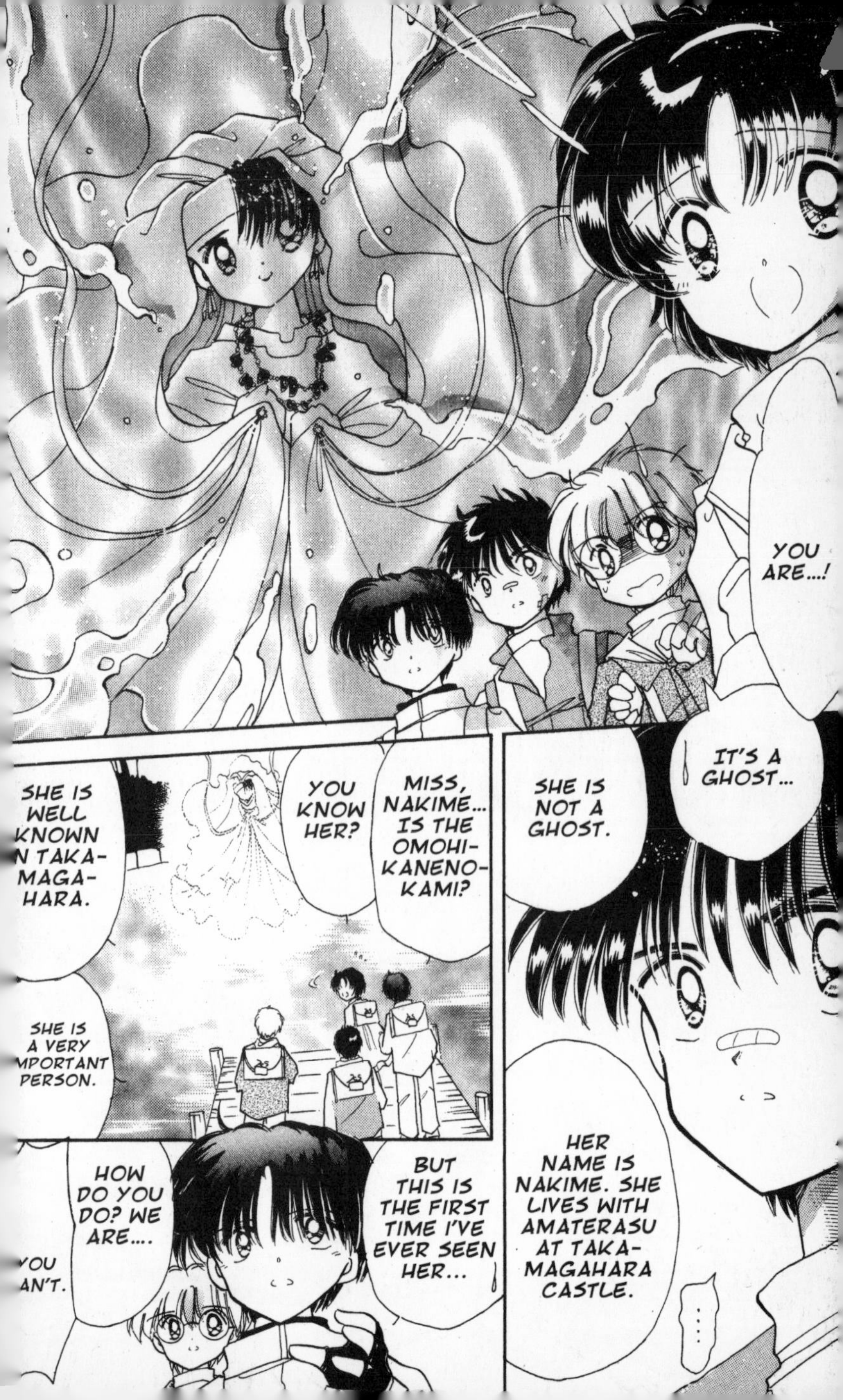
YOU ARE...!
IT'S A GHOST...
SHE IS NOT A GHOST.
HER NAME IS NAKIME. SHE LIVES WITH AMATERASU AT TAKA-MAGAHARA CASTLE.
.....
MISS, NAKIME... IS THE OMOHI-KANENO-KAMI?
YOU KNOW HER?
SHE IS WELL KNOWN N TAKA-MAGA-HARA.
SHE IS A VERY MPORTANT PERSON.
BUT THIS IS THE FIRST TIME I'VE EVER SEEN HER...
HOW DO YOU DO? WE ARE....
'OU AN'T.

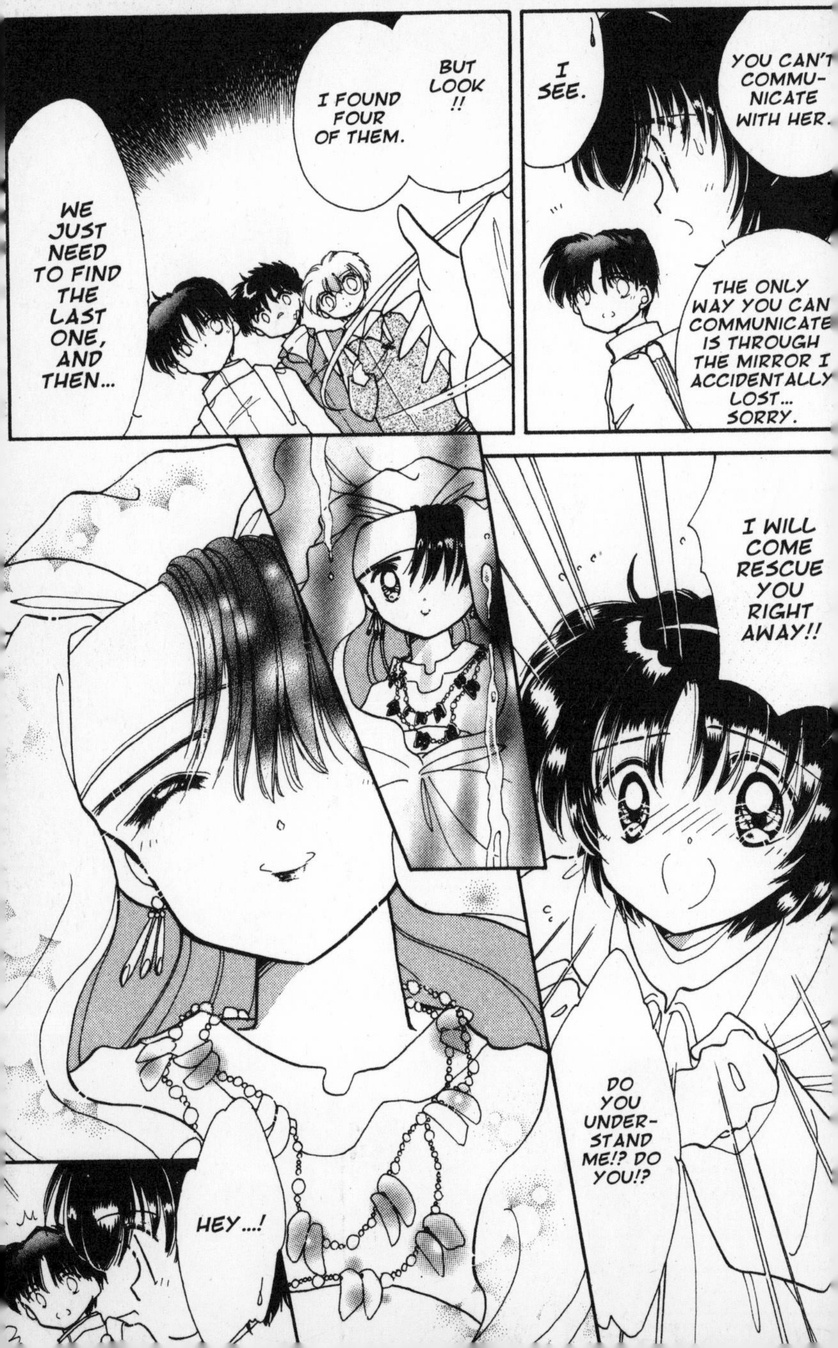
YOU CAN'T COMMUNICATE WITH HER.
I SEE.
THE ONLY WAY YOU CAN COMMUNICATE IS THROUGH THE MIRROR I ACCIDENTALLY LOST... SORRY.
BUT LOOK!!
I FOUND FOUR OF THEM.
WE JUST NEED TO FIND THE LAST ONE, AND THEN...
I WILL COME RESCUE YOU RIGHT AWAY!!
DO YOU UNDERSTAND ME!? DO YOU!?
HEY...!

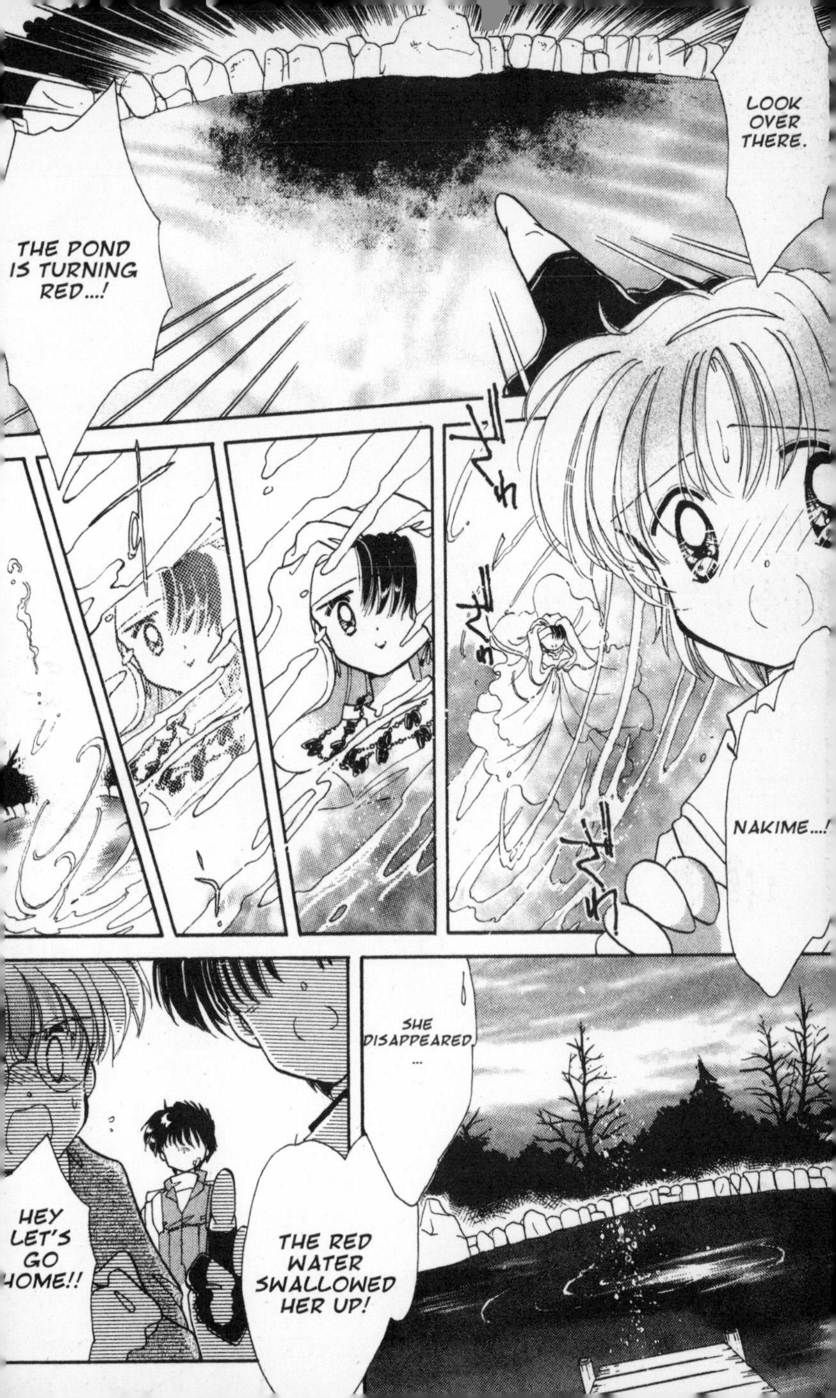
LOOK OVER THERE.
THE POND IS TURNING RED...!
NAKIME...!
SHE DISAPPEARED ...
THE RED WATER SWALLOWED HER UP!
HEY LET'S GO HOME!!

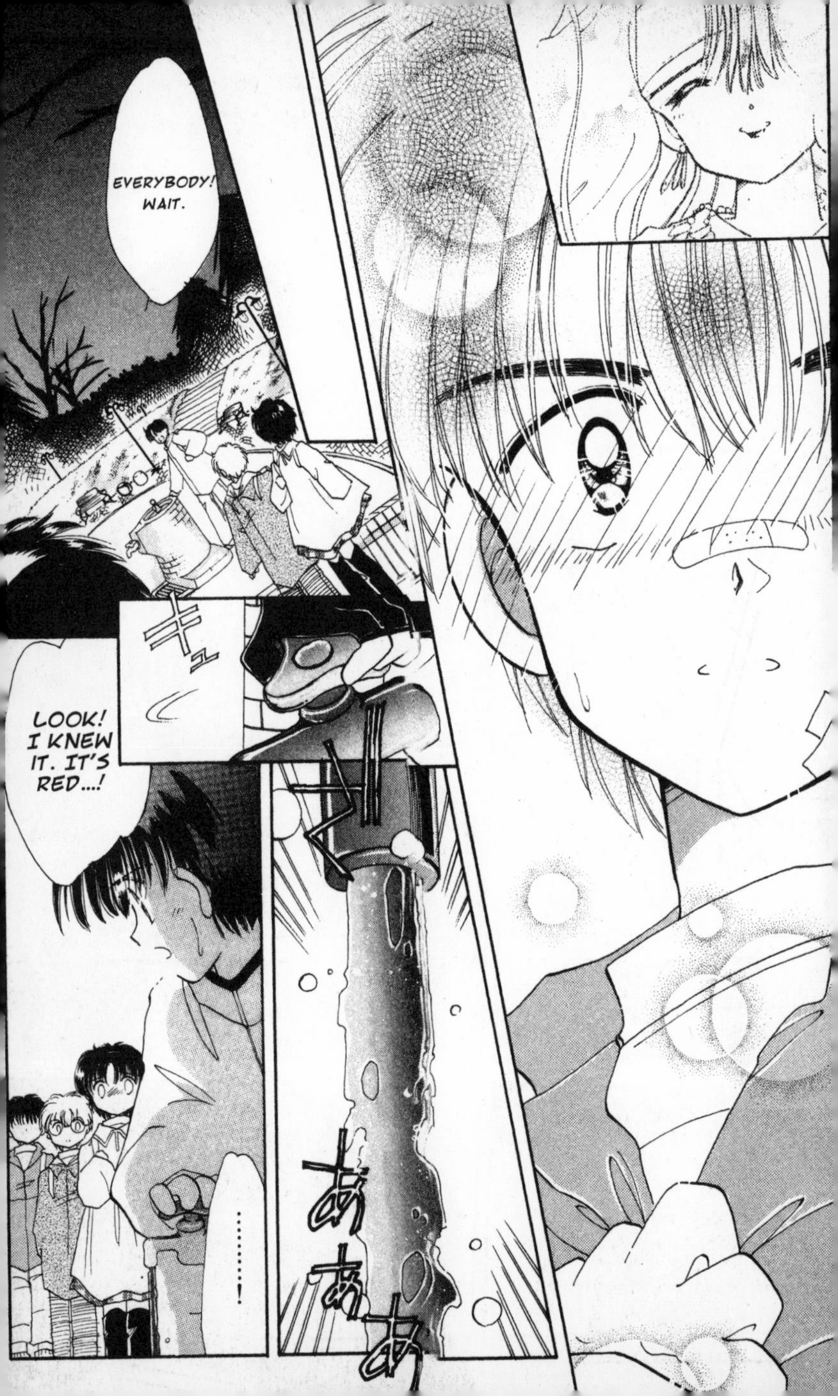
EVERYBODY! WAIT.
キュ
LOOK! I KNEW IT. IT'S RED...!
あああ
......!

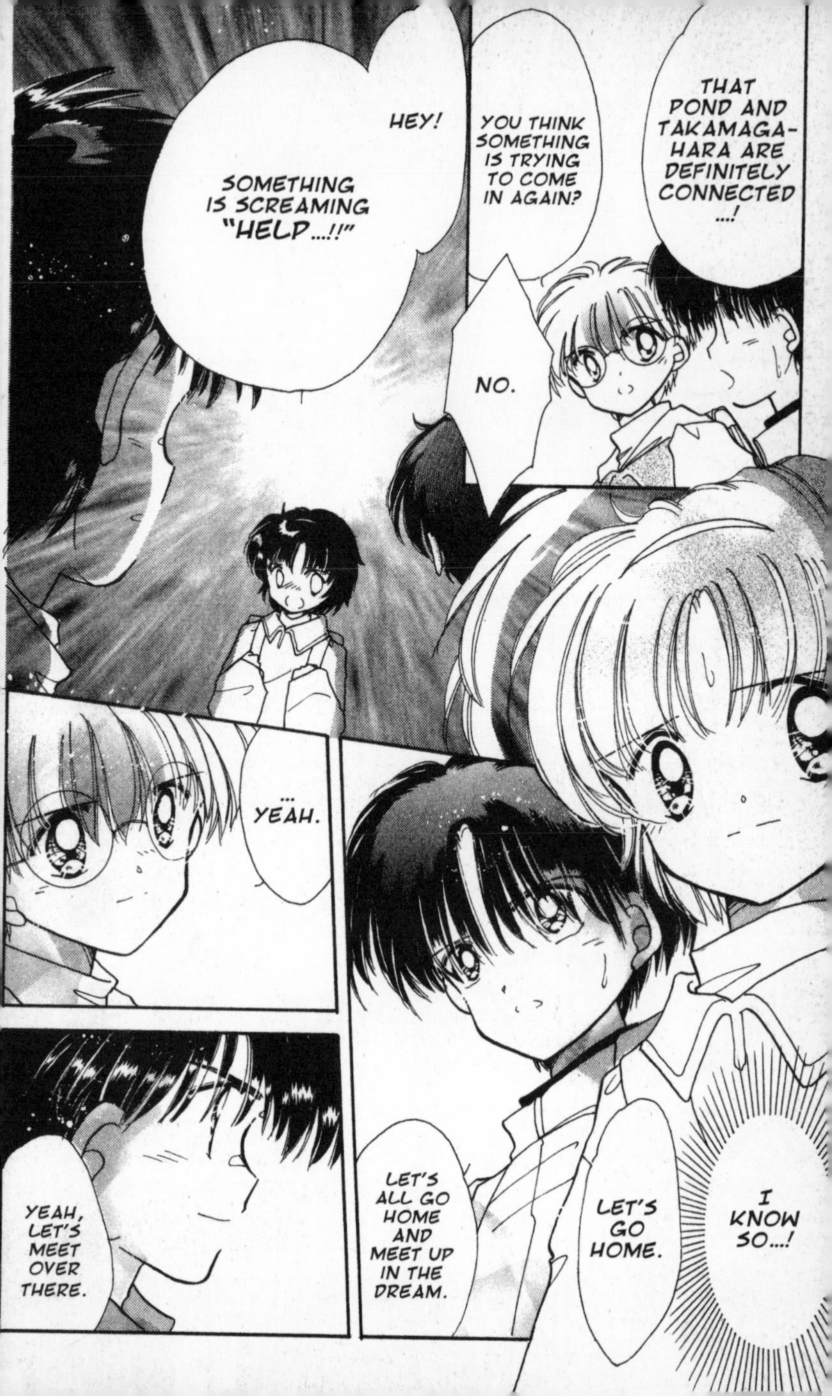
THAT POND AND TAKAMAGA-HARA ARE DEFINITELY CONNECTED ...!
YOU THINK SOMETHING IS TRYING TO COME IN AGAIN?
NO.
HEY!
SOMETHING IS SCREAMING "HELP...!!"
I KNOW SO...!
LET'S GO HOME.
LET'S ALL GO HOME AND MEET UP IN THE DREAM.
... YEAH.
YEAH, LET'S MEET OVER THERE.

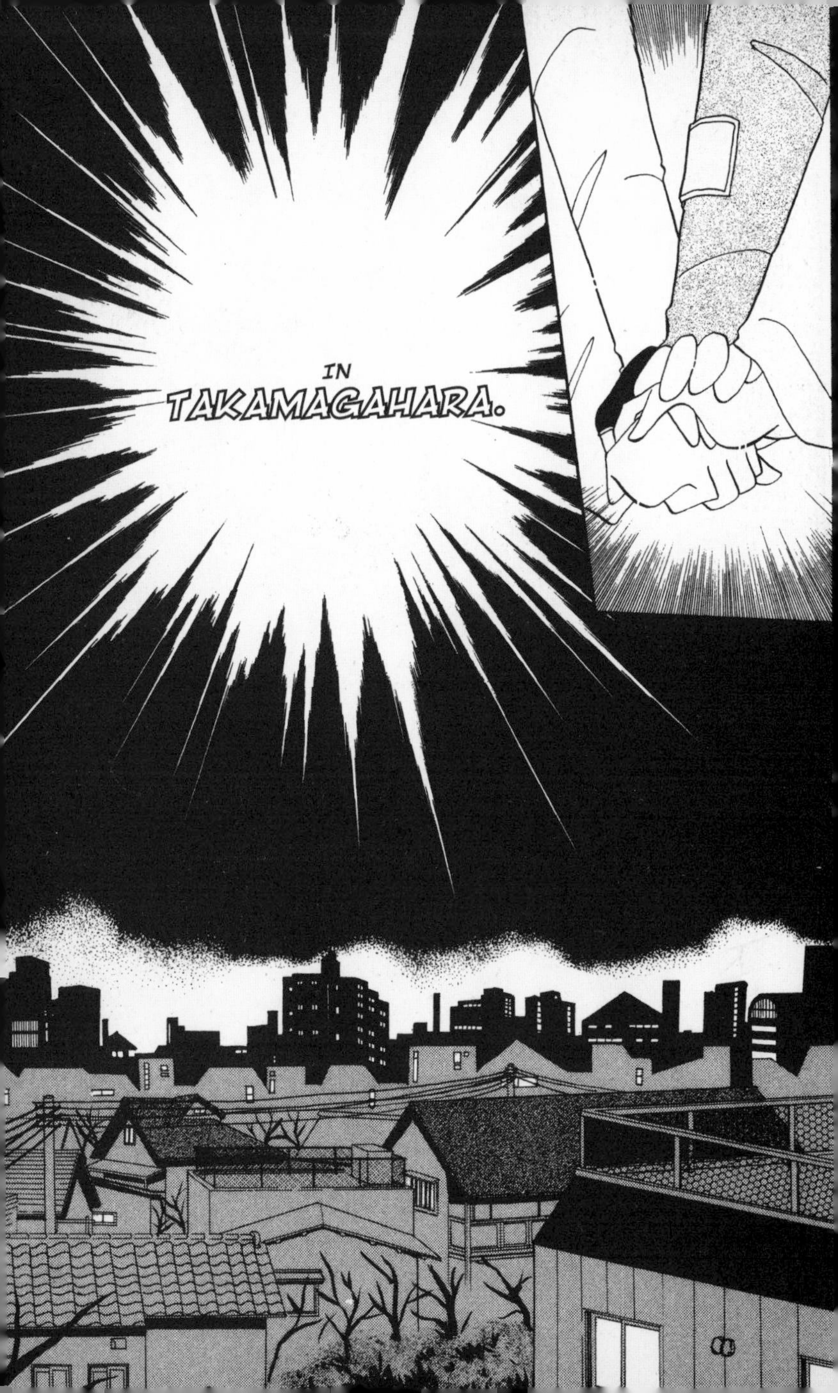
IN
TAKAMAGAHARA.

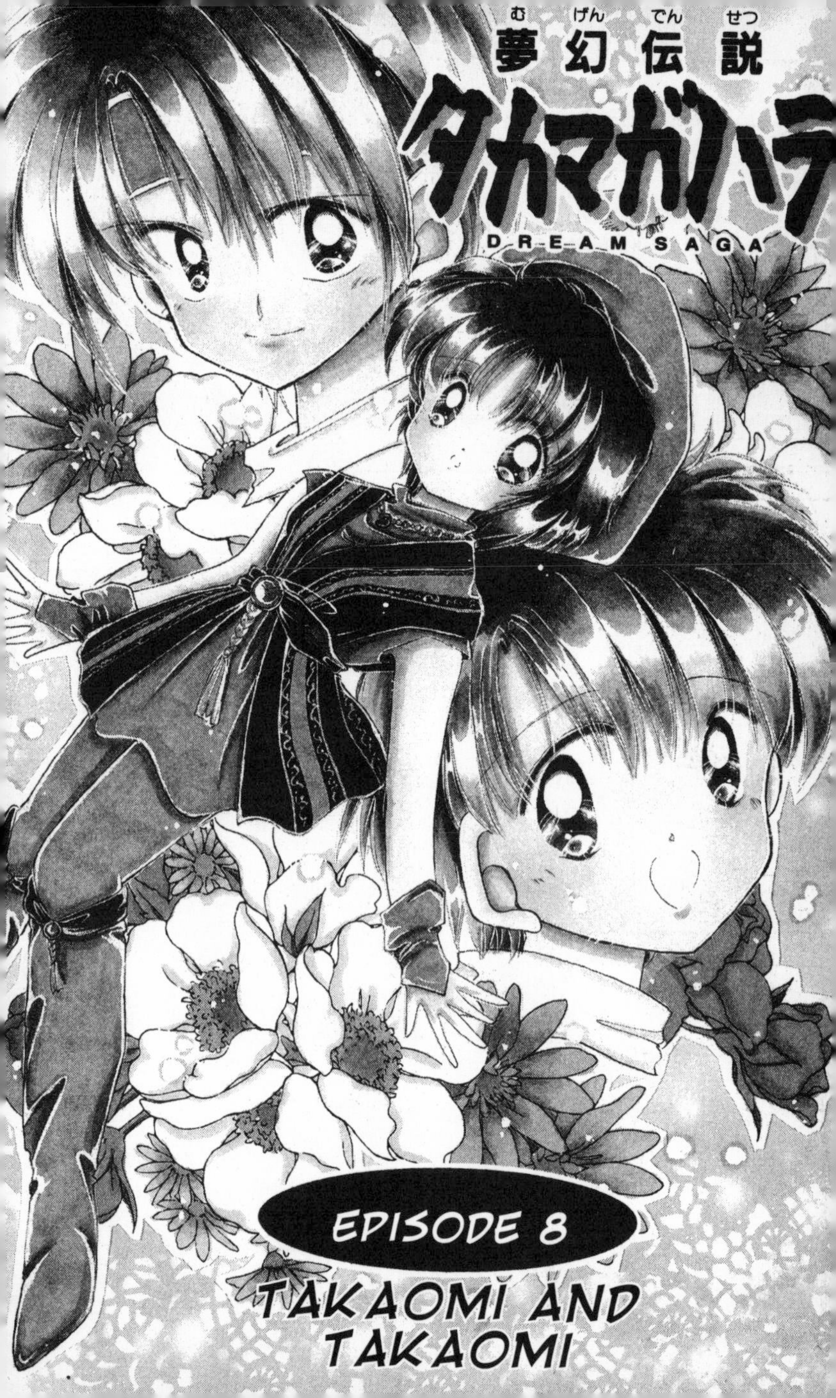

むげん でん せつ
夢幻伝説
タカマガハラ
DREAM SAGA
EPISODE 8
TAKAOMI AND TAKAOMI

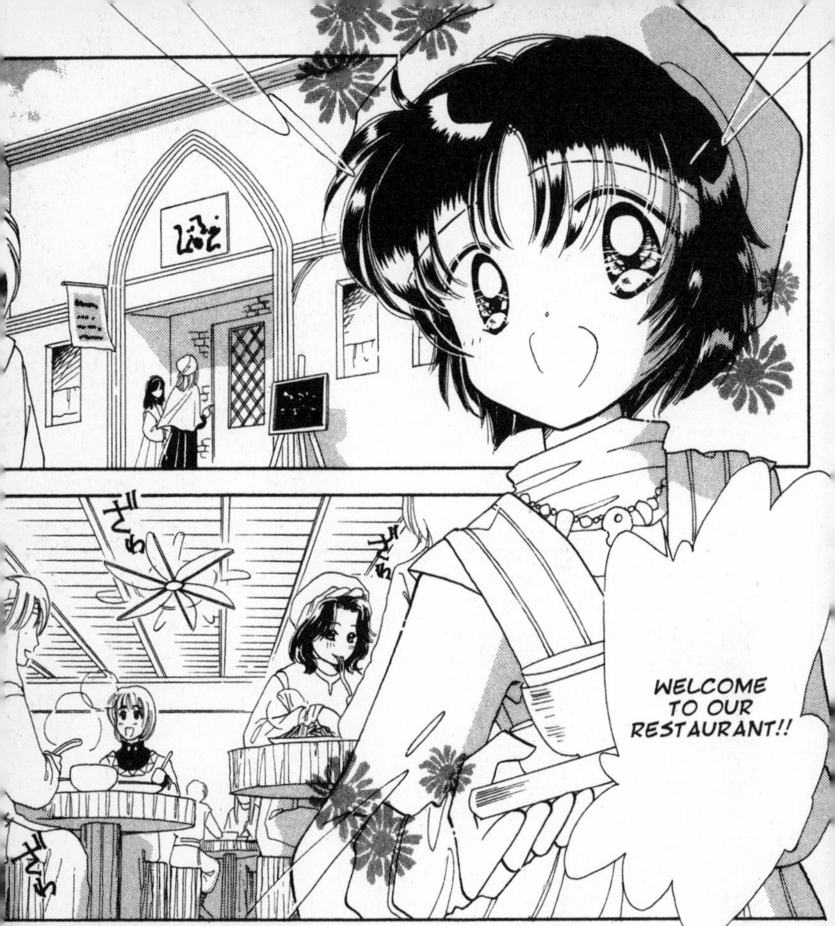
ざわ
ざわ
WELCOME TO OUR RESTAURANT!!
ざわ

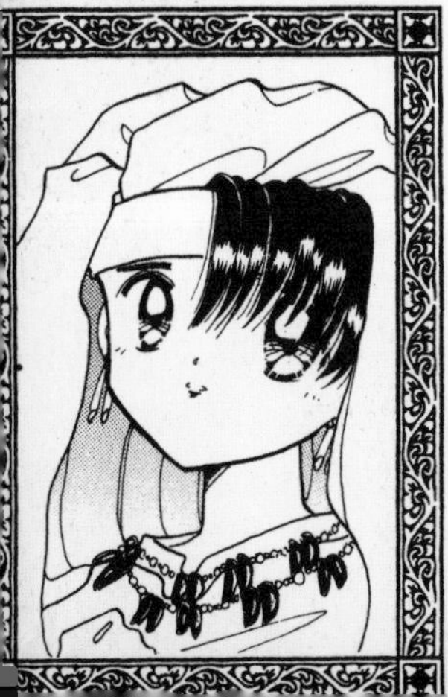

Q: Where does Takamagahara's language (such as the names for the living creatures) come from?

A: I came up with it. I put together sounds from languages everywhere to create these words. So when people ask me where it's from, I have a hard time answering. I mainly used syllables from English, Indian, Turkish, and Spanish. And of course I got some inspiration from Japanese mythology.

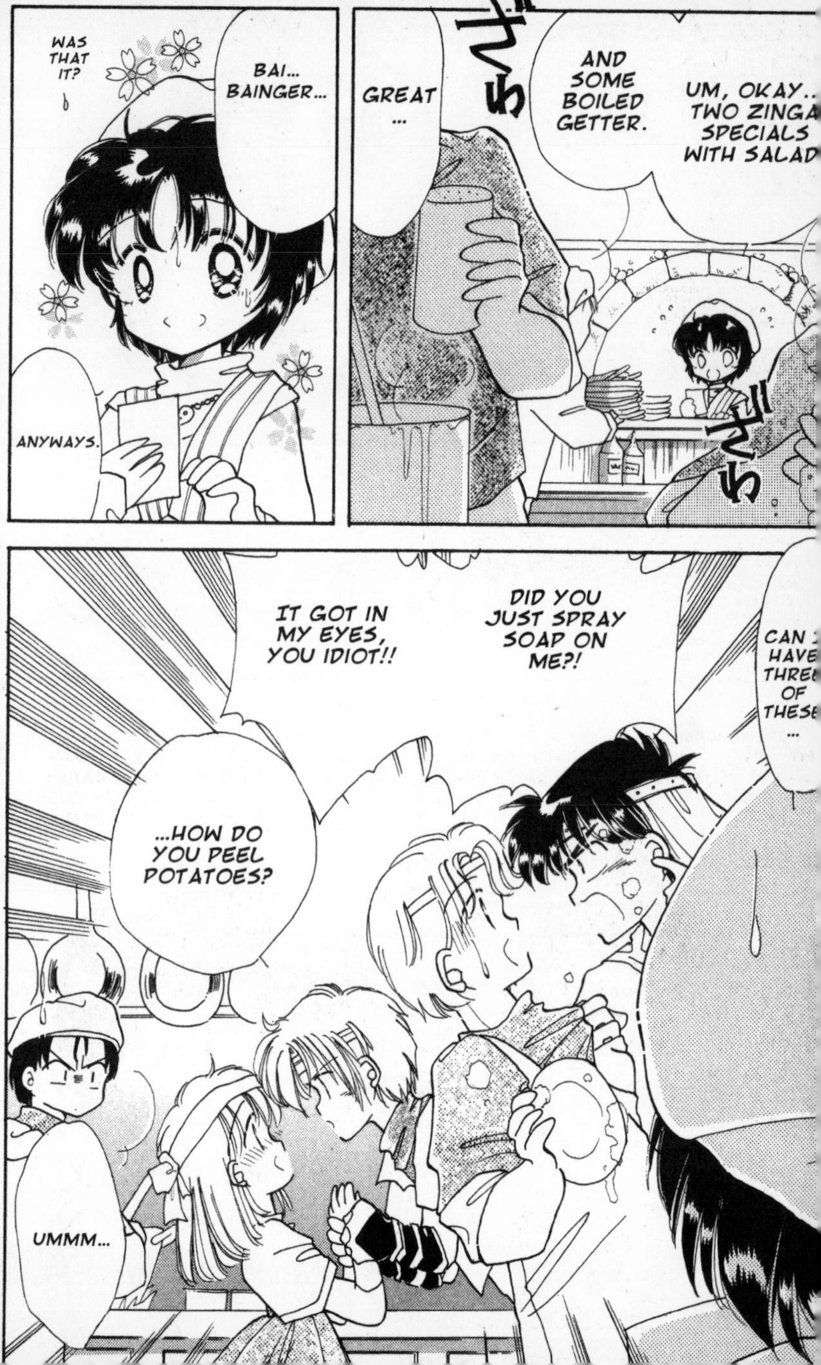

UM, OKAY.. TWO ZINGA SPECIALS WITH SALAD
AND SOME BOILED GETTER.
ざわ
ざわ
GREAT ...
BAI... BAINGER...
WAS THAT IT?
ANYWAYS.
CAN I HAVE THRE OF THES ...
DID YOU JUST SPRAY SOAP ON ME?!
IT GOT IN MY EYES, YOU IDIOT!!
...HOW DO YOU PEEL POTATOES?
UMMM...

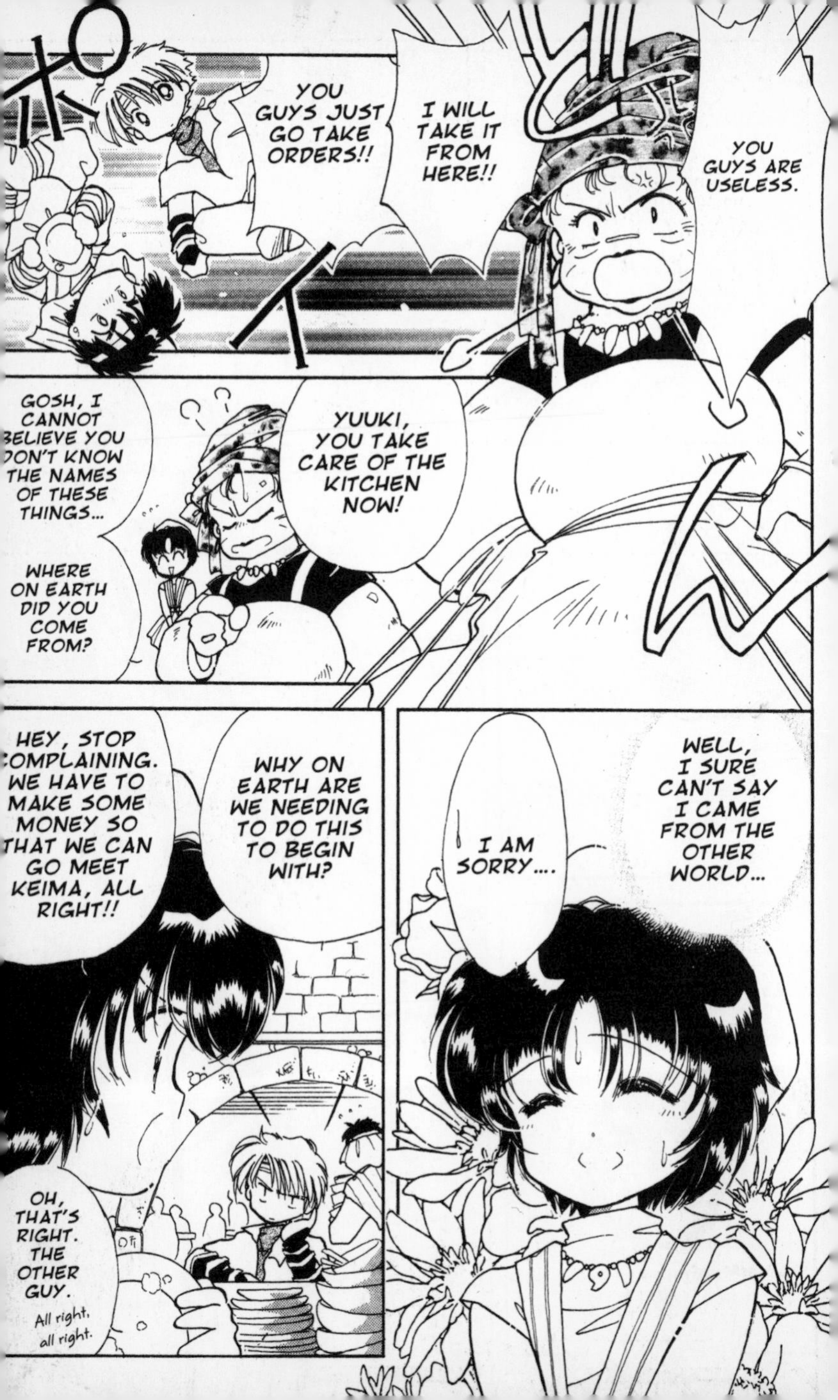
YOU GUYS ARE USELESS.
I WILL TAKE IT FROM HERE!!
YOU GUYS JUST GO TAKE ORDERS!!
YUUKI, YOU TAKE CARE OF THE KITCHEN NOW!
GOSH, I CANNOT BELIEVE YOU DON'T KNOW THE NAMES OF THESE THINGS...
WHERE ON EARTH DID YOU COME FROM?
WELL, I SURE CAN'T SAY I CAME FROM THE OTHER WORLD...
I AM SORRY....
WHY ON EARTH ARE WE NEEDING TO DO THIS TO BEGIN WITH?
HEY, STOP COMPLAINING. WE HAVE TO MAKE SOME MONEY SO THAT WE CAN GO MEET KEIMA, ALL RIGHT!!
OH, THAT'S RIGHT. THE OTHER GUY.
All right, all right.

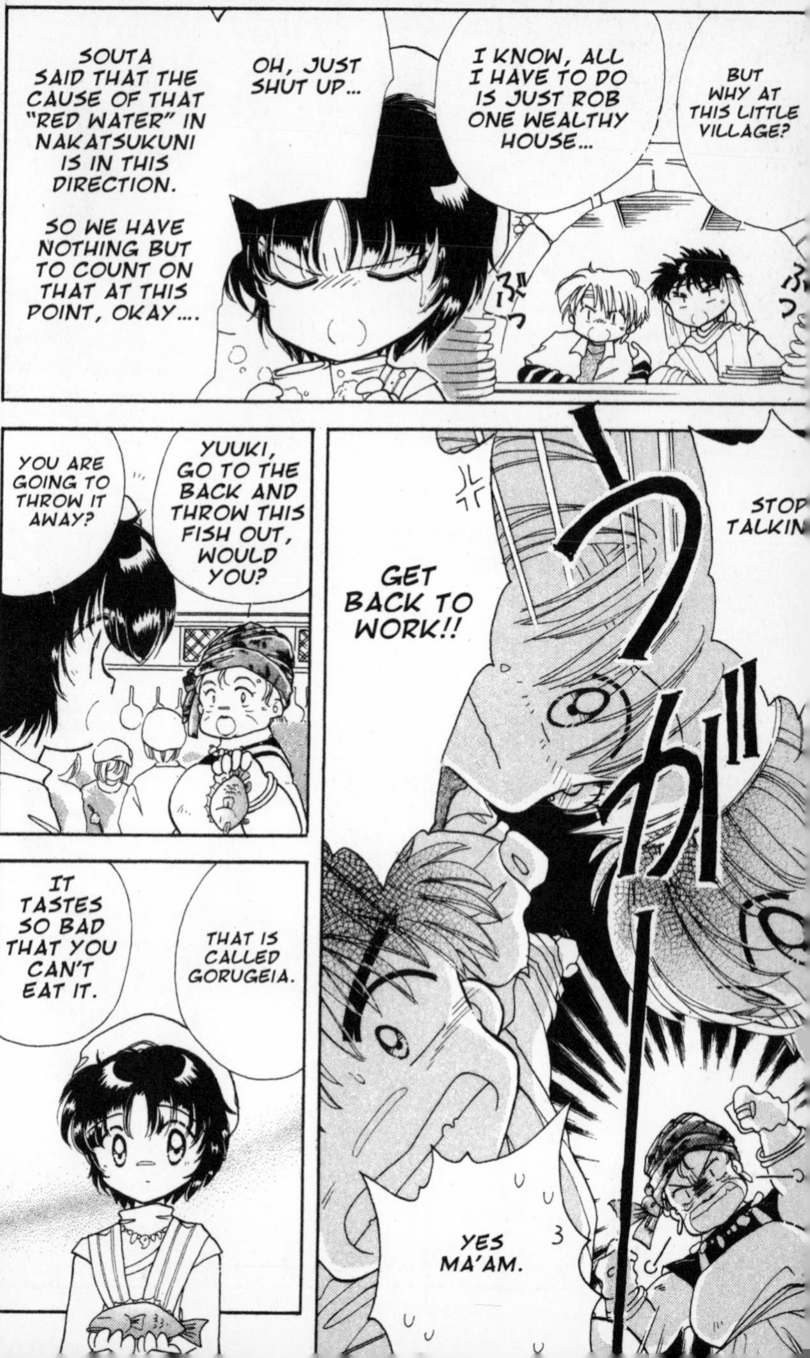
BUT WHY AT THIS LITTLE VILLAGE?
I KNOW, ALL I HAVE TO DO IS JUST ROB ONE WEALTHY HOUSE...
OH, JUST SHUT UP...
SOUTA SAID THAT THE CAUSE OF THAT "RED WATER" IN NAKATSUKUNI IS IN THIS DIRECTION.
SO WE HAVE NOTHING BUT TO COUNT ON THAT AT THIS POINT, OKAY....
STOP TALKIN
GET BACK TO WORK!!
YES MA'AM.
YUUKI, GO TO THE BACK AND THROW THIS FISH OUT, WOULD YOU?
YOU ARE GOING TO THROW IT AWAY?
THAT IS CALLED GORUGEIA.
IT TASTES SO BAD THAT YOU CAN'T EAT IT.

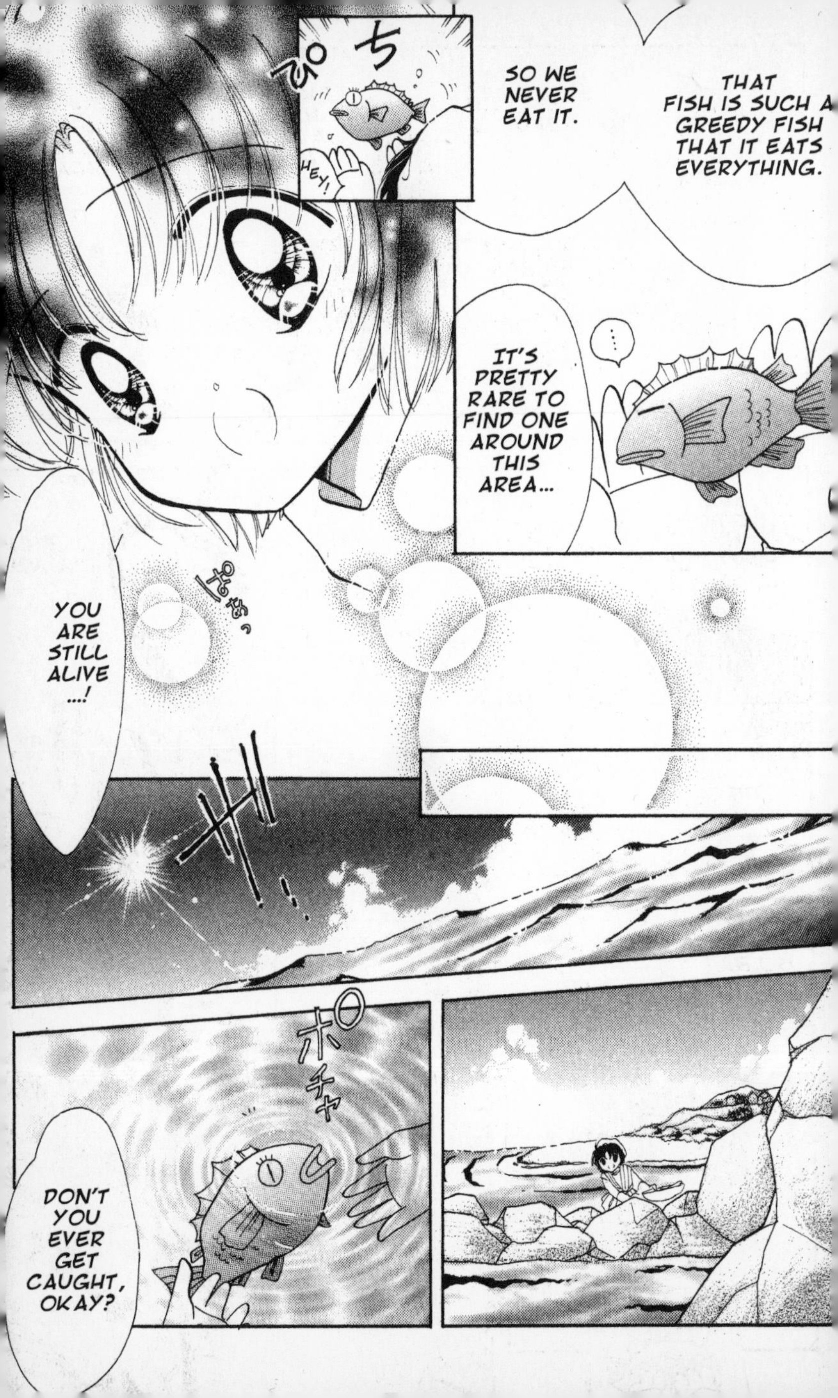
THAT FISH IS SUCH A GREEDY FISH THAT IT EATS EVERYTHING.
SO WE NEVER EAT IT.
ぴち
HEY!
IT'S PRETTY RARE TO FIND ONE AROUND THIS AREA...
...
YOU ARE STILL ALIVE ...!
ポチャ
DON'T YOU EVER GET CAUGHT, OKAY?

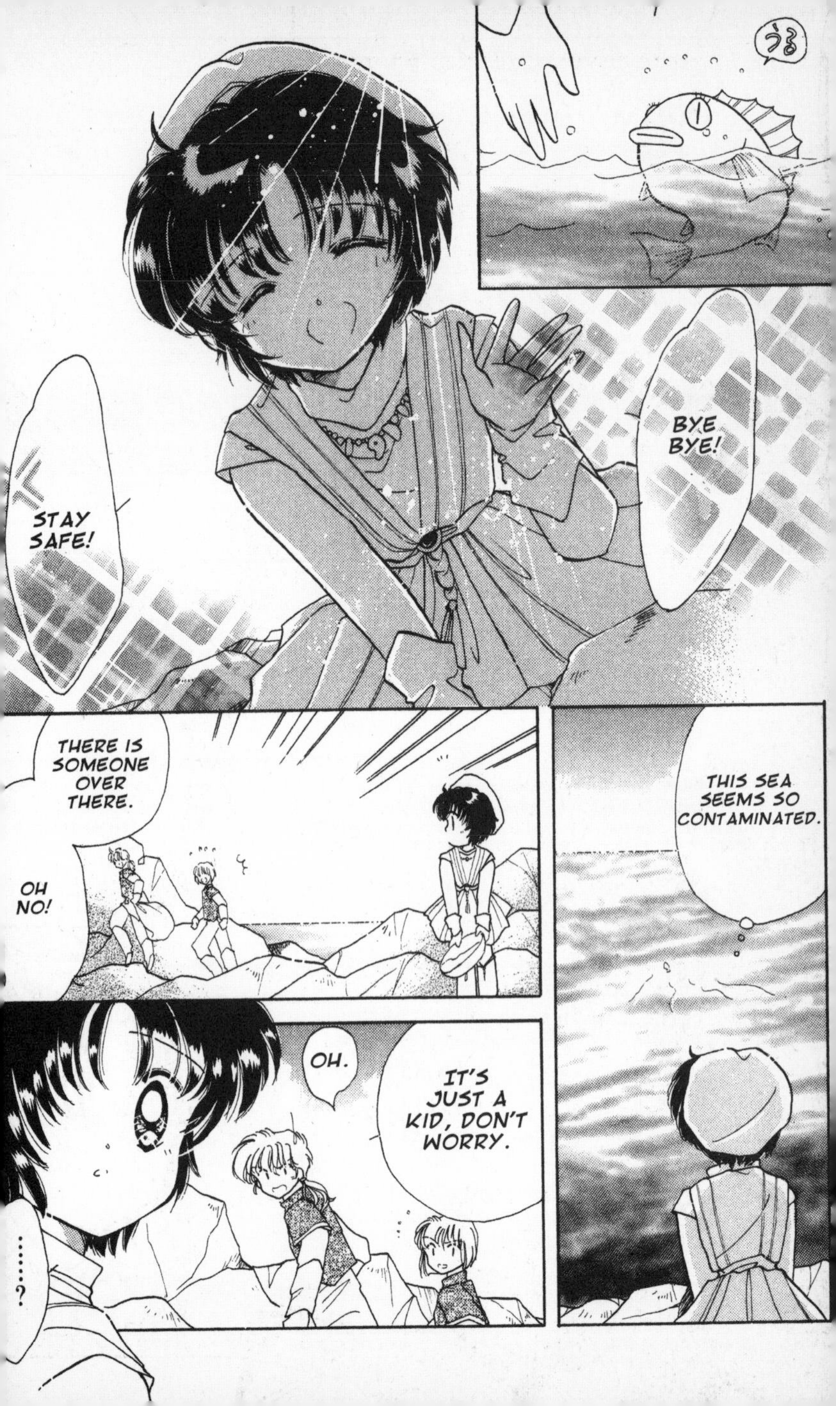
うる
BYE BYE!
STAY SAFE!
THIS SEA SEEMS SO CONTAMINATED.
THERE IS SOMEONE OVER THERE.
OH NO!
IT'S JUST A KID, DON'T WORRY.
OH.
......?

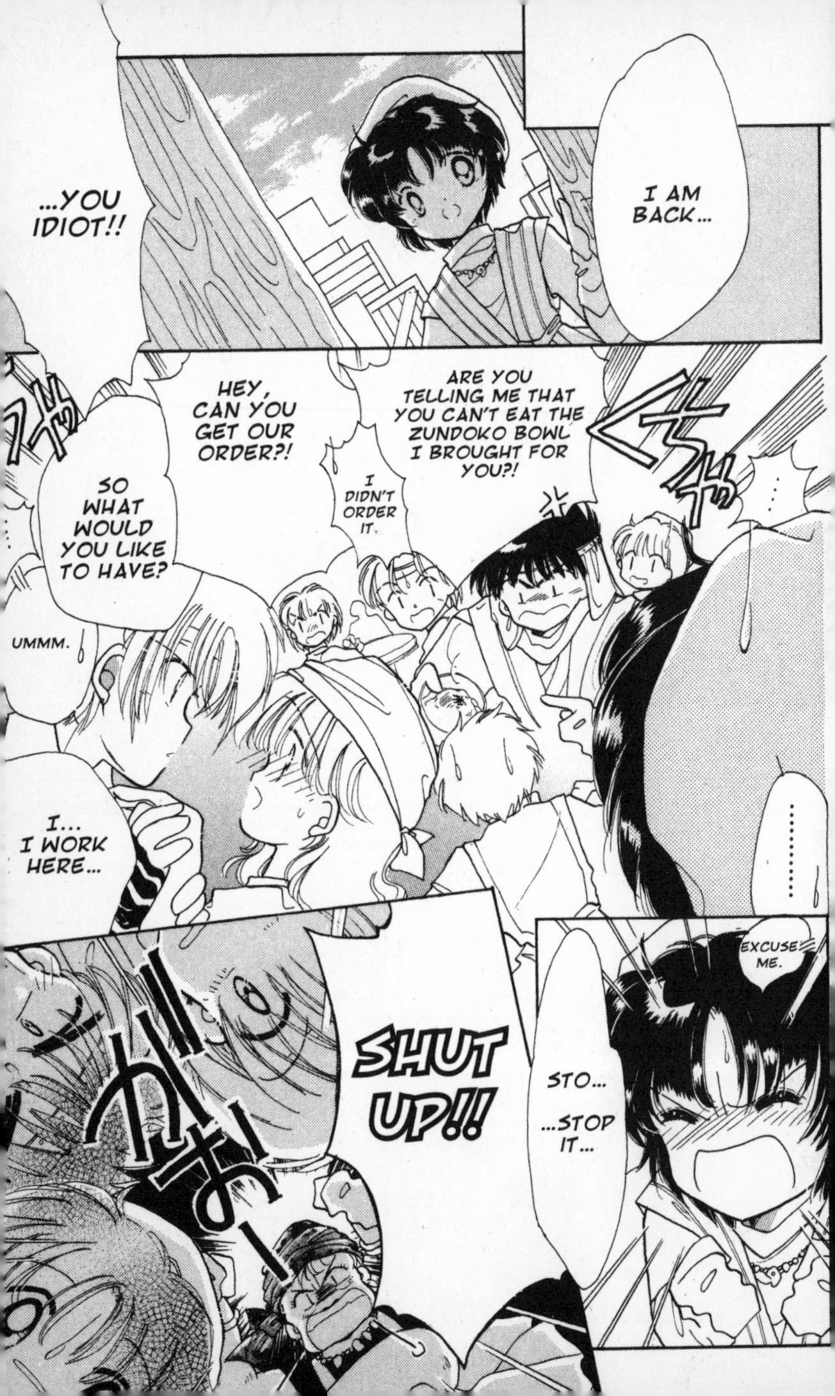

I AM BACK...
...YOU IDIOT!!
ARE YOU TELLING ME THAT YOU CAN'T EAT THE ZUNDOKO BOWL I BROUGHT FOR YOU?!
I DIDN'T ORDER IT.
HEY, CAN YOU GET OUR ORDER?!
SO WHAT WOULD YOU LIKE TO HAVE?
UMMM.
I... I WORK HERE...
EXCUSE ME.
STO...
...STOP IT...
SHUT UP!!

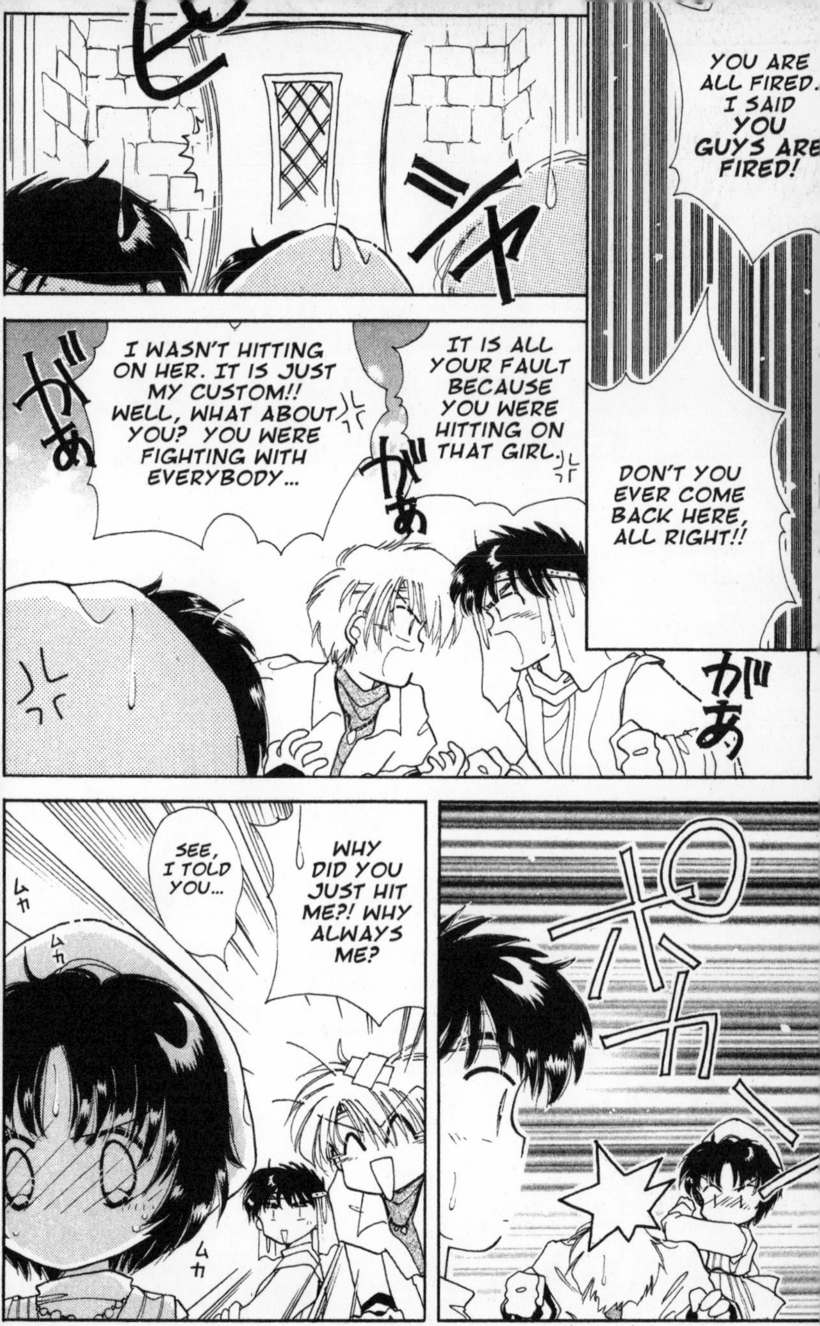
YOU ARE ALL FIRED. I SAID YOU GUYS ARE FIRED!
DON'T YOU EVER COME BACK HERE, ALL RIGHT!!
ピシャ
IT IS ALL YOUR FAULT BECAUSE YOU WERE HITTING ON THAT GIRL.
I WASN'T HITTING ON HER. IT IS JUST MY CUSTOM!! WELL, WHAT ABOUT YOU? YOU WERE FIGHTING WITH EVERYBODY...
があ
があ
があ
ポカ
WHY DID YOU JUST HIT ME?! WHY ALWAYS ME?
SEE, I TOLD YOU...
ムカ
ムカ
ムカ

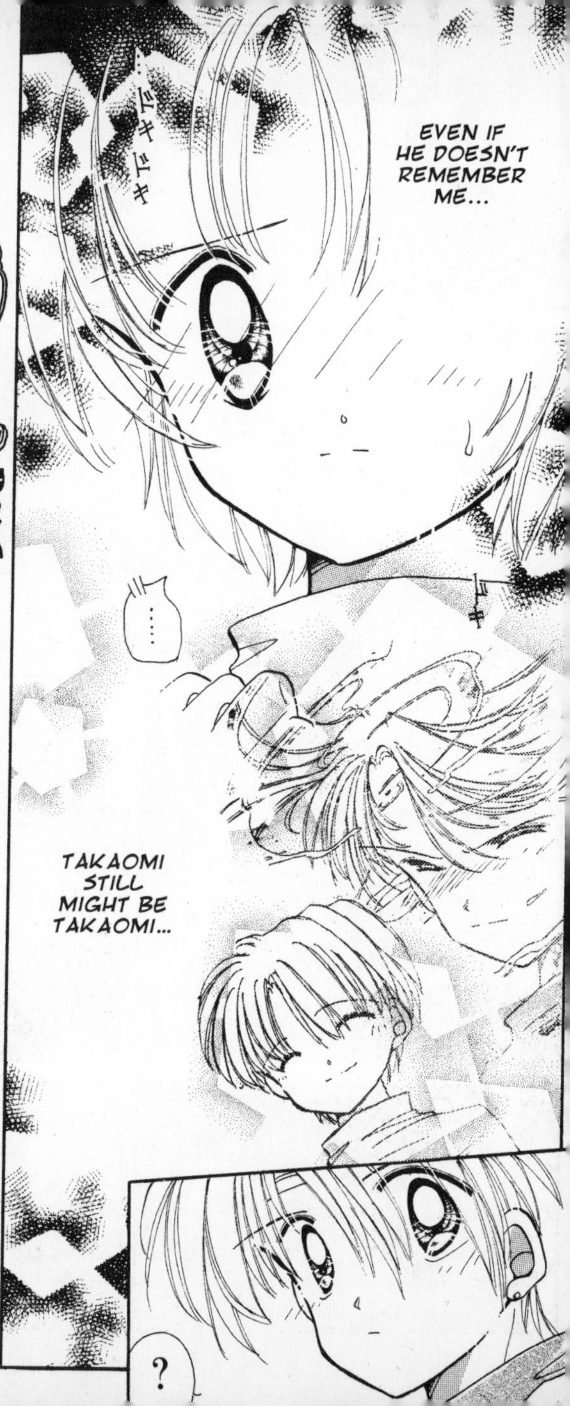
ドキドキ
EVEN IF HE DOESN'T REMEMBER ME...
......
TAKAOMI STILL MIGHT BE TAKAOMI...
?

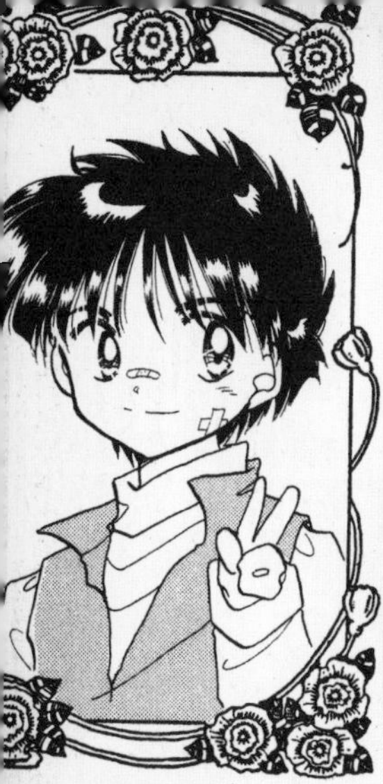

Taizou Hyuga

Born on May 13th.

Blood type: O

He is a 5th grader at the same school where Yuuki goes, but is in a different class. You can say he is kind of a bully at school, but he does have a side of him that is very sweet. He likes competing and fighting with others. He's close with his parents and older sister. It is probably safe to say that he is not that good with studying....

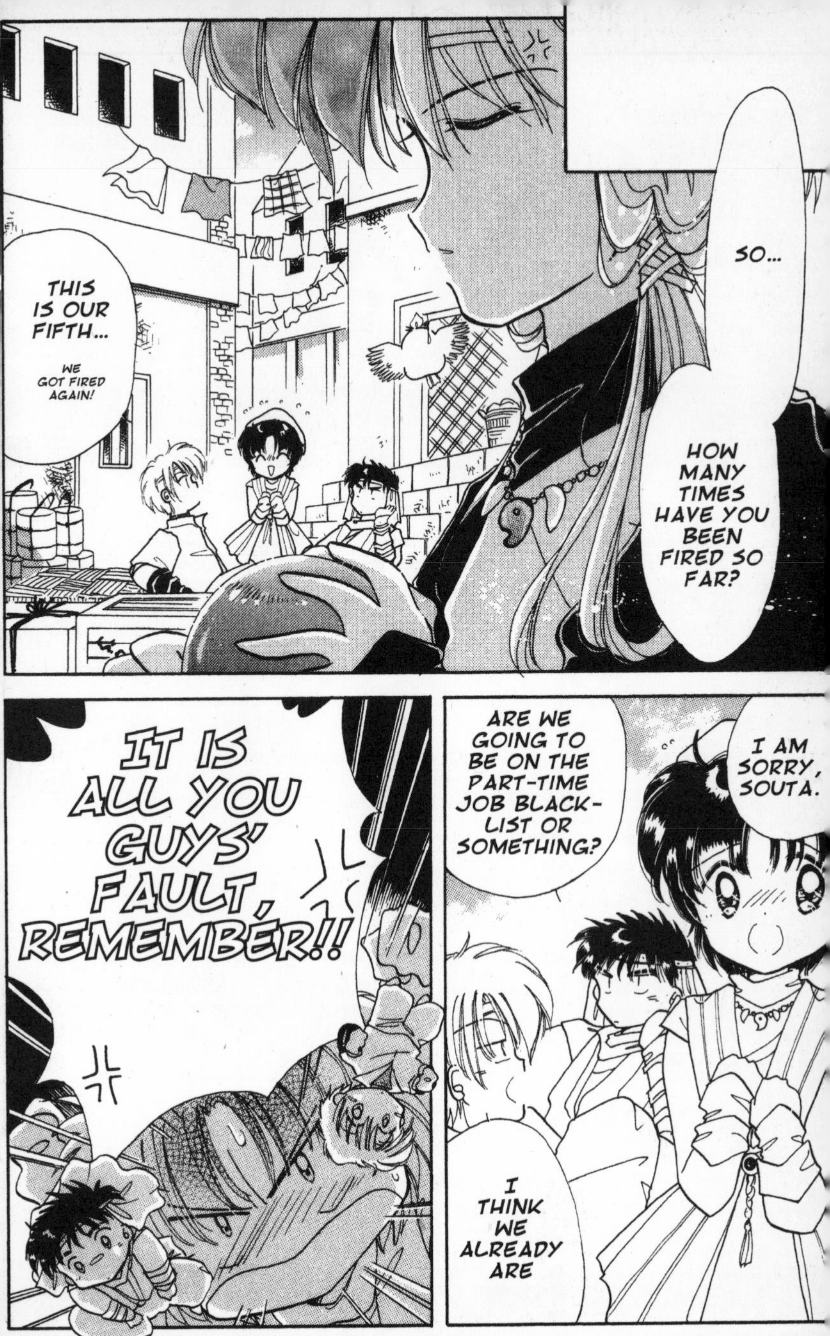

SO...
HOW MANY TIMES HAVE YOU BEEN FIRED SO FAR?
THIS IS OUR FIFTH...
WE GOT FIRED AGAIN!
I AM SORRY, SOUTA.
ARE WE GOING TO BE ON THE PART-TIME JOB BLACK-LIST OR SOMETHING?
I THINK WE ALREADY ARE
IT IS ALL YOU GUYS' FAULT, REMEMBER!!

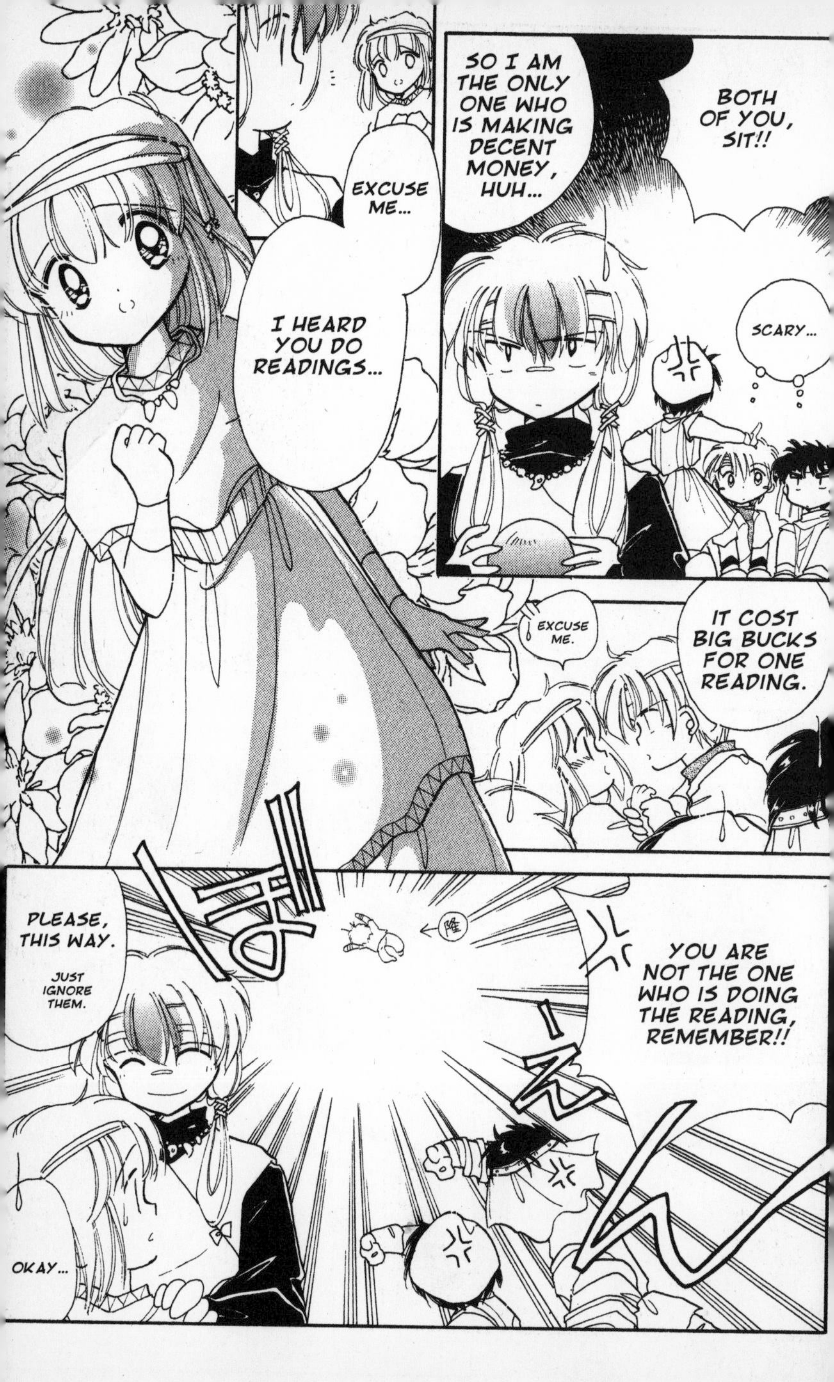

BOTH OF YOU, SIT!!
SO I AM THE ONLY ONE WHO IS MAKING DECENT MONEY, HUH...
SCARY...
IT COST BIG BUCKS FOR ONE READING.
EXCUSE ME.
EXCUSE ME...
I HEARD YOU DO READINGS...
YOU ARE NOT THE ONE WHO IS DOING THE READING, REMEMBER!!
PLEASE, THIS WAY.
JUST IGNORE THEM.
OKAY...

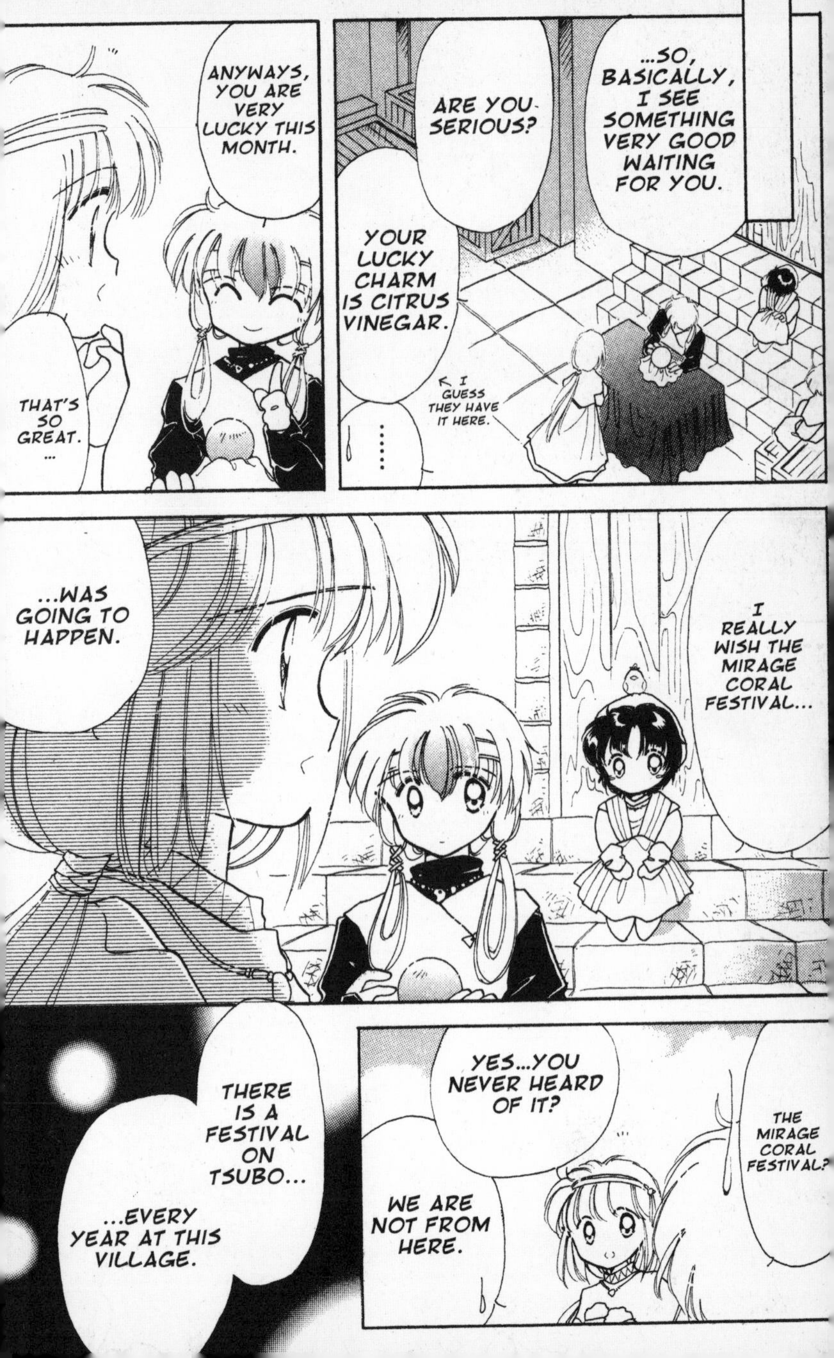

...SO, BASICALLY, I SEE SOMETHING VERY GOOD WAITING FOR YOU.
ARE YOU SERIOUS?
YOUR LUCKY CHARM IS CITRUS VINEGAR.
I GUESS THEY HAVE IT HERE.
......
ANYWAYS, YOU ARE VERY LUCKY THIS MONTH.
THAT'S SO GREAT. ...
I REALLY WISH THE MIRAGE CORAL FESTIVAL...
...WAS GOING TO HAPPEN.
THE MIRAGE CORAL FESTIVAL?
YES...YOU NEVER HEARD OF IT?
WE ARE NOT FROM HERE.
THERE IS A FESTIVAL ON TSUBO...
...EVERY YEAR AT THIS VILLAGE.

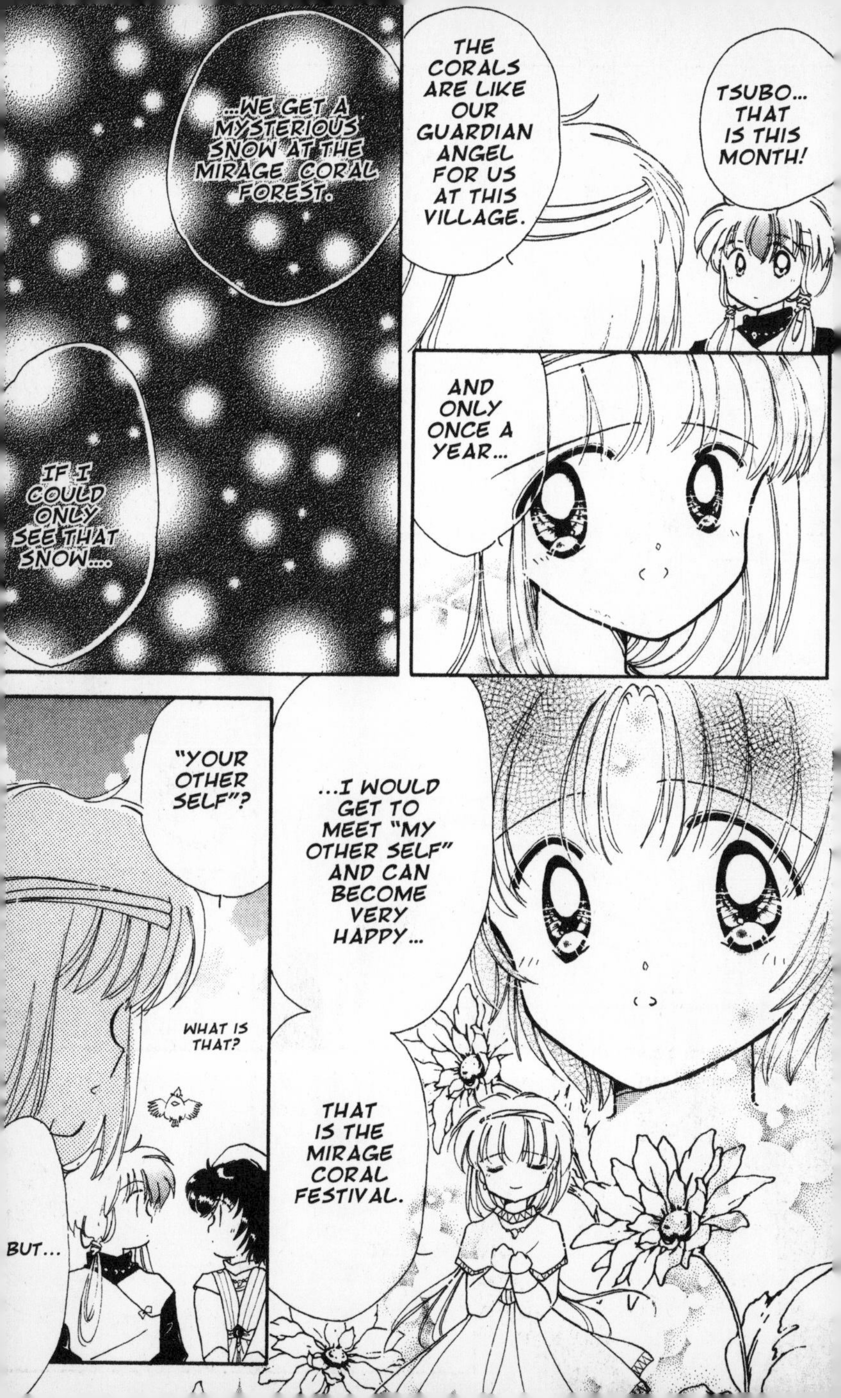
TSUBO... THAT IS THIS MONTH!
THE CORALS ARE LIKE OUR GUARDIAN ANGEL FOR US AT THIS VILLAGE.
AND ONLY ONCE A YEAR...
...WE GET A MYSTERIOUS SNOW AT THE MIRAGE CORAL FOREST.
IF I COULD ONLY SEE THAT SNOW....
...I WOULD GET TO MEET "MY OTHER SELF" AND CAN BECOME VERY HAPPY...
THAT IS THE MIRAGE CORAL FESTIVAL.
"YOUR OTHER SELF"?
WHAT IS THAT?
BUT...

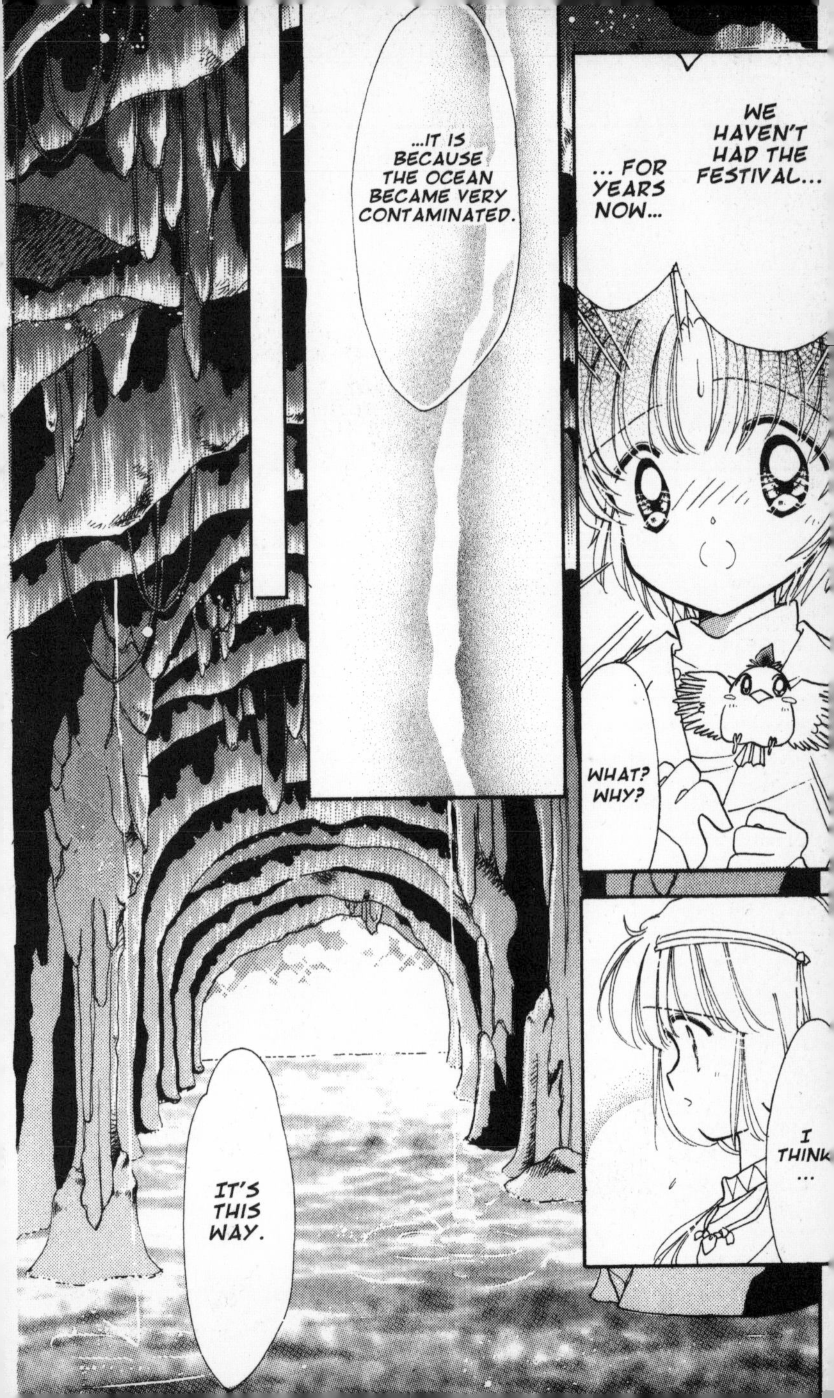
WE HAVEN'T HAD THE FESTIVAL...
... FOR YEARS NOW...
WHAT? WHY?
...IT IS BECAUSE THE OCEAN BECAME VERY CONTAMINATED.
I THINK ...
IT'S THIS WAY.

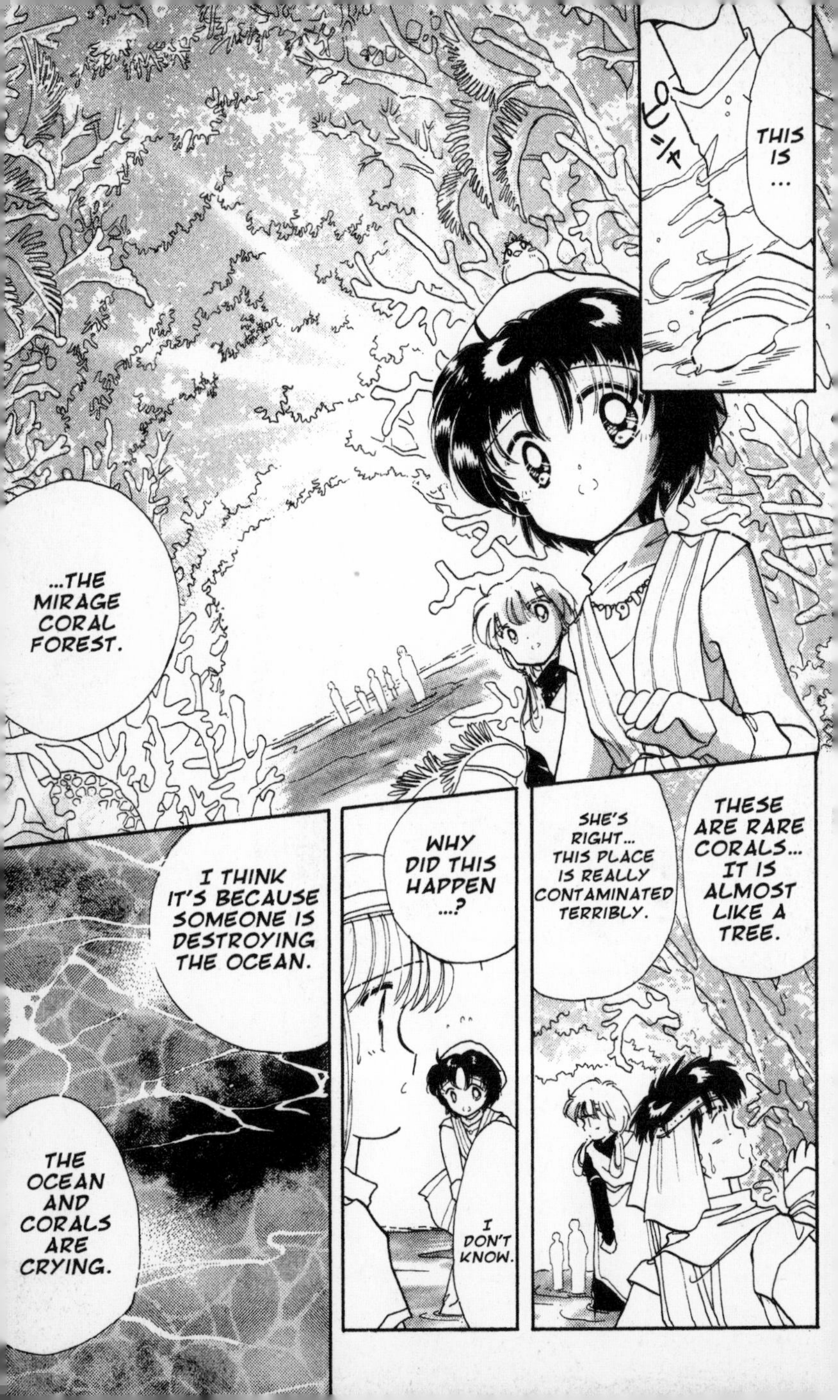
ピシャ
THIS IS ...
...THE MIRAGE CORAL FOREST.
THESE ARE RARE CORALS... IT IS ALMOST LIKE A TREE.
SHE'S RIGHT... THIS PLACE IS REALLY CONTAMINATED TERRIBLY.
WHY DID THIS HAPPEN ...?
I DON'T KNOW.
I THINK IT'S BECAUSE SOMEONE IS DESTROYING THE OCEAN.
THE OCEAN AND CORALS ARE CRYING.

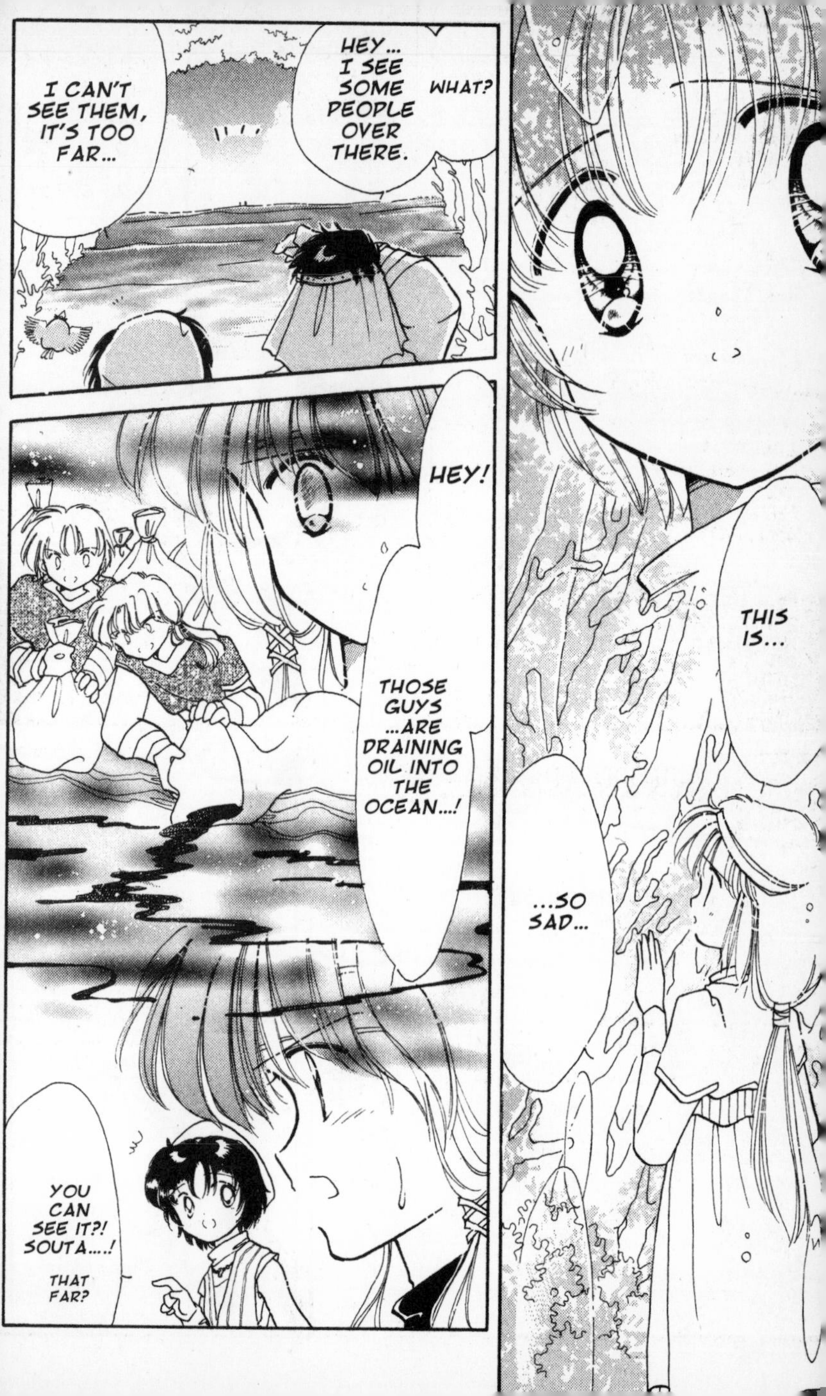
THIS IS...
...SO SAD...
WHAT?
HEY... I SEE SOME PEOPLE OVER THERE.
I CAN'T SEE THEM, IT'S TOO FAR...
HEY!
THOSE GUYS ...ARE DRAINING OIL INTO THE OCEAN...!
YOU CAN SEE IT?! SOUTA....!
THAT FAR?

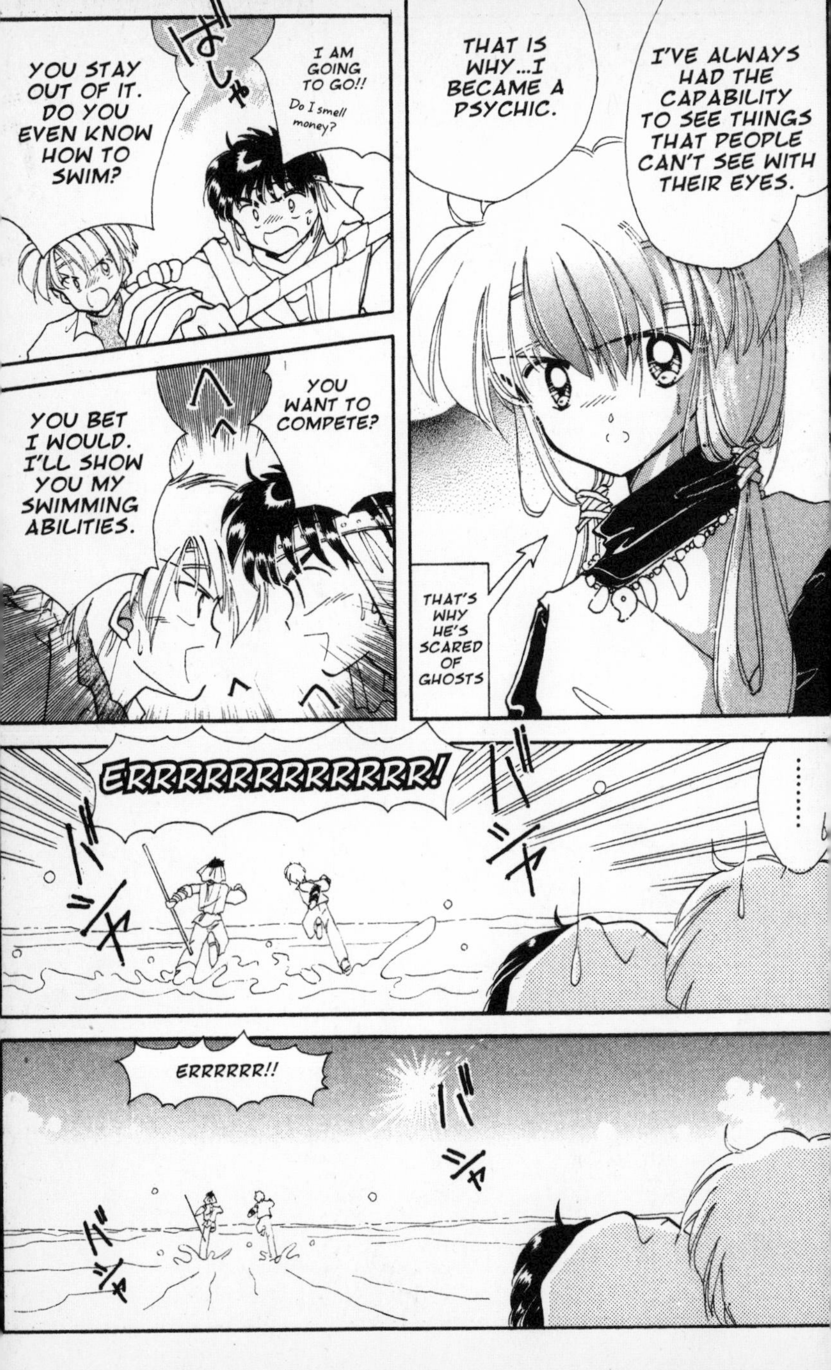
I'VE ALWAYS HAD THE CAPABILITY TO SEE THINGS THAT PEOPLE CAN'T SEE WITH THEIR EYES.
THAT IS WHY...I BECAME A PSYCHIC.
THAT'S WHY HE'S SCARED OF GHOSTS
I AM GOING TO GO!!
Do I smell money?
ばしゃ
YOU STAY OUT OF IT. DO YOU EVEN KNOW HOW TO SWIM?
YOU WANT TO COMPETE?
YOU BET I WOULD. I'LL SHOW YOU MY SWIMMING ABILITIES.
......
バシャ
ERRRRRRRRRRRRRR!
バシャ
ERRRRRR!!
バシャ
バシャ

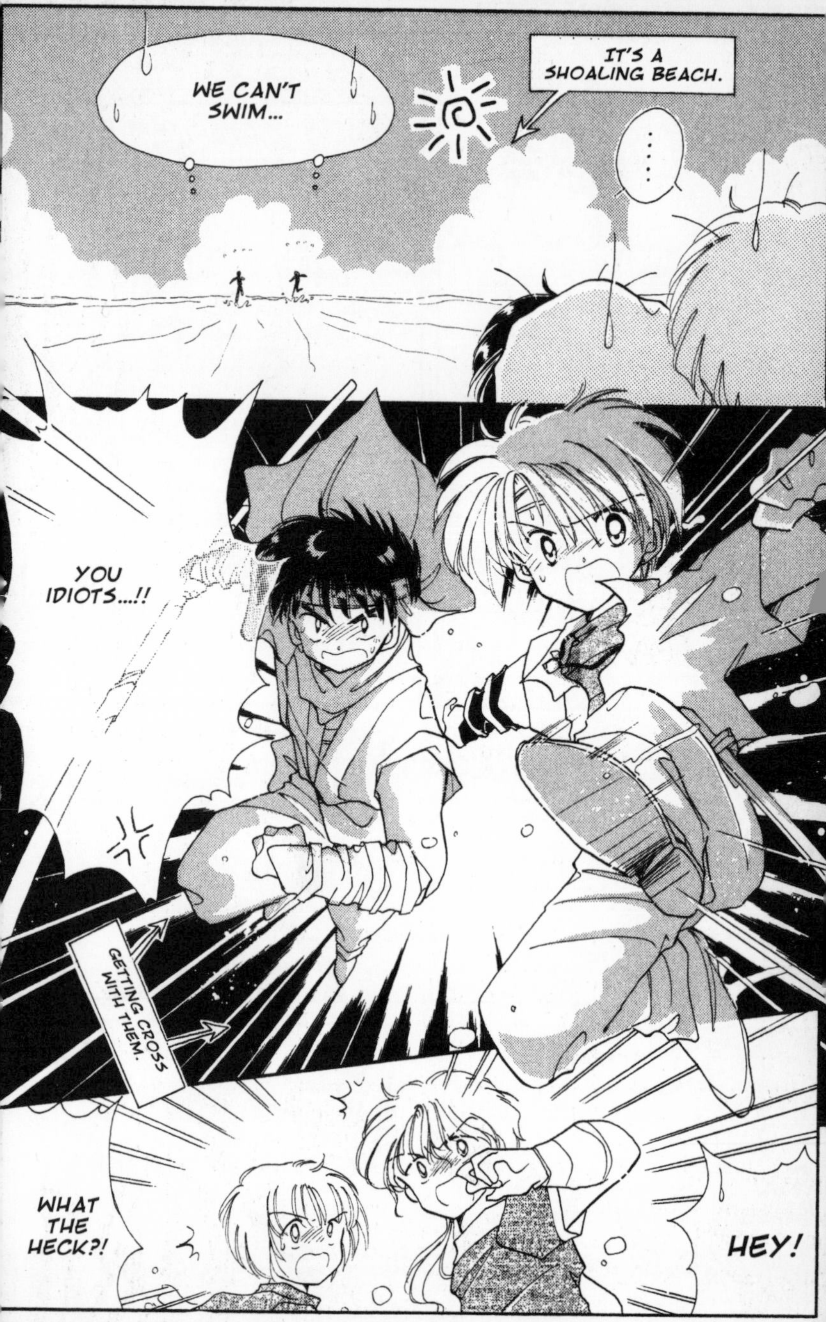

IT'S A SHOALING BEACH.
......
WE CAN'T SWIM...
YOU IDIOTS...!!
GETTING CROSS WITH THEM.
HEY!
WHAT THE HECK?!

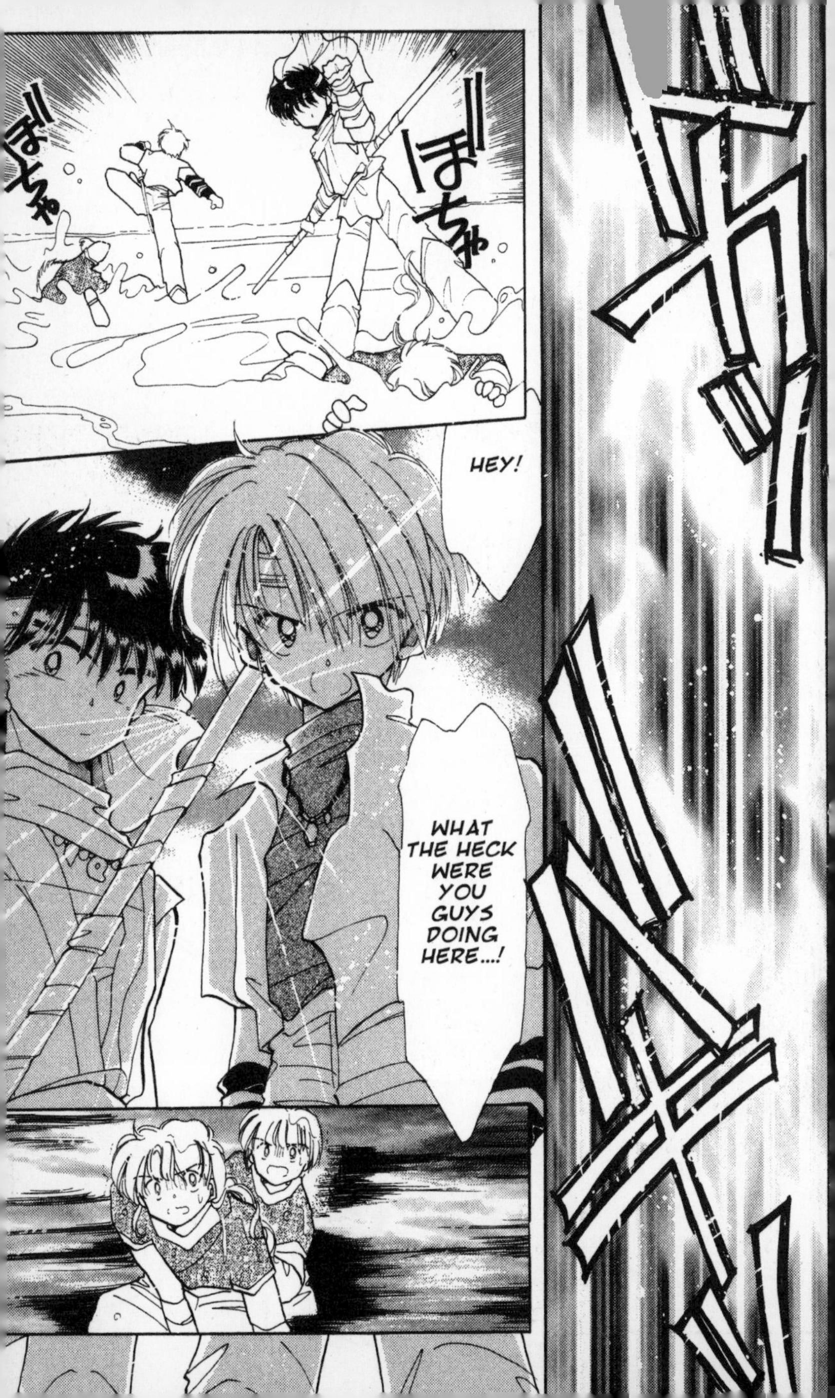
ぼちゃ
ぼちゃ
HEY!
WHAT THE HECK WERE YOU GUYS DOING HERE...!

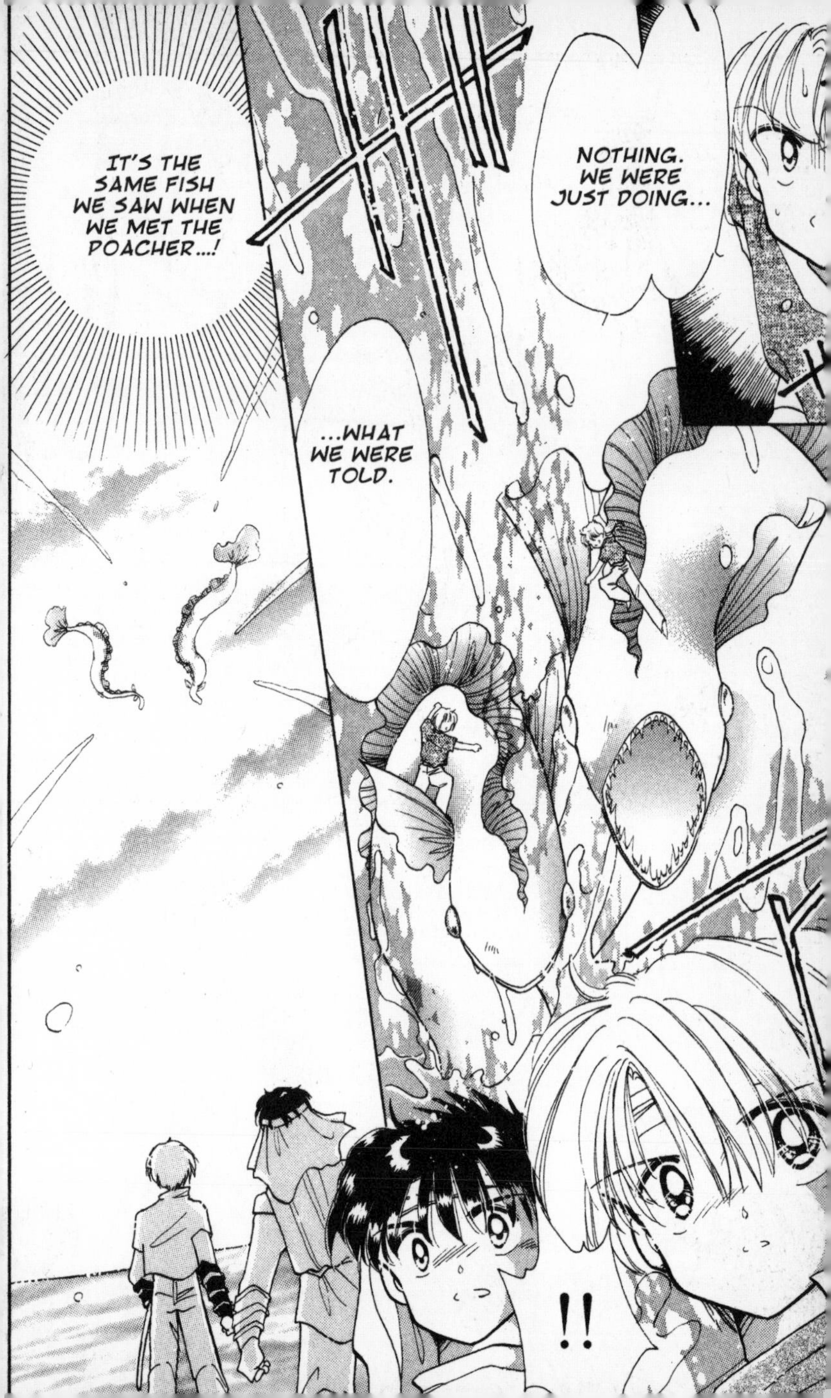
NOTHING. WE WERE JUST DOING...
...WHAT WE WERE TOLD.
!!
IT'S THE SAME FISH WE SAW WHEN WE MET THE POACHER...!

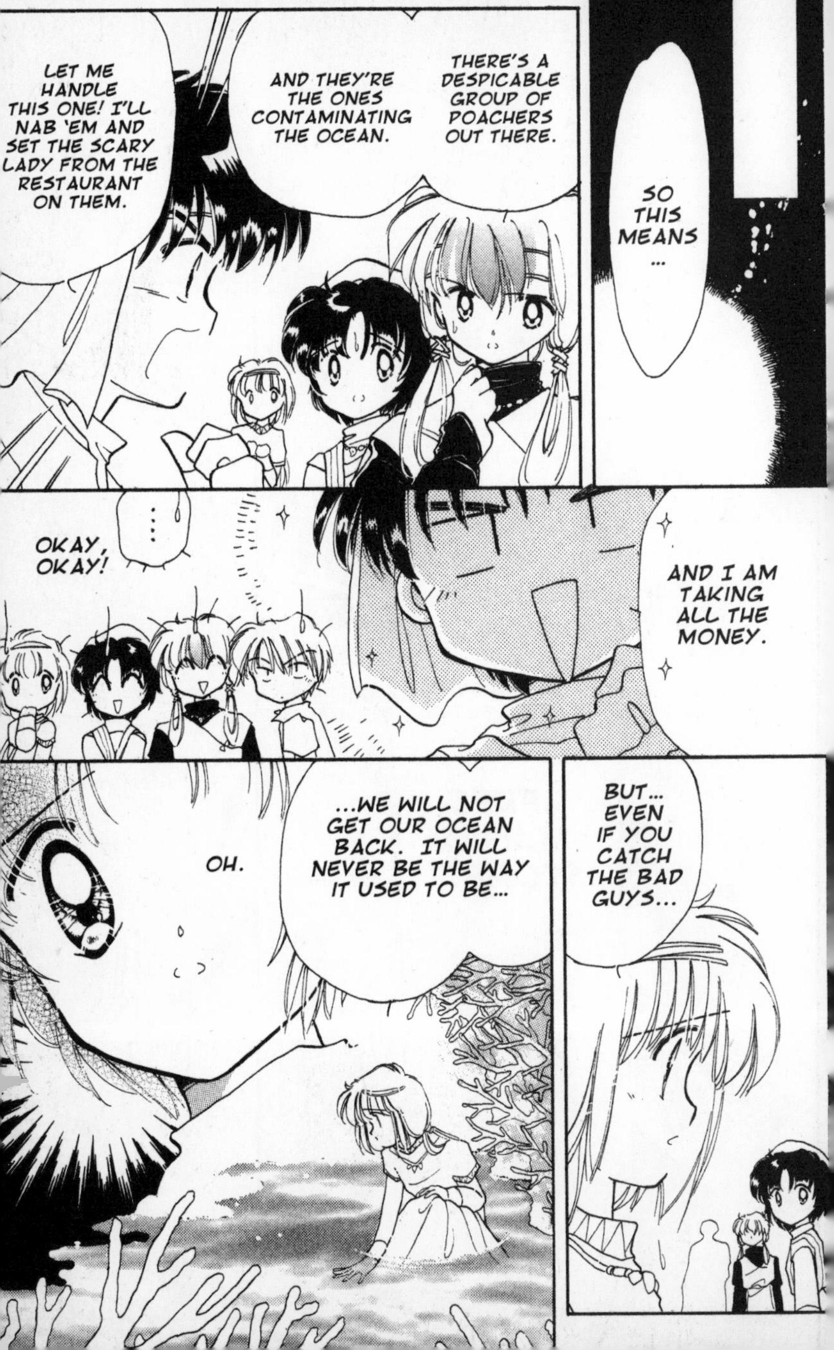
SO THIS MEANS...
THERE'S A DESPICABLE GROUP OF POACHERS OUT THERE.
AND THEY'RE THE ONES CONTAMINATING THE OCEAN.
LET ME HANDLE THIS ONE! I'LL NAB 'EM AND SET THE SCARY LADY FROM THE RESTAURANT ON THEM.
AND I AM TAKING ALL THE MONEY.
....
OKAY, OKAY!
BUT... EVEN IF YOU CATCH THE BAD GUYS...
...WE WILL NOT GET OUR OCEAN BACK. IT WILL NEVER BE THE WAY IT USED TO BE...
OH.

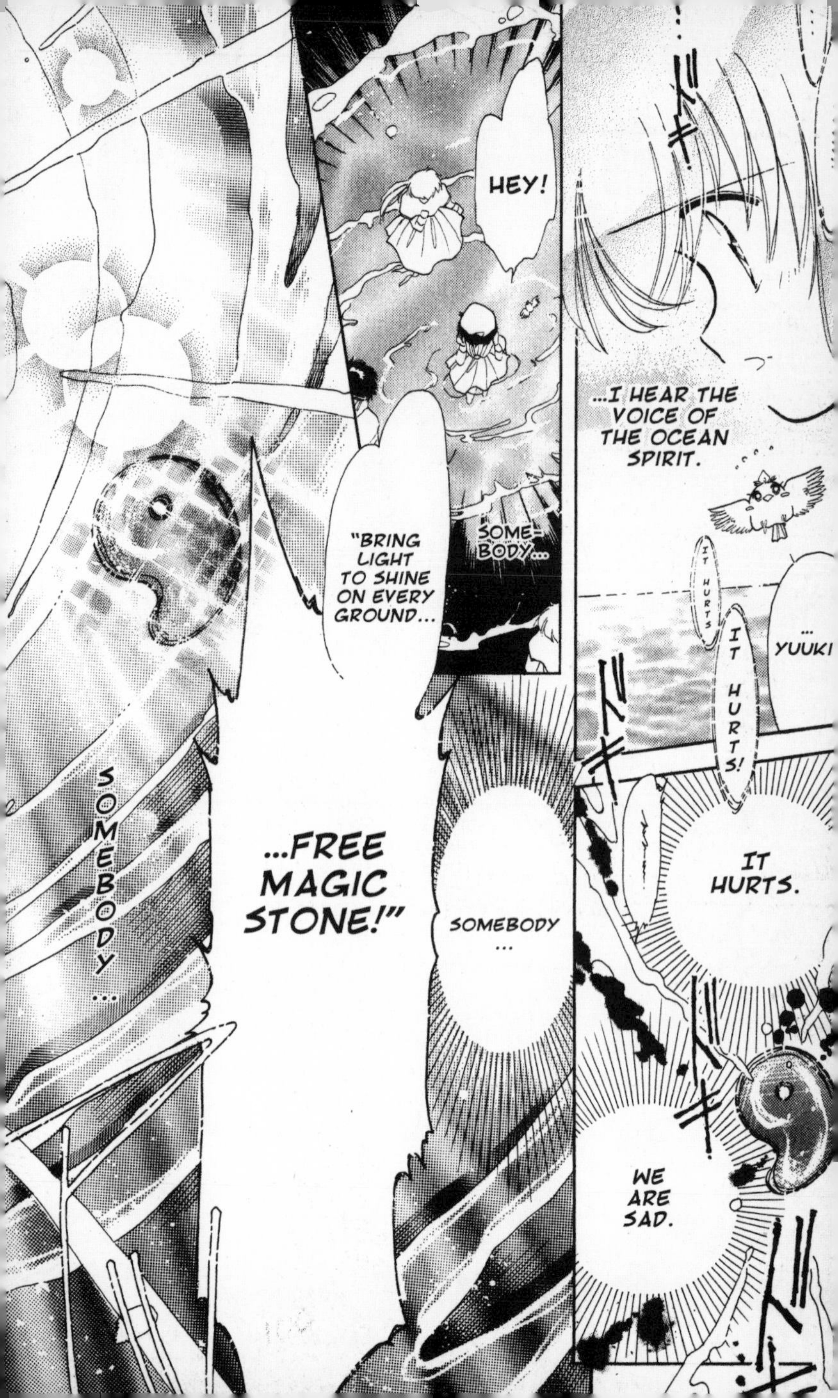
...I HEAR THE VOICE OF THE OCEAN SPIRIT.
... YUUKI
IT HURTS
IT HURTS IT HURTS!
IT HURTS.
WE ARE SAD.
HEY!
SOMEBODY...
"BRING LIGHT TO SHINE ON EVERY GROUND...
...FREE MAGIC STONE!"
SOMEBODY ...
SOMEBODY...

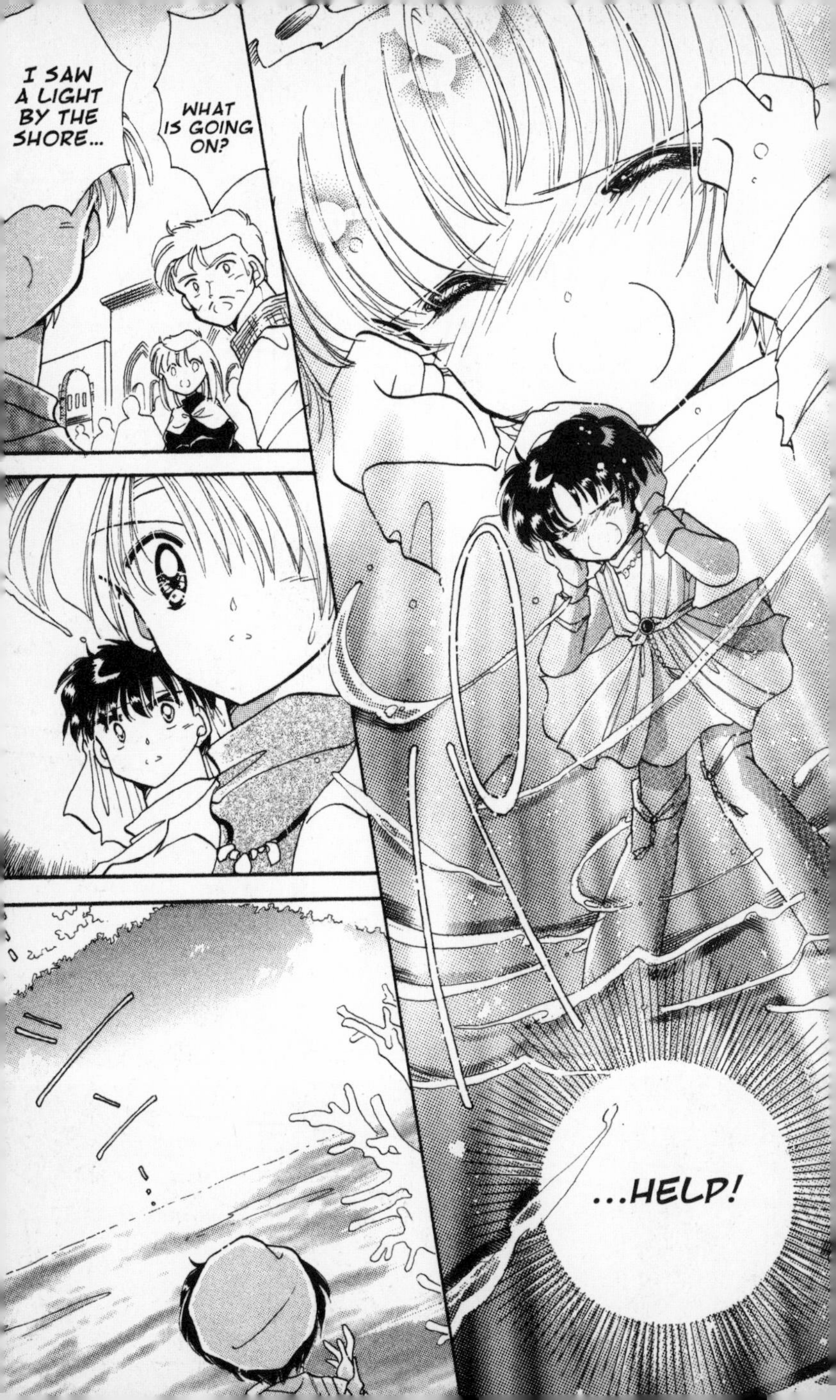

WHAT IS GOING ON?
I SAW A LIGHT BY THE SHORE...
...HELP!

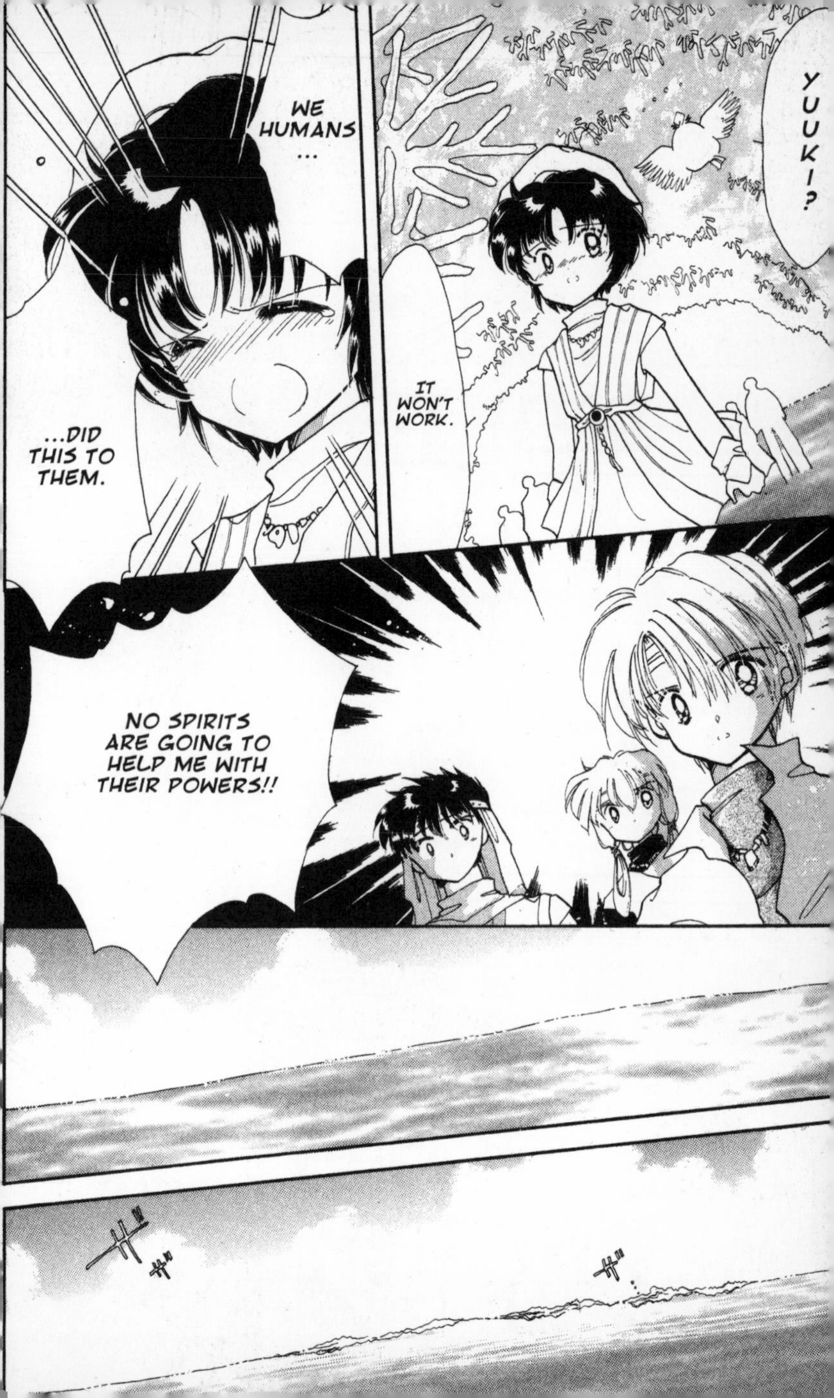
YUUKI?
IT WON'T WORK.
WE HUMANS ...
...DID THIS TO THEM.
NO SPIRITS ARE GOING TO HELP ME WITH THEIR POWERS!!

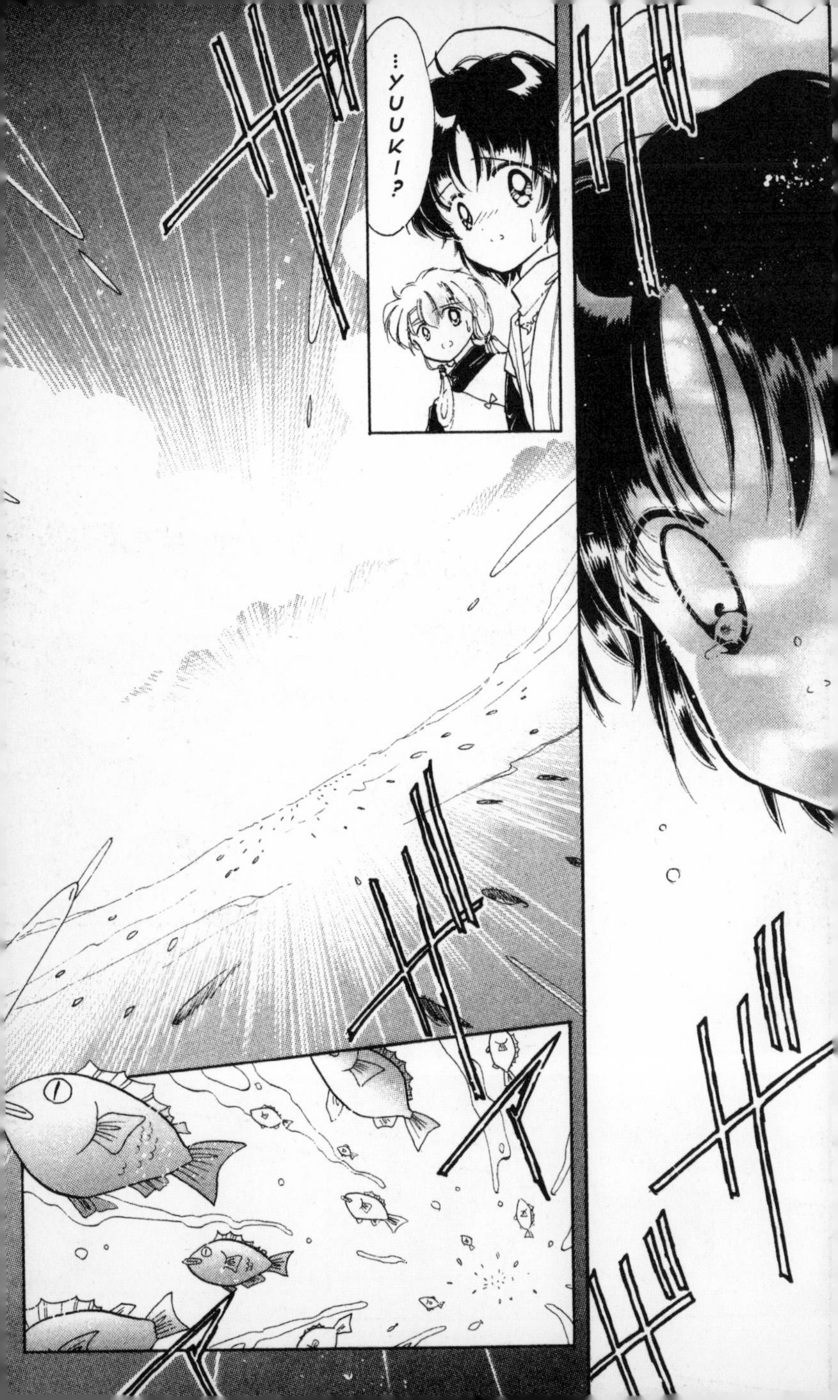
...YUUKI?

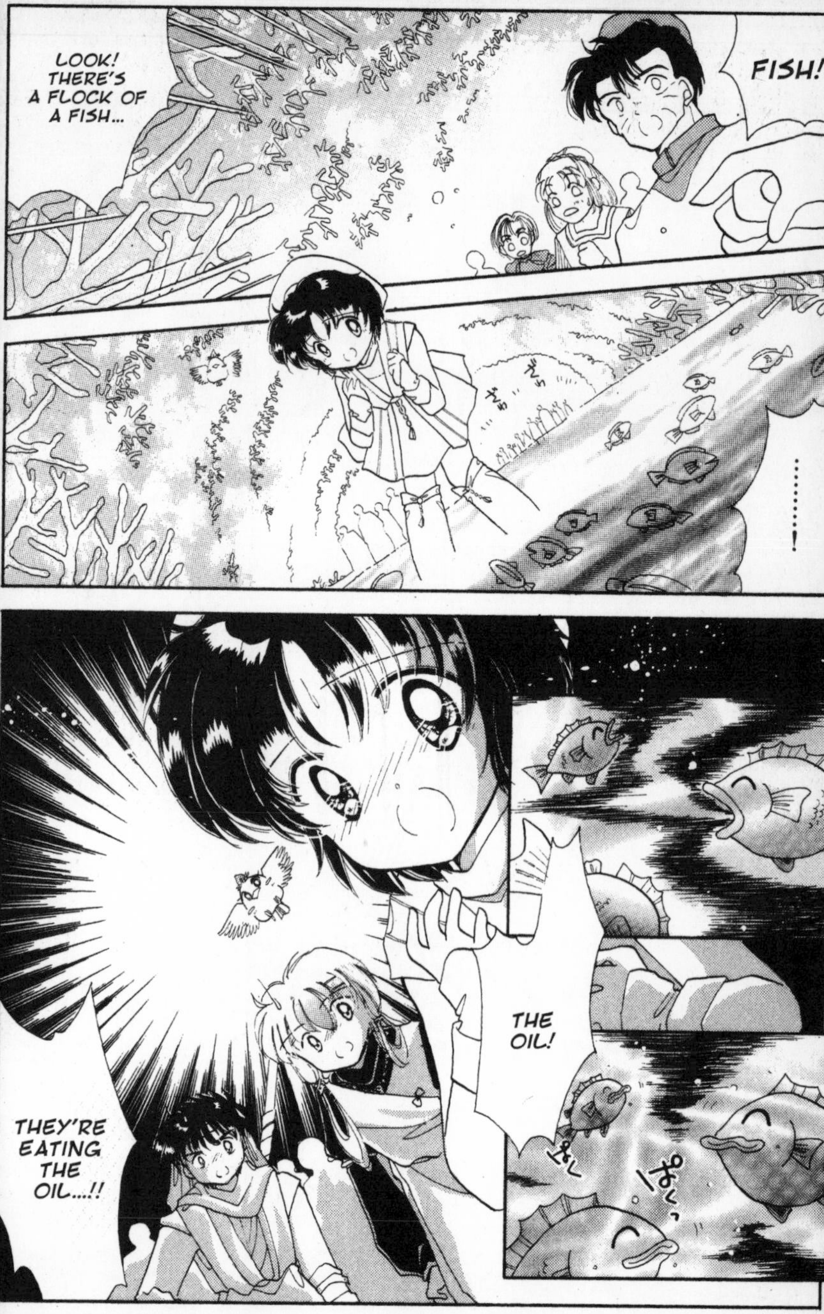
FISH!
LOOK! THERE'S A FLOCK OF A FISH...
......!
THE OIL!
THEY'RE EATING THE OIL...!!

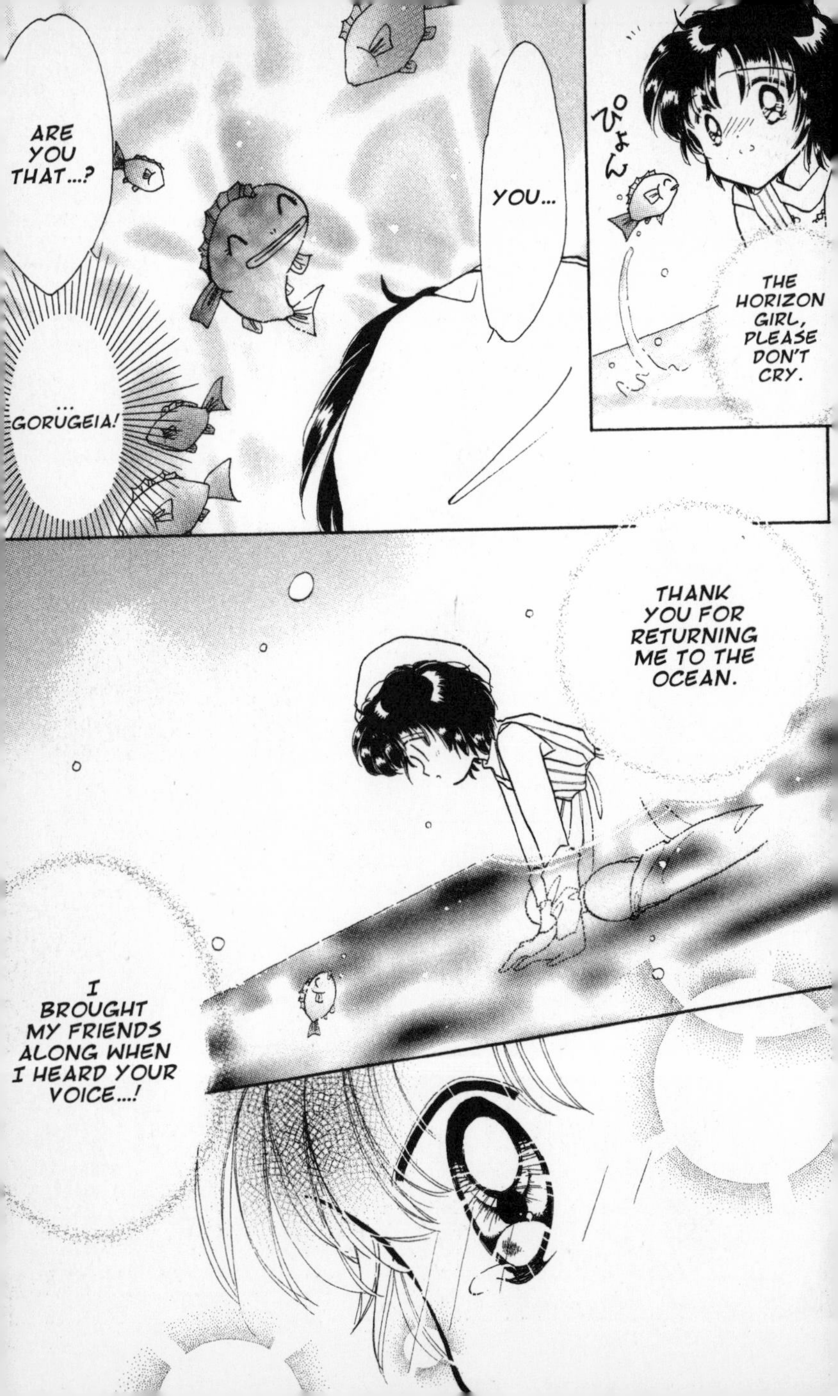
ぴょん
THE HORIZON GIRL, PLEASE DON'T CRY.
YOU...
ARE YOU THAT...?
...GORUGEIA!
THANK YOU FOR RETURNING ME TO THE OCEAN.
I BROUGHT MY FRIENDS ALONG WHEN I HEARD YOUR VOICE...!

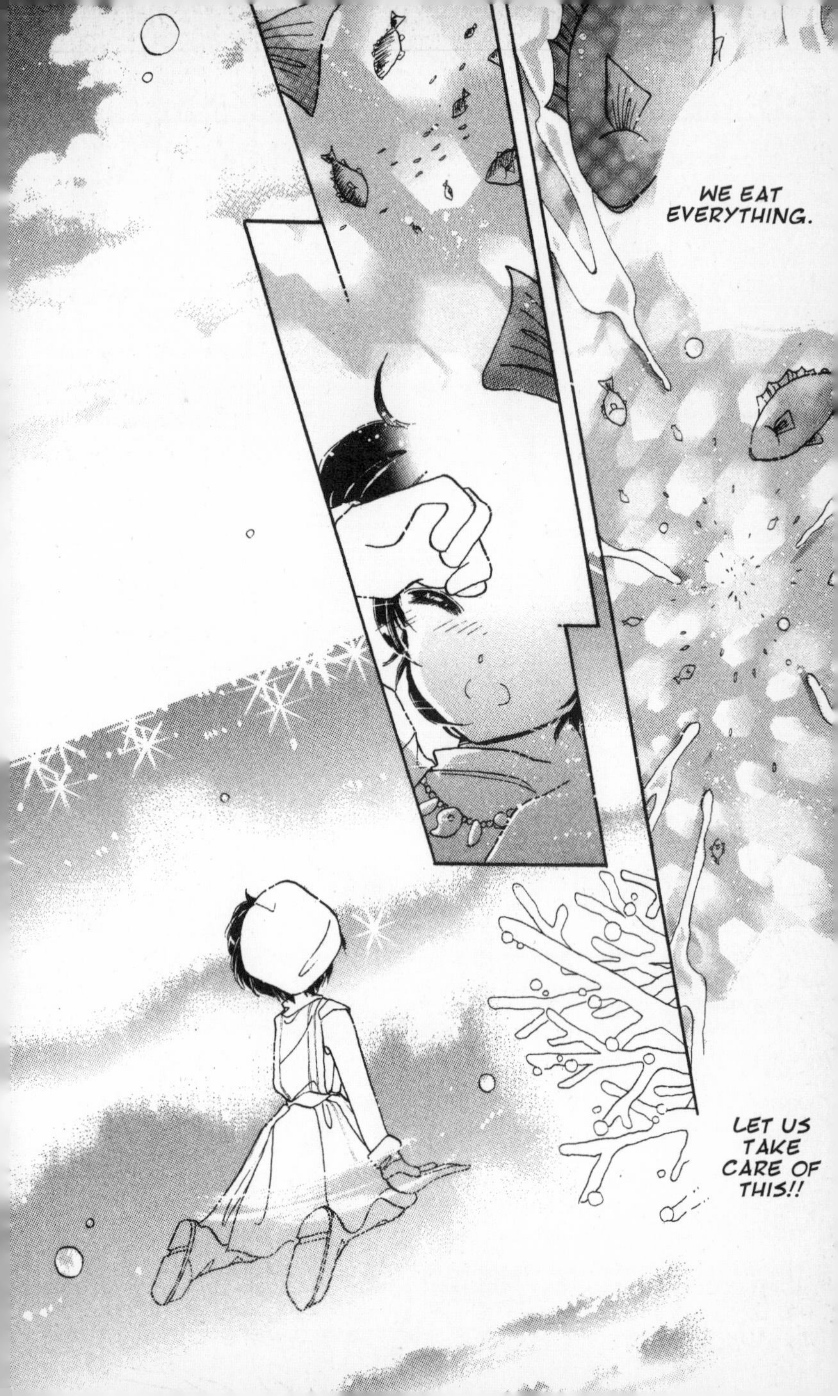
WE EAT EVERYTHING.
LET US TAKE CARE OF THIS!!

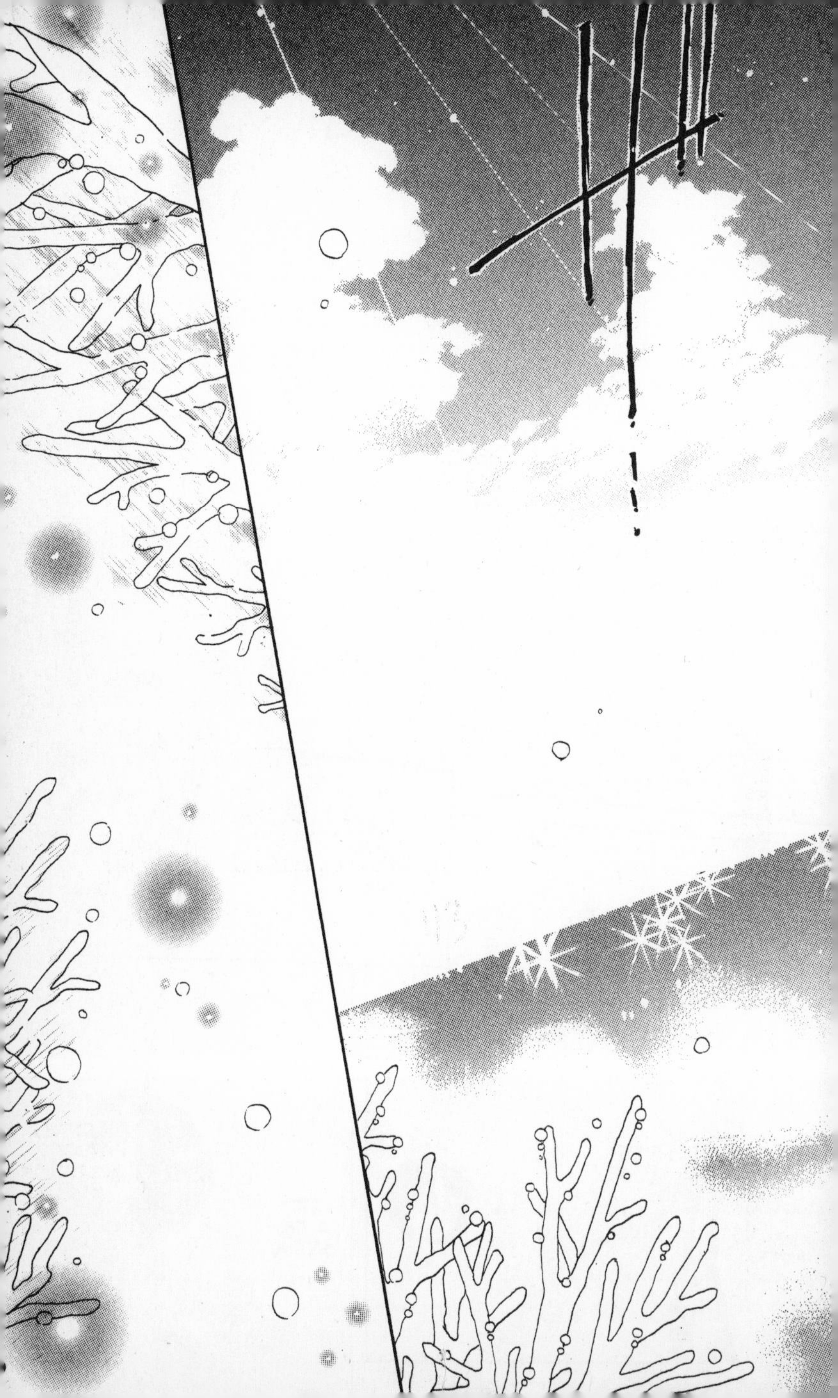

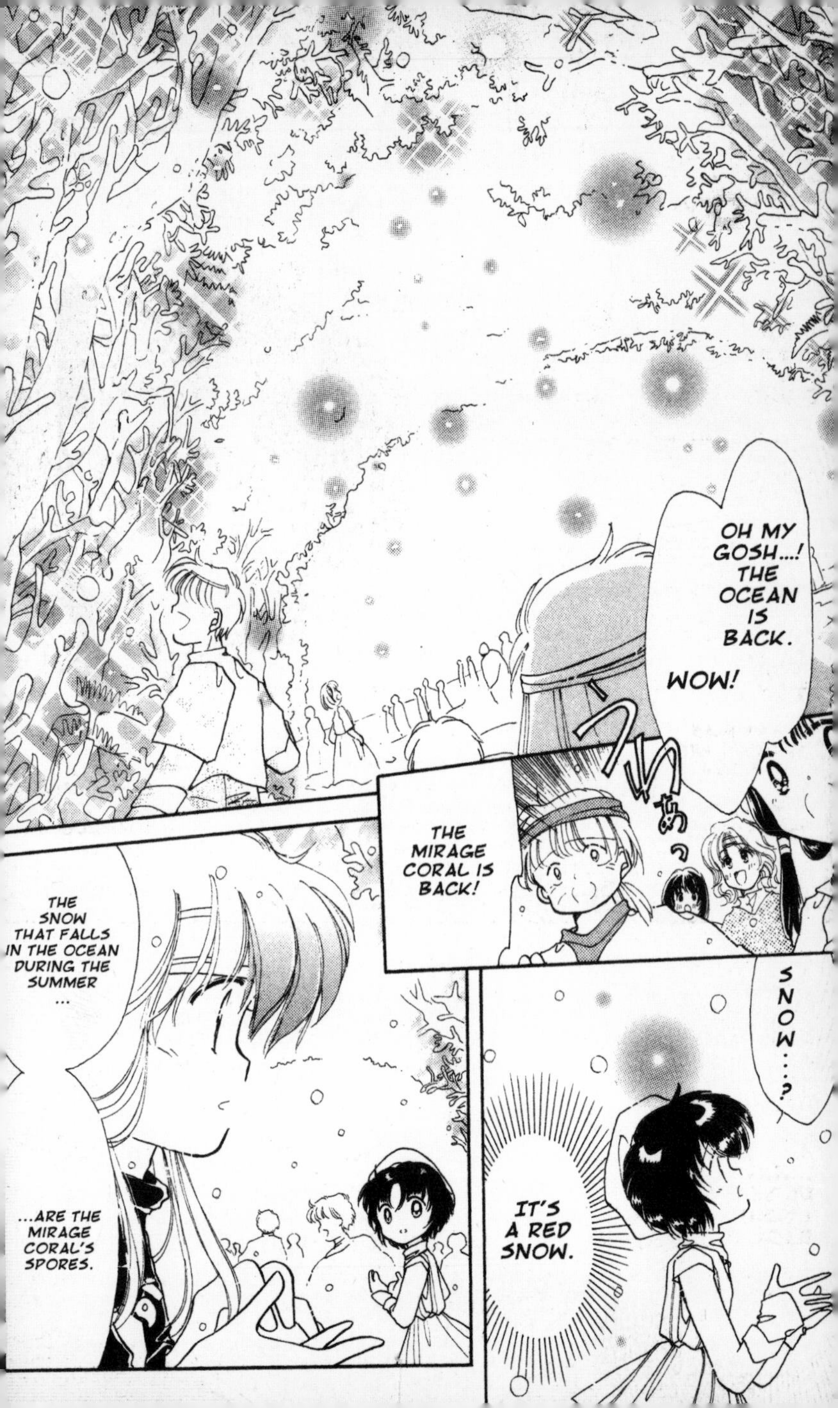
OH MY GOSH...! THE OCEAN IS BACK.
WOW!
うわあっ
THE MIRAGE CORAL IS BACK!
SNOW...?
IT'S A RED SNOW.
THE SNOW THAT FALLS IN THE OCEAN DURING THE SUMMER ...
...ARE THE MIRAGE CORAL'S SPORES.

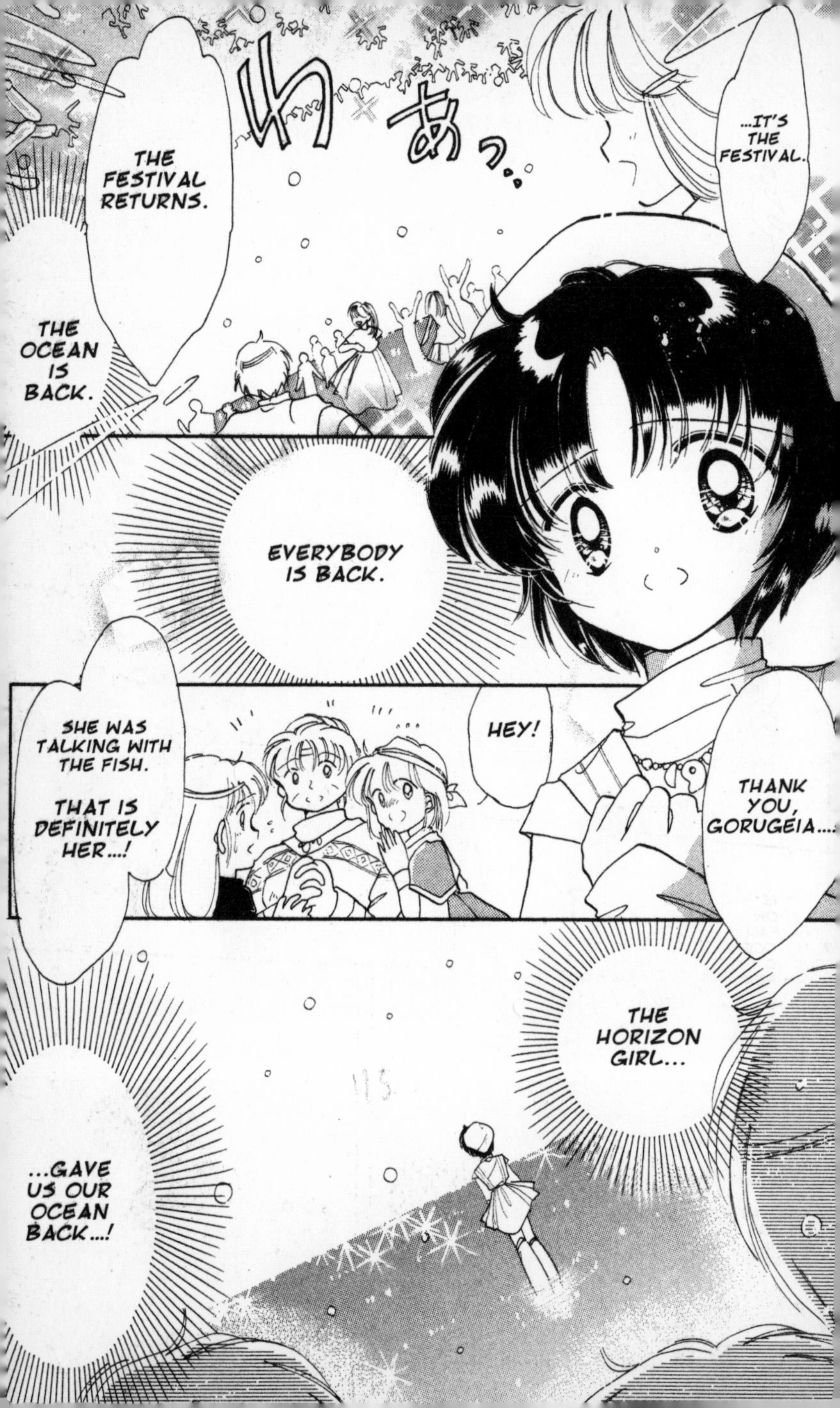
...IT'S THE FESTIVAL.
わあっ
THE FESTIVAL RETURNS.
THE OCEAN IS BACK.
EVERYBODY IS BACK.
THANK YOU, GORUGEIA....
HEY!
SHE WAS TALKING WITH THE FISH.
THAT IS DEFINITELY HER...!
THE HORIZON GIRL...
...GAVE US OUR OCEAN BACK...!

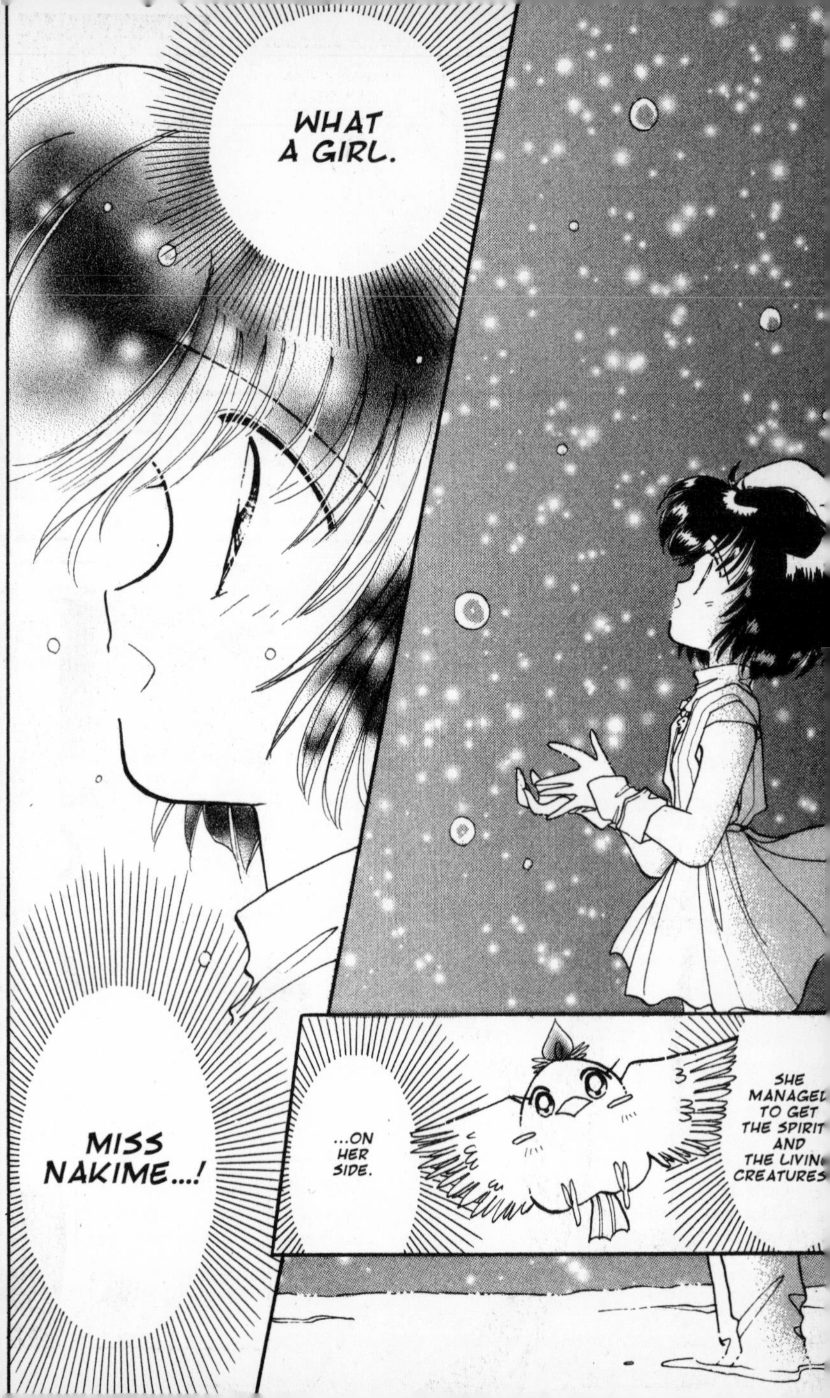
SHE MANAGED TO GET THE SPIRIT AND THE LIVING CREATURES
...ON HER SIDE.
WHAT A GIRL.
MISS NAKIME...!

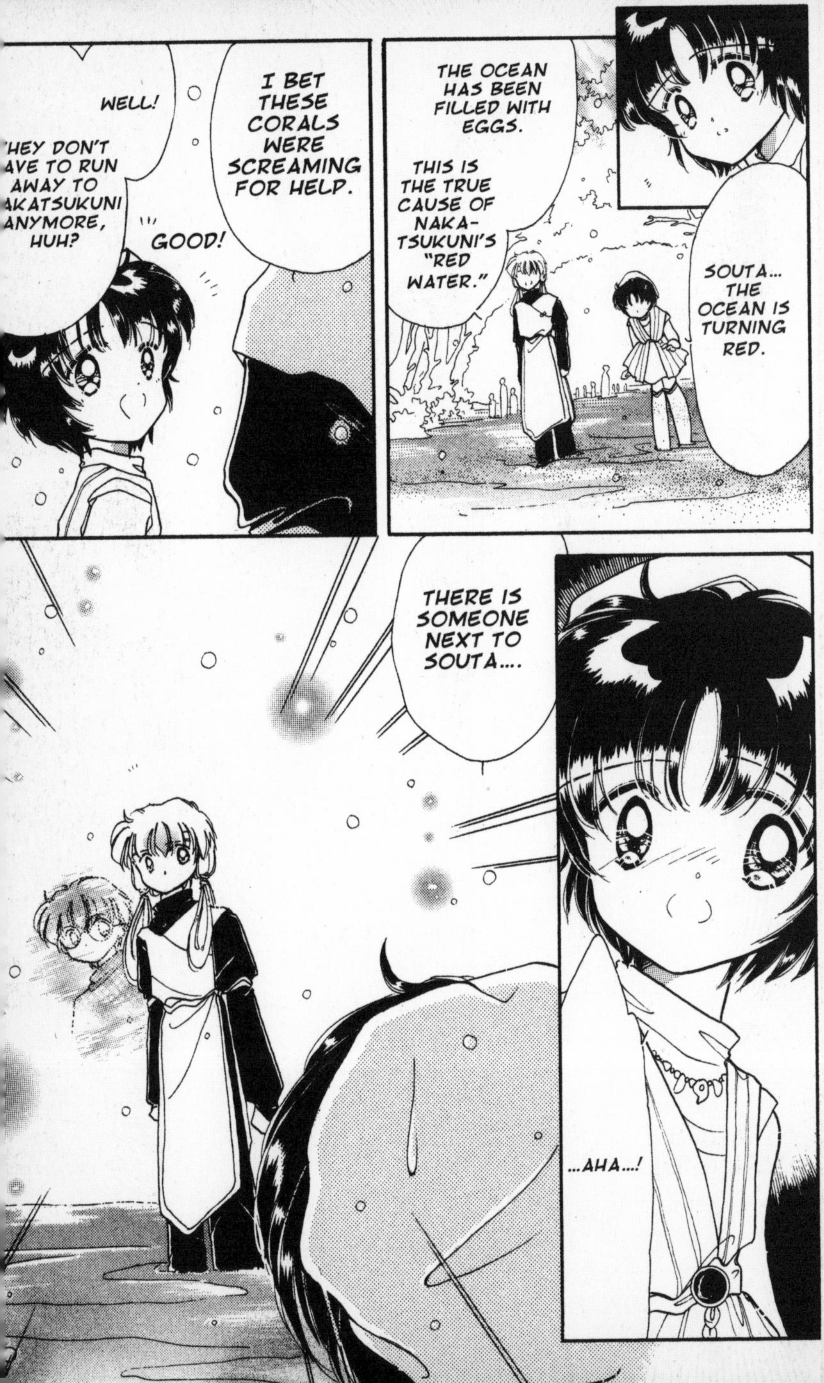
SOUTA... THE OCEAN IS TURNING RED.
THE OCEAN HAS BEEN FILLED WITH EGGS.
THIS IS THE TRUE CAUSE OF NAKA-TSUKUNI'S "RED WATER."
I BET THESE CORALS WERE SCREAMING FOR HELP.
WELL!
'HEY DON'T 'AVE TO RUN AWAY TO 'AKATSUKUNI ANYMORE, HUH?
GOOD!
...AHA...!
THERE IS SOMEONE NEXT TO SOUTA....

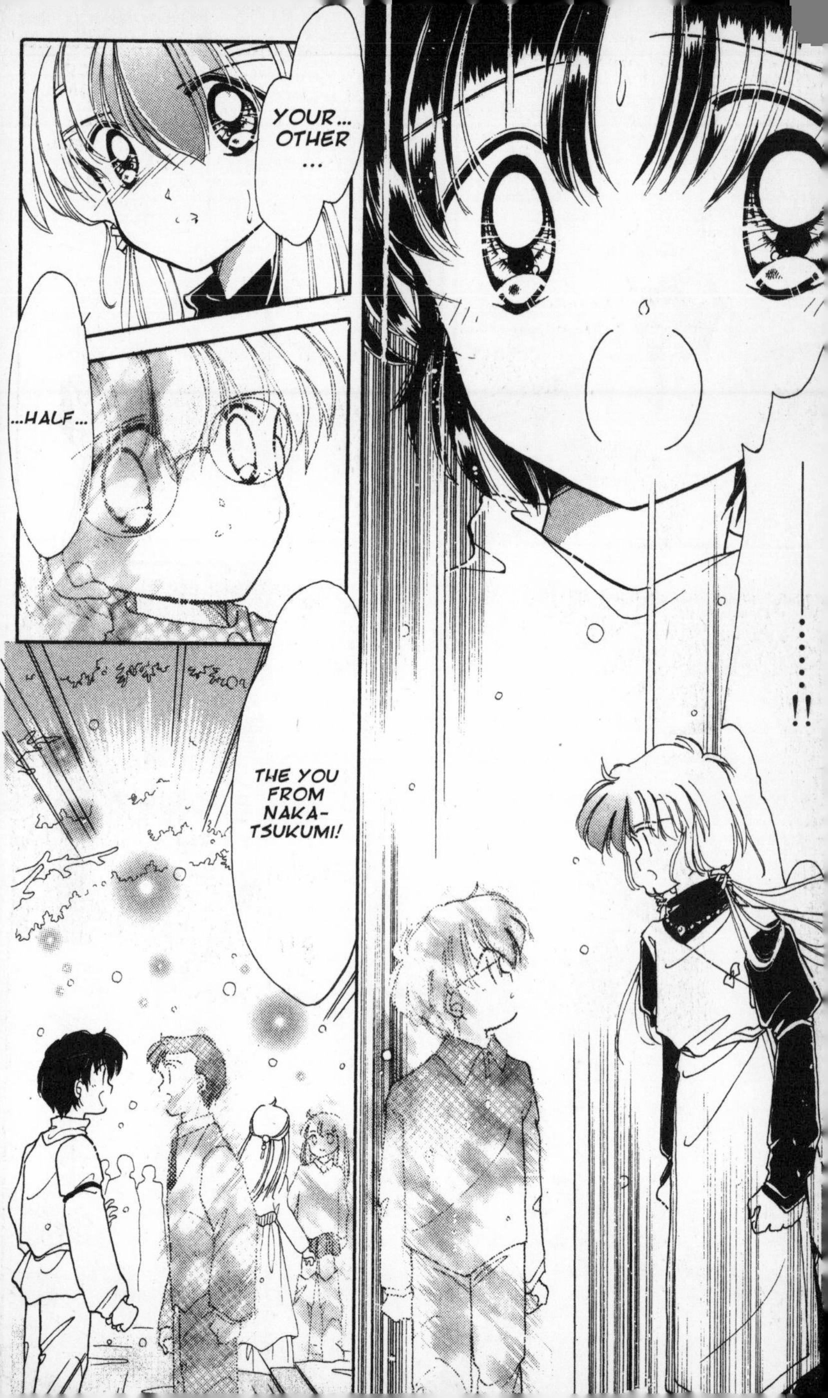
......!!
YOUR... OTHER ...
...HALF...
THE YOU FROM NAKA-TSUKUMI!

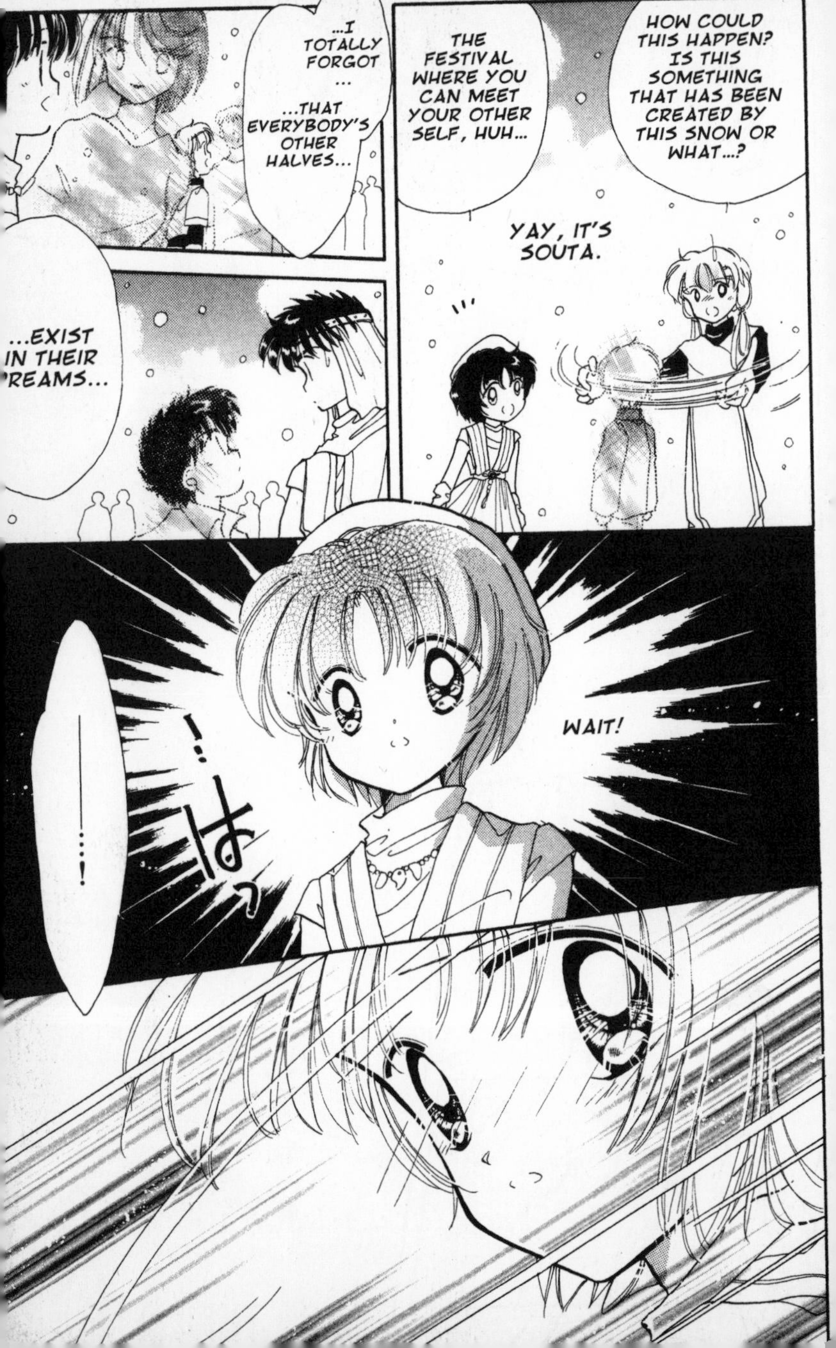

HOW COULD THIS HAPPEN? IS THIS SOMETHING THAT HAS BEEN CREATED BY THIS SNOW OR WHAT...?
THE FESTIVAL WHERE YOU CAN MEET YOUR OTHER SELF, HUH...
YAY, IT'S SOUTA.
...I TOTALLY FORGOT ...
...THAT EVERYBODY'S OTHER HALVES...
...EXIST IN THEIR REAMS...
WAIT!
!! はっ
————...!

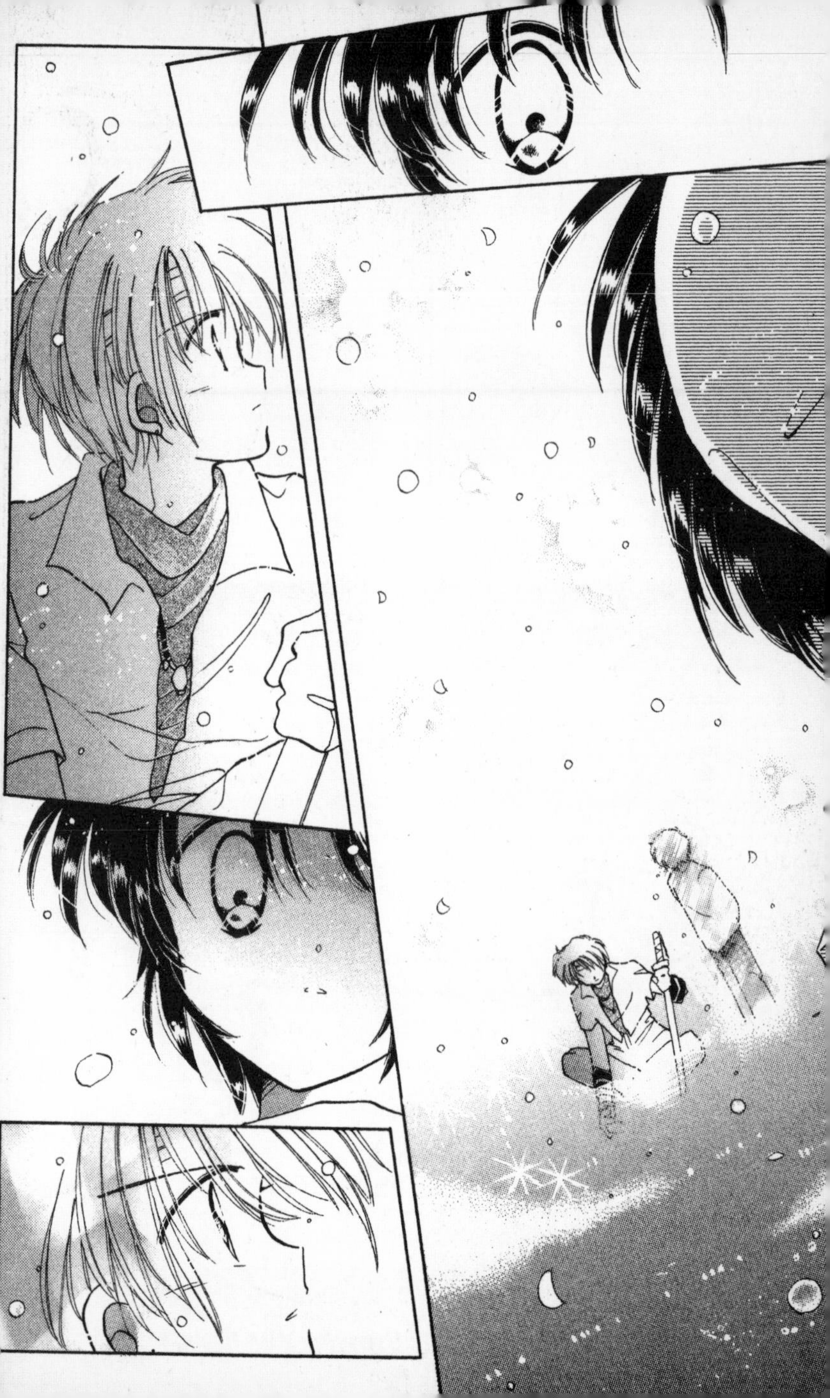

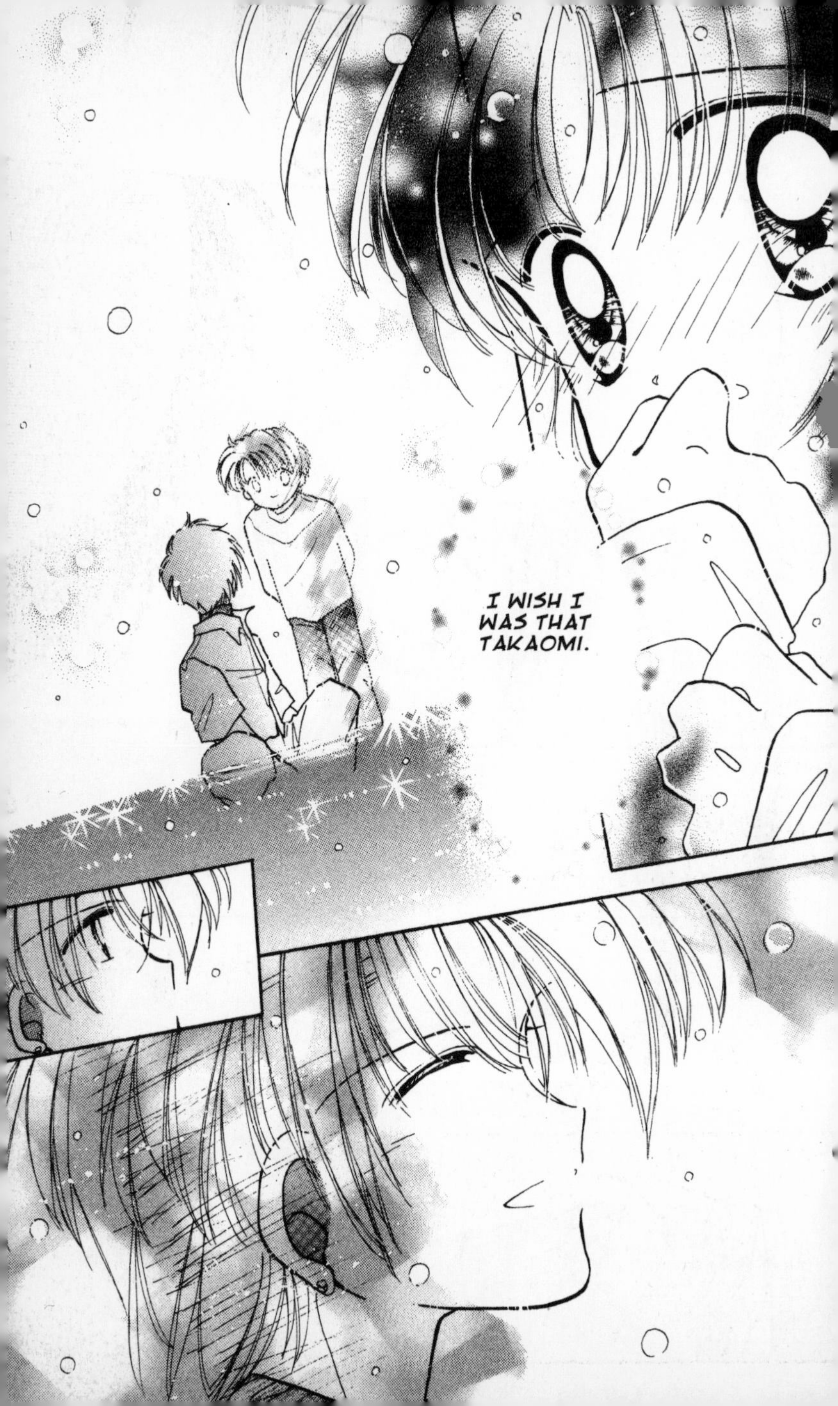
I WISH I WAS THAT TAKAOMI.

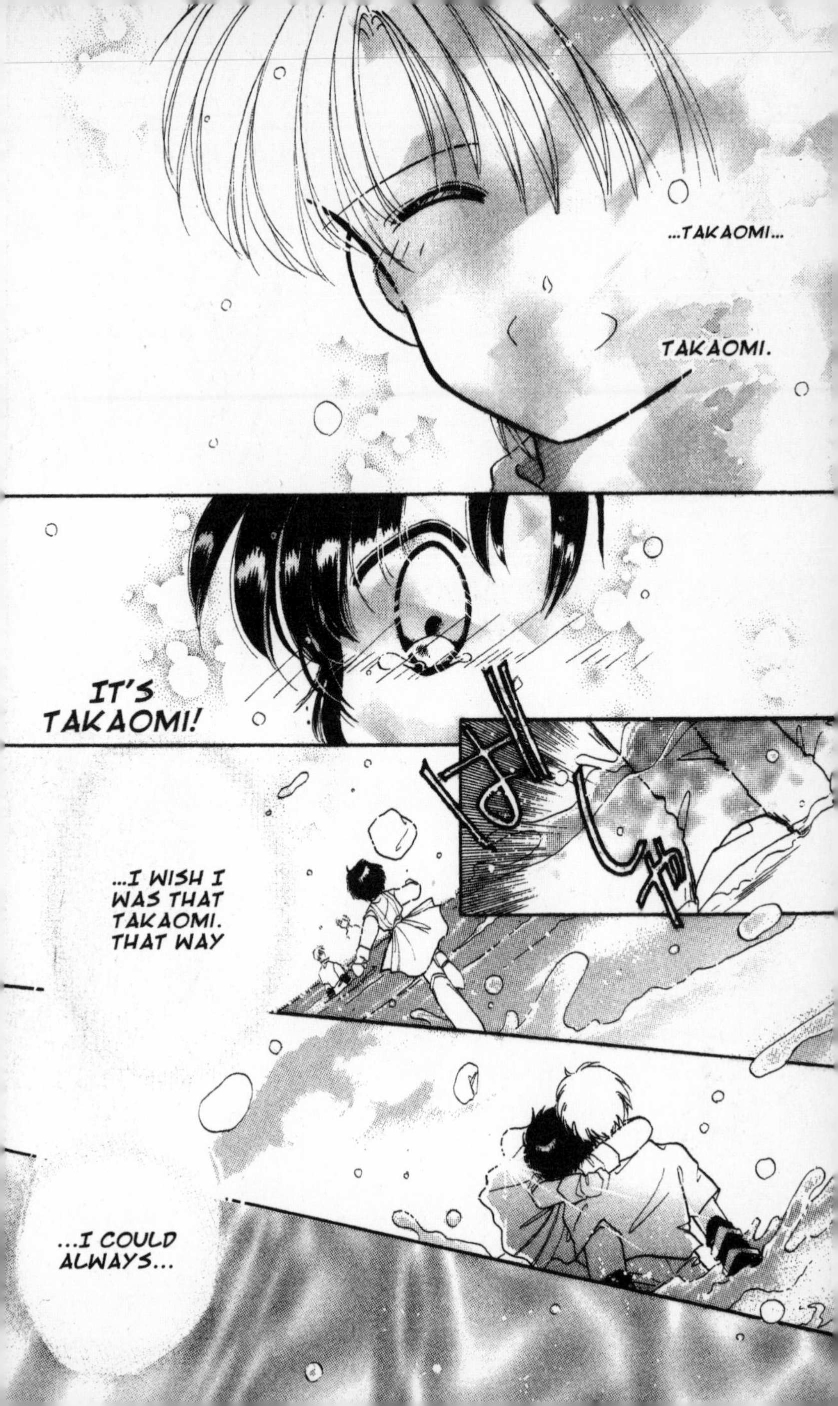
...TAKAOMI...
TAKAOMI.
IT'S TAKAOMI!
...I WISH I WAS THAT TAKAOMI. THAT WAY
...I COULD ALWAYS...

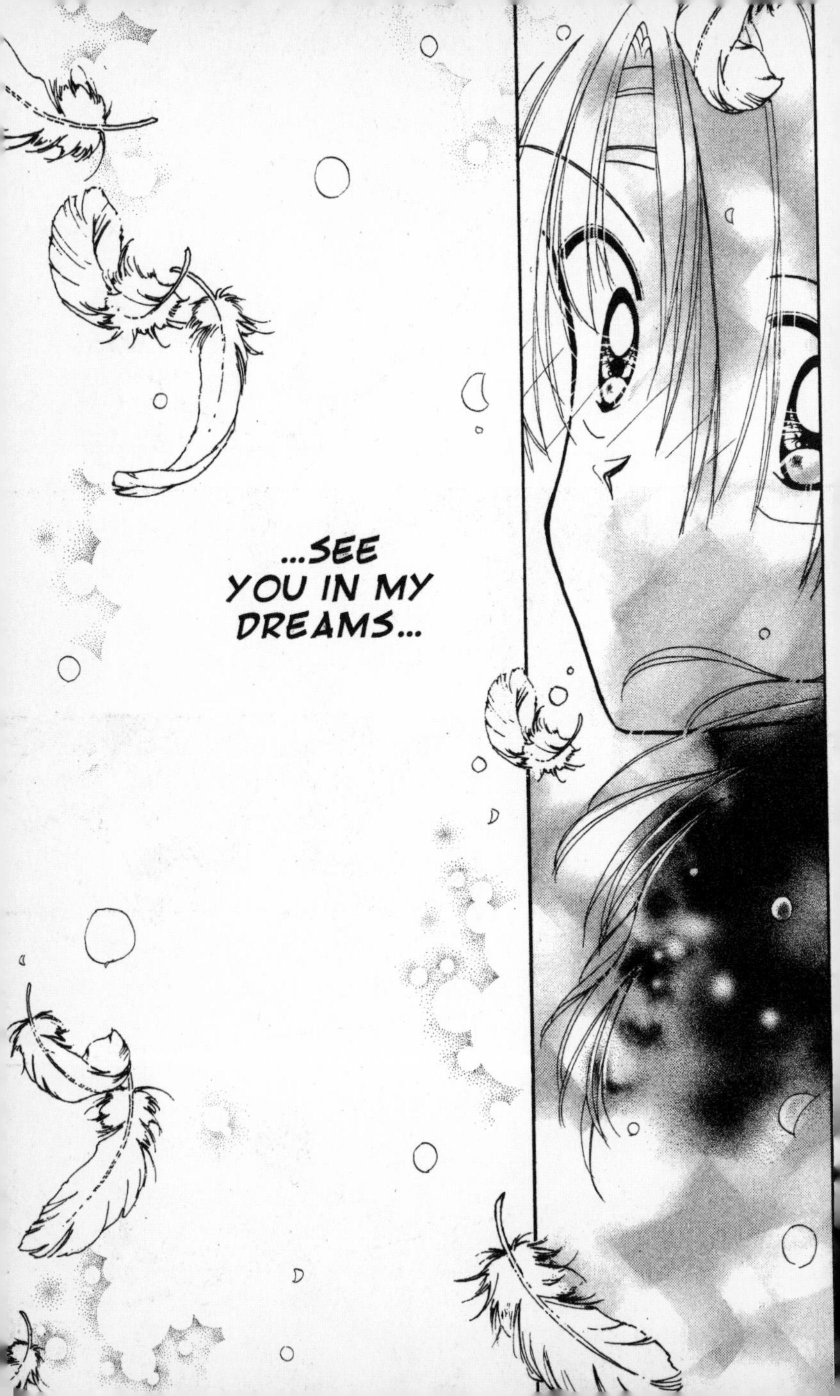
...SEE YOU IN MY DREAMS...

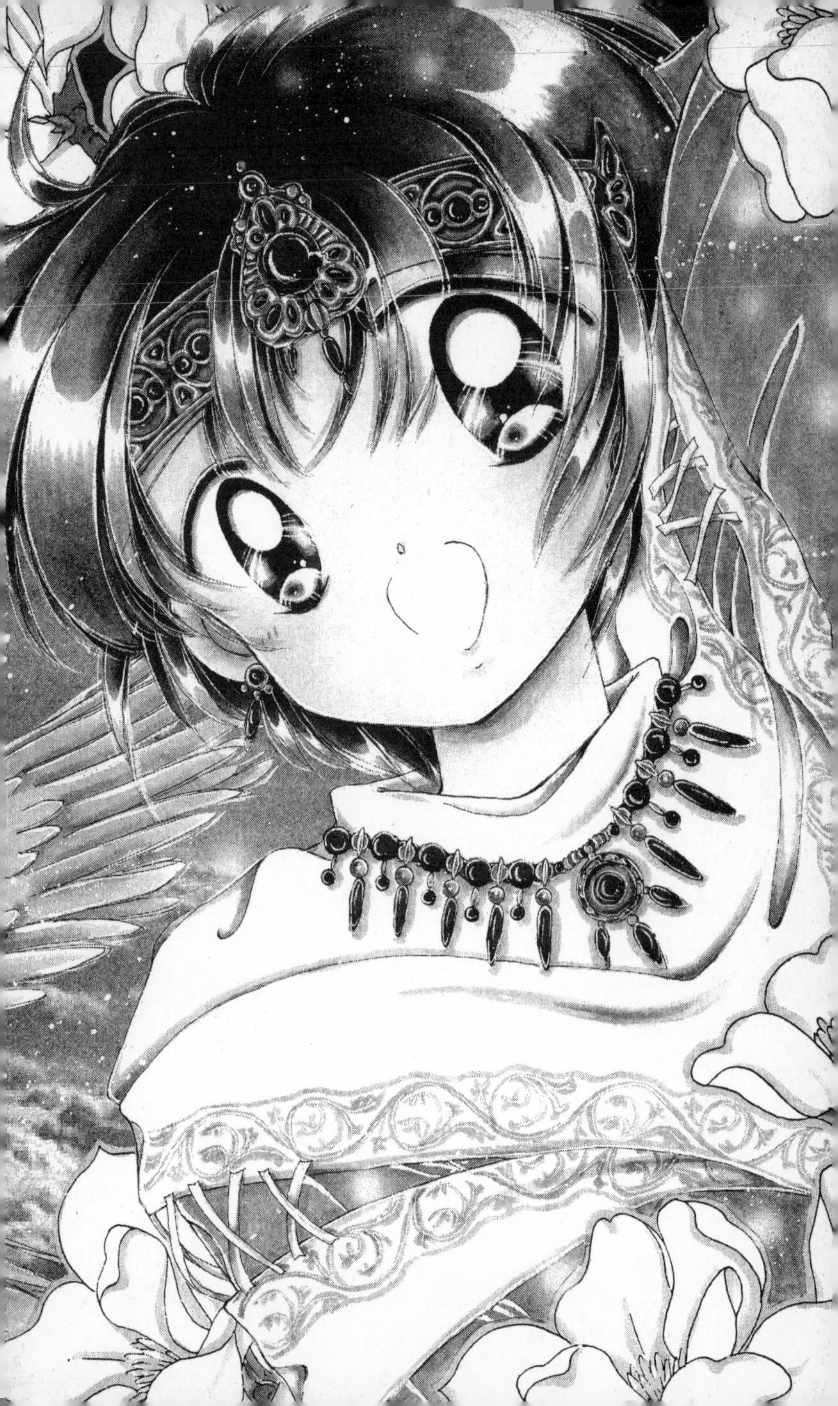

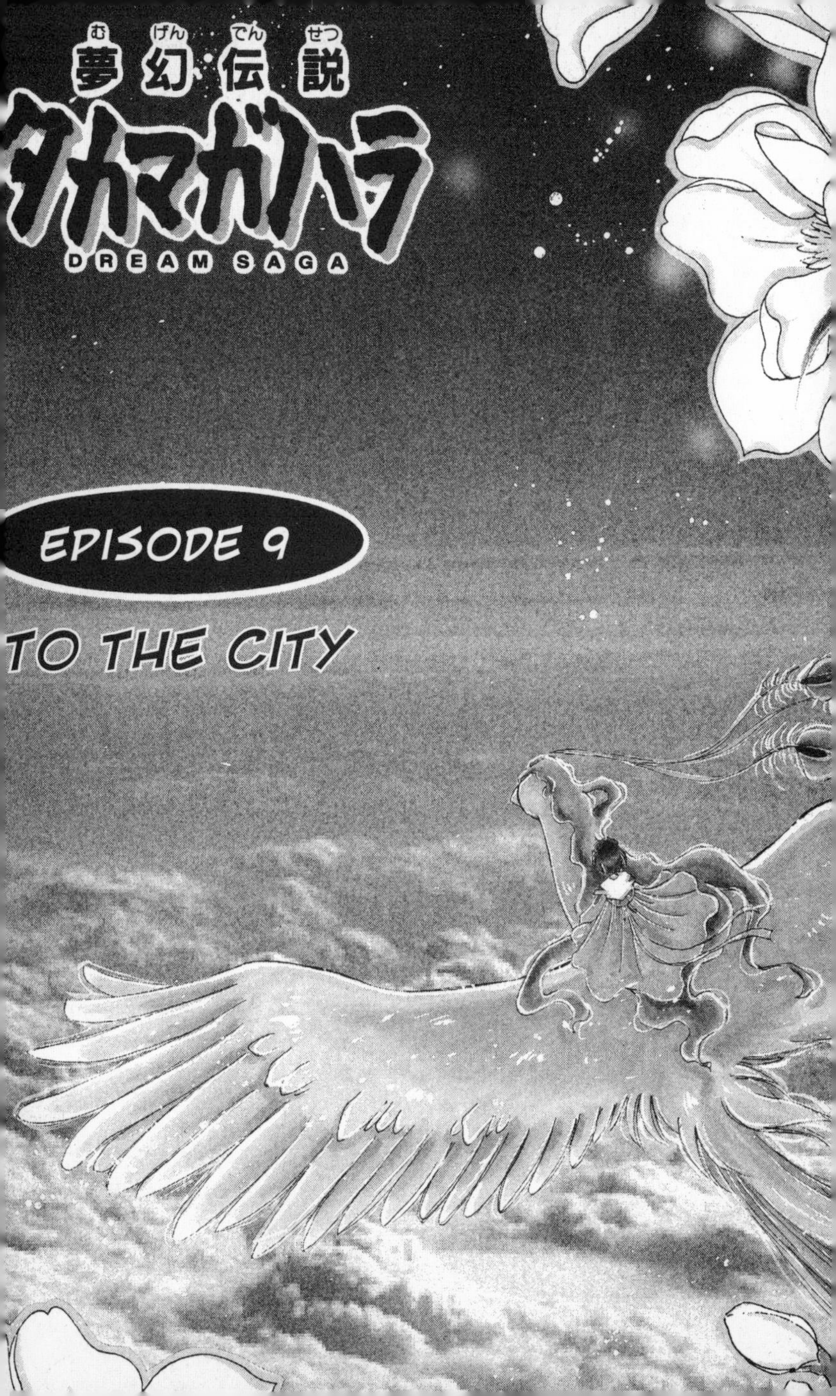
夢(む)幻(げん)伝(でん)説(せつ)
タカマガハラ
DREAM SAGA
EPISODE 9
TO THE CITY

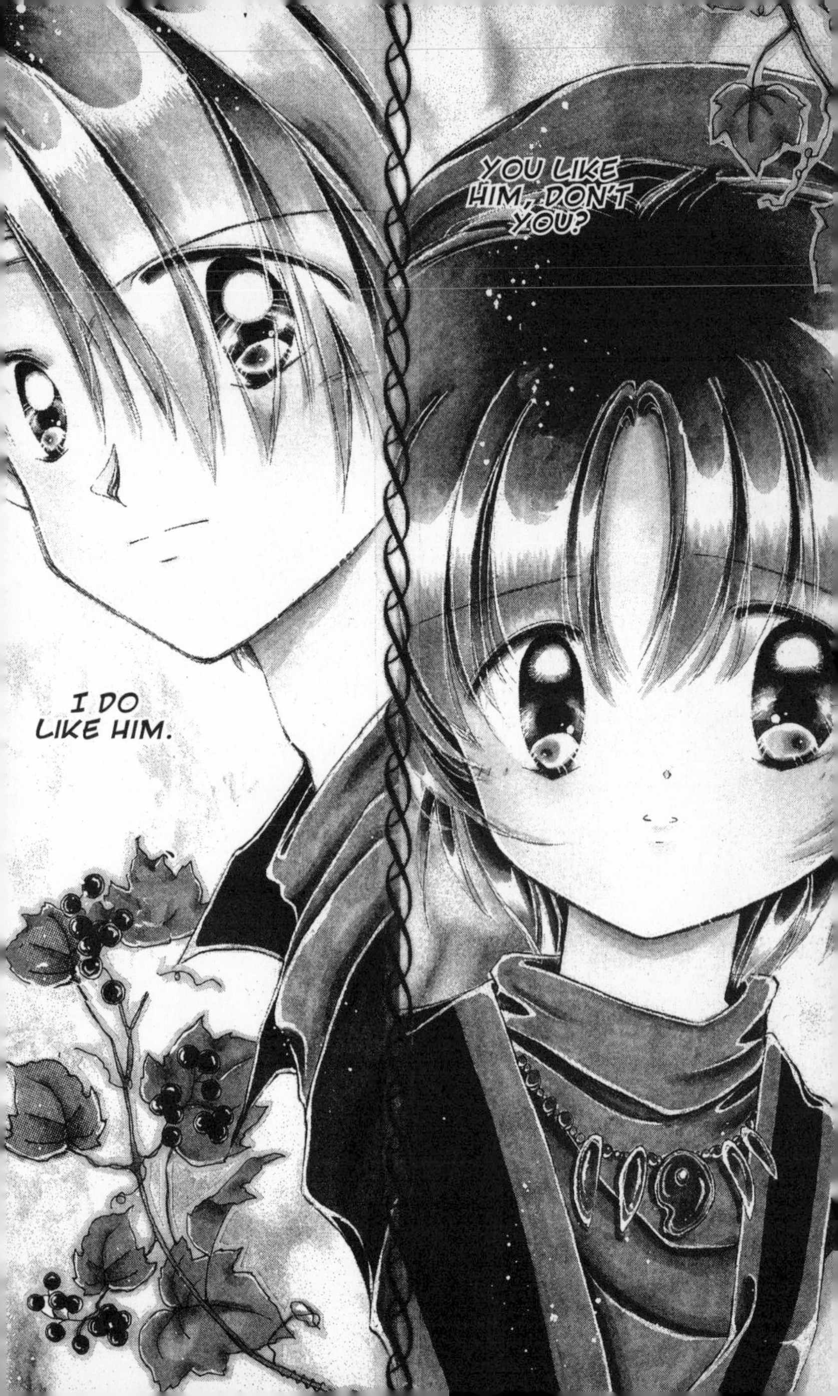
YOU LIKE HIM, DON'T YOU?
I DO LIKE HIM.

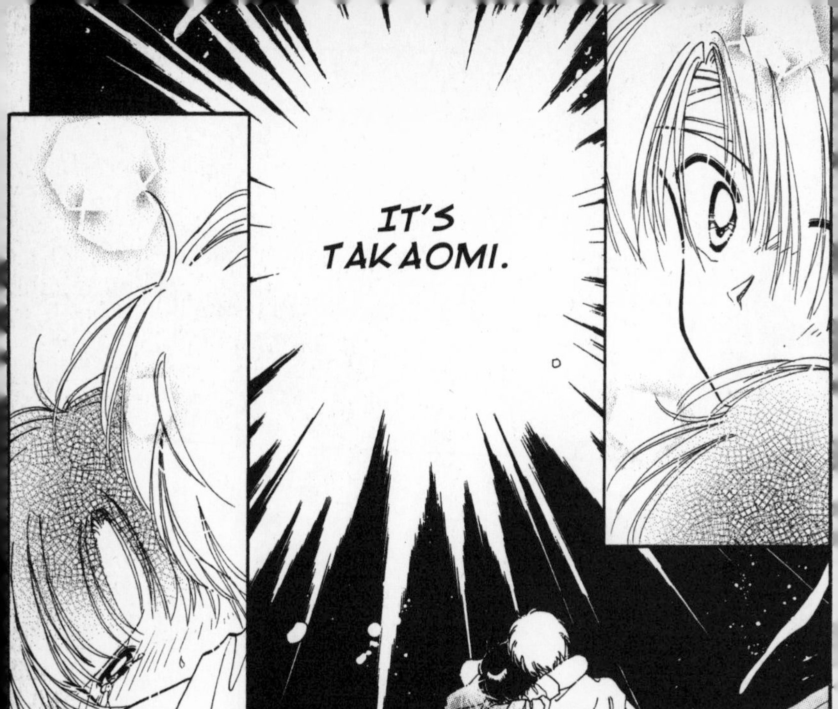
IT'S TAKAOMI.

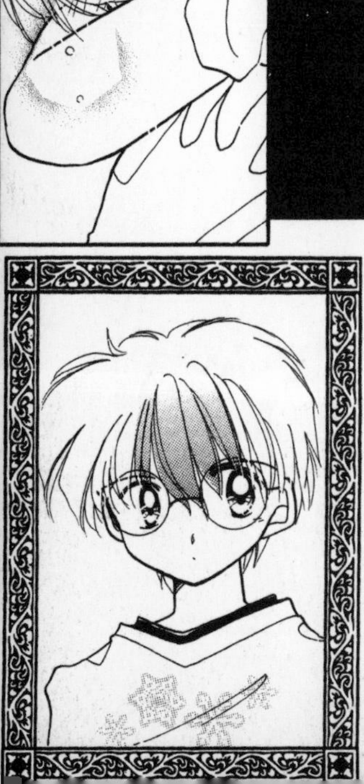

Q: What is the subject you liked most when you were a student?

A: I was into literature so I liked Japanese and English linguistic classes. I wasn't really good with math, science or physics. I wasn't good with physical education either. But regardless of the grade, I always liked music and art classes. I liked my history class, too, just because the professor was funny. Did I ever have a crush on a teacher? Unfortunately, no.

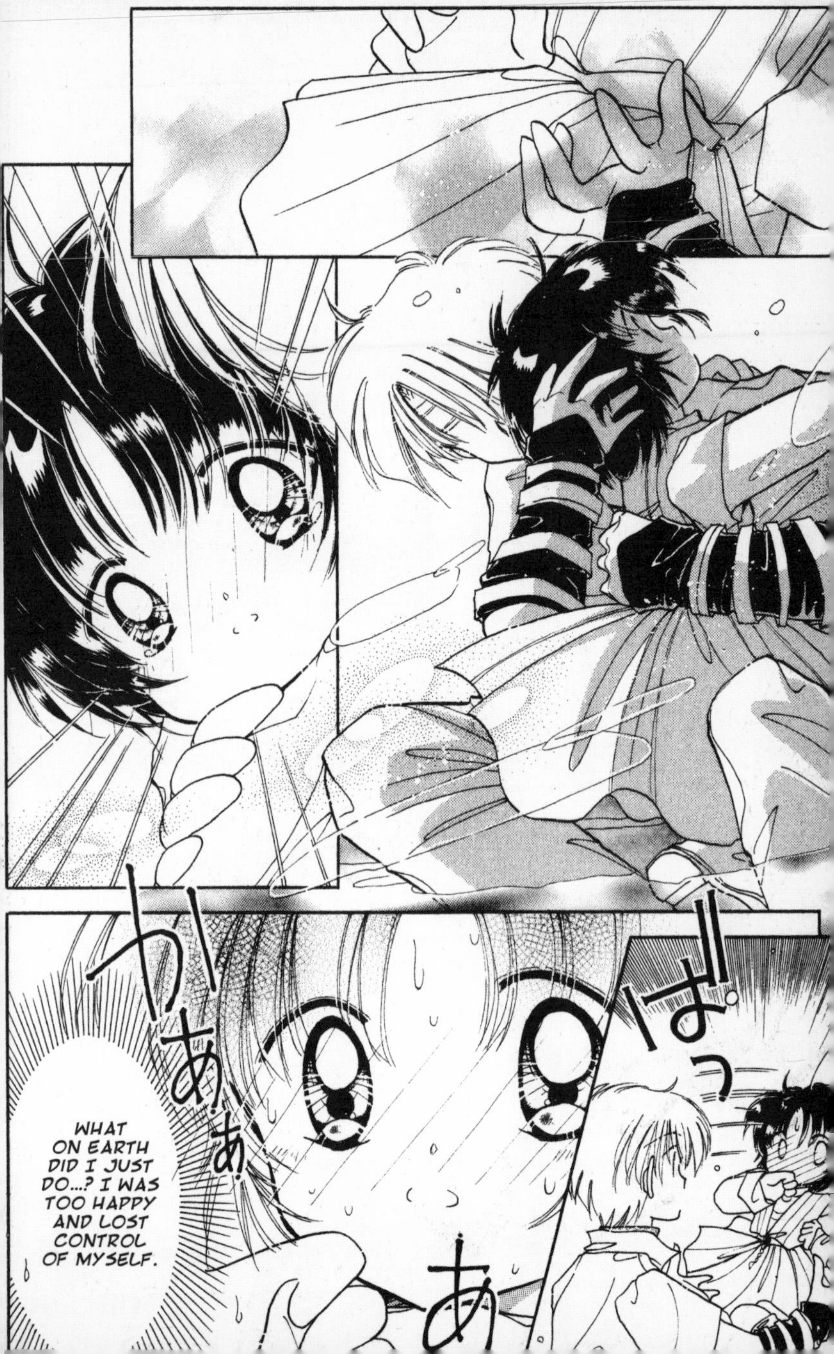

ぱっ
わーああ
WHAT ON EARTH DID I JUST DO...? I WAS TOO HAPPY AND LOST CONTROL OF MYSELF.
あ

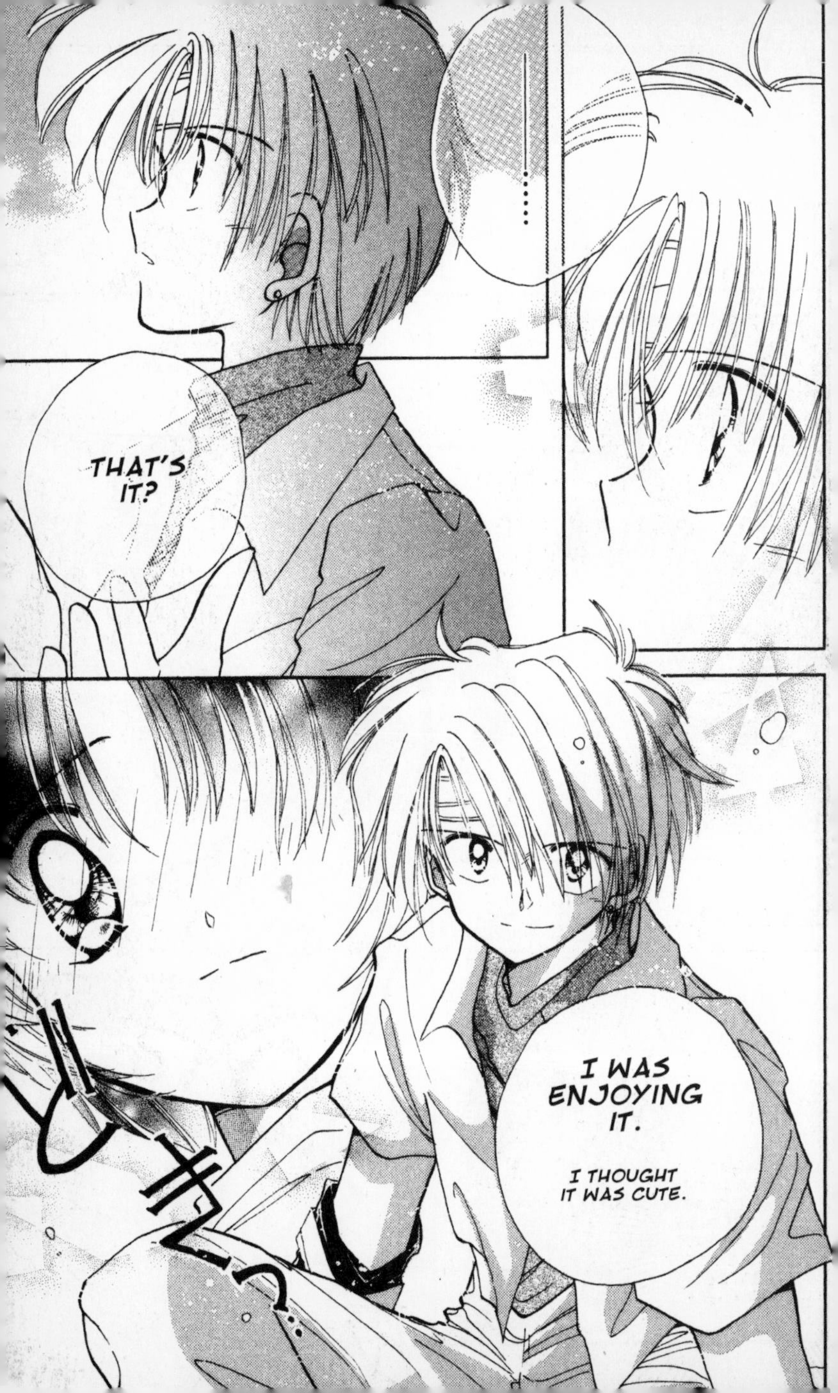
……
THAT'S IT?
I WAS ENJOYING IT.
I THOUGHT IT WAS CUTE.

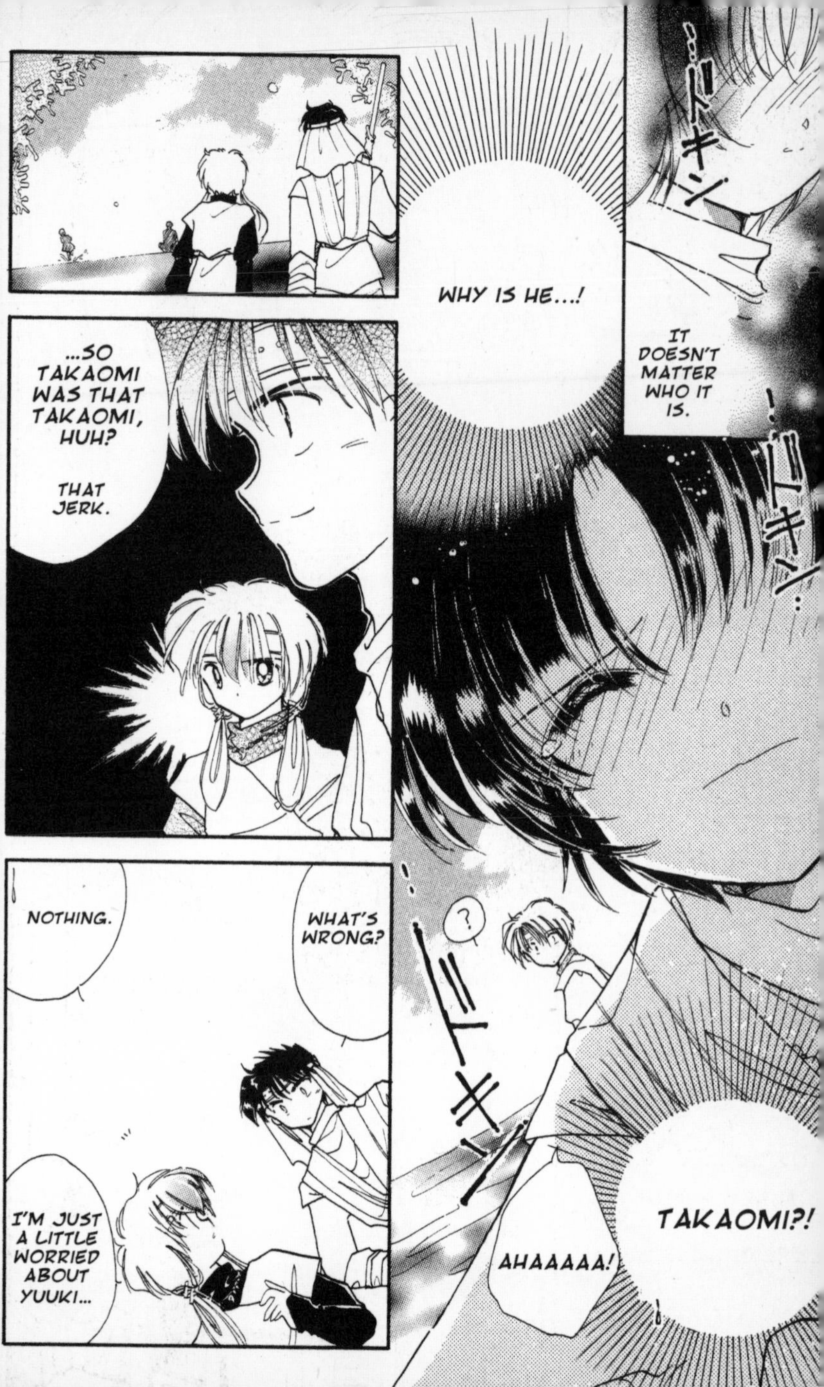

IT DOESN'T MATTER WHO IT IS.
WHY IS HE...!
TAKAOMI?!
AHAAAAA!
...SO TAKAOMI WAS THAT TAKAOMI, HUH?
THAT JERK.
WHAT'S WRONG?
NOTHING.
I'M JUST A LITTLE WORRIED ABOUT YUUKI...

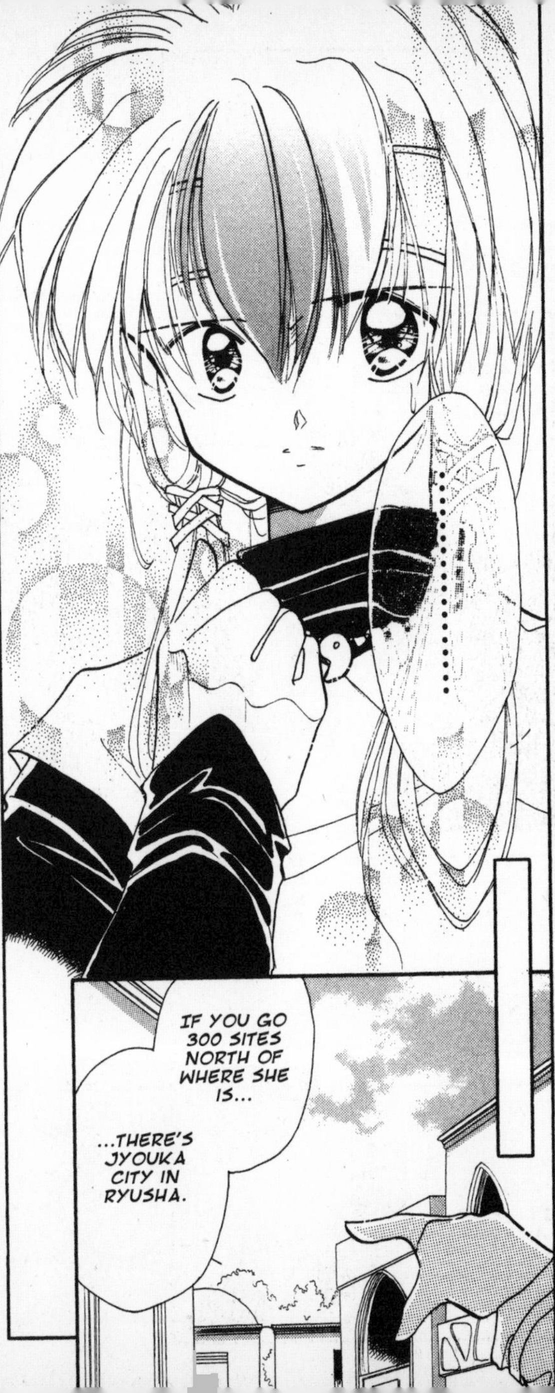
IF YOU GO 300 SITES NORTH OF WHERE SHE IS...
...THERE'S JYOUKA CITY IN RYUSHA.

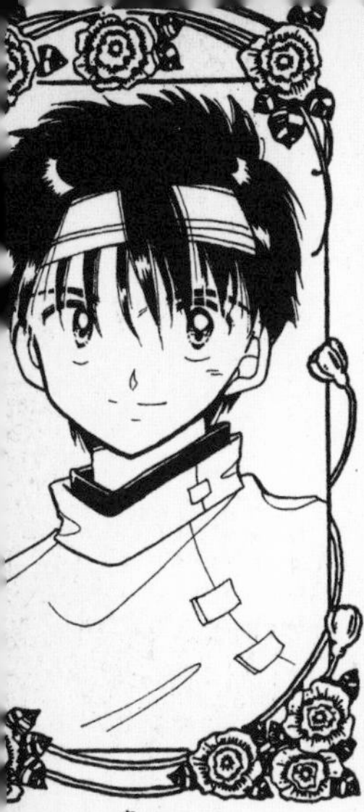

Taizou

Born on May, 6th

Blood type: O

He goes after money in Takamagahara. His personality doesn't differ with Taizou's in Nakatsukuni. He is 17 years old. His hobby is making money. Does he have a crush on Miss. Nakime? Well, please look for clues in the story. There is a model for his character. I named him after his model. (The hint is that he is a comedian.)

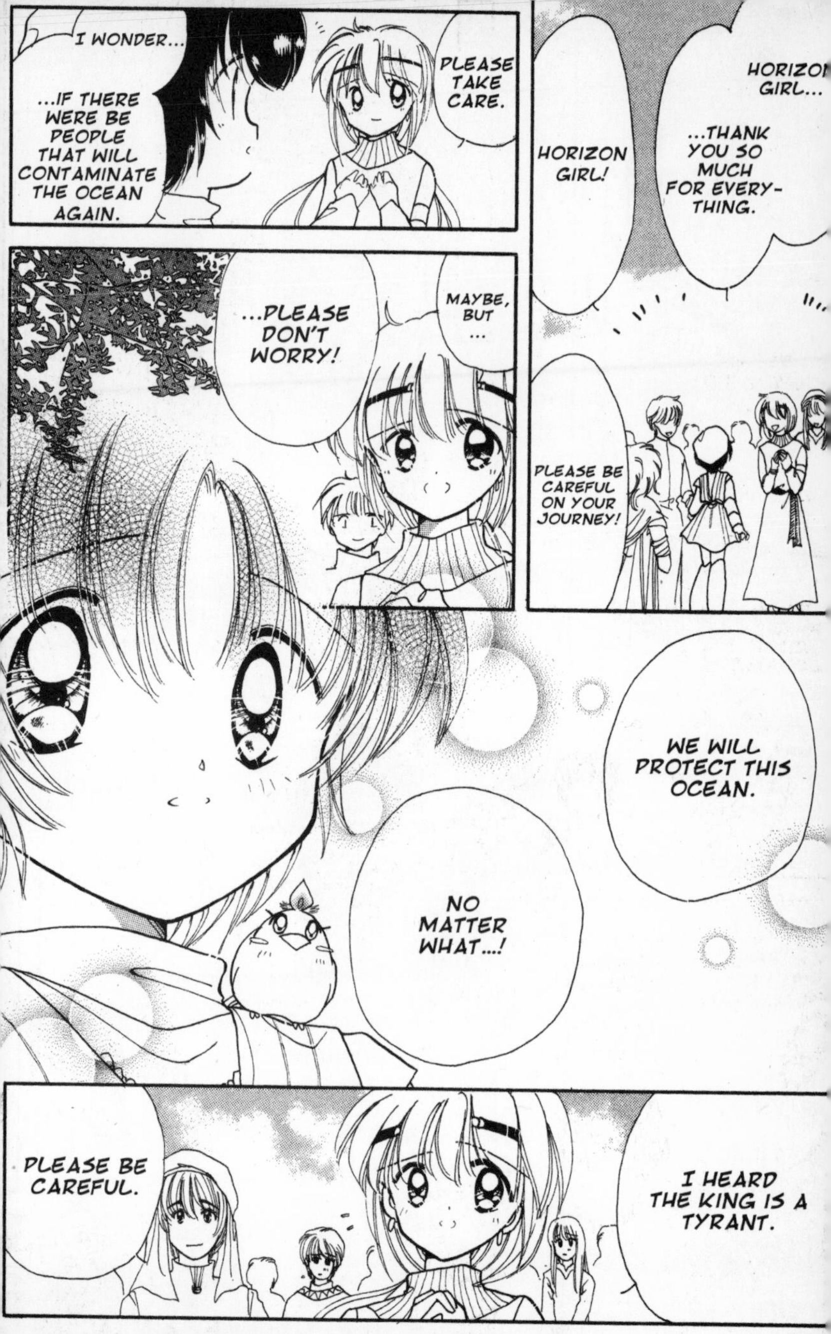
HORIZON GIRL...
...THANK YOU SO MUCH FOR EVERY-THING.
HORIZON GIRL!
PLEASE BE CAREFUL ON YOUR JOURNEY!
PLEASE TAKE CARE.
I WONDER...
...IF THERE WERE BE PEOPLE THAT WILL CONTAMINATE THE OCEAN AGAIN.
MAYBE, BUT ...
...PLEASE DON'T WORRY!
WE WILL PROTECT THIS OCEAN.
NO MATTER WHAT...!
I HEARD THE KING IS A TYRANT.
PLEASE BE CAREFUL.

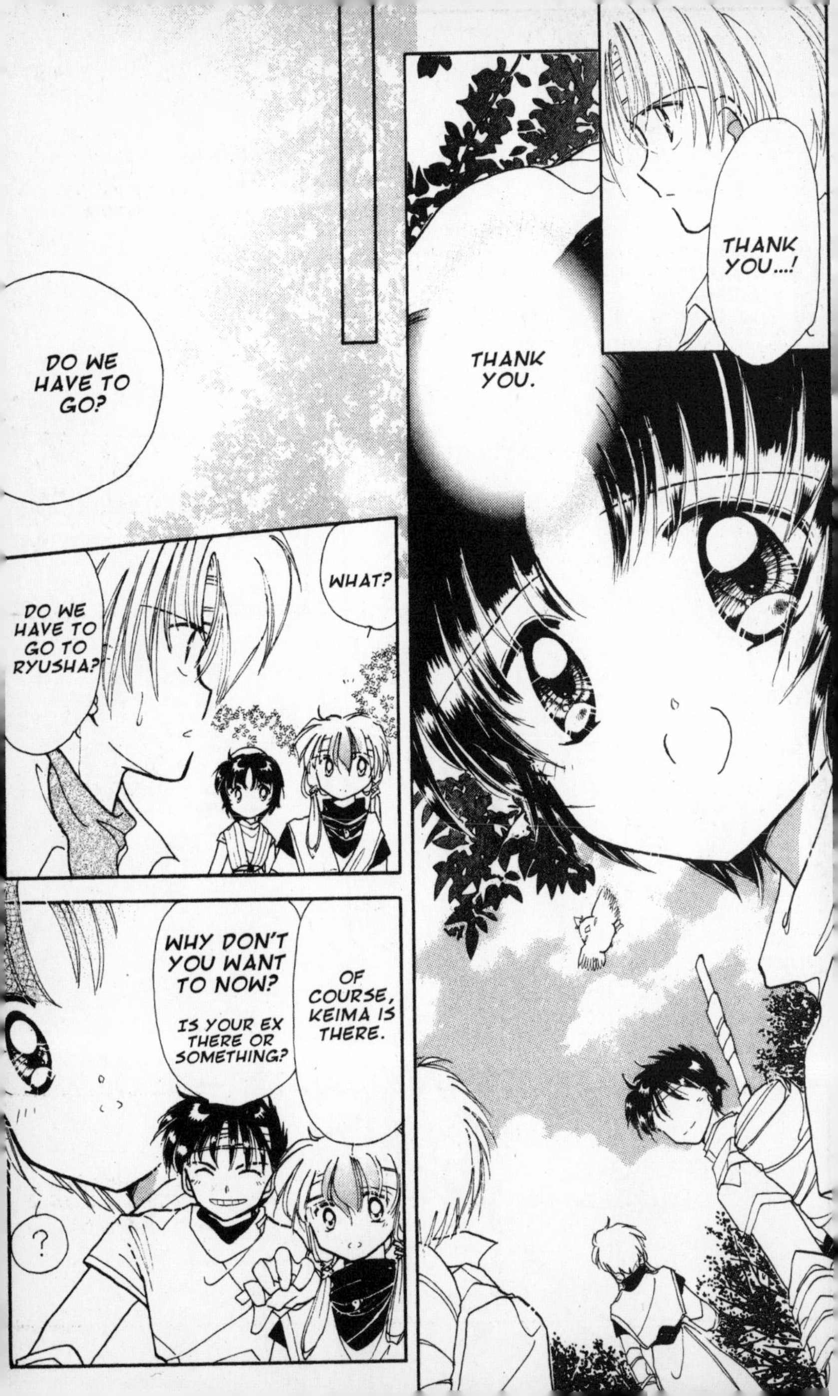
THANK YOU...!
THANK YOU.
DO WE HAVE TO GO?
WHAT?
DO WE HAVE TO GO TO RYUSHA?
OF COURSE, KEIMA IS THERE.
WHY DON'T YOU WANT TO NOW?
IS YOUR EX THERE OR SOMETHING?
?

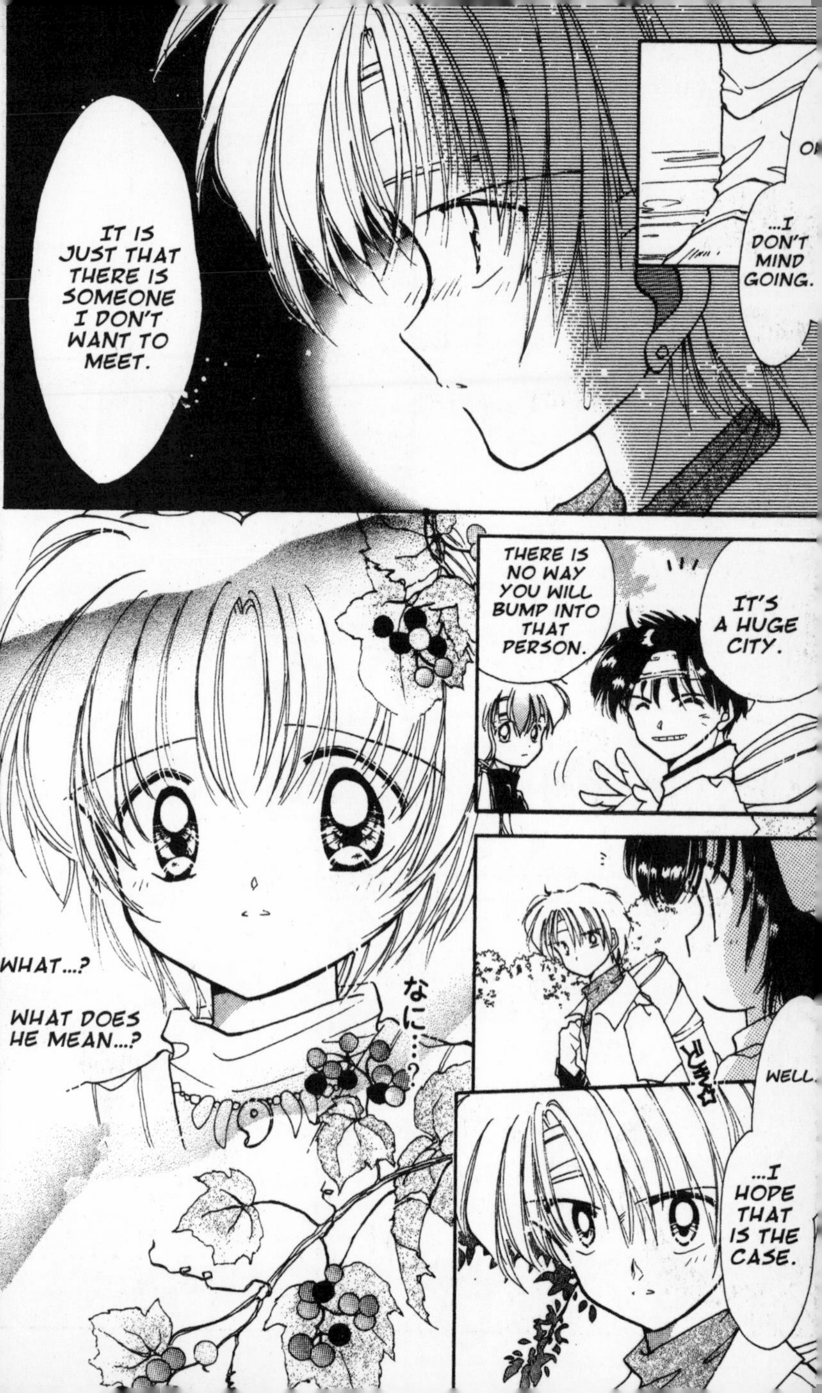

...I DON'T MIND GOING.
IT IS JUST THAT THERE IS SOMEONE I DON'T WANT TO MEET.
IT'S A HUGE CITY.
THERE IS NO WAY YOU WILL BUMP INTO THAT PERSON.
WELL.
...I HOPE THAT IS THE CASE.
なに…？
WHAT...?
WHAT DOES HE MEAN...?

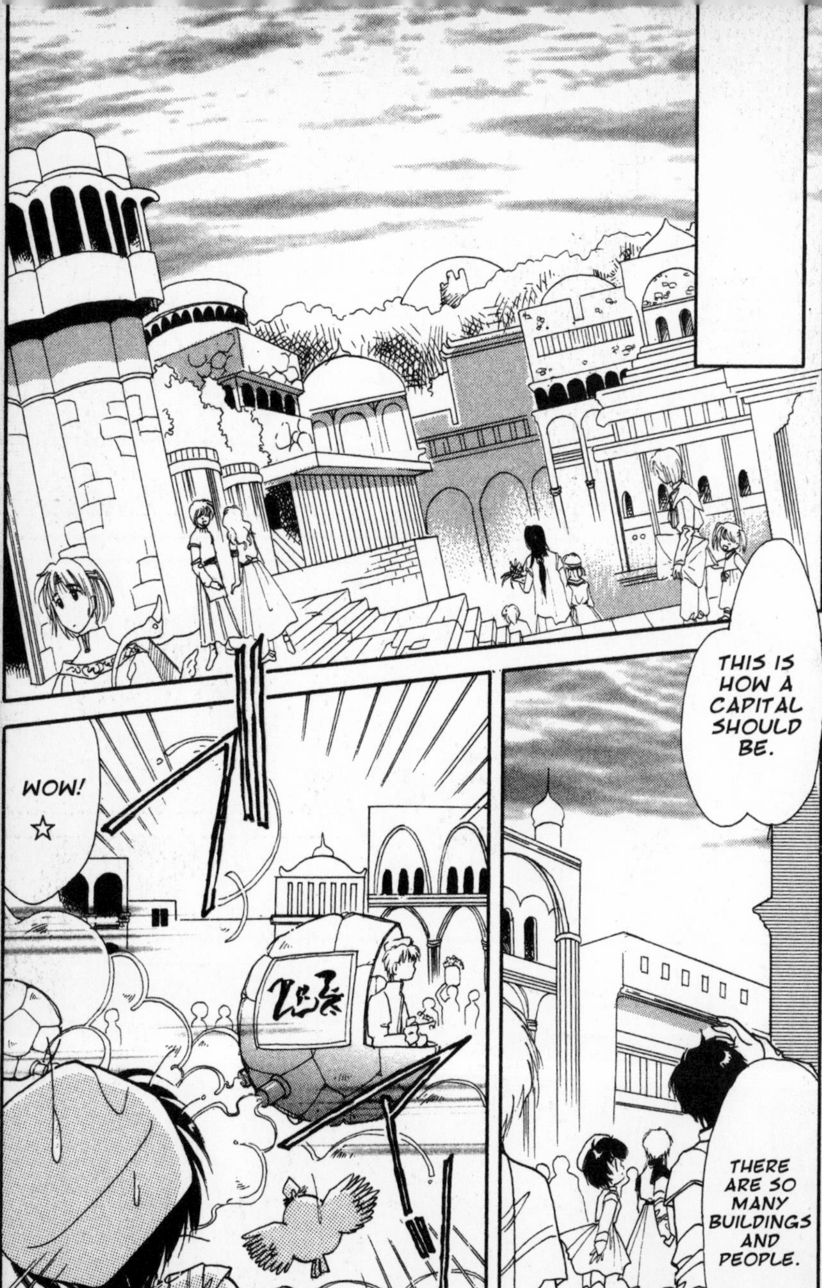
THIS IS HOW A CAPITAL SHOULD BE.
THERE ARE SO MANY BUILDINGS AND PEOPLE.
WOW! ☆

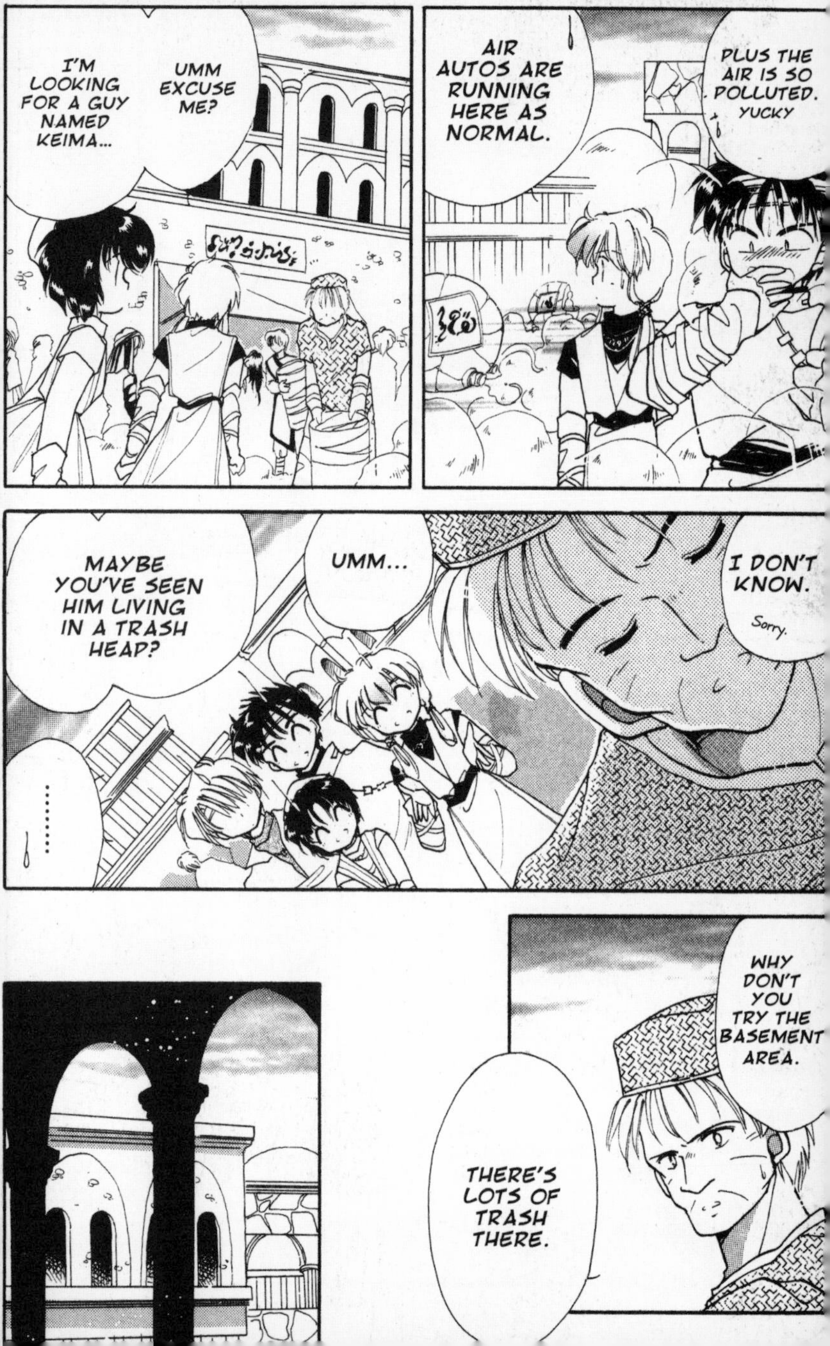
PLUS THE AIR IS SO POLLUTED.
YUCKY
AIR AUTOS ARE RUNNING HERE AS NORMAL.
UMM EXCUSE ME?
I'M LOOKING FOR A GUY NAMED KEIMA...
I DON'T KNOW.
Sorry.
UMM...
MAYBE YOU'VE SEEN HIM LIVING IN A TRASH HEAP?
......
WHY DON'T YOU TRY THE BASEMENT AREA.
THERE'S LOTS OF TRASH THERE.

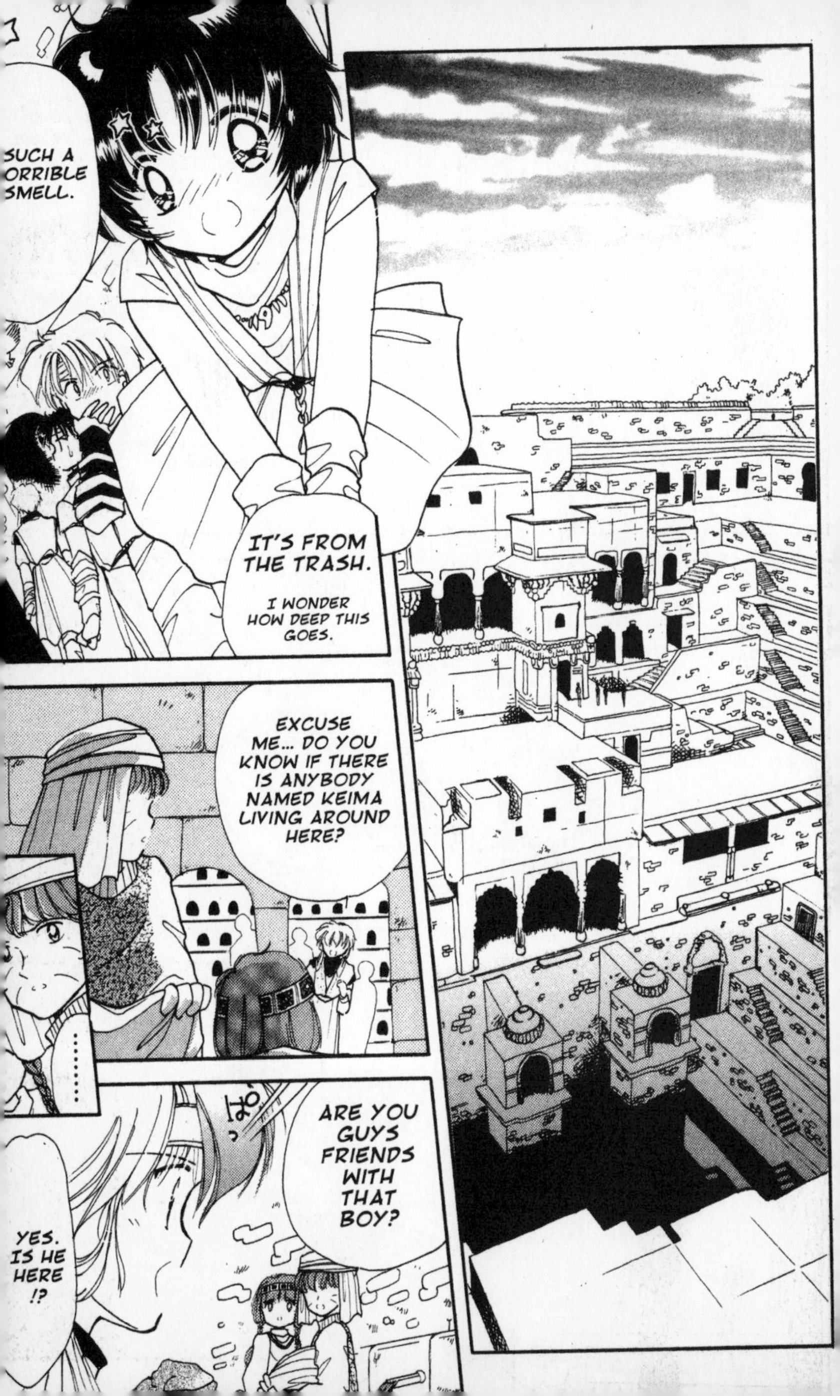
SUCH A ORRIBLE SMELL.
IT'S FROM THE TRASH.
I WONDER HOW DEEP THIS GOES.
EXCUSE ME... DO YOU KNOW IF THERE IS ANYBODY NAMED KEIMA LIVING AROUND HERE?
......
ARE YOU GUYS FRIENDS WITH THAT BOY?
YES. IS HE HERE !?

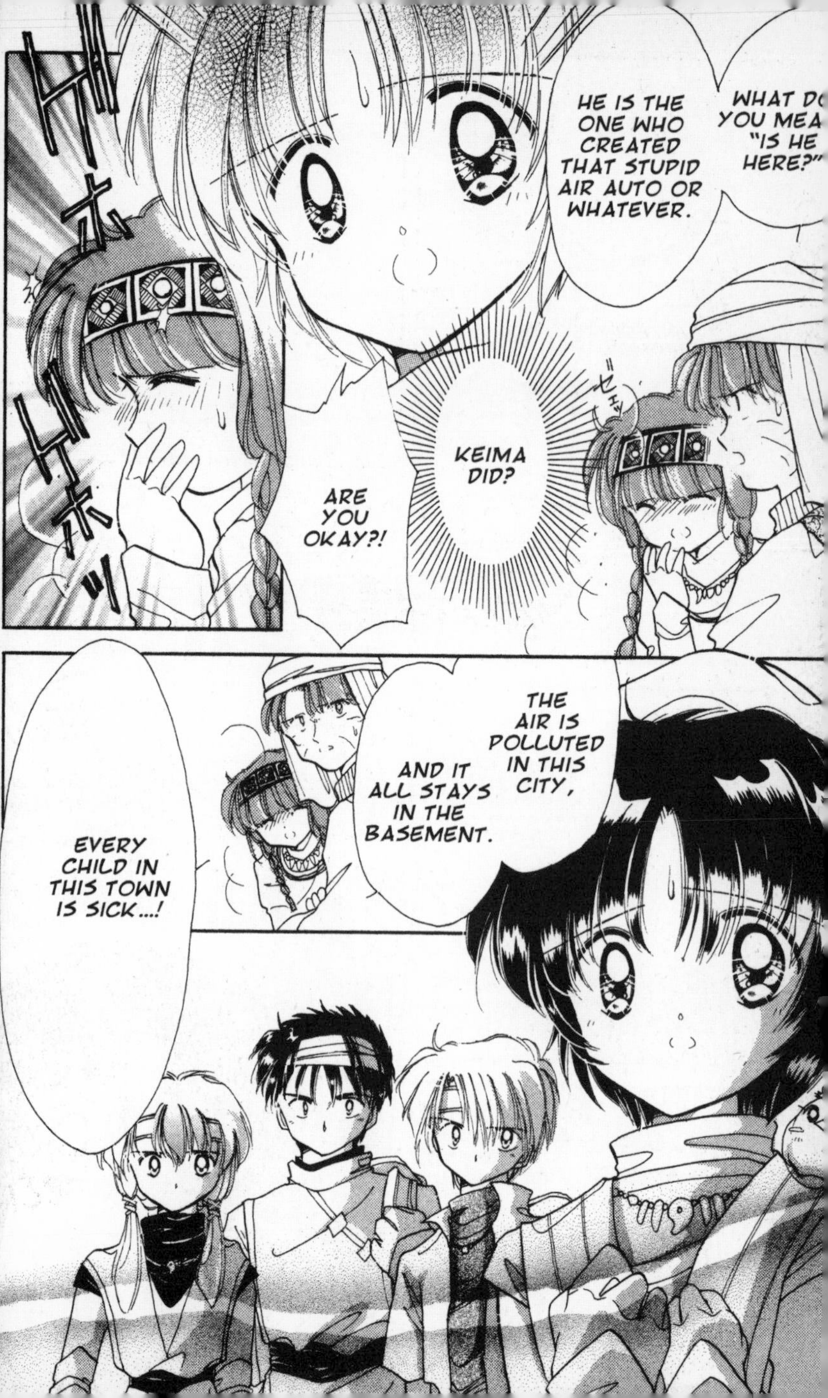
WHAT DO YOU MEA "IS HE HERE?"
HE IS THE ONE WHO CREATED THAT STUPID AIR AUTO OR WHATEVER.
KEIMA DID?
ARE YOU OKAY?!
THE AIR IS POLLUTED IN THIS CITY,
AND IT ALL STAYS IN THE BASEMENT.
EVERY CHILD IN THIS TOWN IS SICK...!

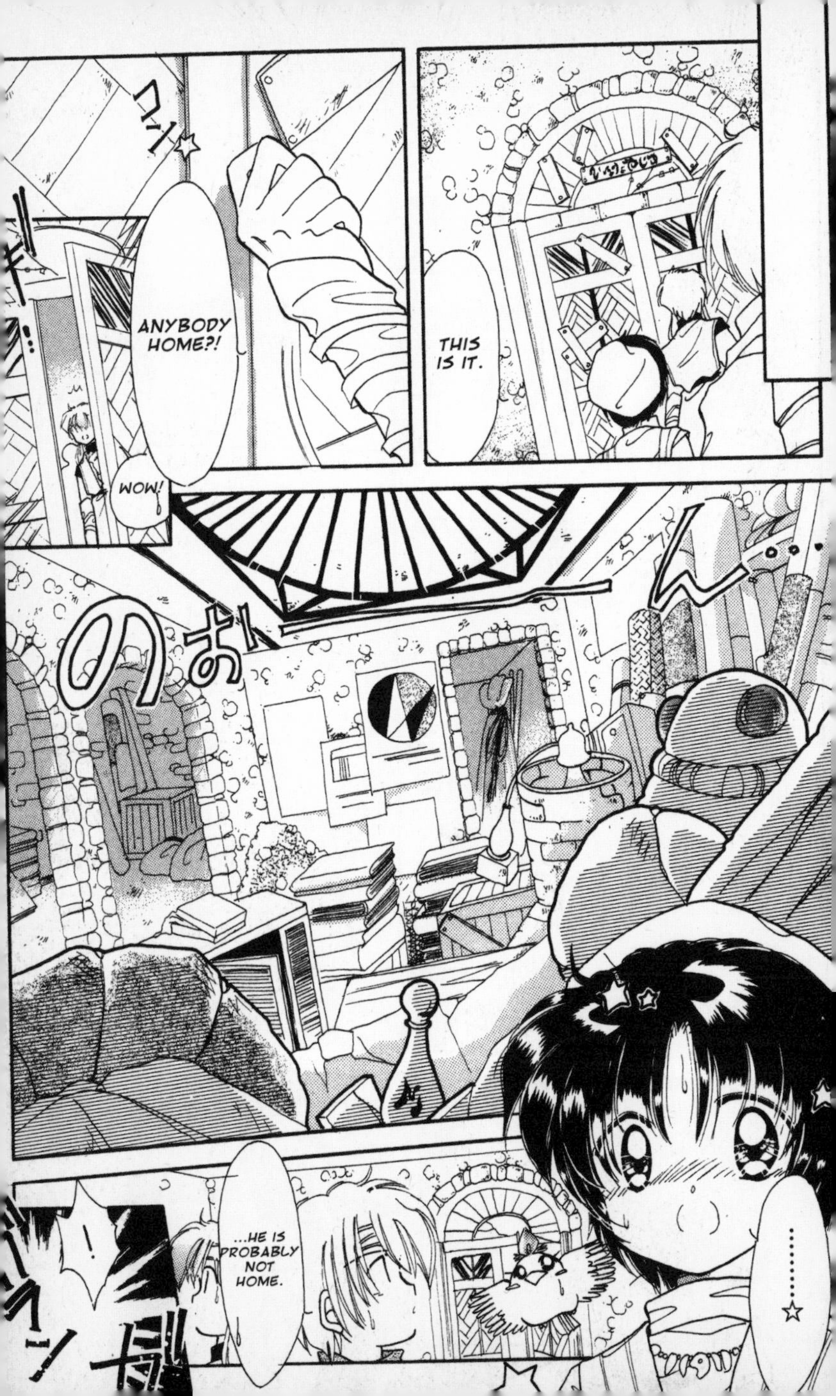
THIS IS IT.
ANYBODY HOME?!
WOW!
......☆
...HE IS PROBABLY NOT HOME.
!

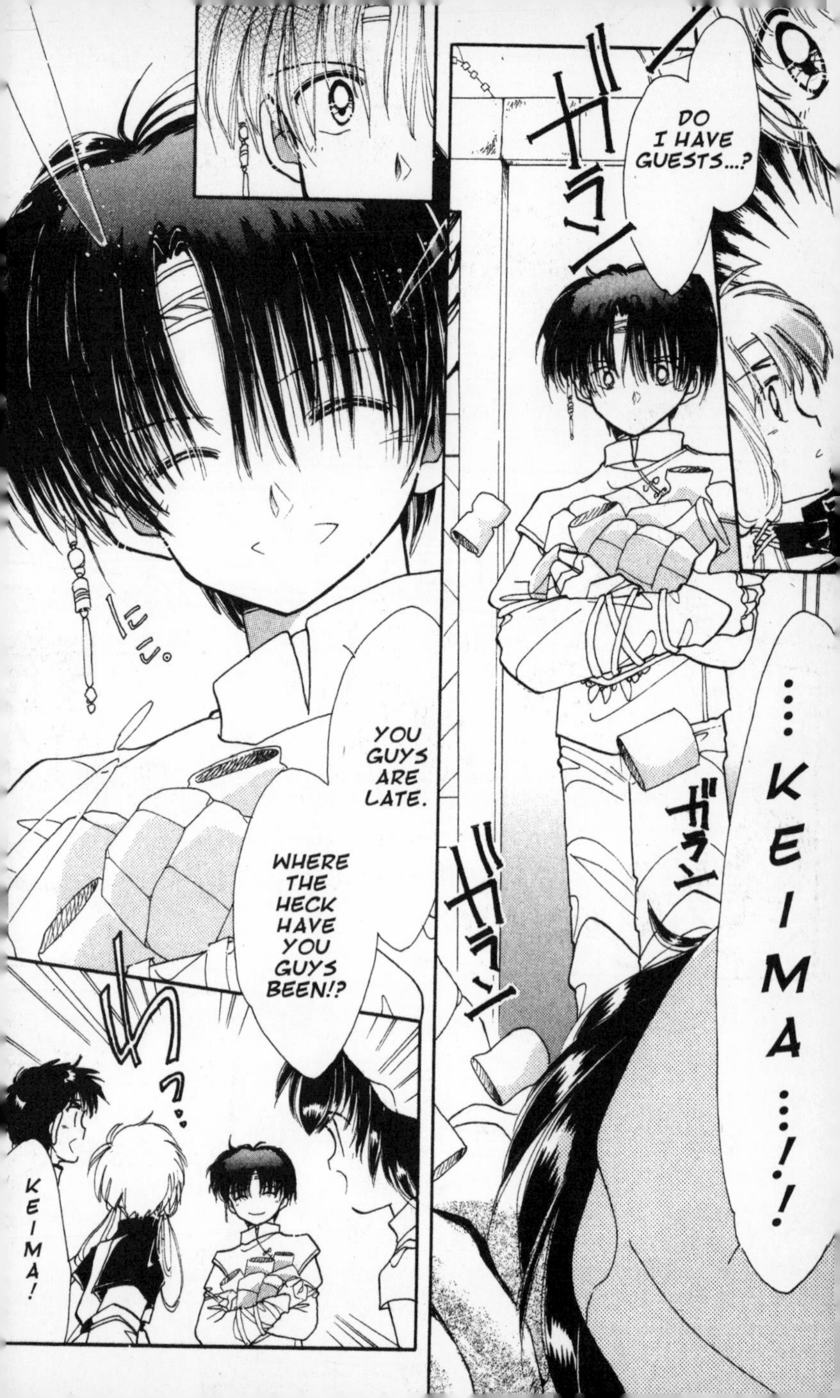

ガラン
DO I HAVE GUESTS...?
...KEIMA...!!
ガラン
ガラン
にこ。
YOU GUYS ARE LATE.
WHERE THE HECK HAVE YOU GUYS BEEN!?
わっ
KEIMA!

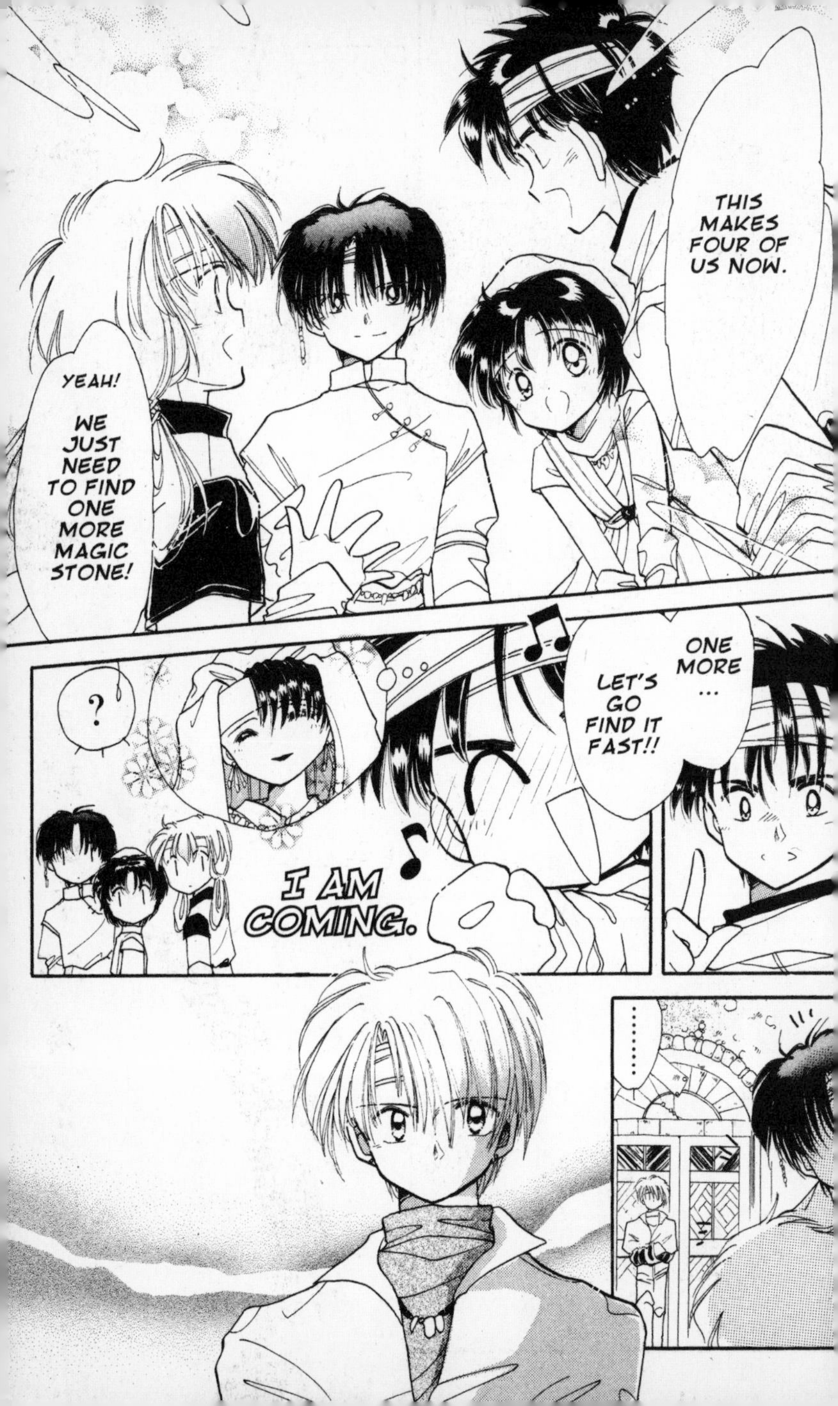
THIS MAKES FOUR OF US NOW.
YEAH!
WE JUST NEED TO FIND ONE MORE MAGIC STONE!
ONE MORE ...
LET'S GO FIND IT FAST!!
I AM COMING.
?
......

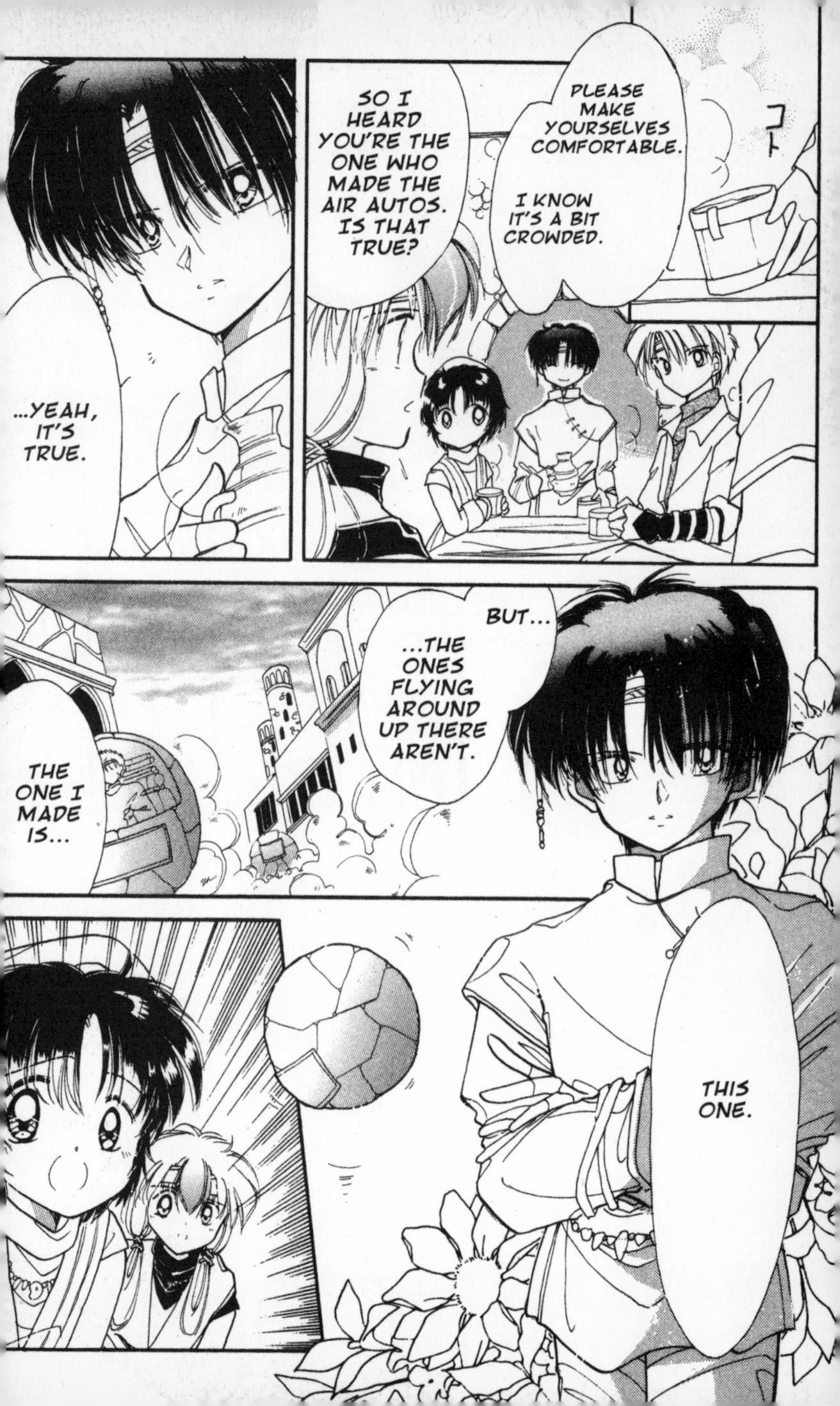

コト
PLEASE MAKE YOURSELVES COMFORTABLE.
I KNOW IT'S A BIT CROWDED.
SO I HEARD YOU'RE THE ONE WHO MADE THE AIR AUTOS. IS THAT TRUE?
...YEAH, IT'S TRUE.
BUT...
...THE ONES FLYING AROUND UP THERE AREN'T.
THE ONE I MADE IS...
THIS ONE.

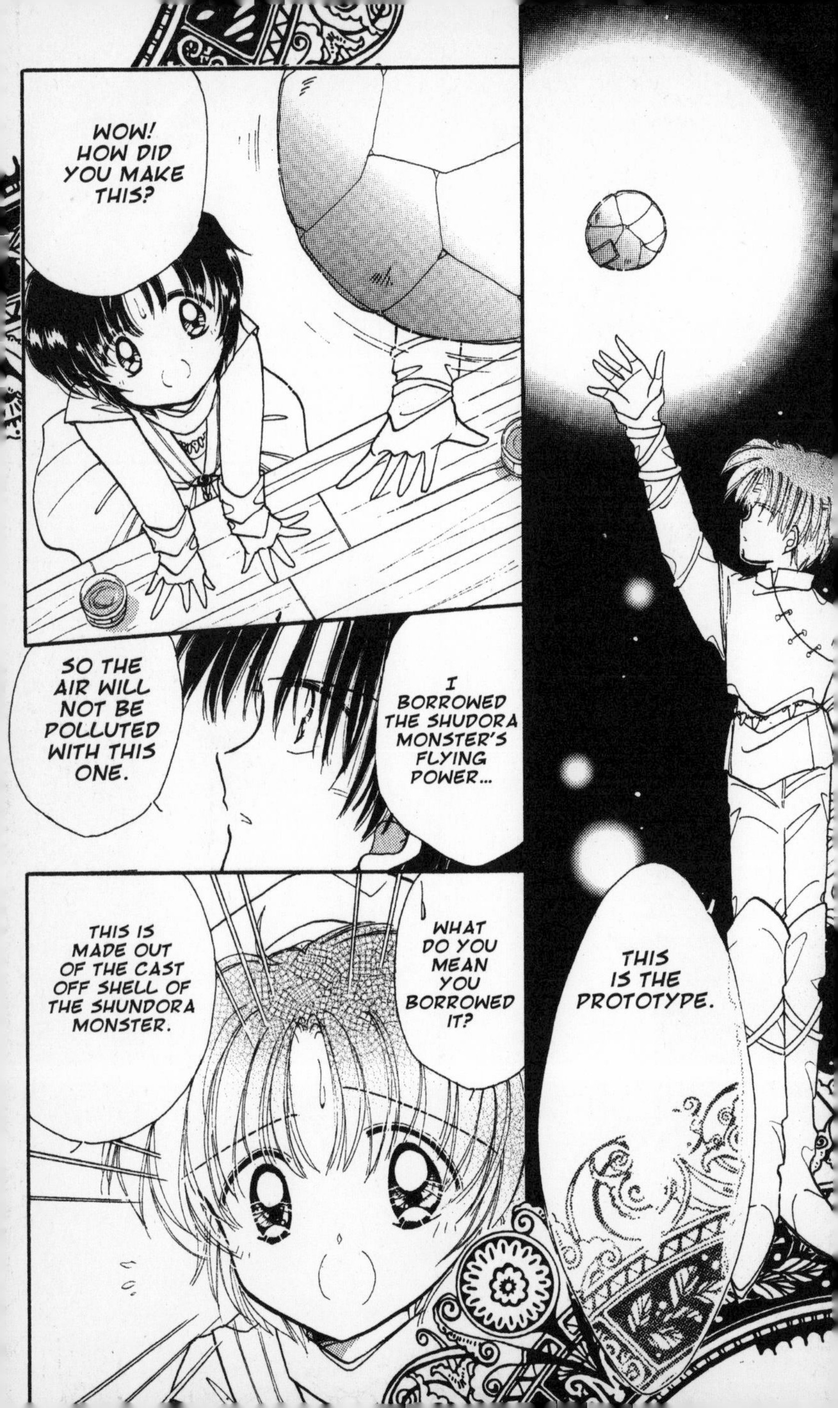
THIS IS THE PROTOTYPE.
WOW! HOW DID YOU MAKE THIS?
I BORROWED THE SHUDORA MONSTER'S FLYING POWER...
SO THE AIR WILL NOT BE POLLUTED WITH THIS ONE.
WHAT DO YOU MEAN YOU BORROWED IT?
THIS IS MADE OUT OF THE CAST OFF SHELL OF THE SHUNDORA MONSTER.

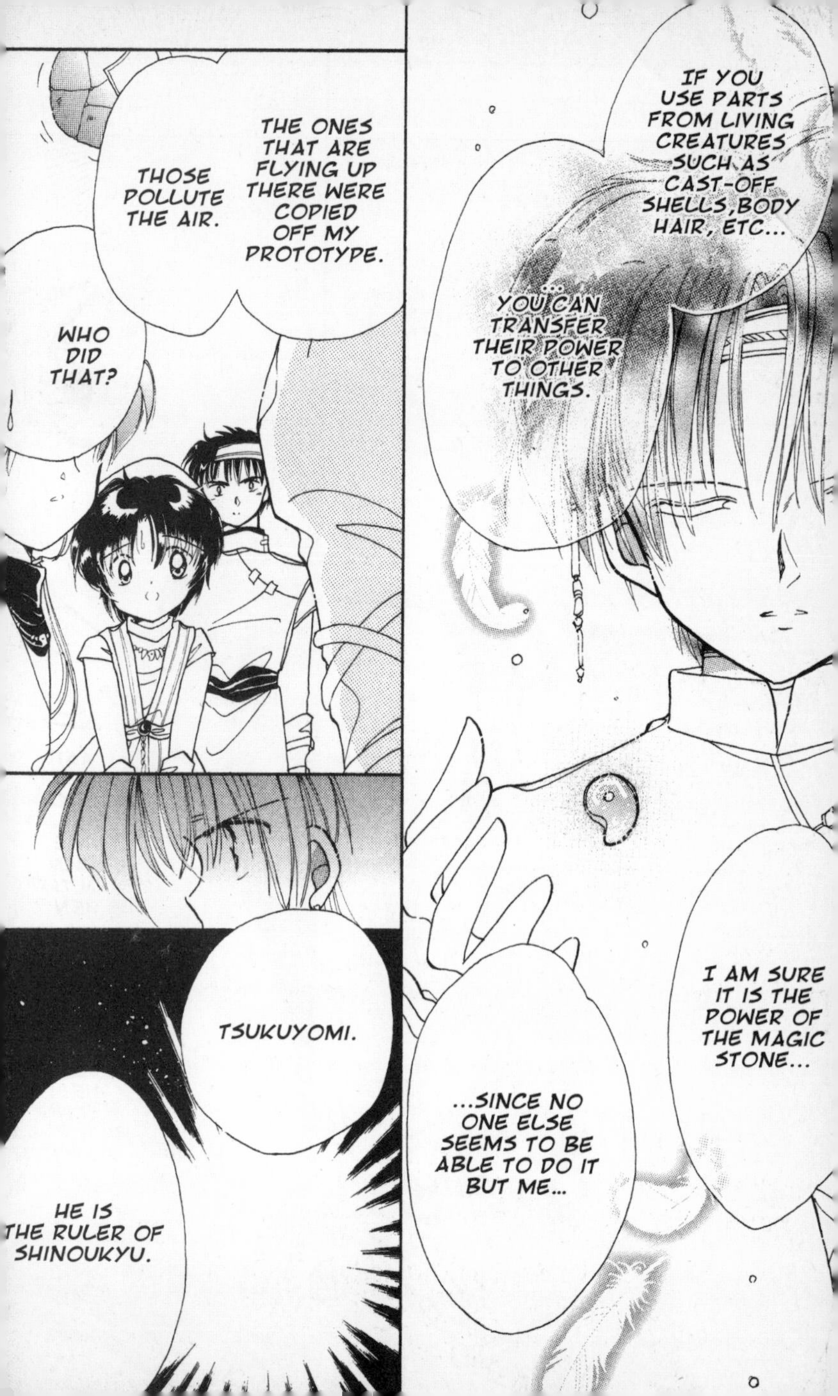
IF YOU USE PARTS FROM LIVING CREATURES SUCH AS CAST-OFF SHELLS, BODY HAIR, ETC...
...YOU CAN TRANSFER THEIR POWER TO OTHER THINGS.
I AM SURE IT IS THE POWER OF THE MAGIC STONE...
...SINCE NO ONE ELSE SEEMS TO BE ABLE TO DO IT BUT ME...
THE ONES THAT ARE FLYING UP THERE WERE COPIED OFF MY PROTOTYPE.
THOSE POLLUTE THE AIR.
WHO DID THAT?
TSUKUYOMI.
HE IS THE RULER OF SHINOUKYU.

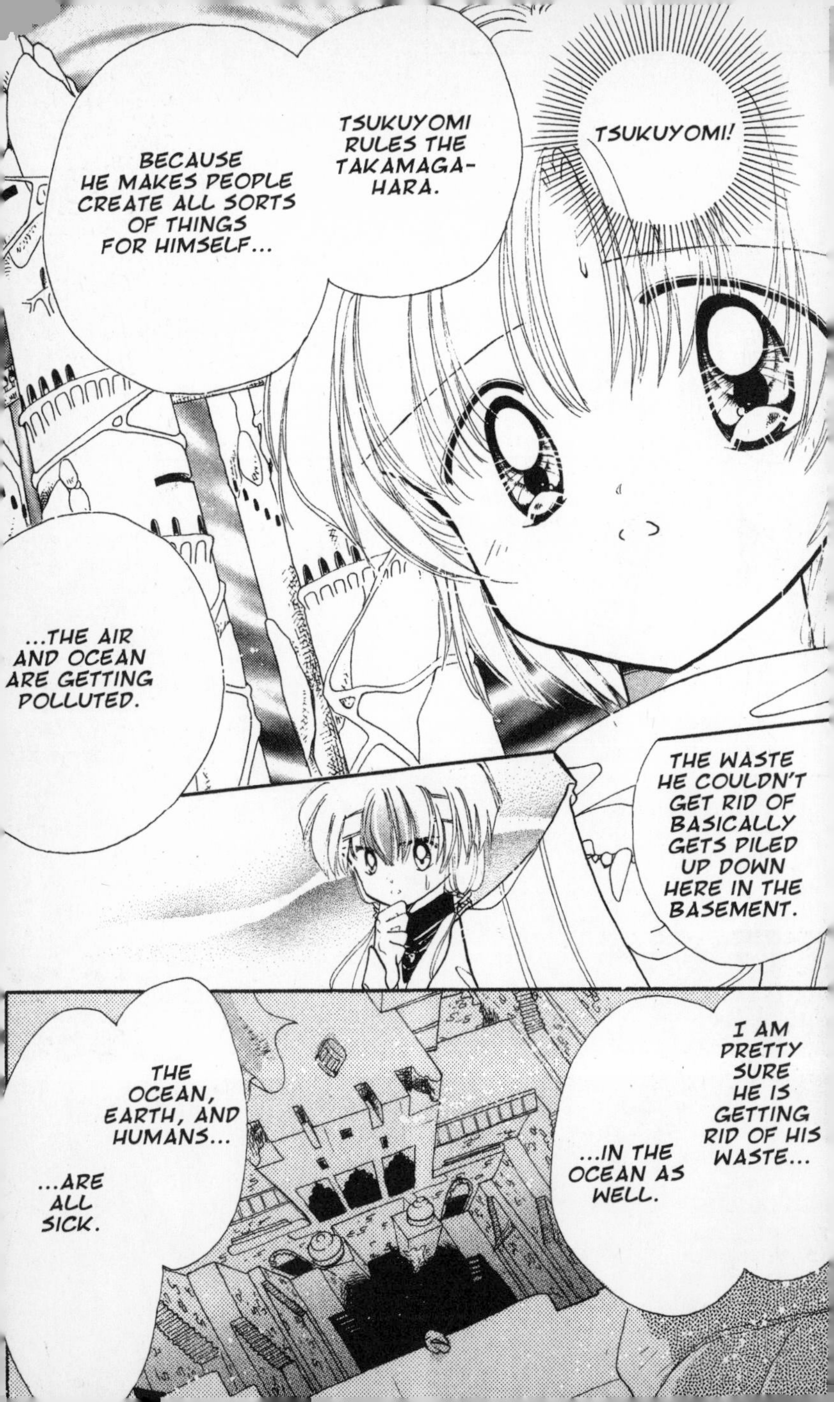

TSUKUYOMI!
TSUKUYOMI RULES THE TAKAMAGA-HARA.
BECAUSE HE MAKES PEOPLE CREATE ALL SORTS OF THINGS FOR HIMSELF...
...THE AIR AND OCEAN ARE GETTING POLLUTED.
THE WASTE HE COULDN'T GET RID OF BASICALLY GETS PILED UP DOWN HERE IN THE BASEMENT.
I AM PRETTY SURE HE IS GETTING RID OF HIS WASTE...
...IN THE OCEAN AS WELL.
THE OCEAN, EARTH, AND HUMANS...
...ARE ALL SICK.

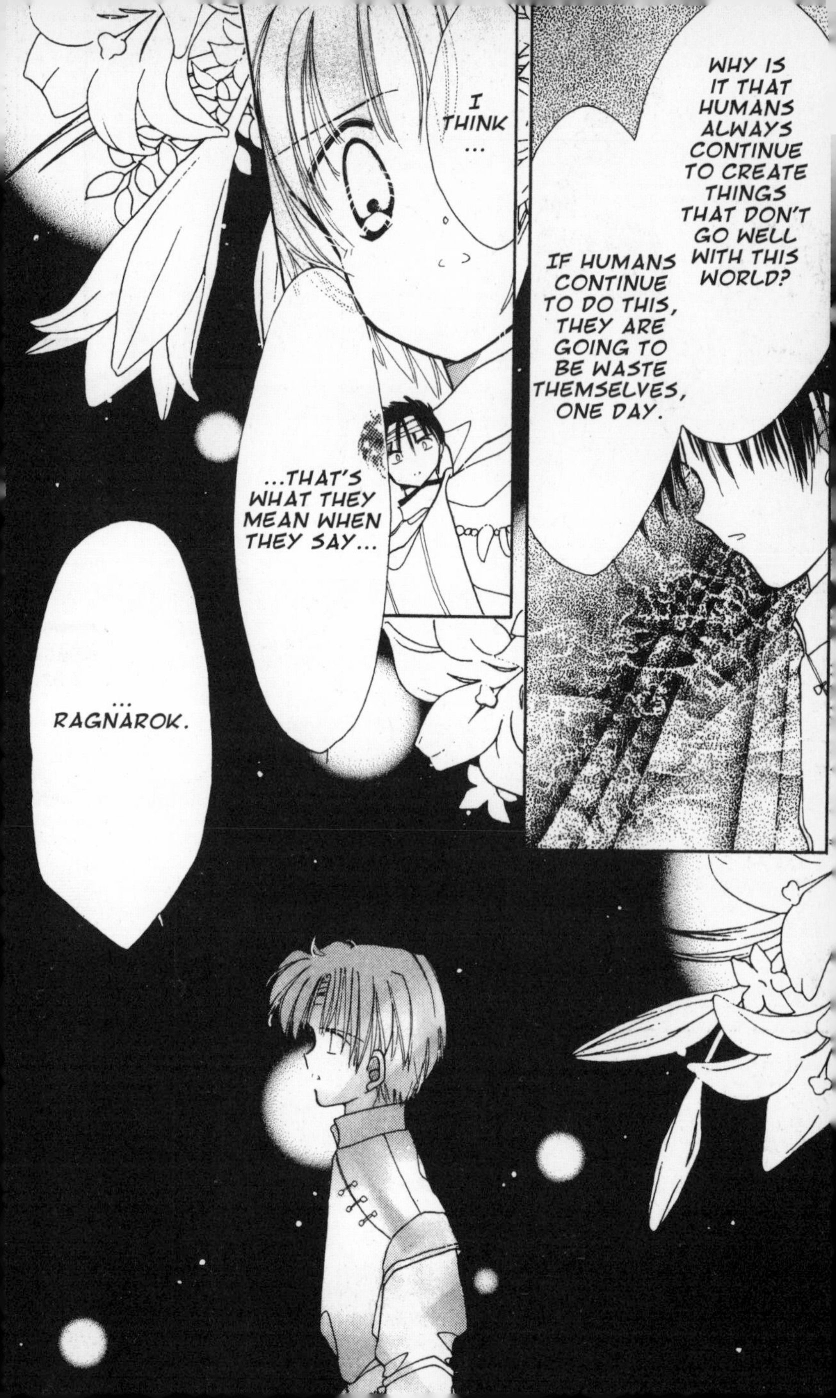
WHY IS IT THAT HUMANS ALWAYS CONTINUE TO CREATE THINGS THAT DON'T GO WELL WITH THIS WORLD?
IF HUMANS CONTINUE TO DO THIS, THEY ARE GOING TO BE WASTE THEMSELVES, ONE DAY.
I THINK ...
...THAT'S WHAT THEY MEAN WHEN THEY SAY...
... RAGNÄROK.

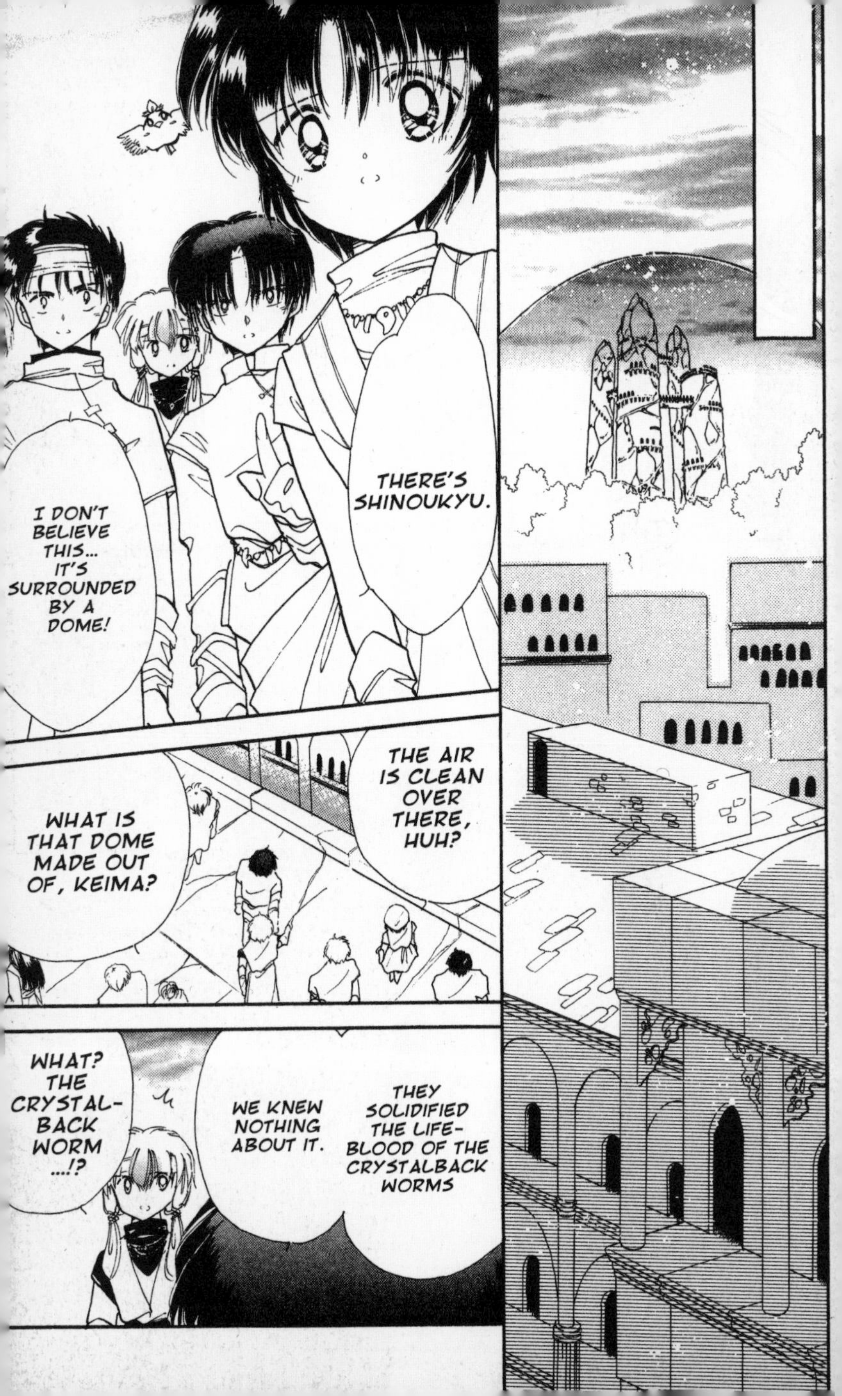
THERE'S SHINOUKYU.
I DON'T BELIEVE THIS... IT'S SURROUNDED BY A DOME!
THE AIR IS CLEAN OVER THERE, HUH?
WHAT IS THAT DOME MADE OUT OF, KEIMA?
THEY SOLIDIFIED THE LIFE-BLOOD OF THE CRYSTALBACK WORMS
WE KNEW NOTHING ABOUT IT.
WHAT? THE CRYSTAL-BACK WORM ...!?

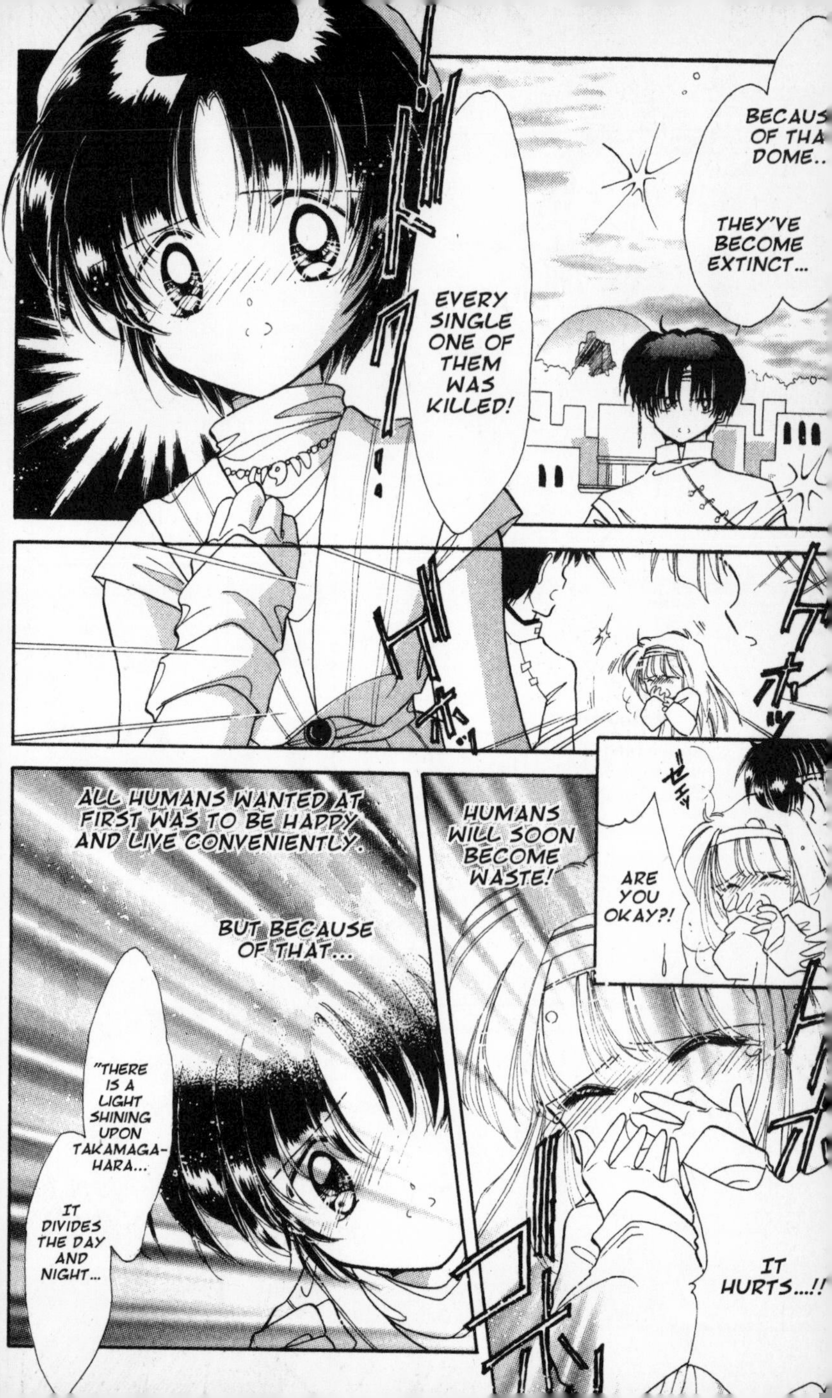
BECAUS OF THA DOME..
THEY'VE BECOME EXTINCT...
EVERY SINGLE ONE OF THEM WAS KILLED!
ARE YOU OKAY?!
IT HURTS...!!
HUMANS WILL SOON BECOME WASTE!
ALL HUMANS WANTED AT FIRST WAS TO BE HAPPY AND LIVE CONVENIENTLY.
BUT BECAUSE OF THAT...
"THERE IS A LIGHT SHINING UPON TAKAMAGA-HARA...
IT DIVIDES THE DAY AND NIGHT...

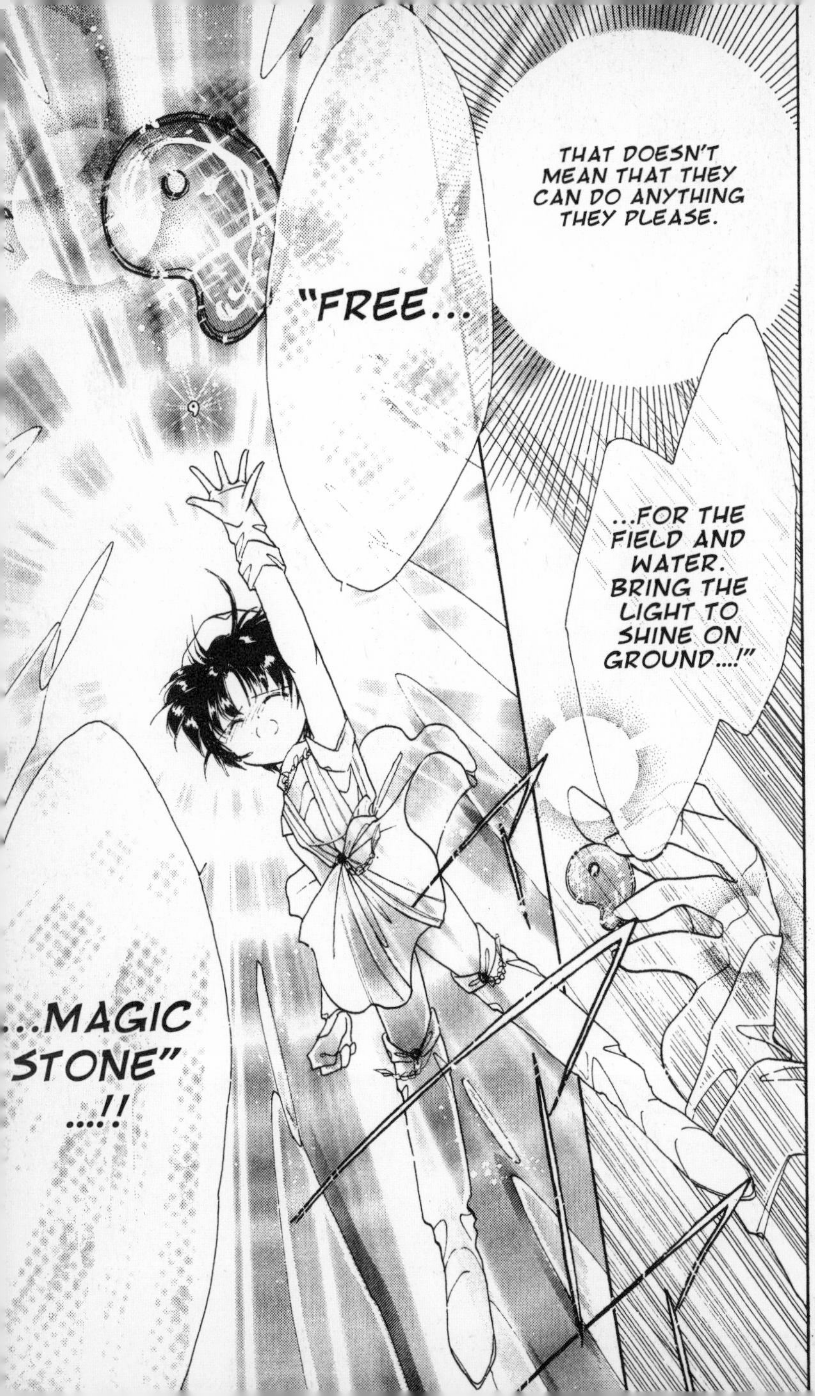
THAT DOESN'T MEAN THAT THEY CAN DO ANYTHING THEY PLEASE.
"FREE...
...FOR THE FIELD AND WATER. BRING THE LIGHT TO SHINE ON GROUND...!"
...MAGIC STONE"
...!!

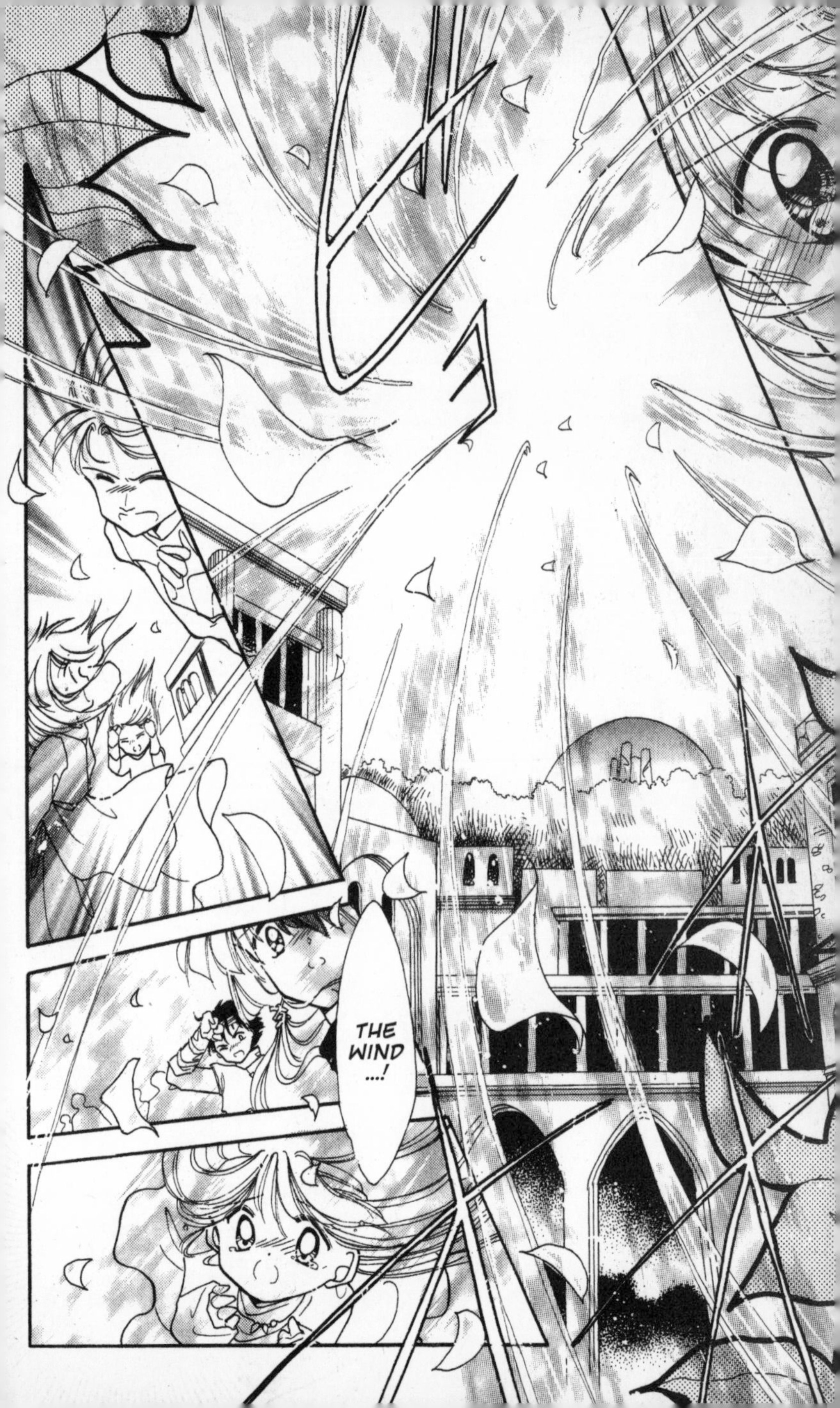
THE WIND ...!

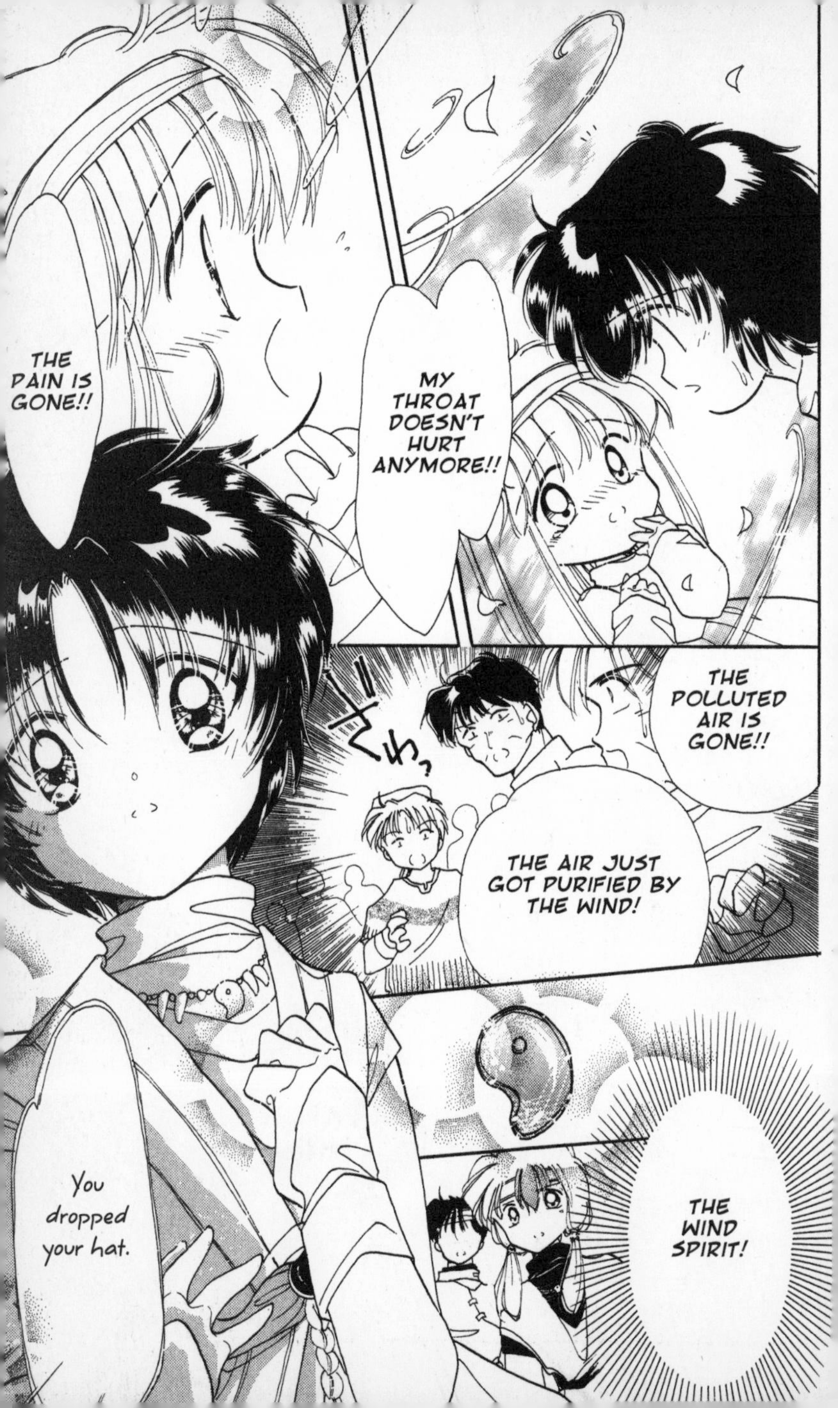
MY THROAT DOESN'T HURT ANYMORE!!
THE PAIN IS GONE!!
THE POLLUTED AIR IS GONE!!
ざわっ
THE AIR JUST GOT PURIFIED BY THE WIND!
THE WIND SPIRIT!
You dropped your hat.

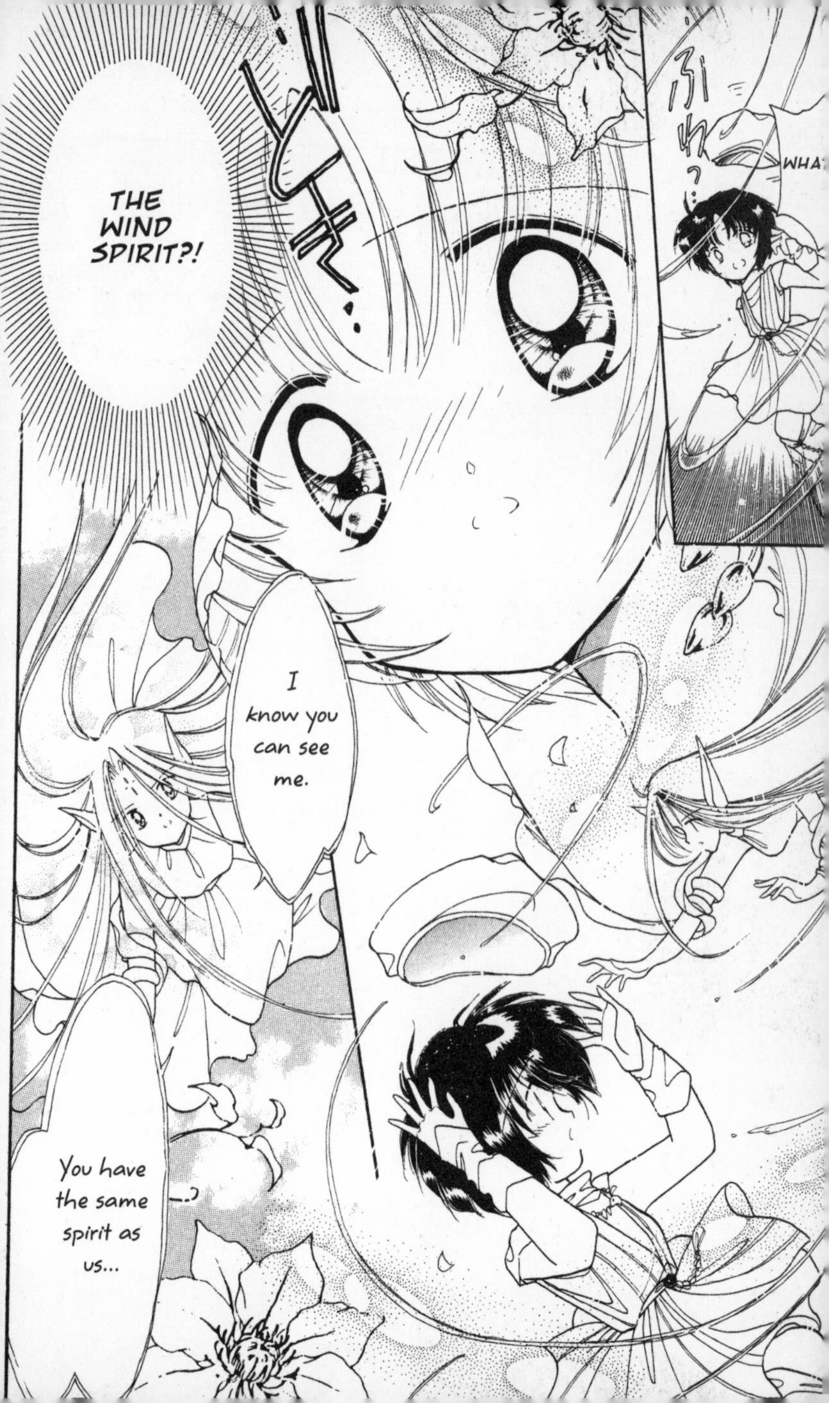

ふわっ…
WHA
THE WIND SPIRIT?!
I know you can see me.
You have the same spirit as us...

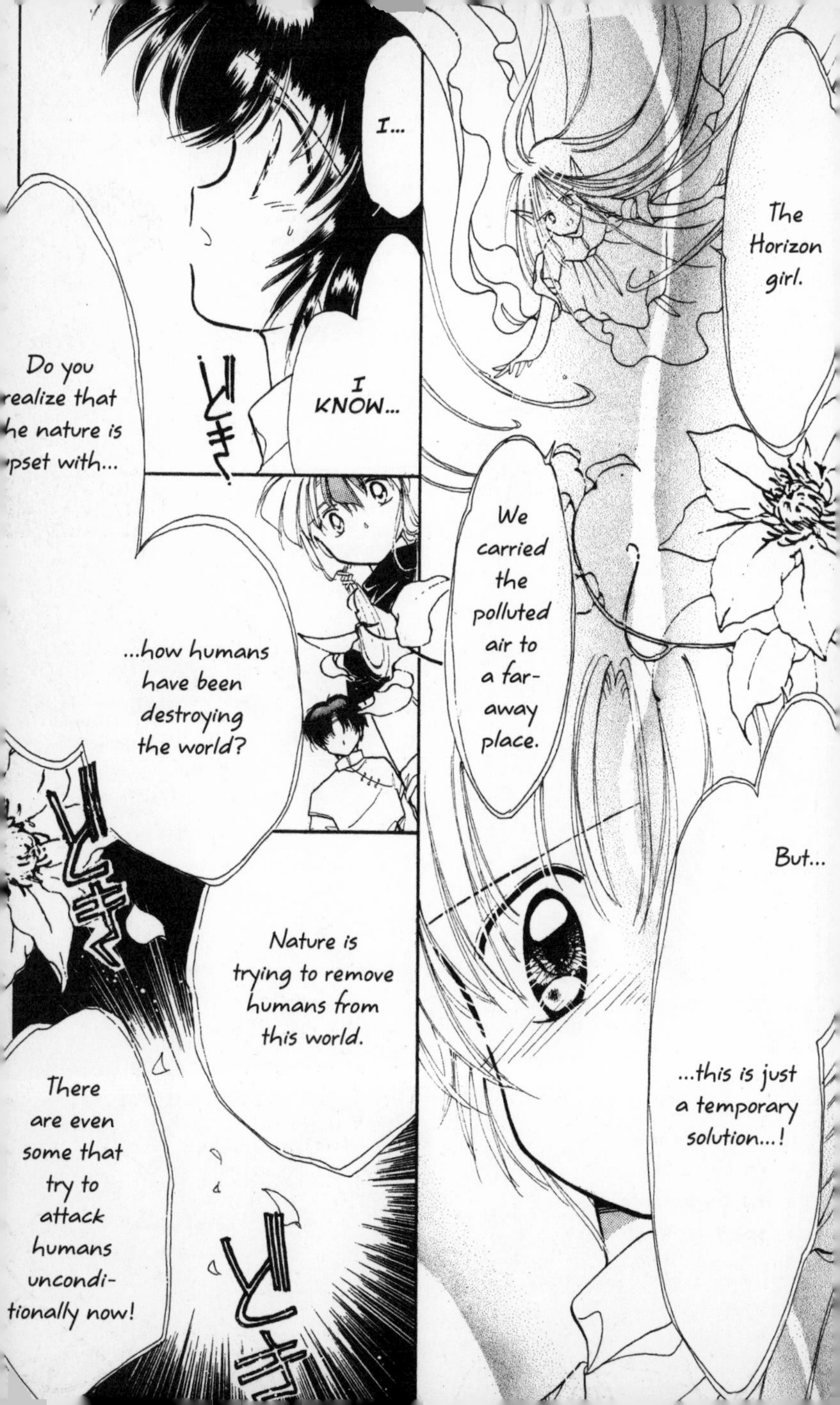
The Horizon girl.
We carried the polluted air to a far-away place.
But...
...this is just a temporary solution...!
I...
I KNOW...
Do you realize that he nature is pset with...
...how humans have been destroying the world?
Nature is trying to remove humans from this world.
There are even some that try to attack humans unconditionally now!

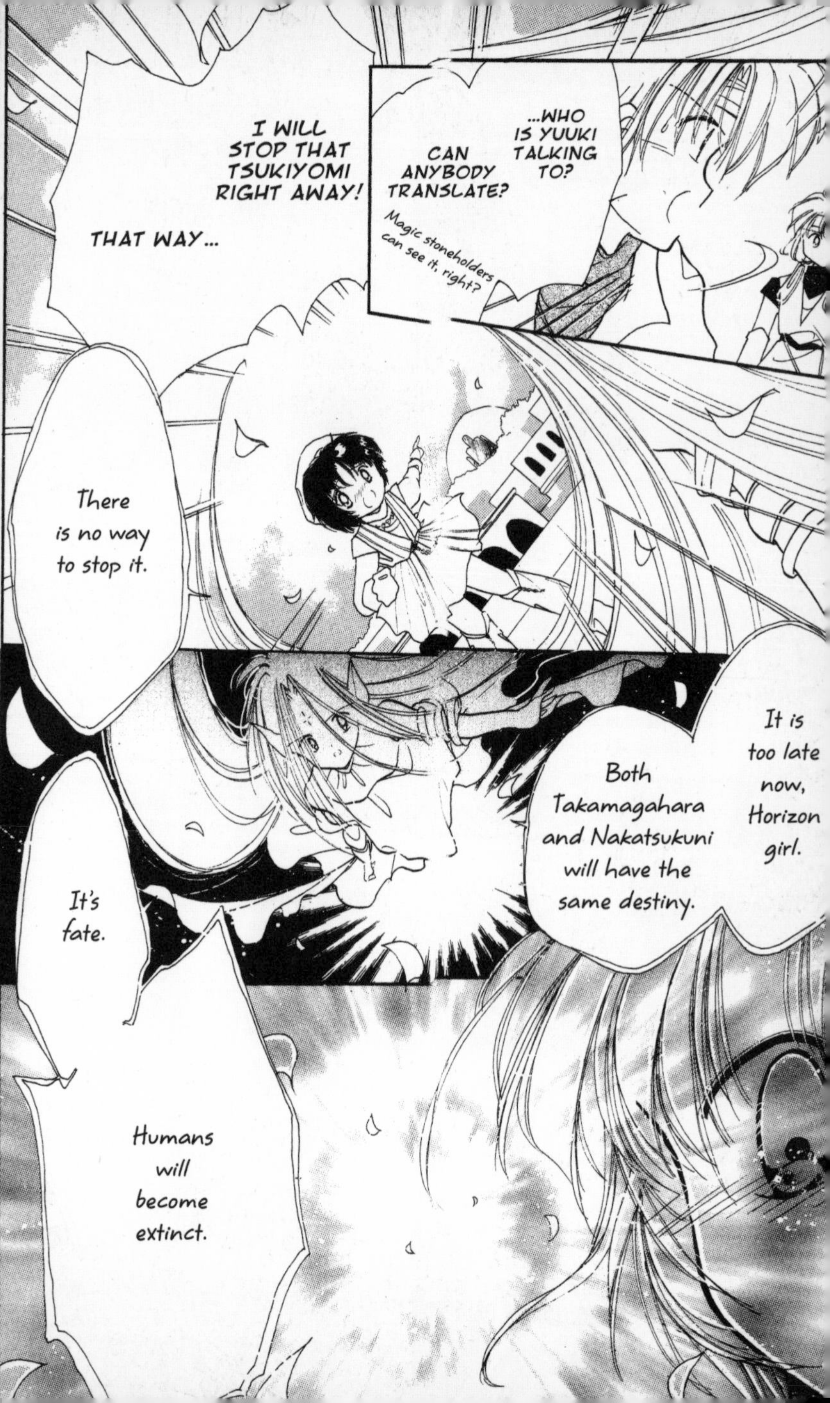
...WHO IS YUUKI TALKING TO?
CAN ANYBODY TRANSLATE?
Magic stoneholders can see it, right?
I WILL STOP THAT TSUKIYOMI RIGHT AWAY!
THAT WAY...
There is no way to stop it.
It is too late now, Horizon girl.
Both Takamagahara and Nakatsukuni will have the same destiny.
It's fate.
Humans will become extinct.

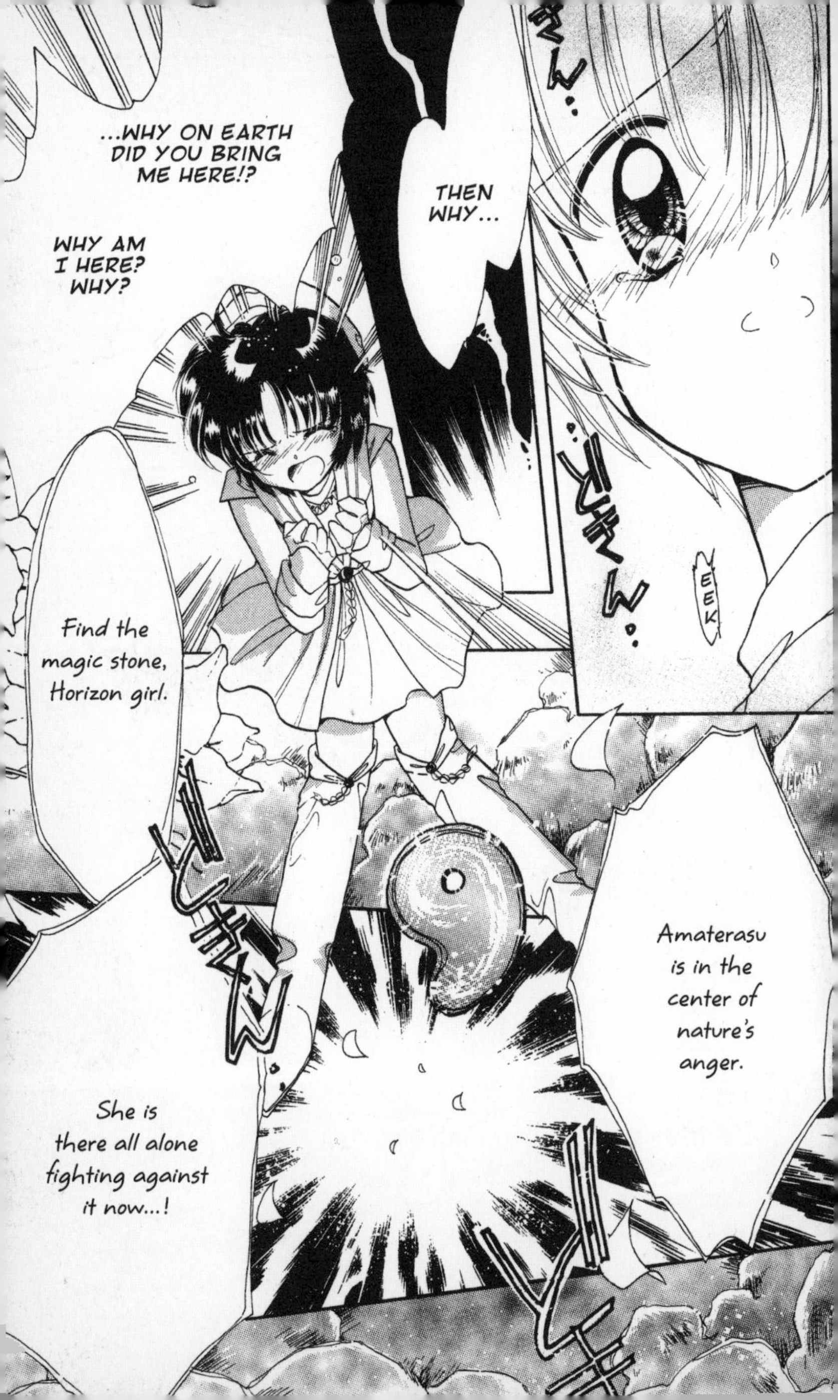
THEN WHY...
EEK
...WHY ON EARTH DID YOU BRING ME HERE!?
WHY AM I HERE? WHY?
Find the magic stone, Horizon girl.
Amaterasu is in the center of nature's anger.
She is there all alone fighting against it now...!

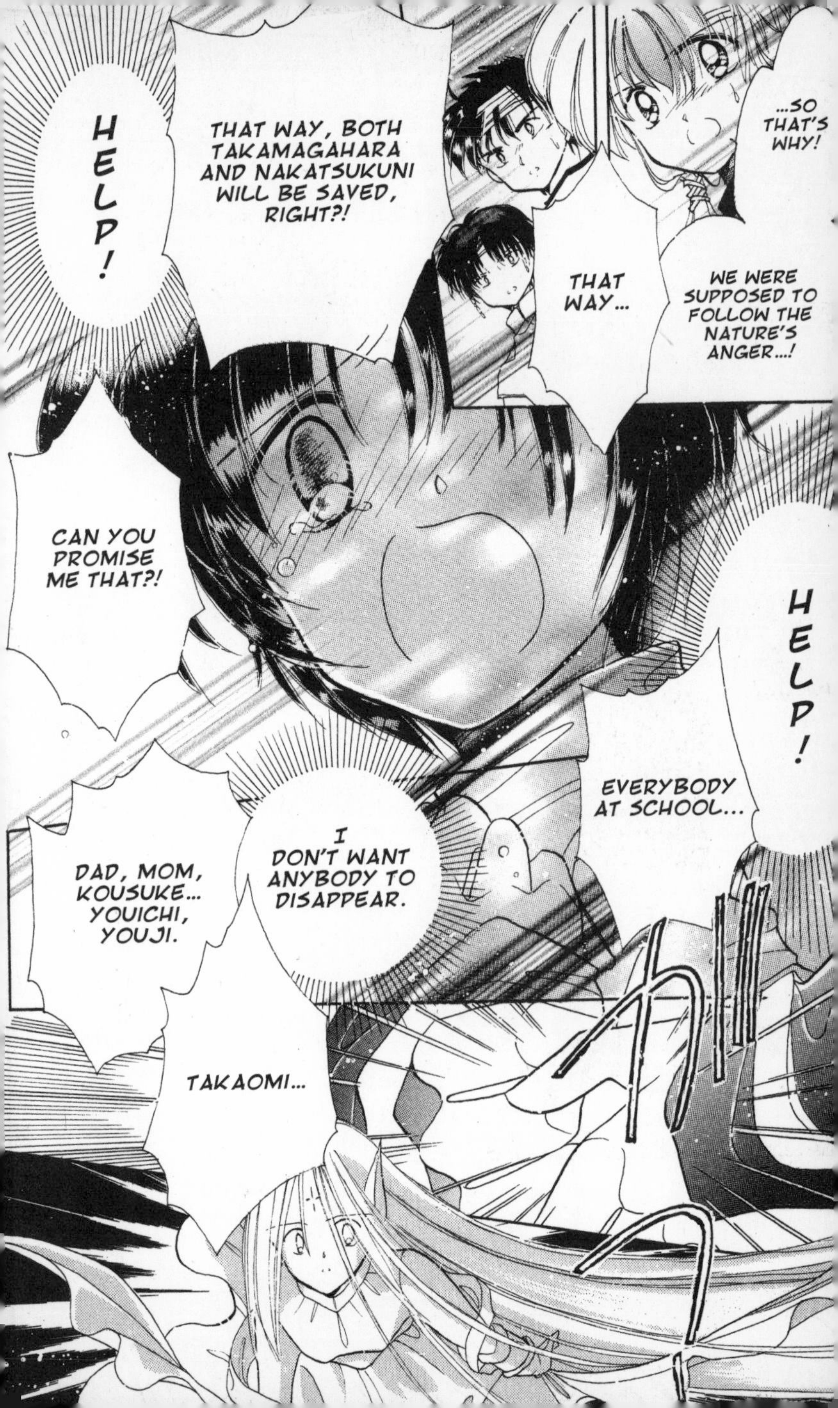
...SO THAT'S WHY!
WE WERE SUPPOSED TO FOLLOW THE NATURE'S ANGER...!
THAT WAY...
THAT WAY, BOTH TAKAMAGAHARA AND NAKATSUKUNI WILL BE SAVED, RIGHT?!
HELP!
HELP!
CAN YOU PROMISE ME THAT?!
EVERYBODY AT SCHOOL...
I DON'T WANT ANYBODY TO DISAPPEAR.
DAD, MOM, KOUSUKE... YOUICHI, YOUJI.
TAKAOMI...

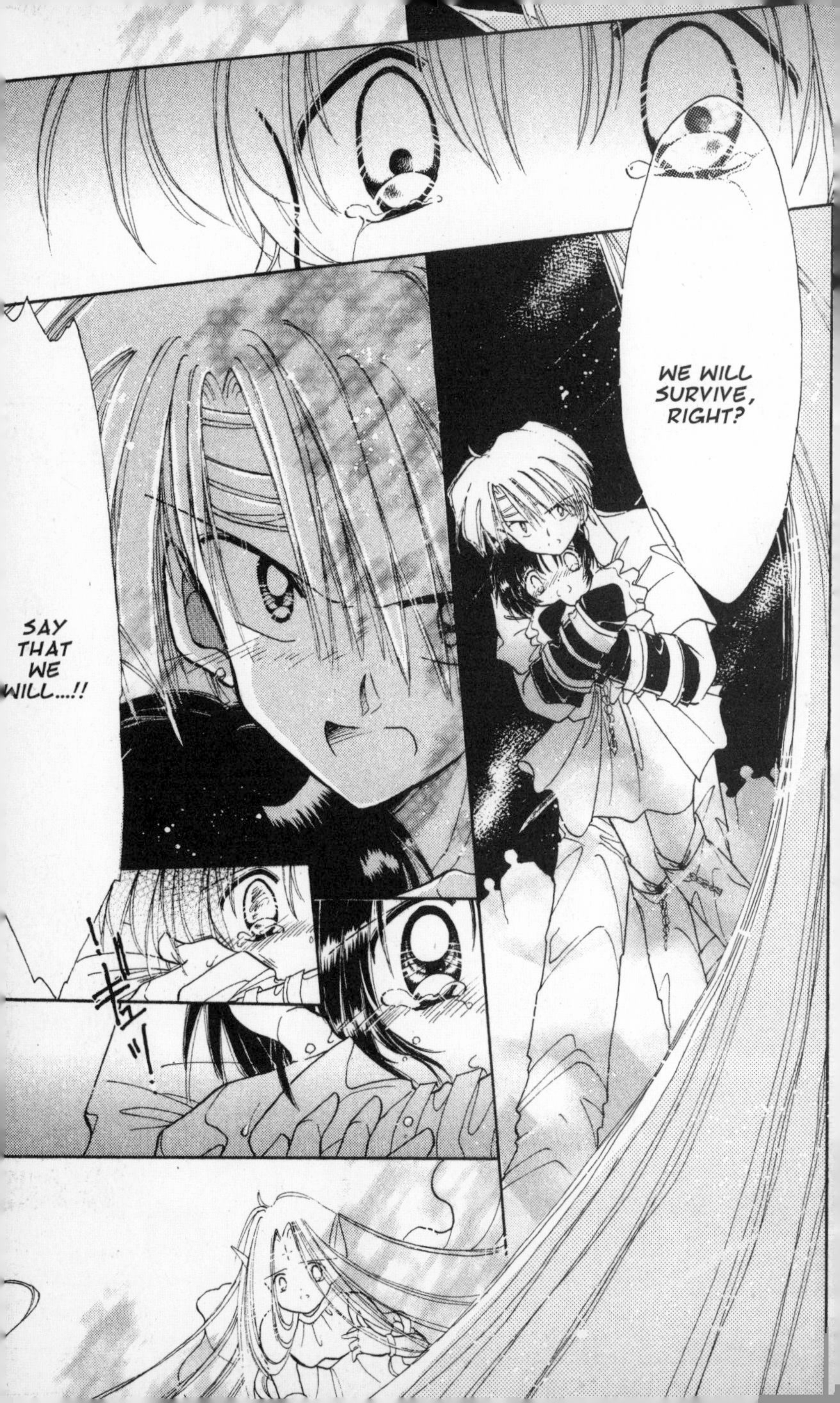
WE WILL SURVIVE, RIGHT?
SAY THAT WE WILL...!!

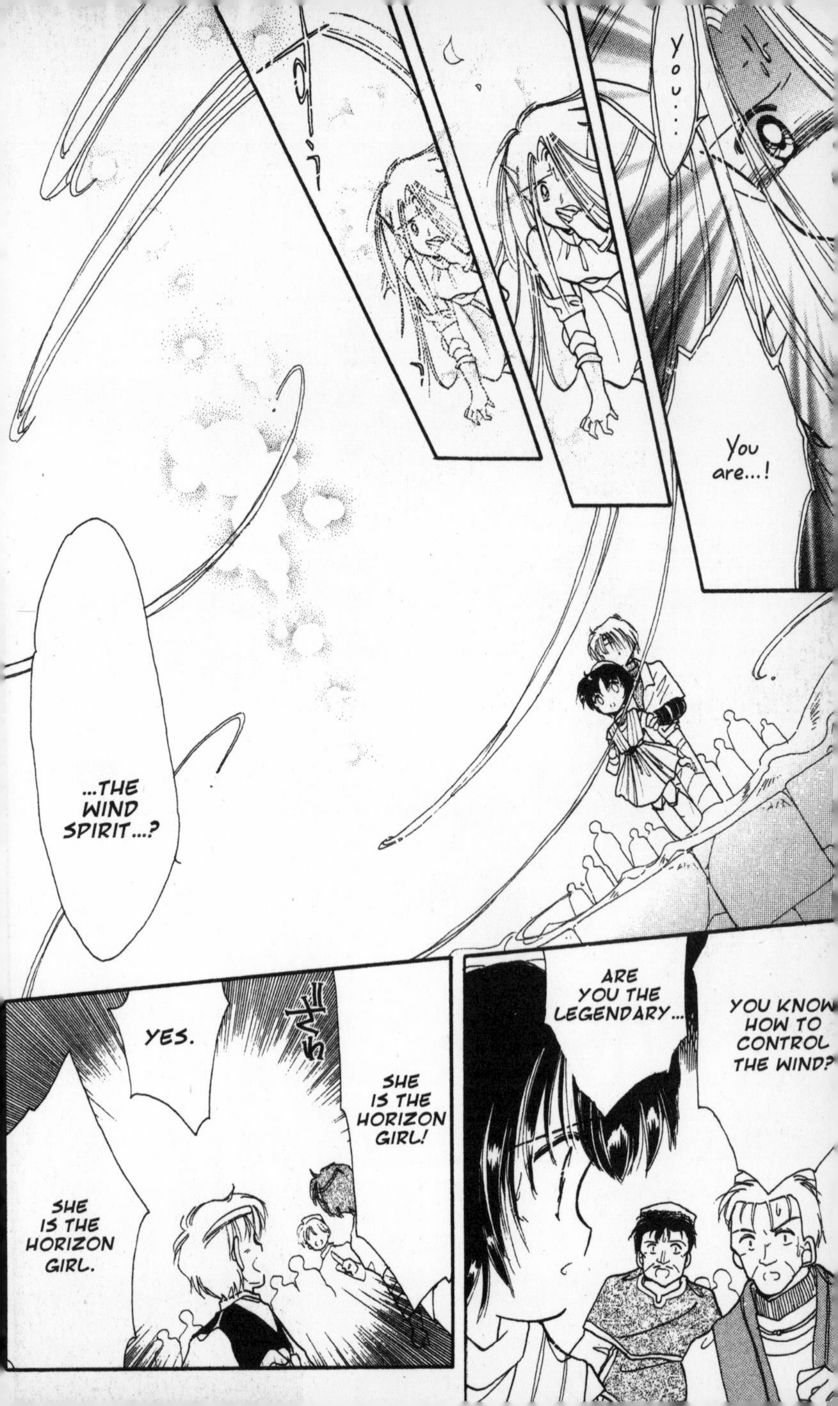

You...
You are...!
...THE WIND SPIRIT...?
YOU KNOW HOW TO CONTROL THE WIND?
ARE YOU THE LEGENDARY...
YES.
SHE IS THE HORIZON GIRL!
SHE IS THE HORIZON GIRL.

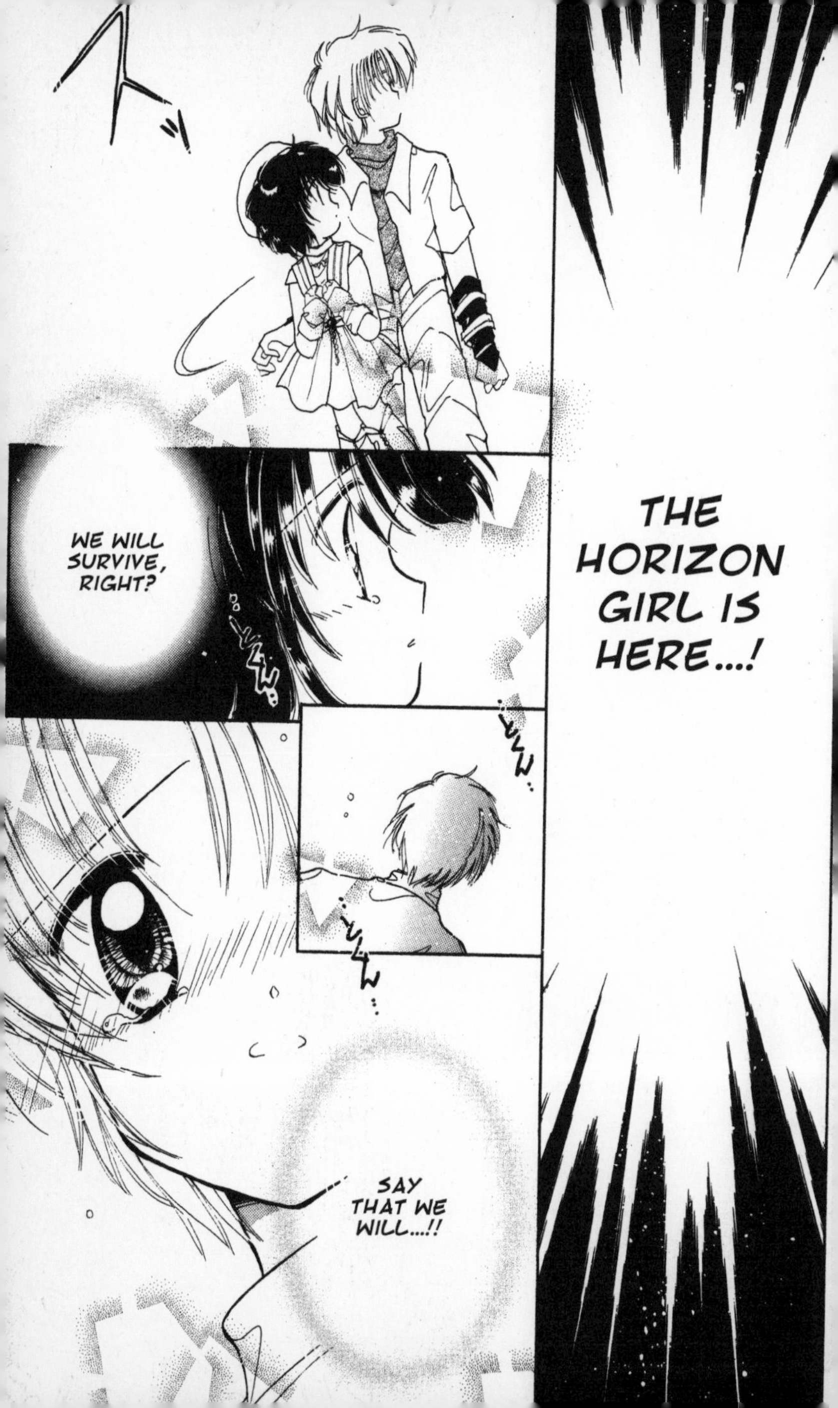
THE HORIZON GIRL IS HERE...!
WE WILL SURVIVE, RIGHT?
SAY THAT WE WILL...!!

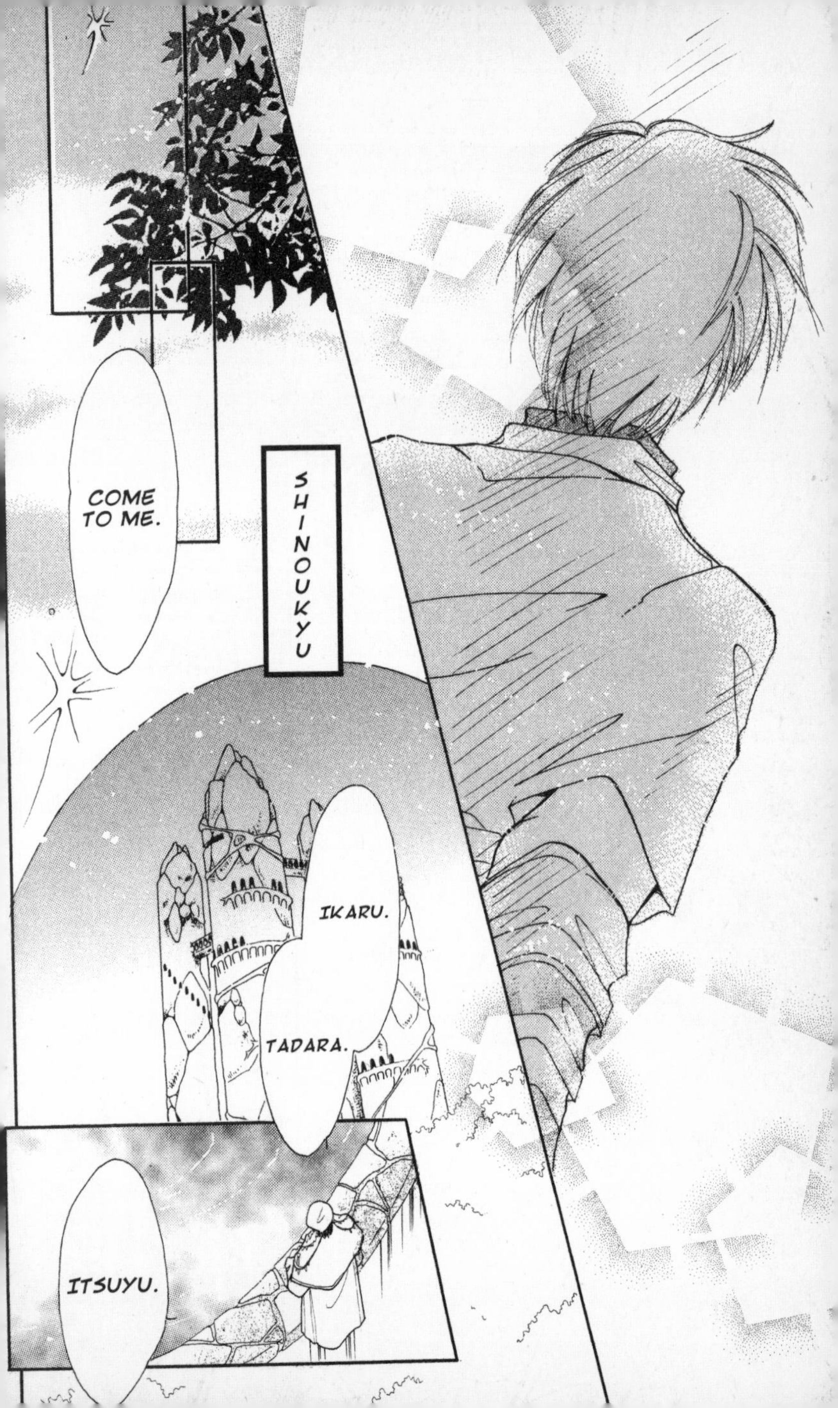
COME TO ME.
SHINOUKYU
IKARU.
TADARA.
ITSUYU.

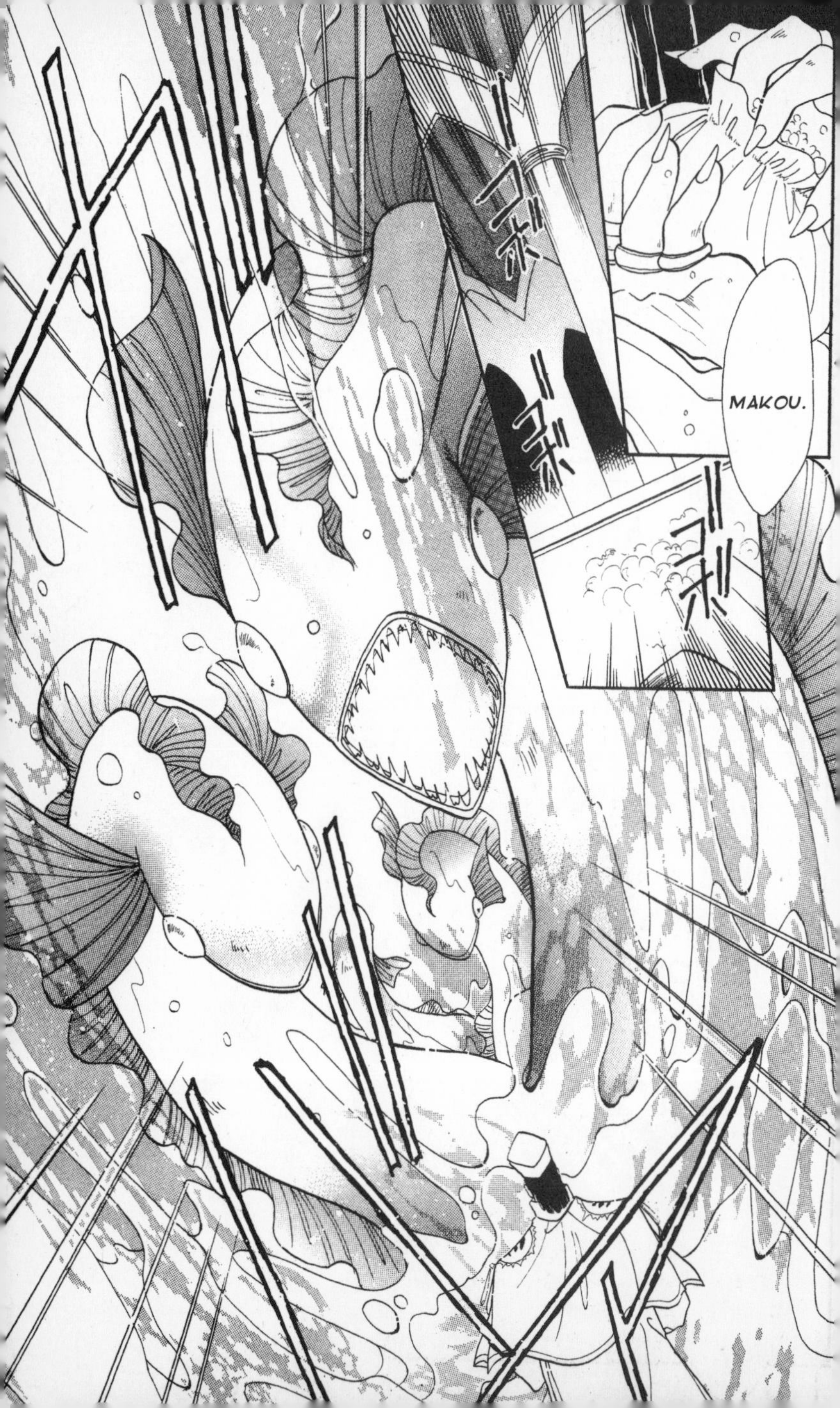
MAKOU.
ゴボ
ゴボ
ゴボ

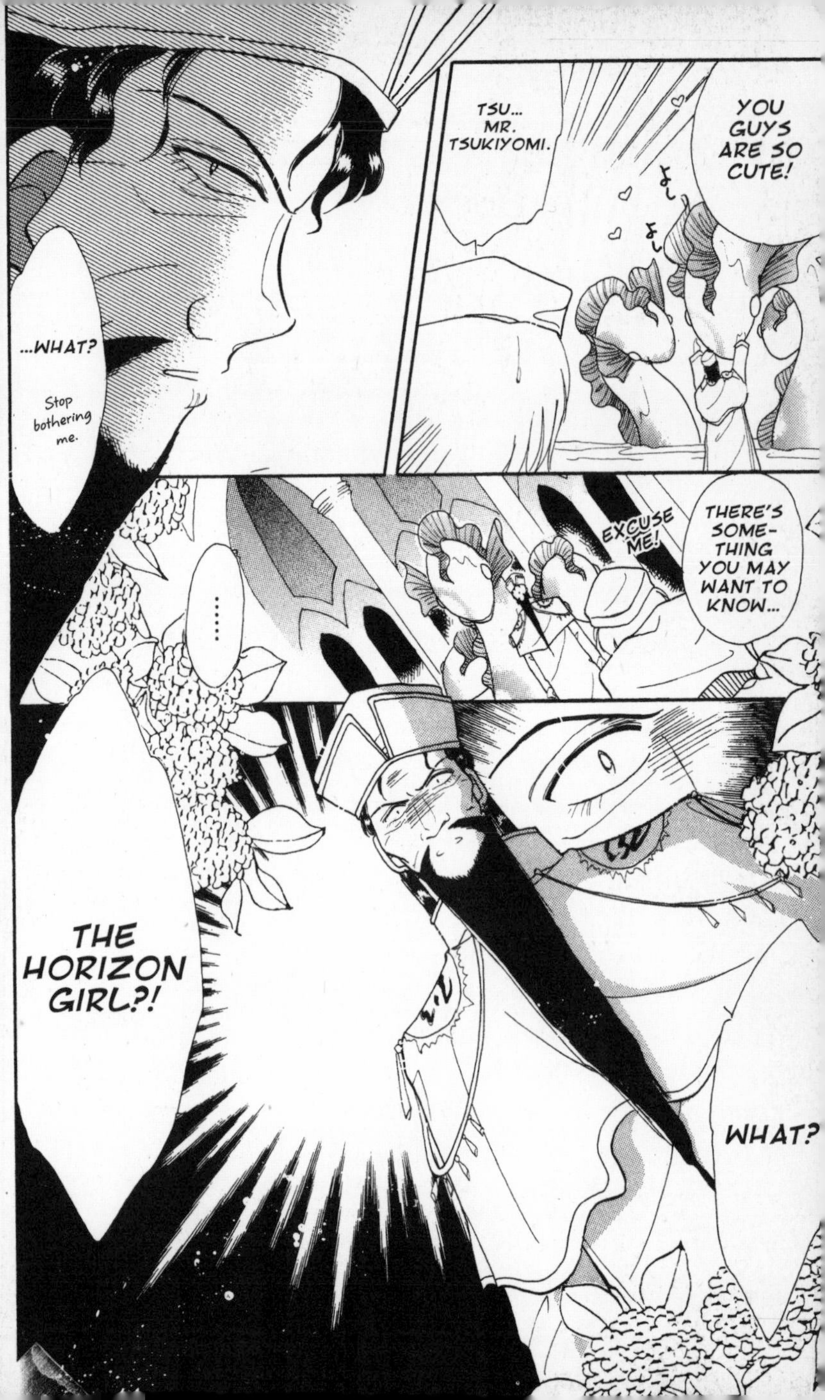

YOU GUYS ARE SO CUTE!
よし
よし
TSU... MR. TSUKIYOMI.
...WHAT?
Stop bothering me.
EXCUSE ME!
THERE'S SOME-THING YOU MAY WANT TO KNOW...
......
WHAT?
THE HORIZON GIRL?!

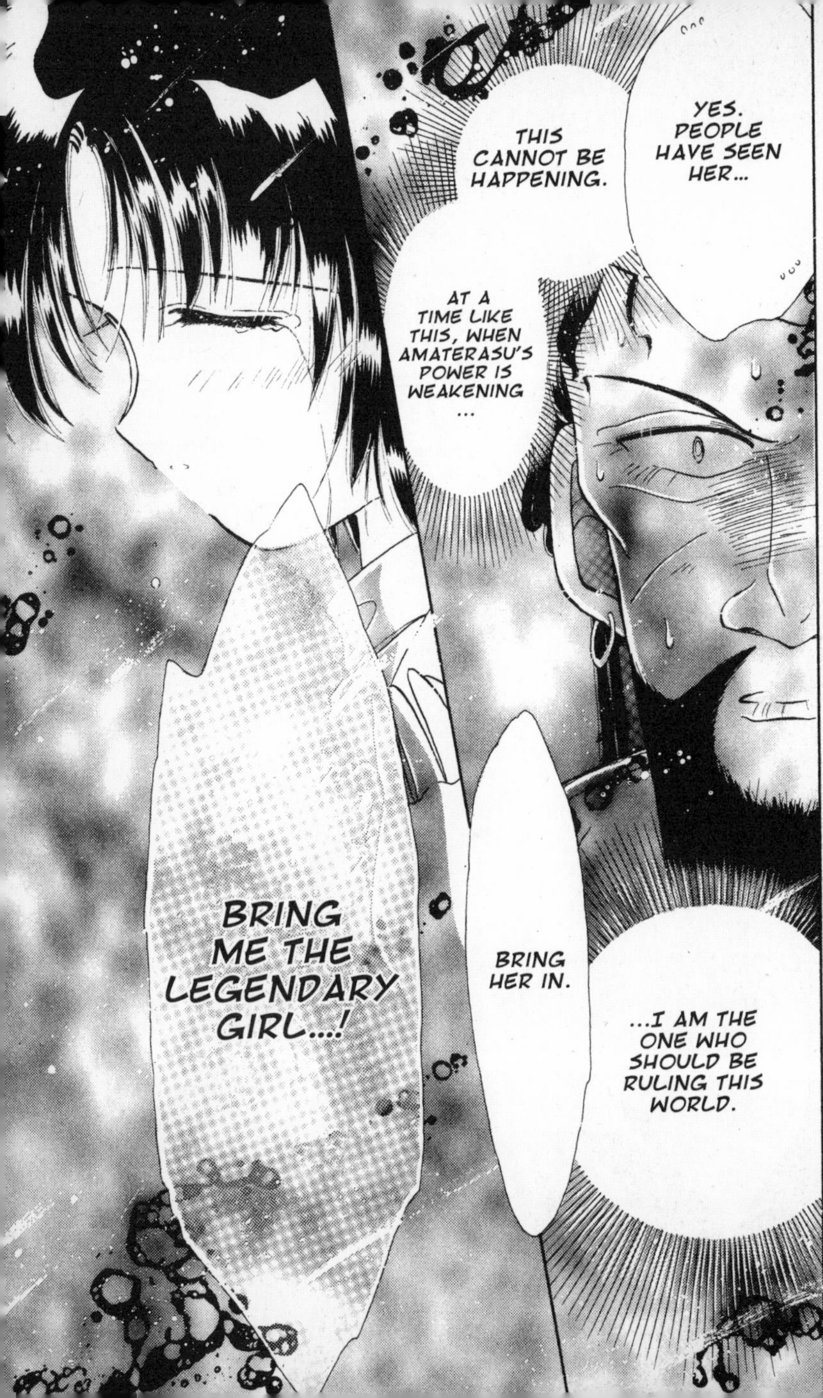
YES. PEOPLE HAVE SEEN HER...
THIS CANNOT BE HAPPENING.
AT A TIME LIKE THIS, WHEN AMATERASU'S POWER IS WEAKENING...
...I AM THE ONE WHO SHOULD BE RULING THIS WORLD.
BRING HER IN.
BRING ME THE LEGENDARY GIRL...!

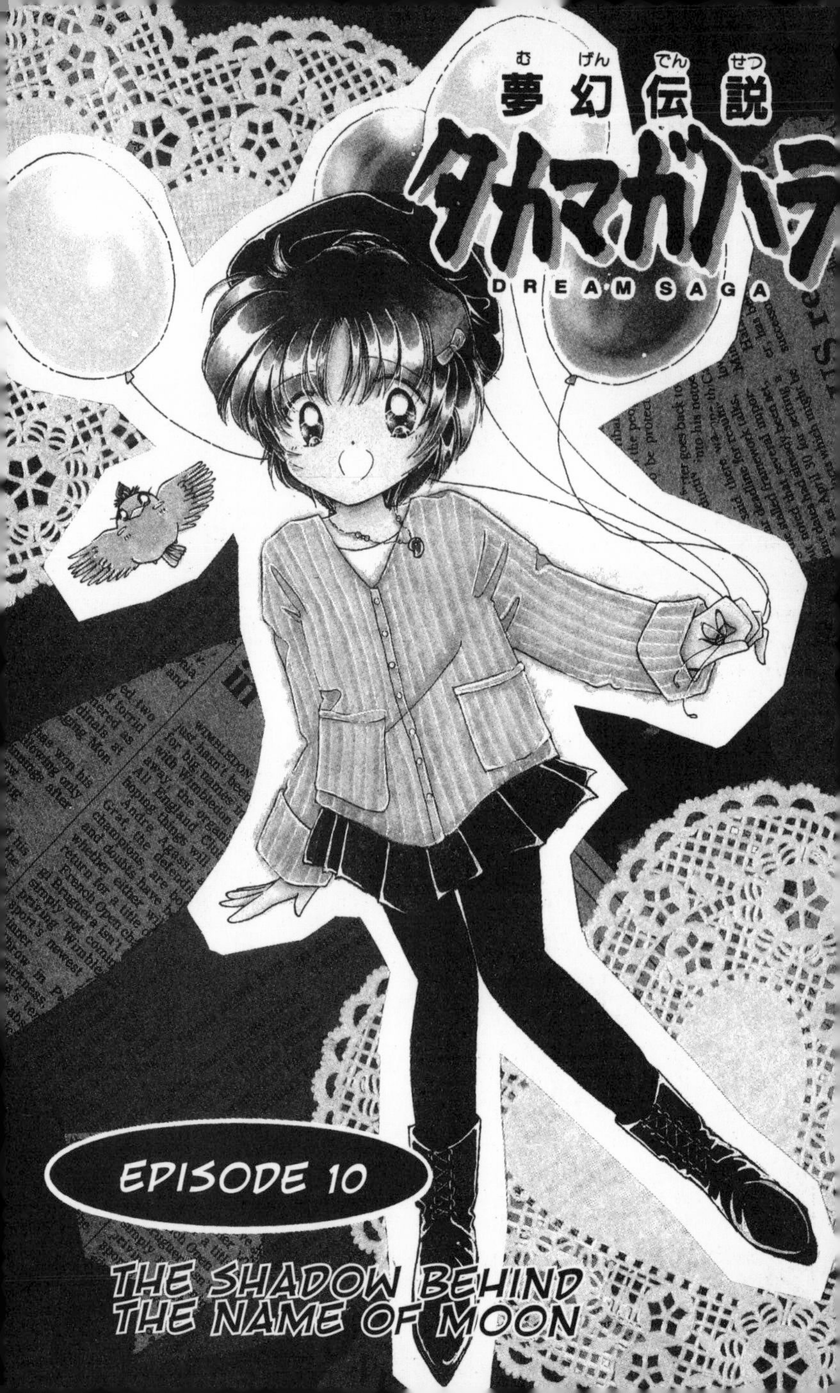

夢幻伝説
タカマガハラ
DREAM SAGA
EPISODE 10
THE SHADOW BEHIND
THE NAME OF MOON

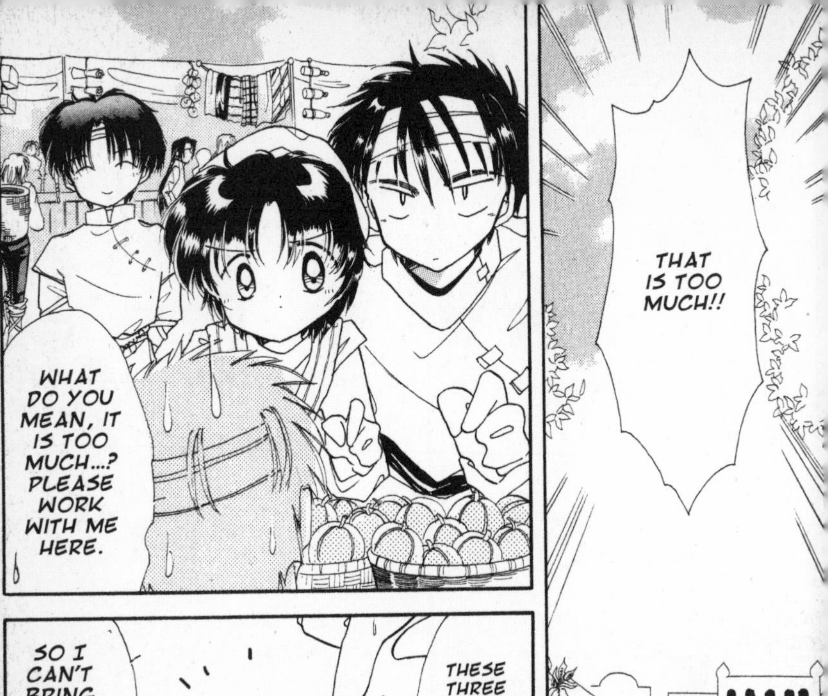
THAT IS TOO MUCH!!
WHAT DO YOU MEAN, IT IS TOO MUCH...? PLEASE WORK WITH ME HERE.
THESE THREE TOGETHER COST ME A FORTUNE!
SO I CAN'T BRING THE PRICE LOWER THAN THAT!

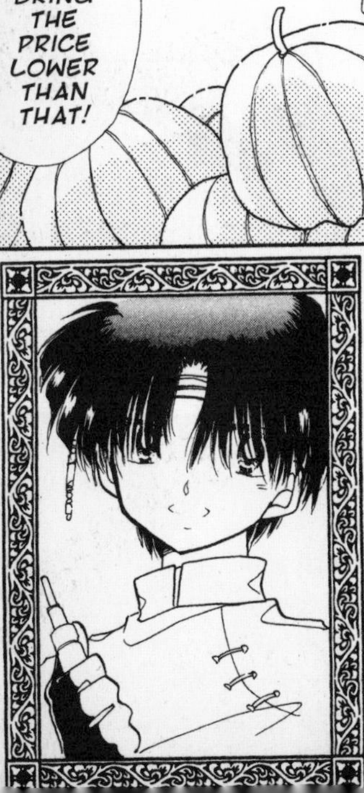

Q. Which soap operas and animation do you watch these days?

A: It is currently December, 1997. The soap operas I watch are "Narita Divorce," "Eve," "One-way Ticket for Love" and "Love Generation." I especially like Gorou Inagaki in "One-way Ticket f Love". His glasses and hairstyle look great. Actually, I used him as an image when I drew Keima... I know they don't look alike all. I don't watch any particular animation at this point. Sorry.

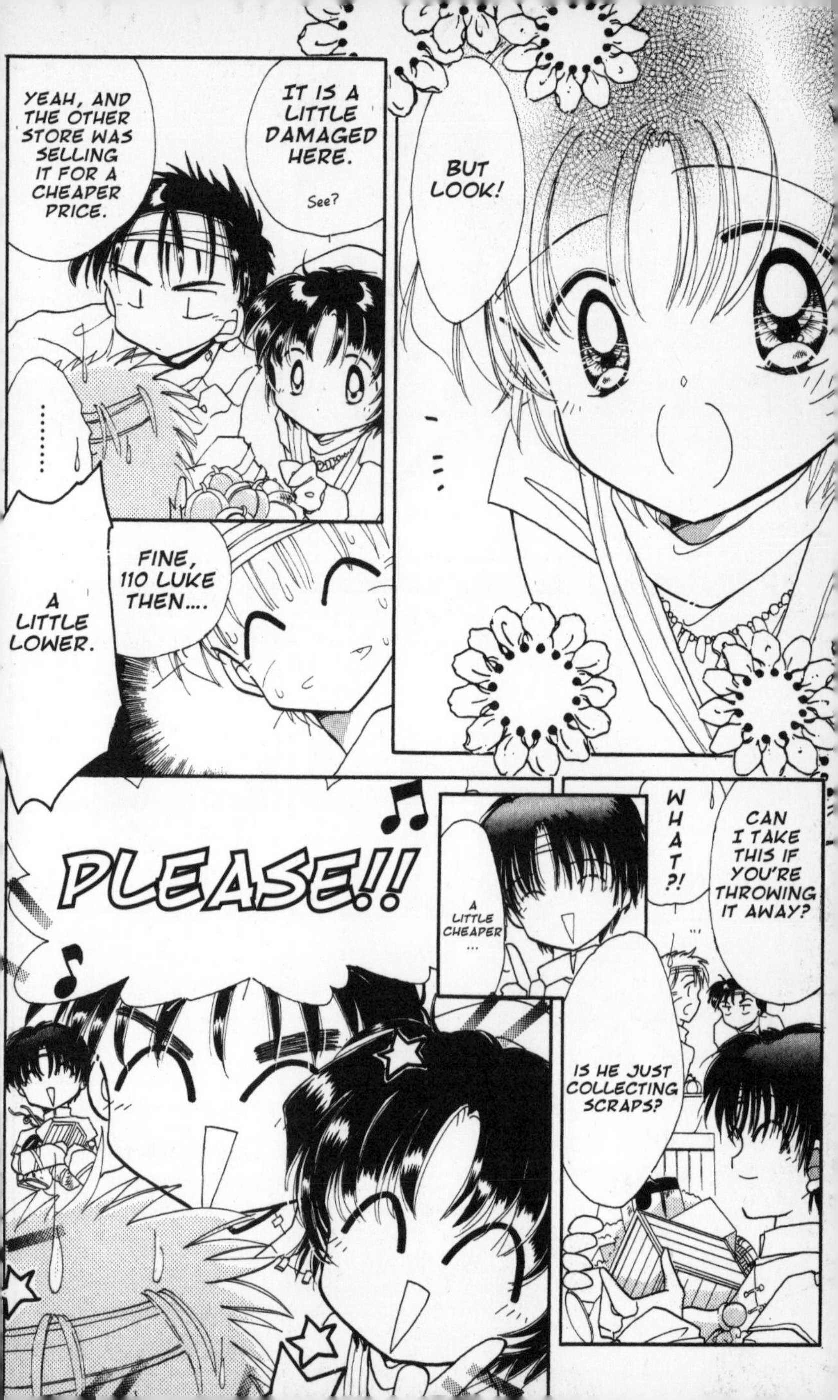
BUT LOOK!
IT IS A LITTLE DAMAGED HERE.
See?
YEAH, AND THE OTHER STORE WAS SELLING IT FOR A CHEAPER PRICE.
......
FINE, 110 LUKE THEN....
A LITTLE LOWER.
CAN I TAKE THIS IF YOU'RE THROWING IT AWAY?
WHAT?!
IS HE JUST COLLECTING SCRAPS?
A LITTLE CHEAPER ...
PLEASE!!

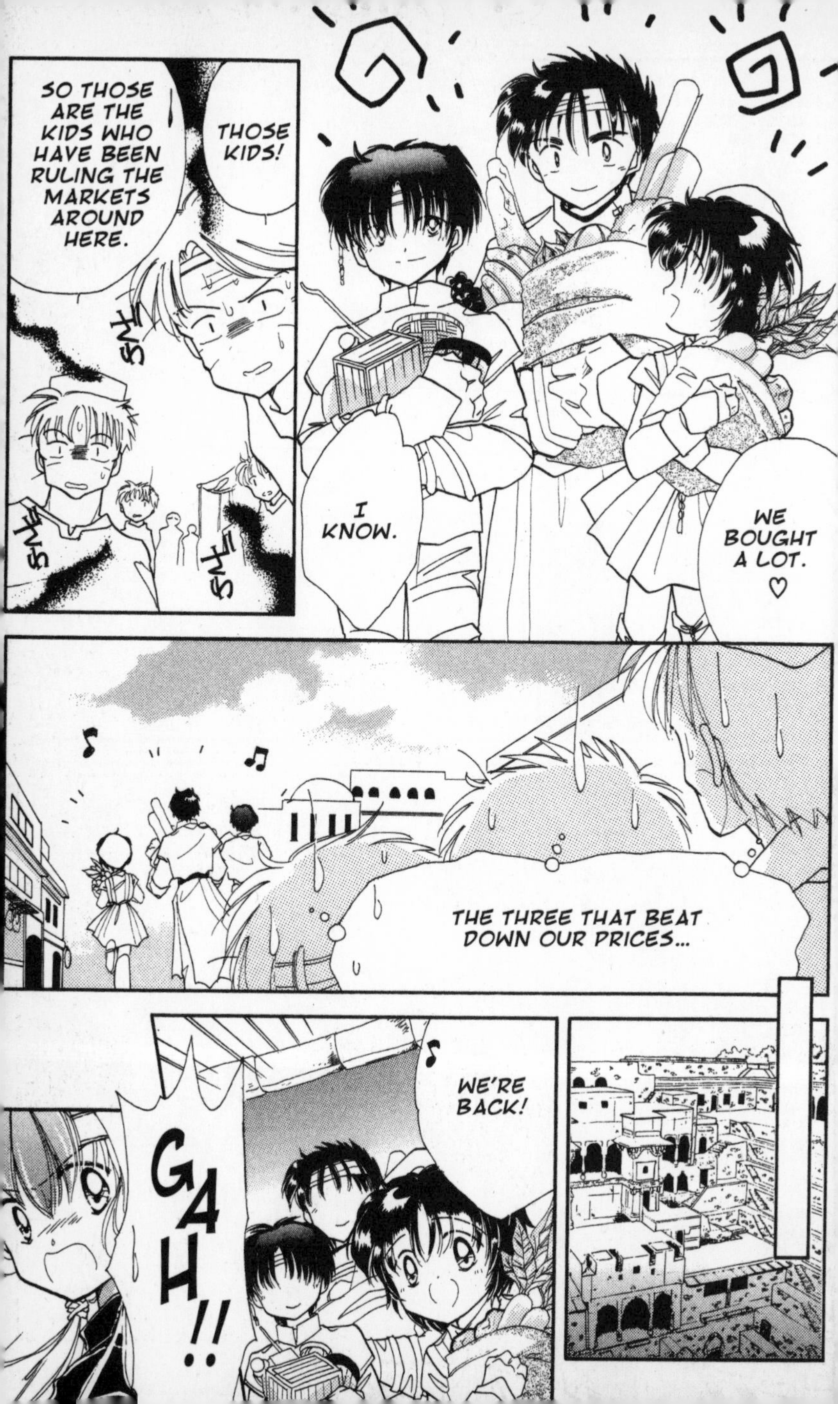
WE BOUGHT A LOT. ♡
I KNOW.
THOSE KIDS!
SO THOSE ARE THE KIDS WHO HAVE BEEN RULING THE MARKETS AROUND HERE.
THE THREE THAT BEAT DOWN OUR PRICES...
WE'RE BACK!
GAH!!

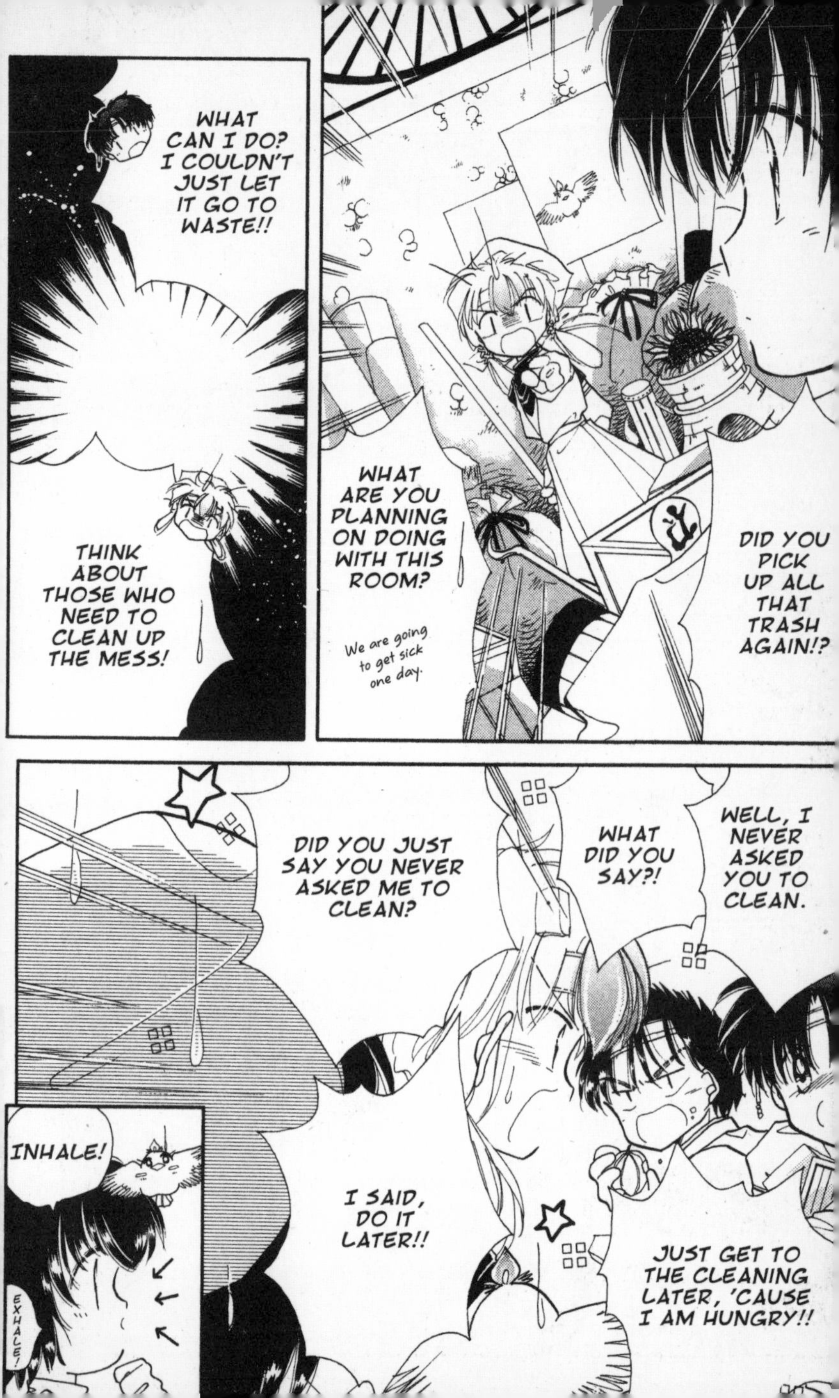
DID YOU PICK UP ALL THAT TRASH AGAIN!?
WHAT ARE YOU PLANNING ON DOING WITH THIS ROOM?
We are going to get sick one day.
WHAT CAN I DO? I COULDN'T JUST LET IT GO TO WASTE!!
THINK ABOUT THOSE WHO NEED TO CLEAN UP THE MESS!
WELL, I NEVER ASKED YOU TO CLEAN.
WHAT DID YOU SAY?!
DID YOU JUST SAY YOU NEVER ASKED ME TO CLEAN?
JUST GET TO THE CLEANING LATER, 'CAUSE I AM HUNGRY!!
I SAID, DO IT LATER!!
INHALE!
EXHALE!

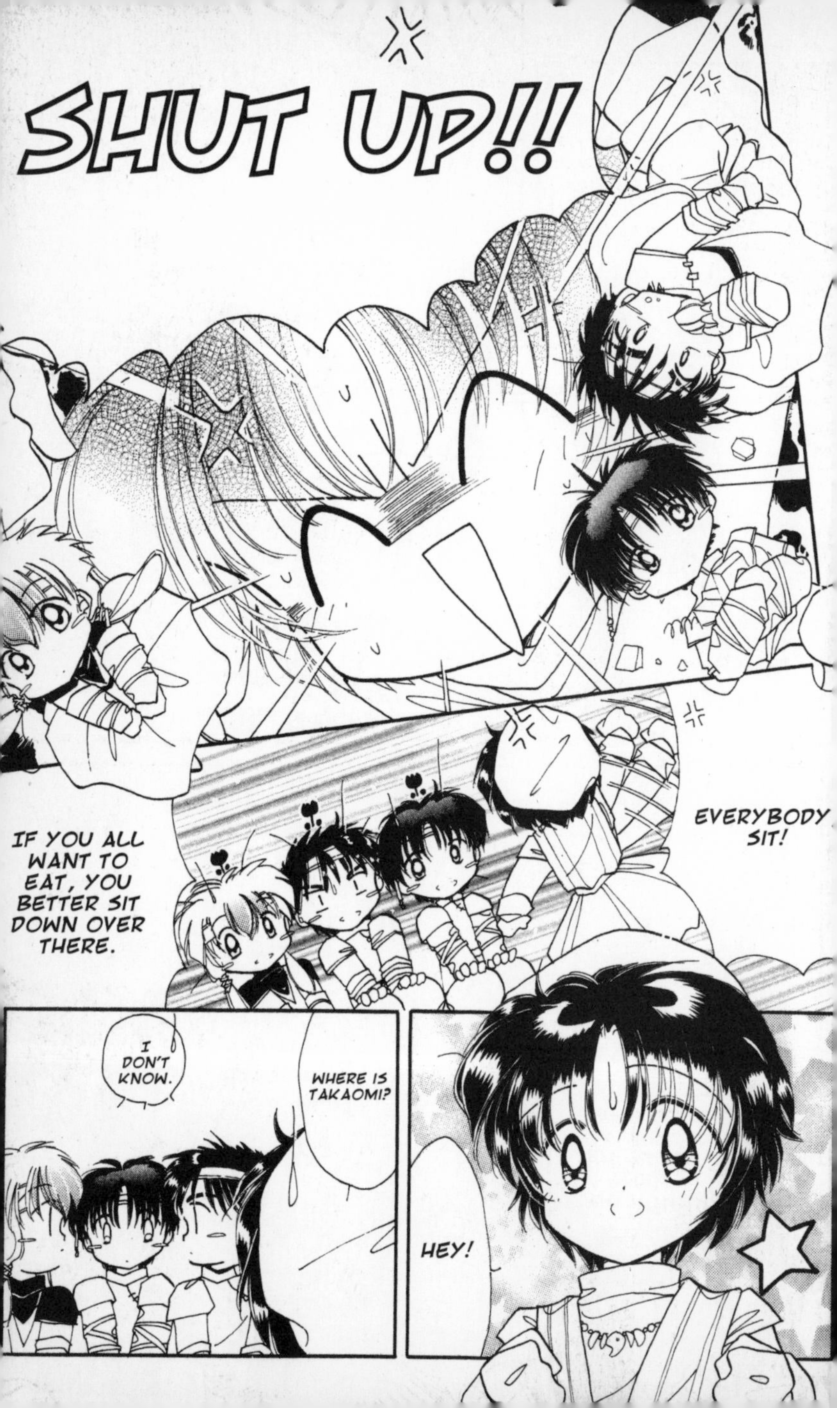
SHUT UP!!
EVERYBODY SIT!
IF YOU ALL WANT TO EAT, YOU BETTER SIT DOWN OVER THERE.
HEY!
WHERE IS TAKAOMI?
I DON'T KNOW.

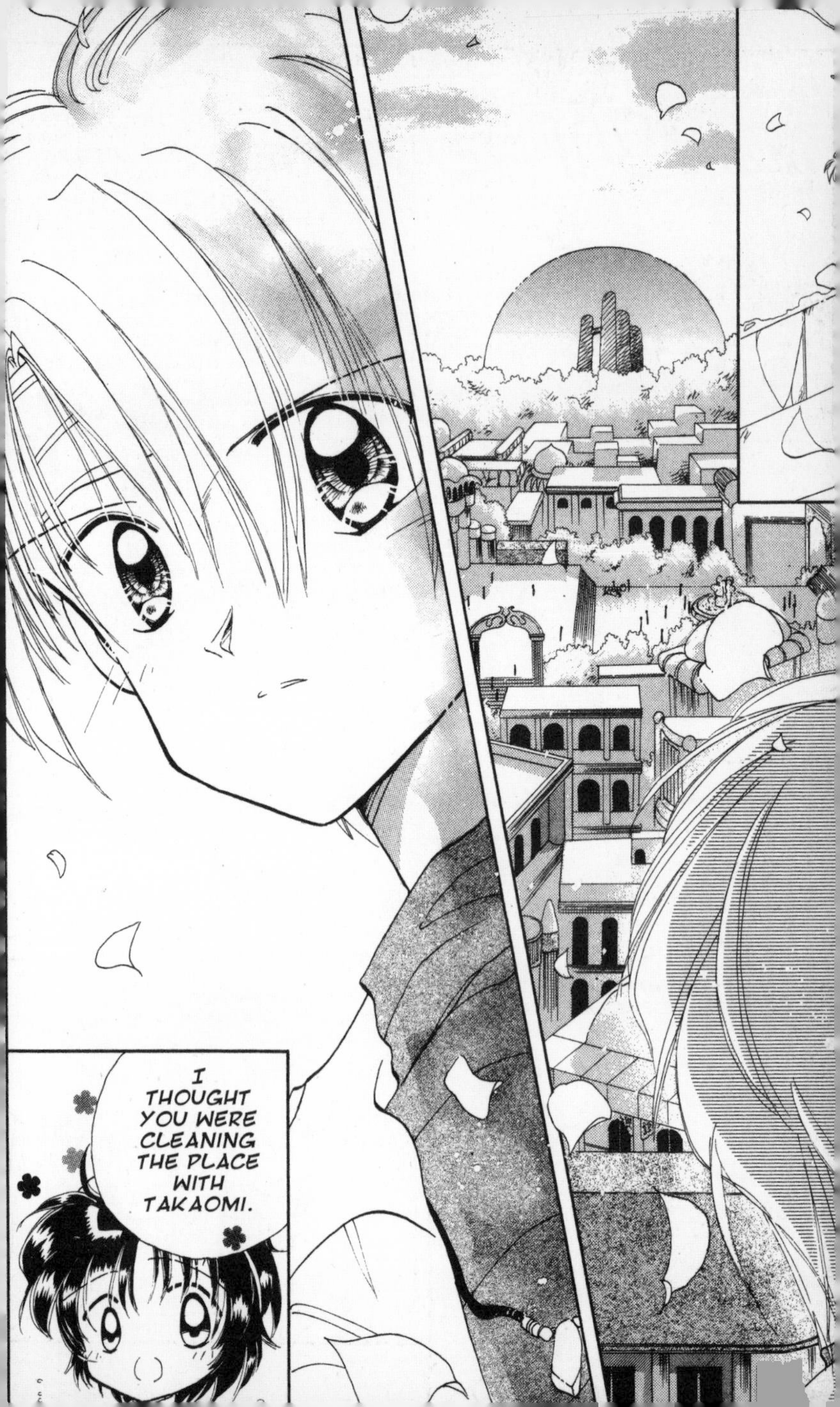
I THOUGHT YOU WERE CLEANING THE PLACE WITH TAKAOMI.

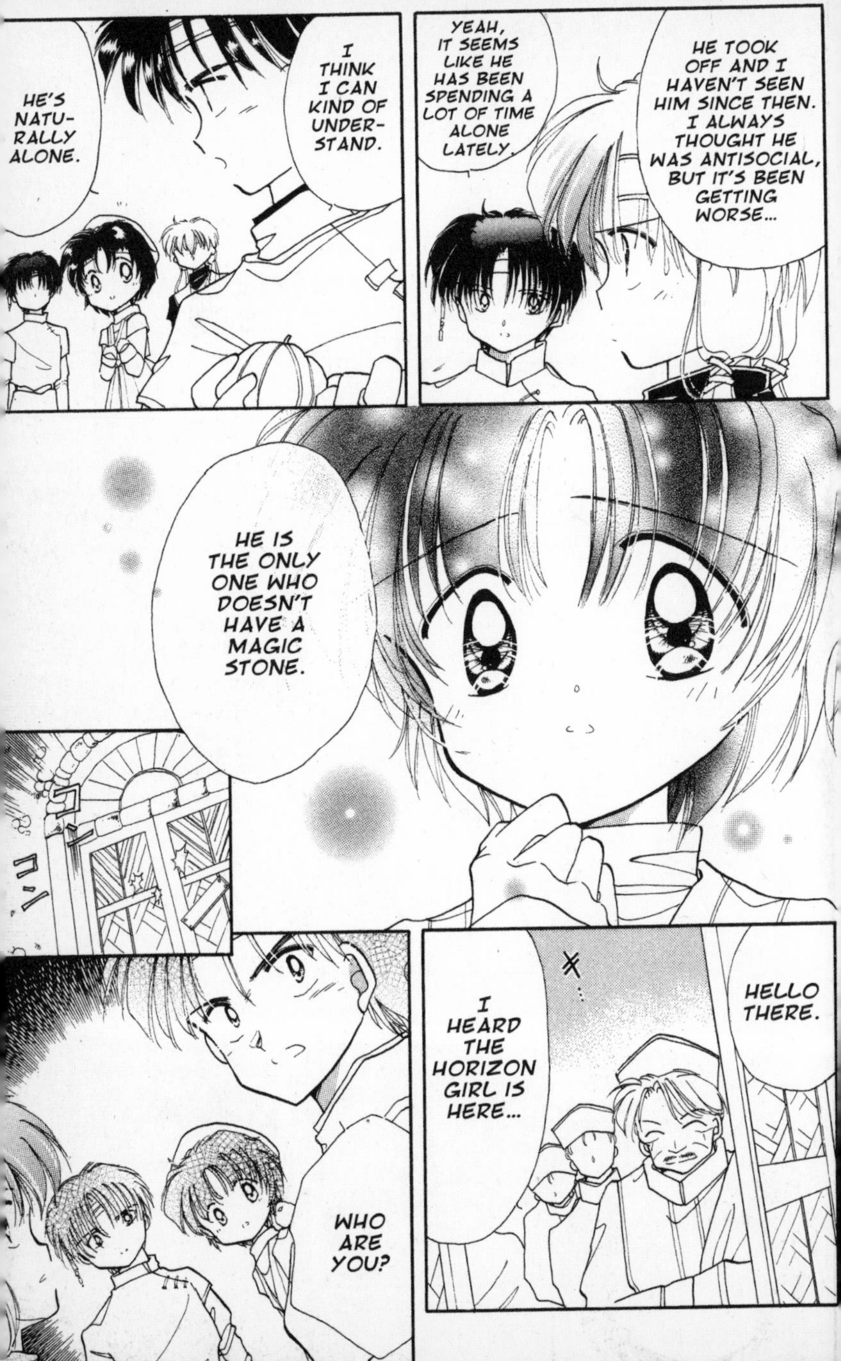

HE TOOK OFF AND I HAVEN'T SEEN HIM SINCE THEN. I ALWAYS THOUGHT HE WAS ANTISOCIAL, BUT IT'S BEEN GETTING WORSE...
YEAH, IT SEEMS LIKE HE HAS BEEN SPENDING A LOT OF TIME ALONE LATELY.
I THINK I CAN KIND OF UNDER-STAND.
HE'S NATU-RALLY ALONE.
HE IS THE ONLY ONE WHO DOESN'T HAVE A MAGIC STONE.
HELLO THERE.
I HEARD THE HORIZON GIRL IS HERE...
WHO ARE YOU?

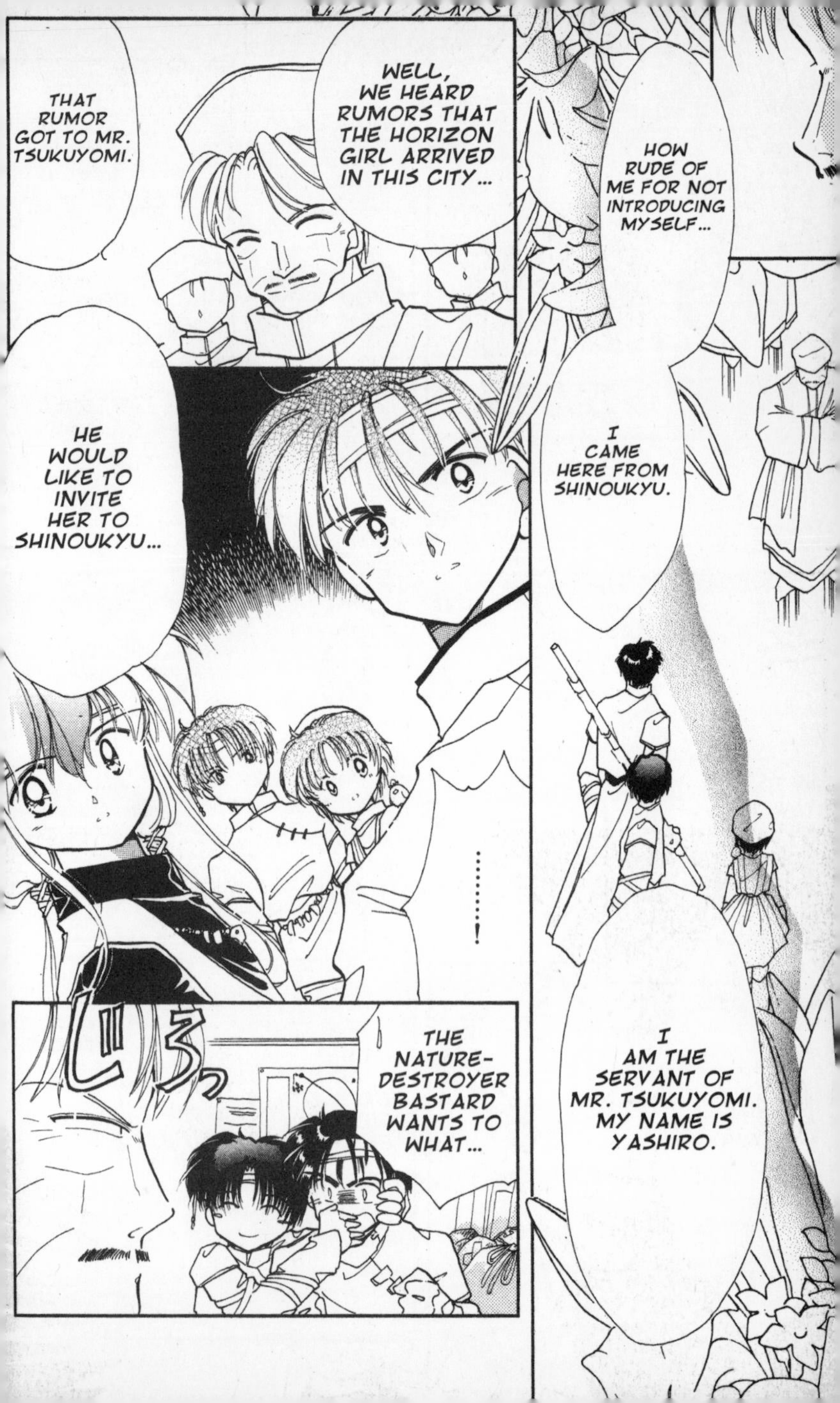

HOW RUDE OF ME FOR NOT INTRODUCING MYSELF...
I CAME HERE FROM SHINOUKYU.
I AM THE SERVANT OF MR. TSUKUYOMI. MY NAME IS YASHIRO.
WELL, WE HEARD RUMORS THAT THE HORIZON GIRL ARRIVED IN THIS CITY...
THAT RUMOR GOT TO MR. TSUKUYOMI.
HE WOULD LIKE TO INVITE HER TO SHINOUKYU...
......!
THE NATURE-DESTROYER BASTARD WANTS TO WHAT...

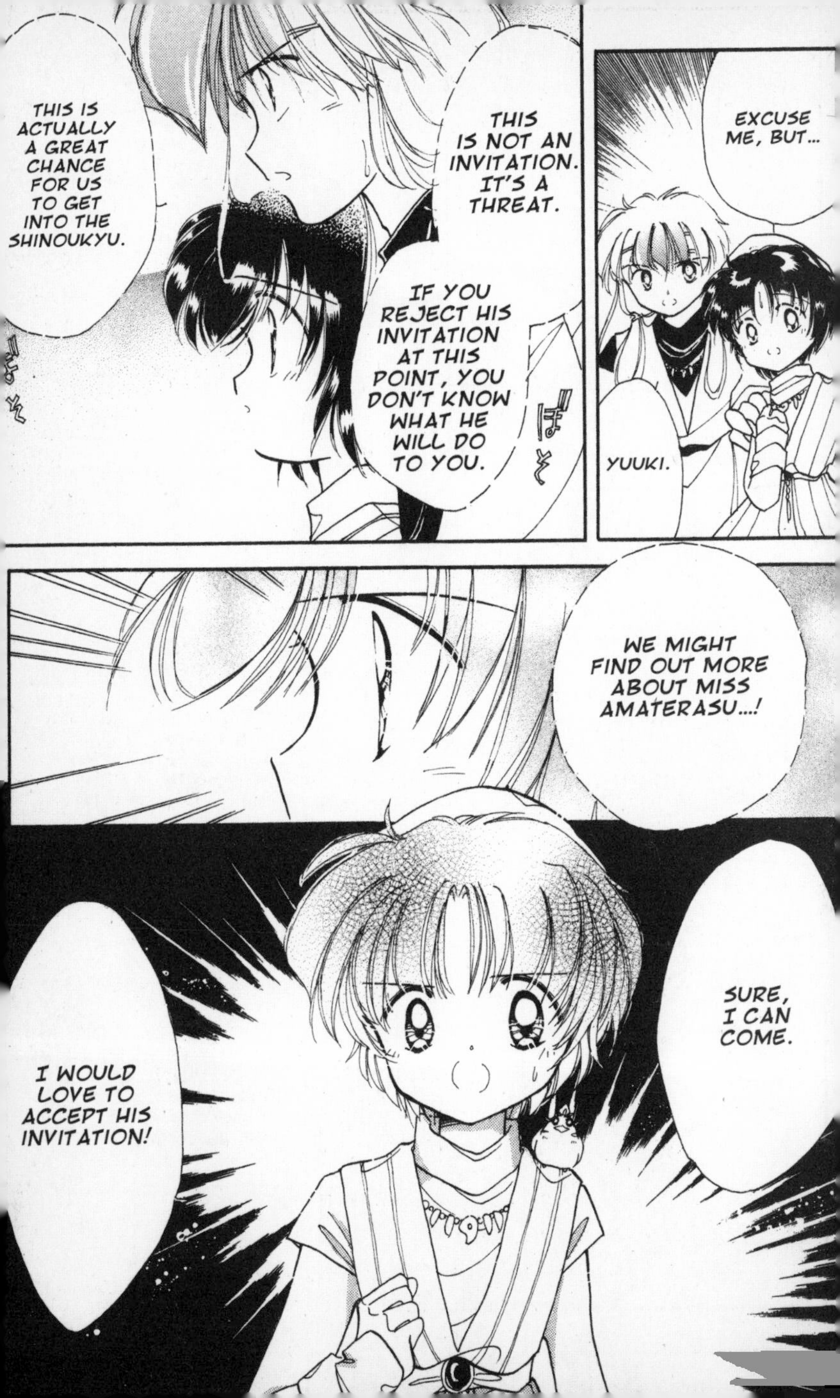
EXCUSE ME, BUT...
YUUKI.
THIS IS NOT AN INVITATION. IT'S A THREAT.
IF YOU REJECT HIS INVITATION AT THIS POINT, YOU DON'T KNOW WHAT HE WILL DO TO YOU.
THIS IS ACTUALLY A GREAT CHANCE FOR US TO GET INTO THE SHINOUKYU.
WE MIGHT FIND OUT MORE ABOUT MISS AMATERASU...!
SURE, I CAN COME.
I WOULD LOVE TO ACCEPT HIS INVITATION!

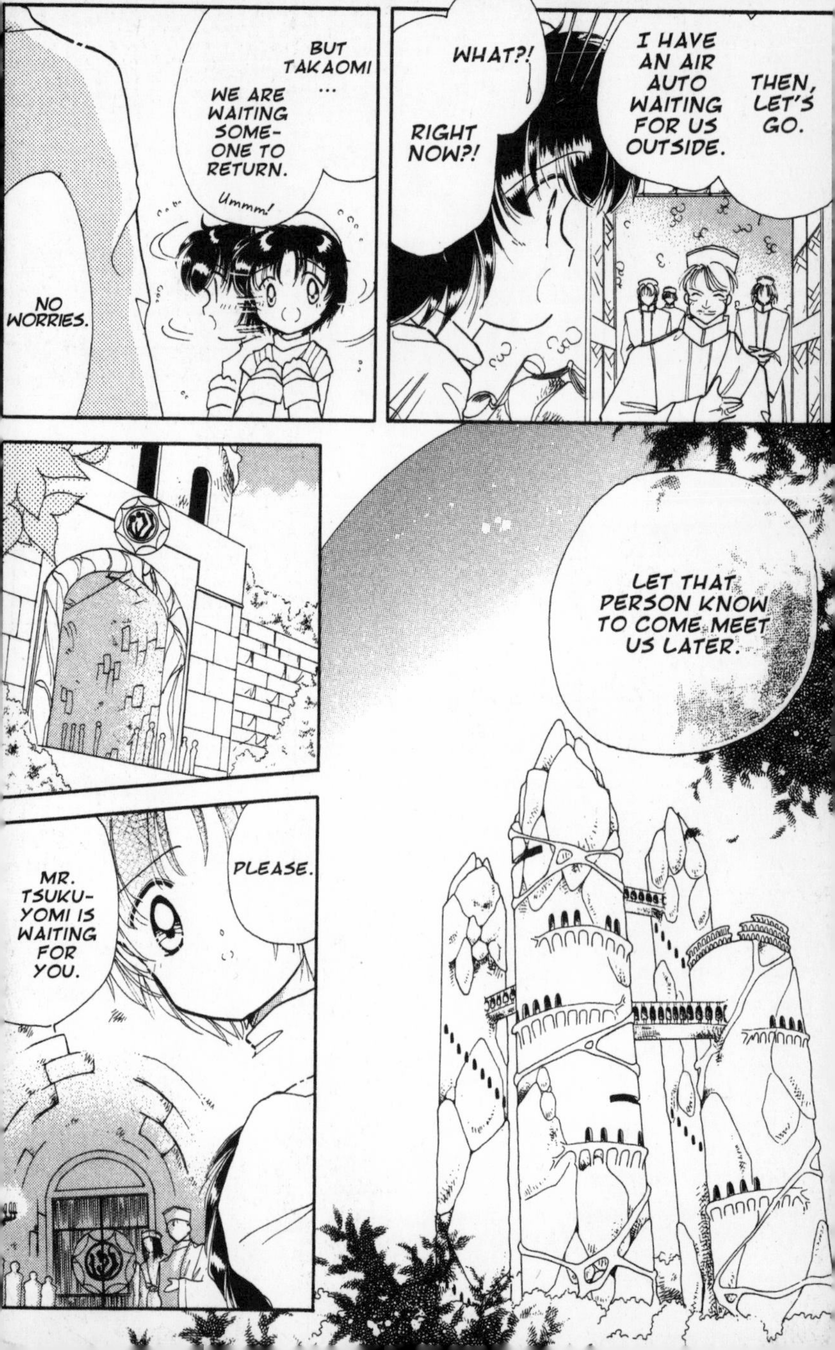
THEN, LET'S GO.
I HAVE AN AIR AUTO WAITING FOR US OUTSIDE.
WHAT?!
RIGHT NOW?!
BUT TAKAOMI ...
WE ARE WAITING SOME-ONE TO RETURN.
Ummm!
NO WORRIES.
LET THAT PERSON KNOW TO COME MEET US LATER.
PLEASE.
MR. TSUKU-YOMI IS WAITING FOR YOU.

TAKAOMI.

COME QUICKLY...

は っ

・・・・・

・・!!

WHO IS IT...?

!

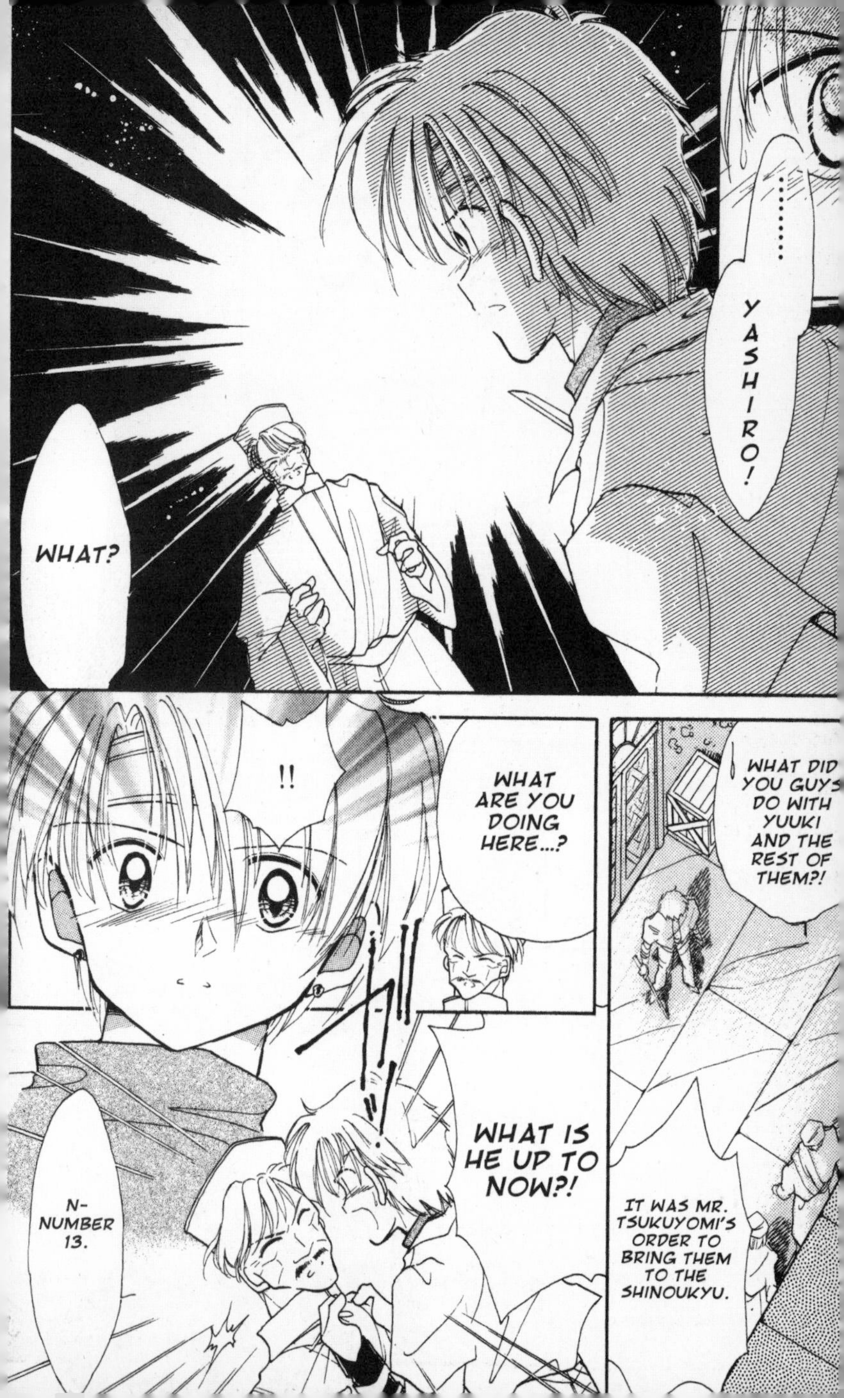
......YASHIRO!
WHAT?
WHAT DID YOU GUYS DO WITH YUUKI AND THE REST OF THEM?!
IT WAS MR. TSUKUYOMI'S ORDER TO BRING THEM TO THE SHINOUKYU.
WHAT ARE YOU DOING HERE...?
!!
WHAT IS HE UP TO NOW?!
N- NUMBER 13.

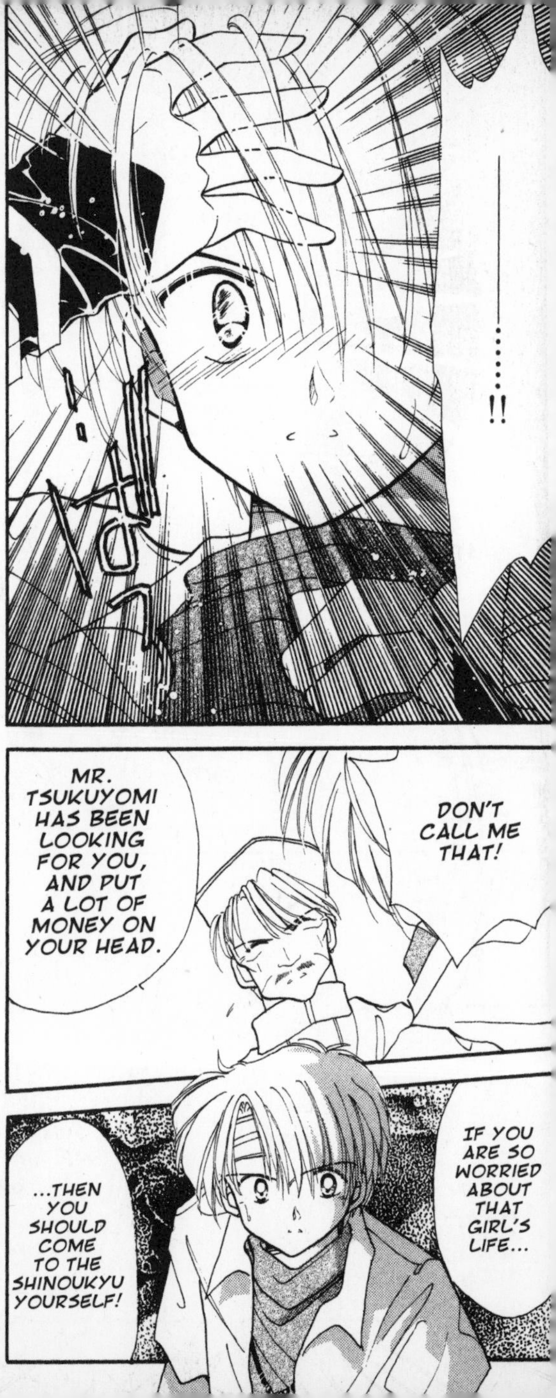
......!!
DON'T CALL ME THAT!
MR. TSUKUYOMI HAS BEEN LOOKING FOR YOU, AND PUT A LOT OF MONEY ON YOUR HEAD.
IF YOU ARE SO WORRIED ABOUT THAT GIRL'S LIFE...
...THEN YOU SHOULD COME TO THE SHINOUKYU YOURSELF!

his time's BGM.

Aovin on" by Favorite Blue

Escape" by Moon Child

Calling" by B'z

Let's Dance in a Circle" by V6

Forever" by Zard

Mr. Lonely" by Kouji Tamaki

Everything will be Okay"

y Touko Furuuchi

Sythia" by Tomoyo Harada

There is Something I Want to

Tell You" by Kazumasa Oda

"Smiling" by Noriyuki Makihara

"Realize" by Rie Ohashi

"Un" by Rie Tomosaka

"Hybrid" by Curio

"Moon," "Real Time," and

"Guitar Land" by Michiya Haruhata

"Zard Blend - Sun & Stone" by Zard

"Wool" by Smap

I liked Haruhata's songs the best.

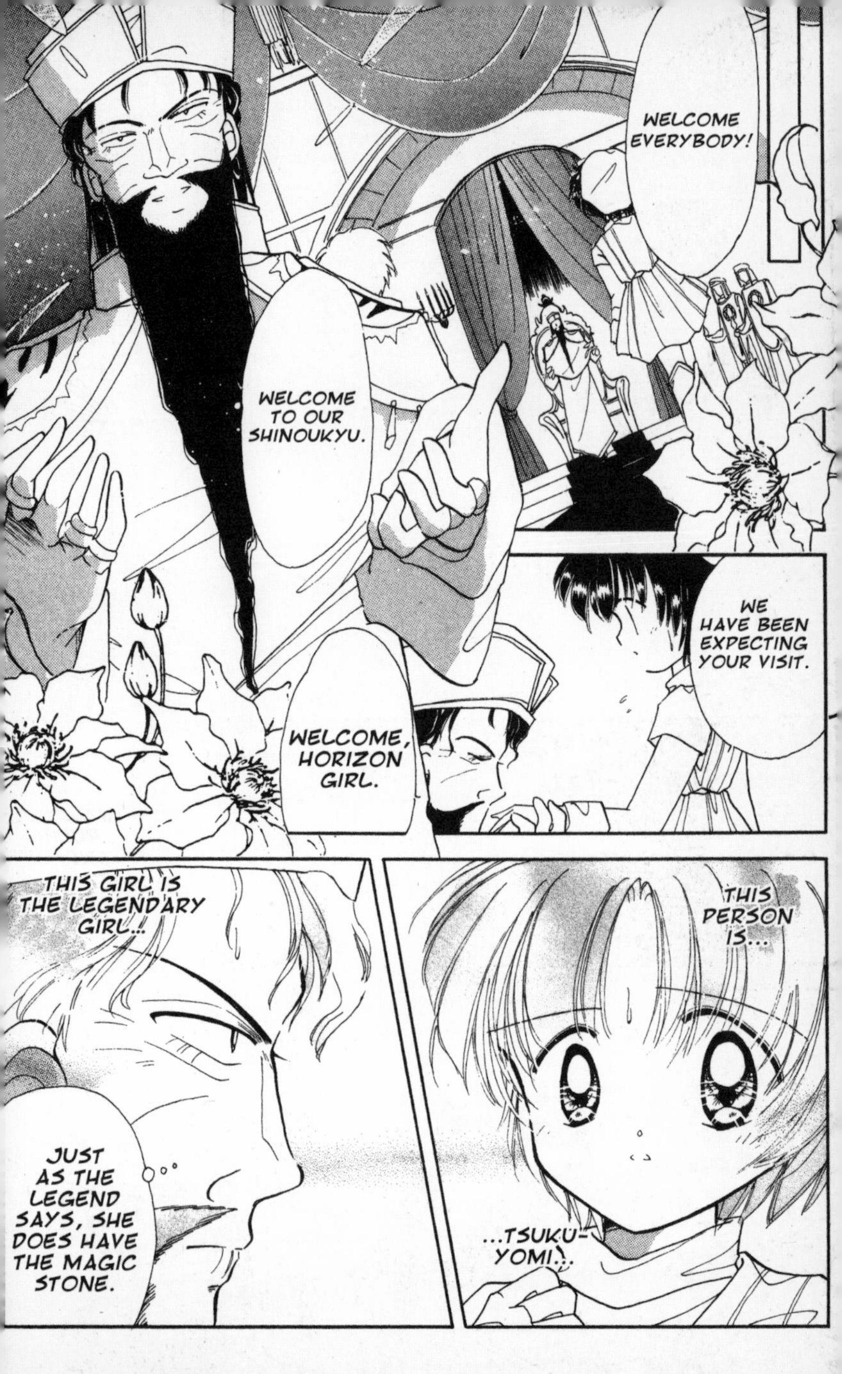
WELCOME EVERYBODY!
WE HAVE BEEN EXPECTING YOUR VISIT.
WELCOME TO OUR SHINOUKYU.
WELCOME, HORIZON GIRL.
THIS PERSON IS...
...TSUKU-YOMI...
THIS GIRL IS THE LEGENDARY GIRL...
JUST AS THE LEGEND SAYS, SHE DOES HAVE THE MAGIC STONE.

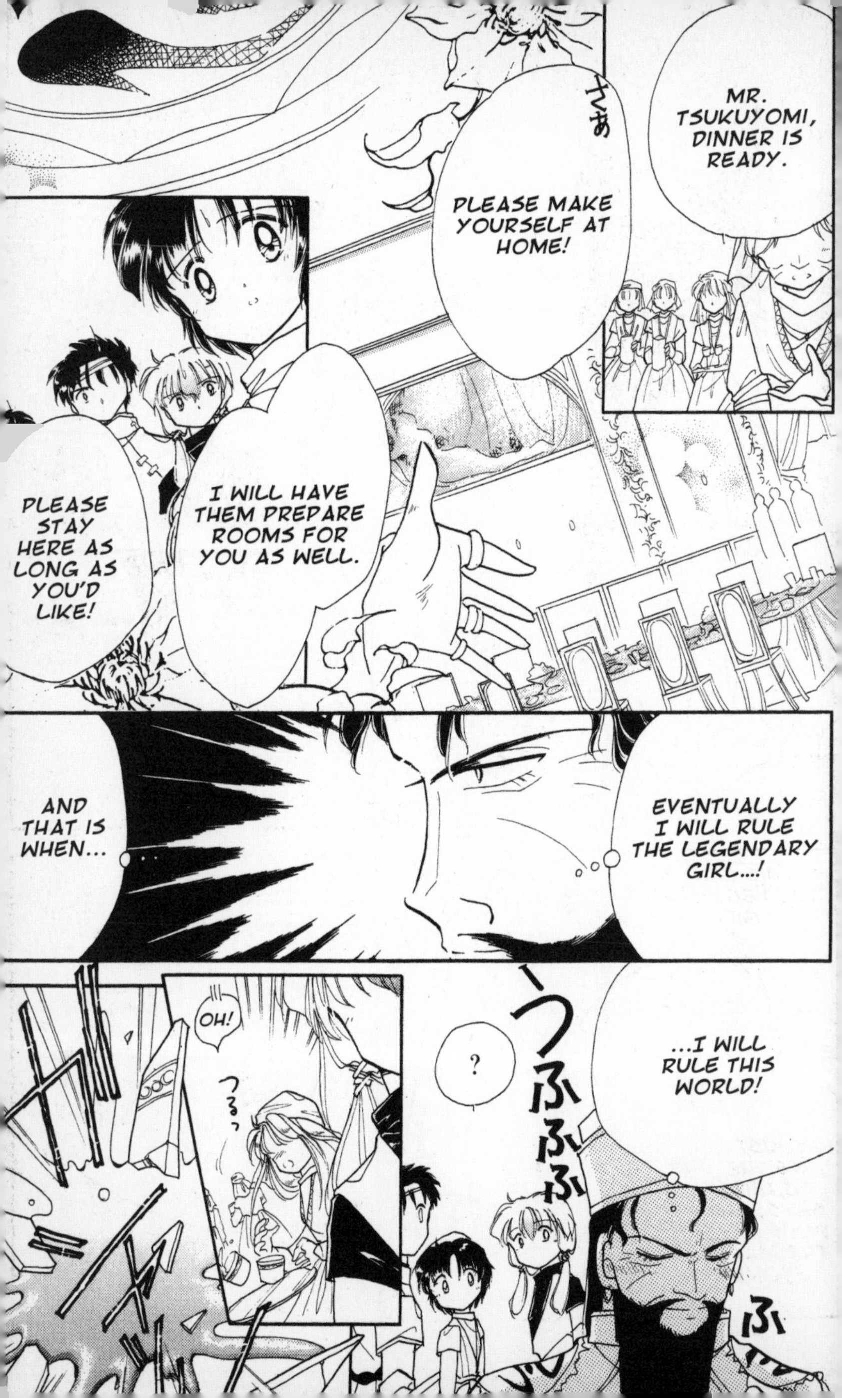

MR. TSUKUYOMI, DINNER IS READY.
さぁ
PLEASE MAKE YOURSELF AT HOME!
I WILL HAVE THEM PREPARE ROOMS FOR YOU AS WELL.
PLEASE STAY HERE AS LONG AS YOU'D LIKE!
EVENTUALLY I WILL RULE THE LEGENDARY GIRL...!
AND THAT IS WHEN...
...I WILL RULE THIS WORLD!
うふふふ
ふ
?
OH!
つるっ

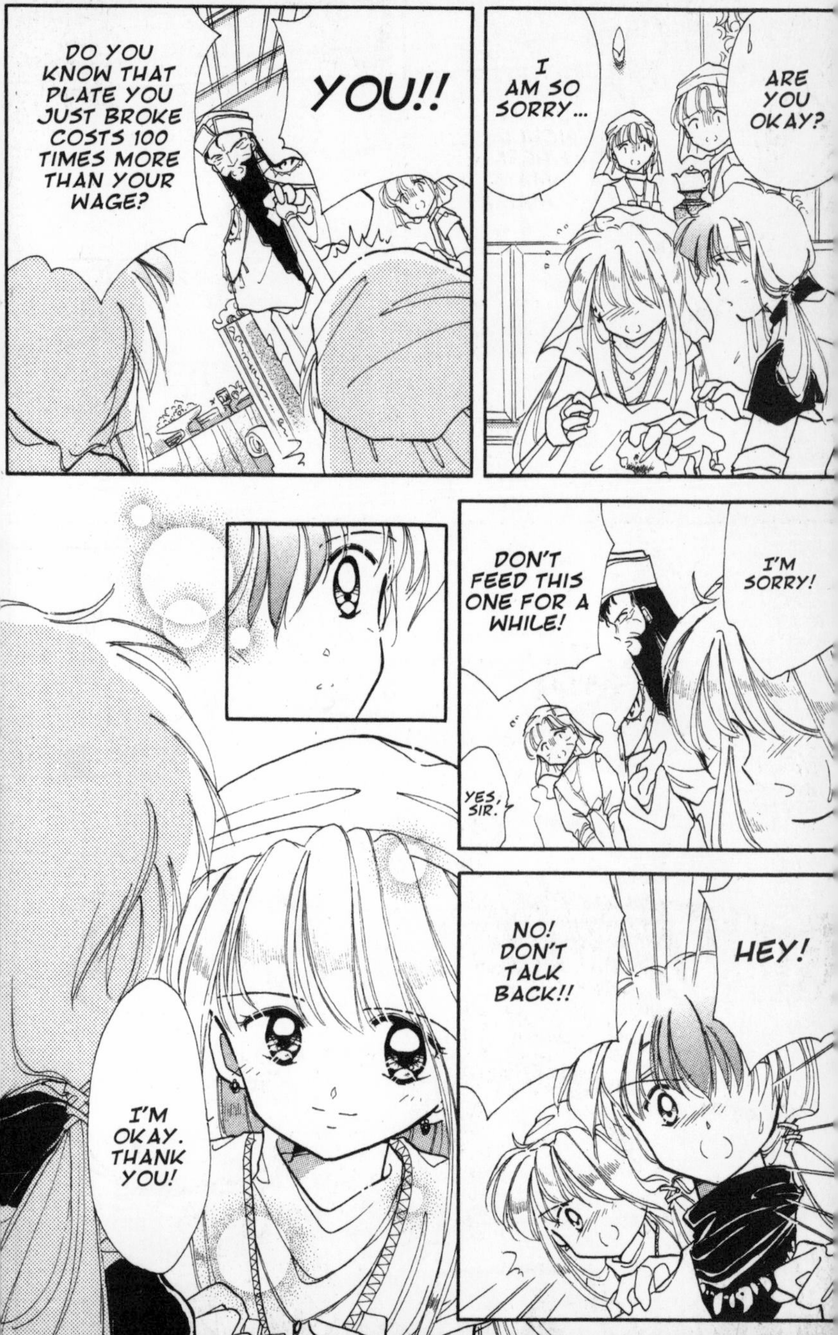
ARE YOU OKAY?
I AM SO SORRY...
YOU!!
DO YOU KNOW THAT PLATE YOU JUST BROKE COSTS 100 TIMES MORE THAN YOUR WAGE?
I'M SORRY!
DON'T FEED THIS ONE FOR A WHILE!
YES, SIR.
HEY!
NO! DON'T TALK BACK!!
I'M OKAY. THANK YOU!

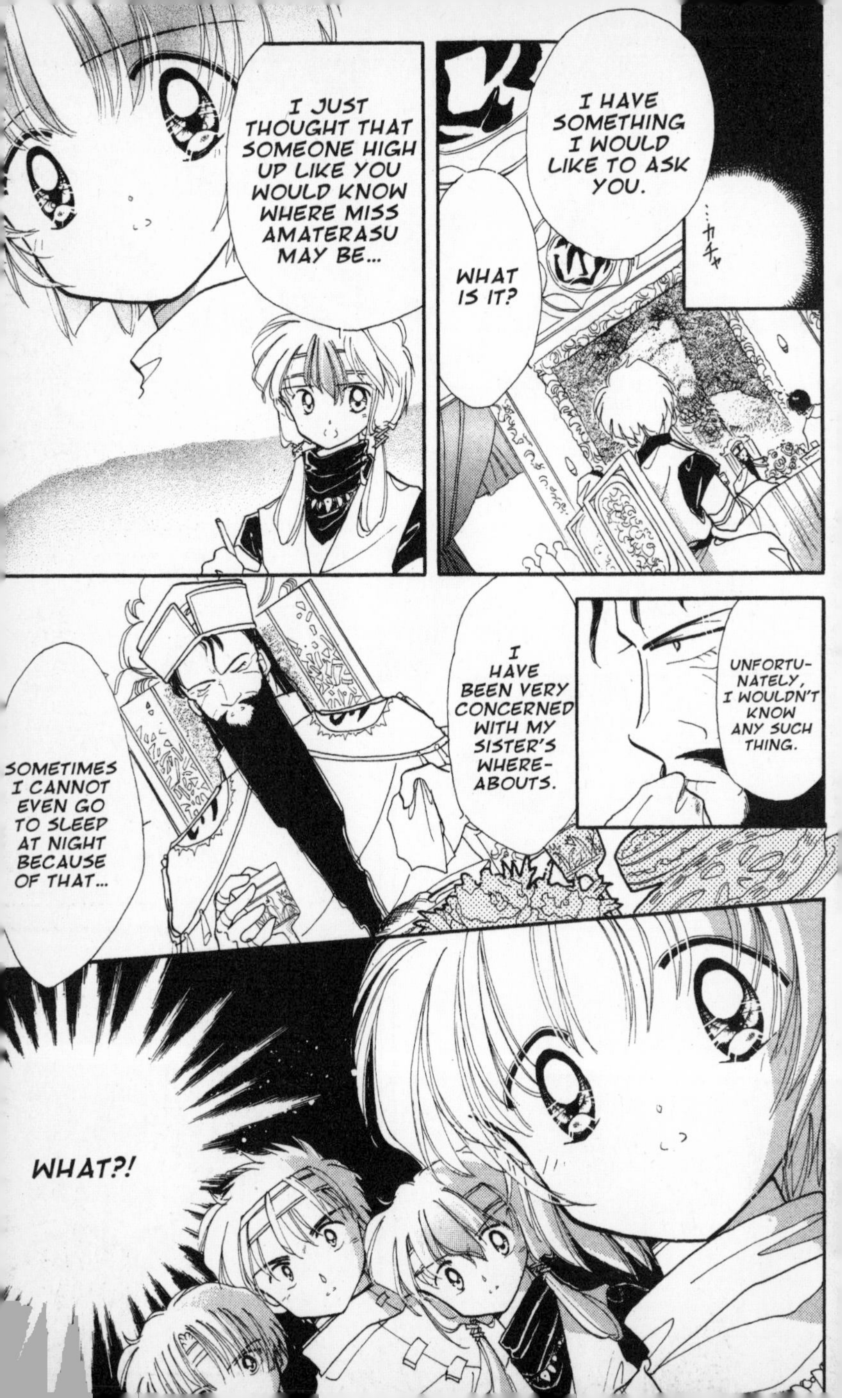
…カチャ
I HAVE SOMETHING I WOULD LIKE TO ASK YOU.
WHAT IS IT?
I JUST THOUGHT THAT SOMEONE HIGH UP LIKE YOU WOULD KNOW WHERE MISS AMATERASU MAY BE...
UNFORTUNATELY, I WOULDN'T KNOW ANY SUCH THING.
I HAVE BEEN VERY CONCERNED WITH MY SISTER'S WHEREABOUTS.
SOMETIMES I CANNOT EVEN GO TO SLEEP AT NIGHT BECAUSE OF THAT...
WHAT?!

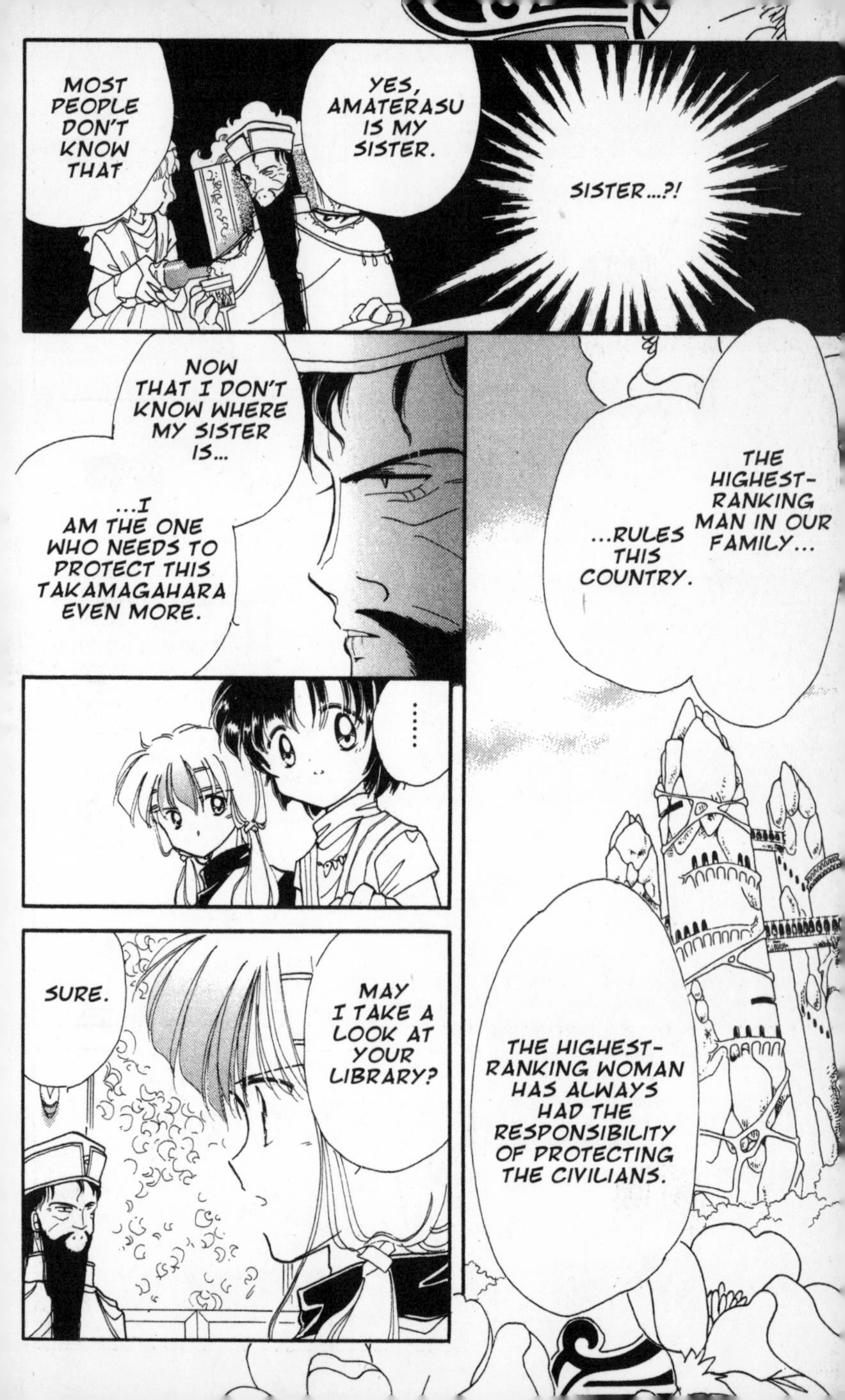
SISTER...?!
YES, AMATERASU IS MY SISTER.
MOST PEOPLE DON'T KNOW THAT
THE HIGHEST-RANKING MAN IN OUR FAMILY...
...RULES THIS COUNTRY.
THE HIGHEST-RANKING WOMAN HAS ALWAYS HAD THE RESPONSIBILITY OF PROTECTING THE CIVILIANS.
NOW THAT I DON'T KNOW WHERE MY SISTER IS...
...I AM THE ONE WHO NEEDS TO PROTECT THIS TAKAMAGAHARA EVEN MORE.
......
MAY I TAKE A LOOK AT YOUR LIBRARY?
SURE.

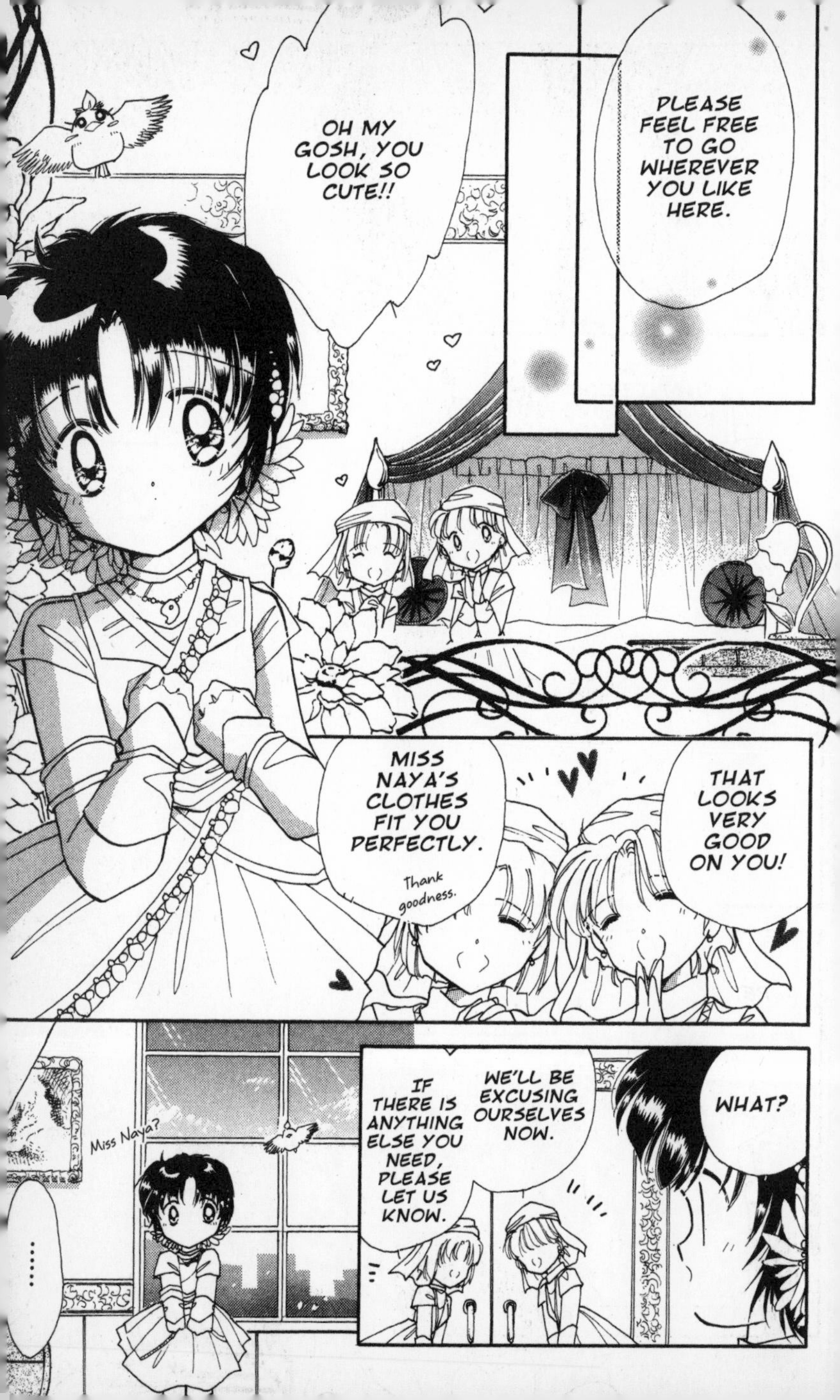
PLEASE FEEL FREE TO GO WHEREVER YOU LIKE HERE.
OH MY GOSH, YOU LOOK SO CUTE!!
THAT LOOKS VERY GOOD ON YOU!
MISS NAYA'S CLOTHES FIT YOU PERFECTLY.
Thank goodness.
WHAT?
WE'LL BE EXCUSING OURSELVES NOW.
IF THERE IS ANYTHING ELSE YOU NEED, PLEASE LET US KNOW.
Miss Naya?
......

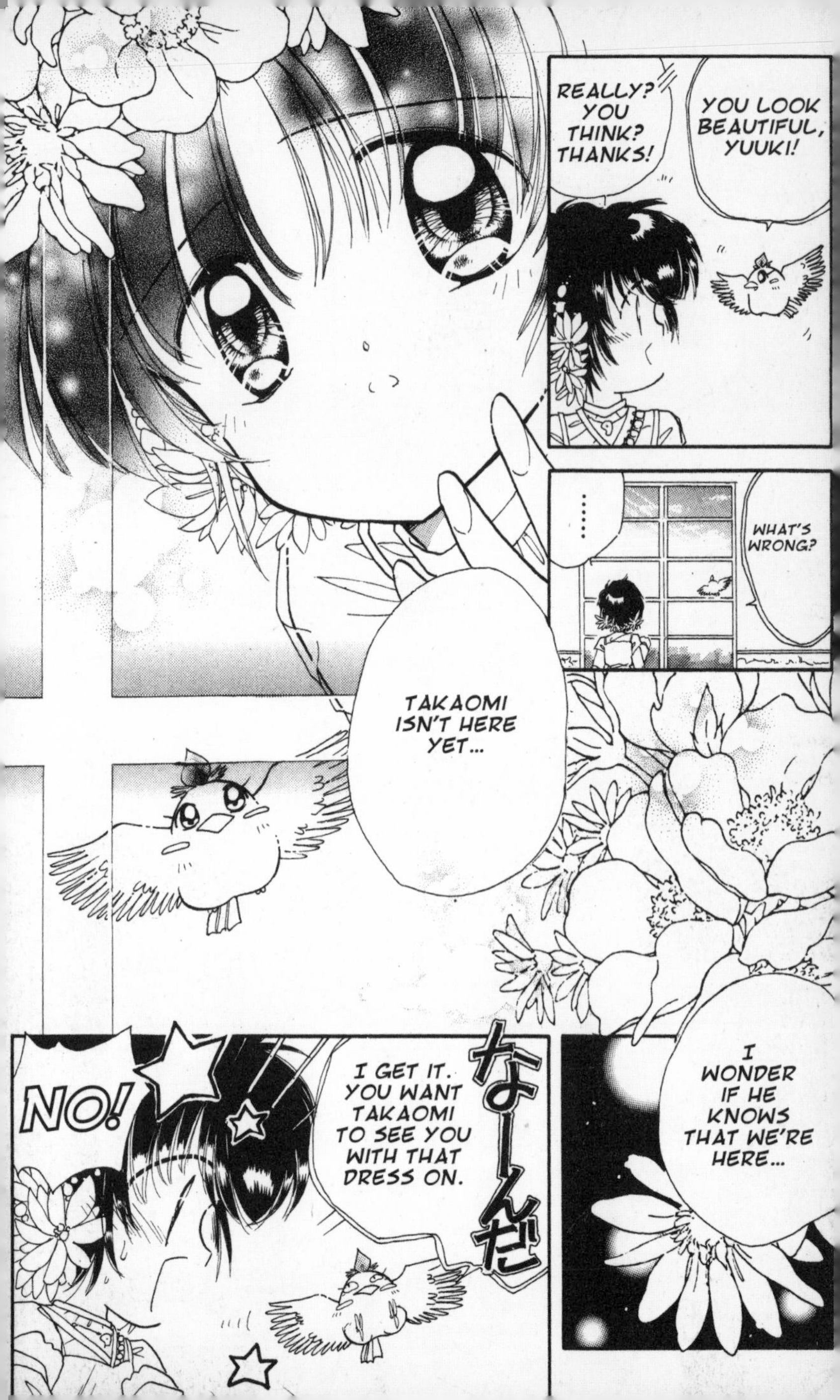
YOU LOOK BEAUTIFUL, YUUKI!
REALLY? YOU THINK? THANKS!
WHAT'S WRONG?
……
TAKAOMI ISN'T HERE YET...
I WONDER IF HE KNOWS THAT WE'RE HERE...
なーんだ
I GET IT. YOU WANT TAKAOMI TO SEE YOU WITH THAT DRESS ON.
NO!

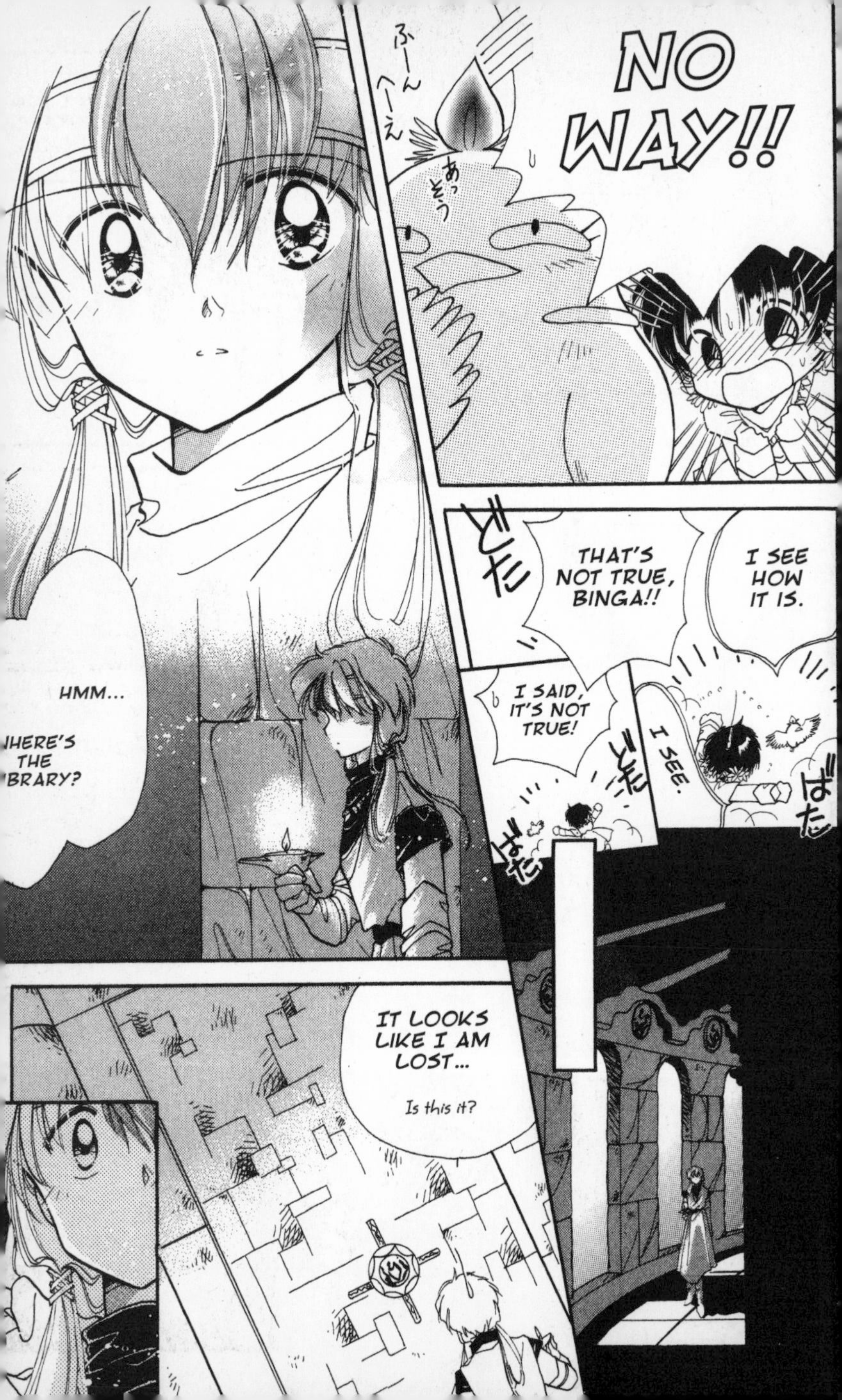

NO WAY!!
ふーん
へーえ
あっそう
I SEE HOW IT IS.
THAT'S NOT TRUE, BINGA!!
ばた
I SEE.
I SAID, IT'S NOT TRUE!
HMM...
HERE'S THE BRARY?
IT LOOKS LIKE I AM LOST...
Is this it?

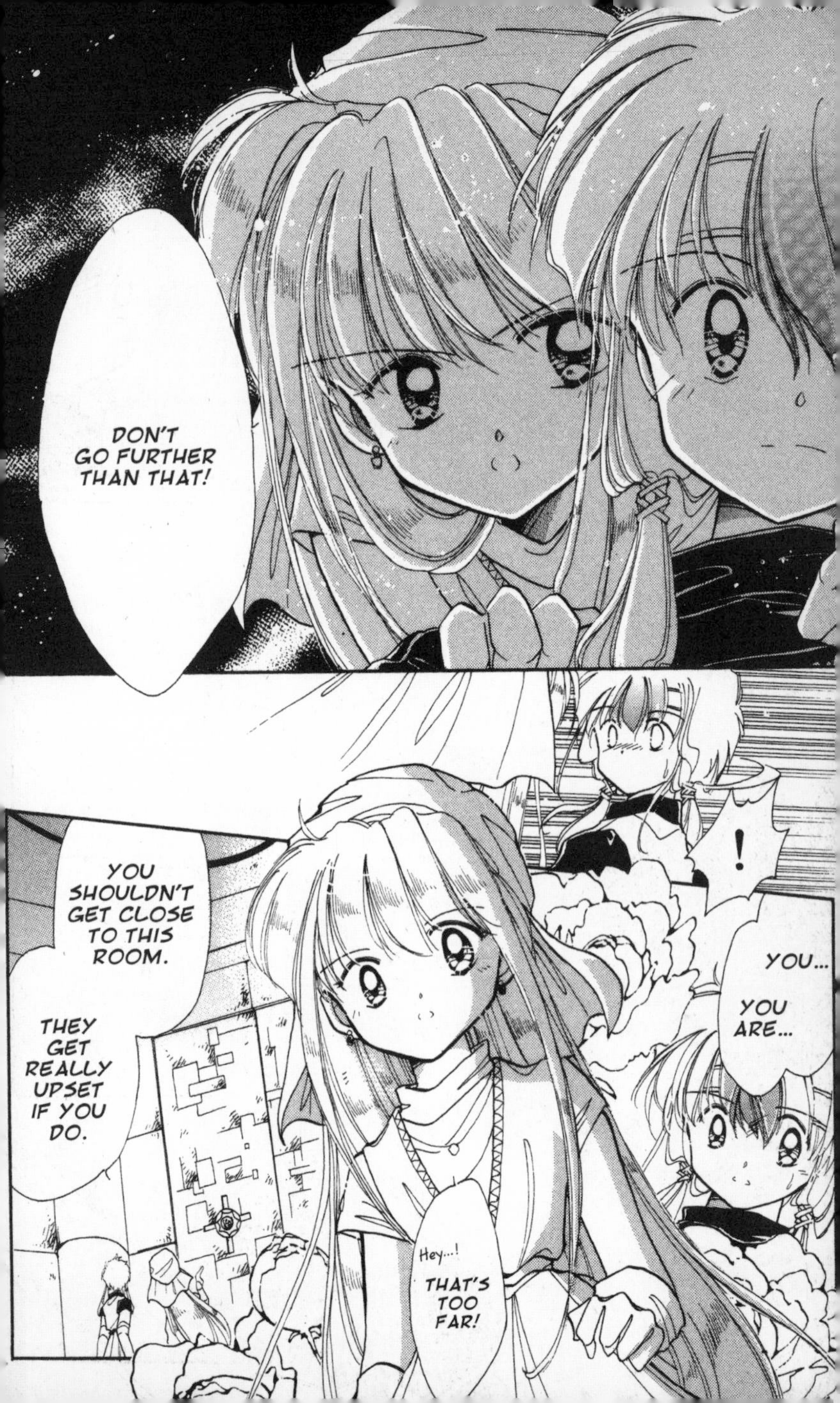
DON'T GO FURTHER THAN THAT!
!
YOU...
YOU ARE...
Hey...!
THAT'S TOO FAR!
YOU SHOULDN'T GET CLOSE TO THIS ROOM.
THEY GET REALLY UPSET IF YOU DO.

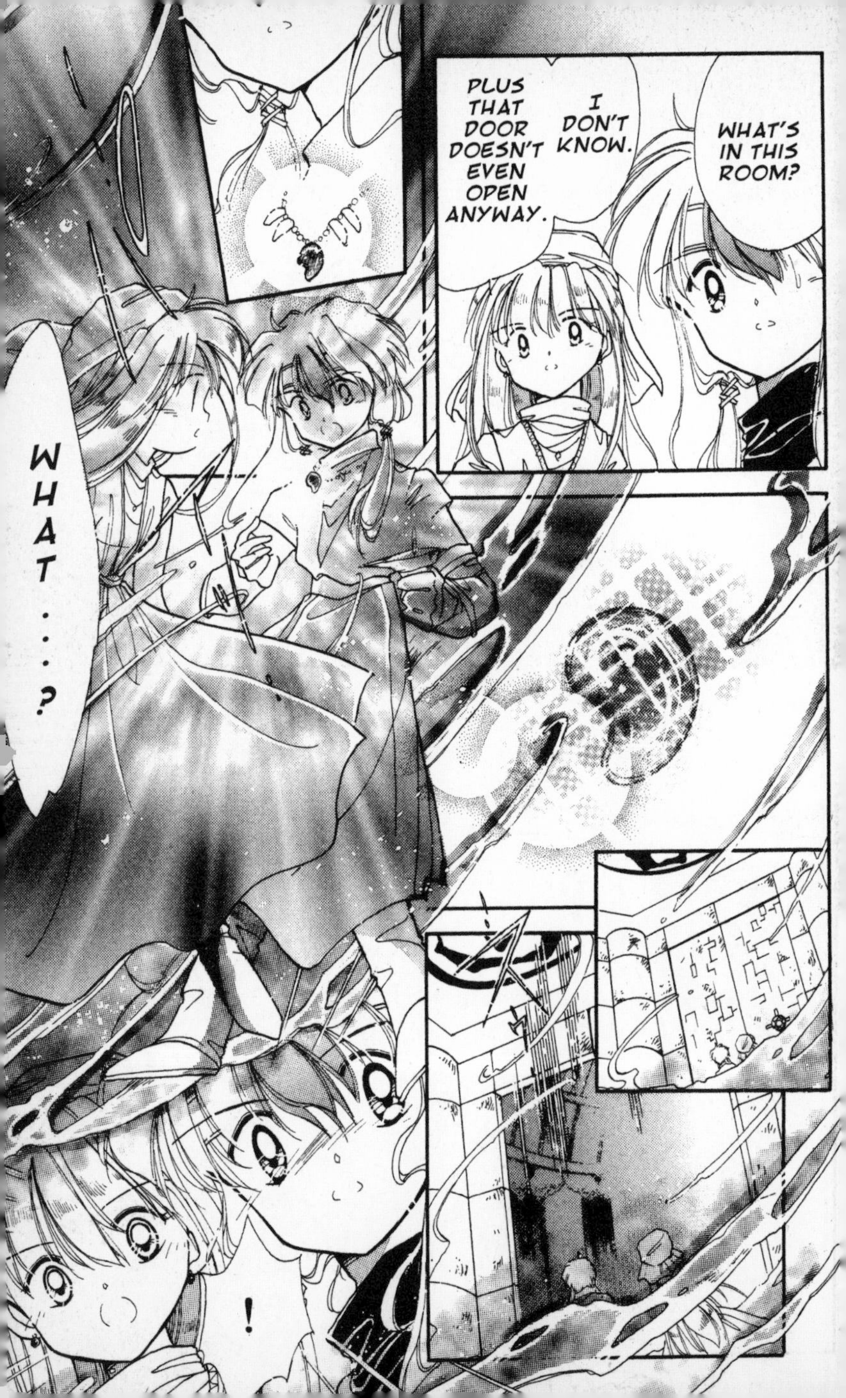
WHAT'S IN THIS ROOM?
I DON'T KNOW.
PLUS THAT DOOR DOESN'T EVEN OPEN ANYWAY.
WHAT...?
!

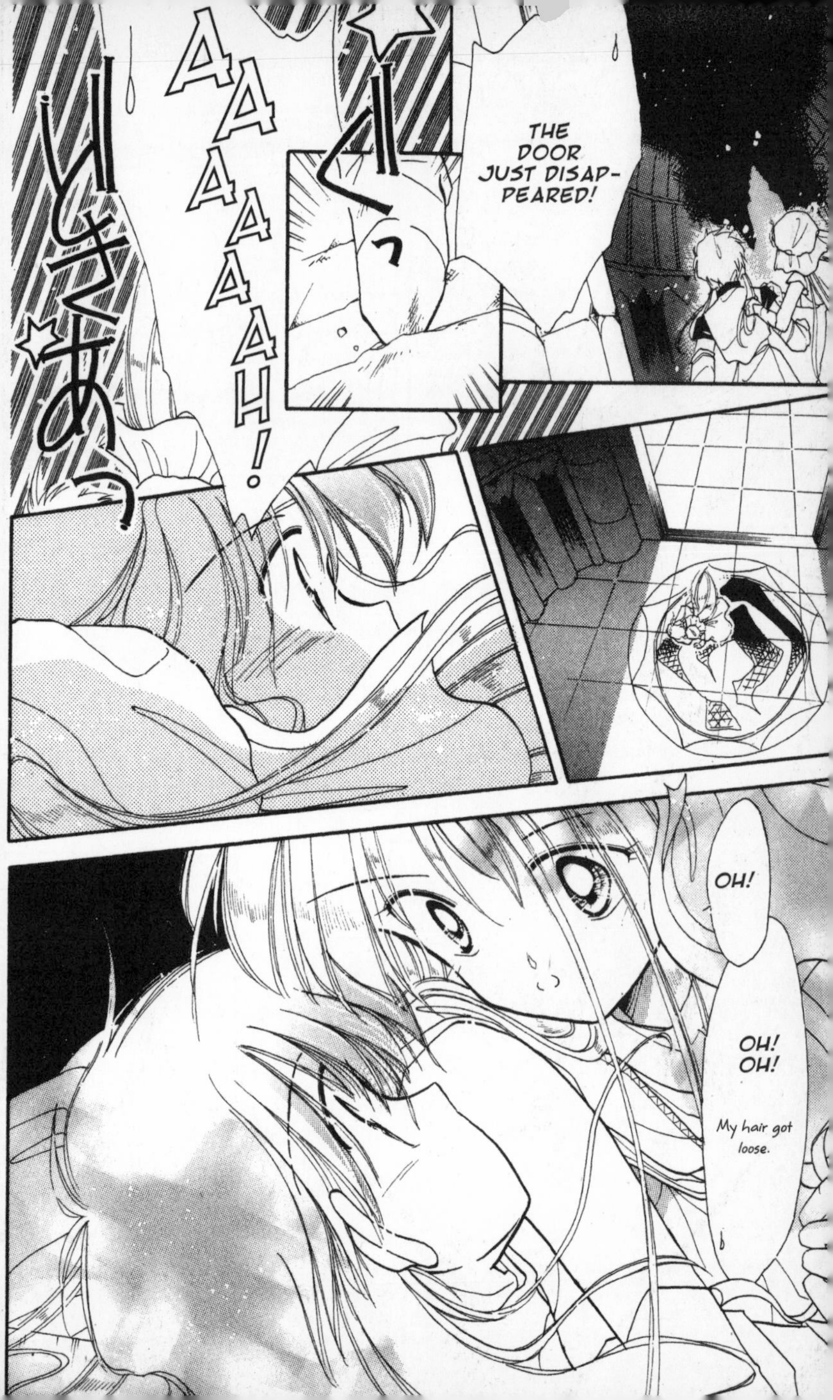
THE DOOR JUST DISAPPEARED!
AAAAAAH!
OH!
OH! OH!
My hair got loose.

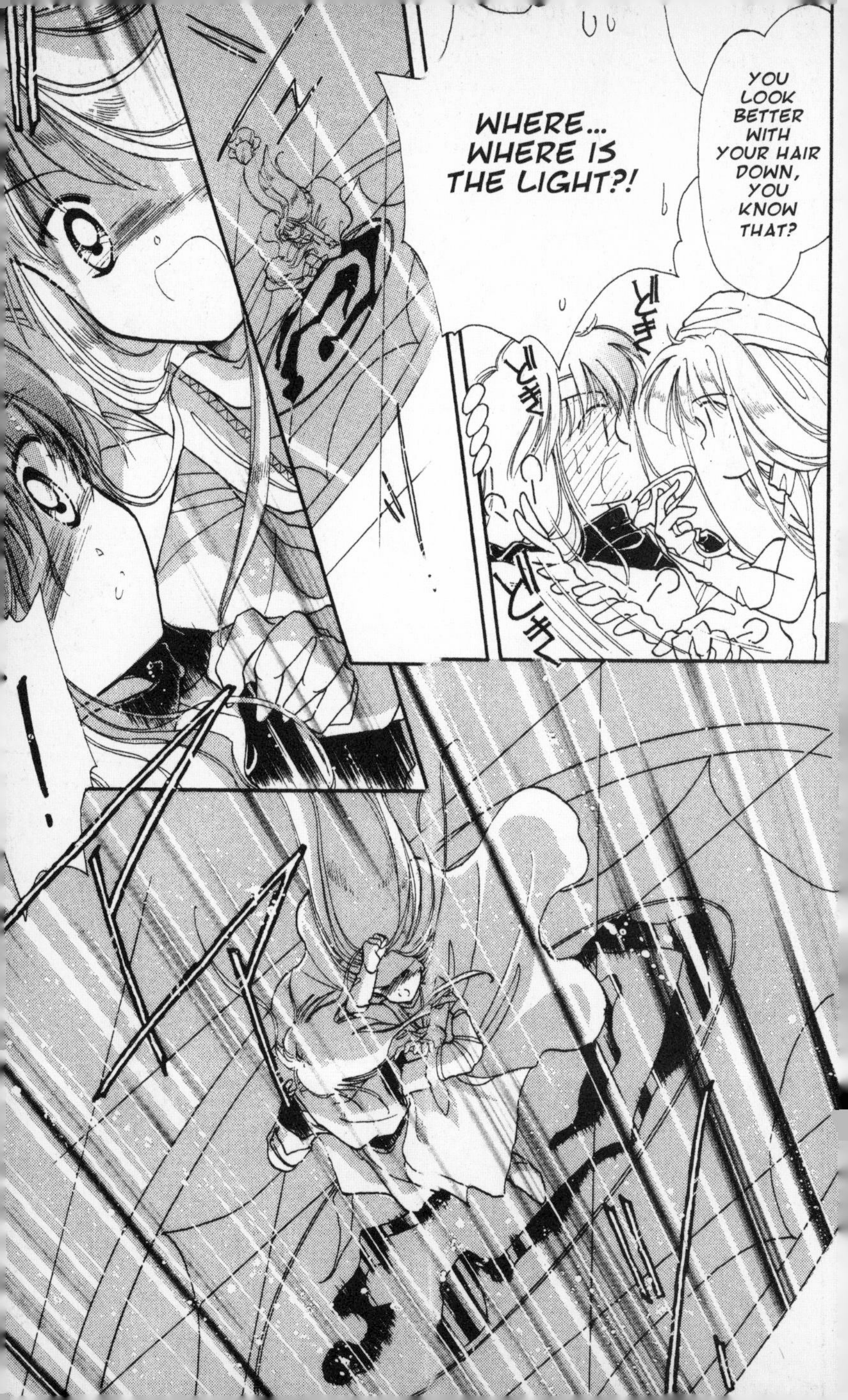
YOU LOOK BETTER WITH YOUR HAIR DOWN, YOU KNOW THAT?
WHERE... WHERE IS THE LIGHT?!

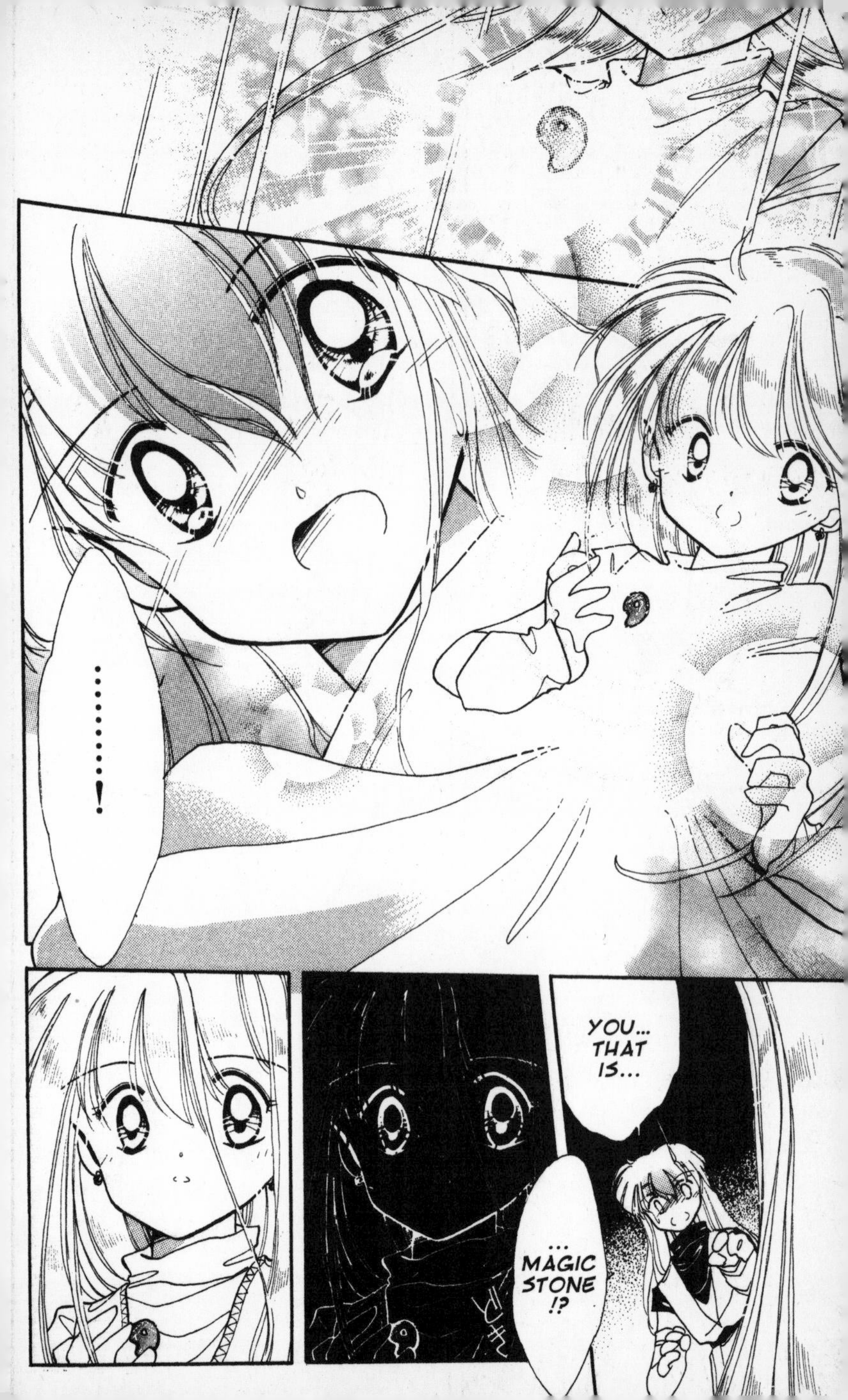
......!
YOU... THAT IS...
...MAGIC STONE !?

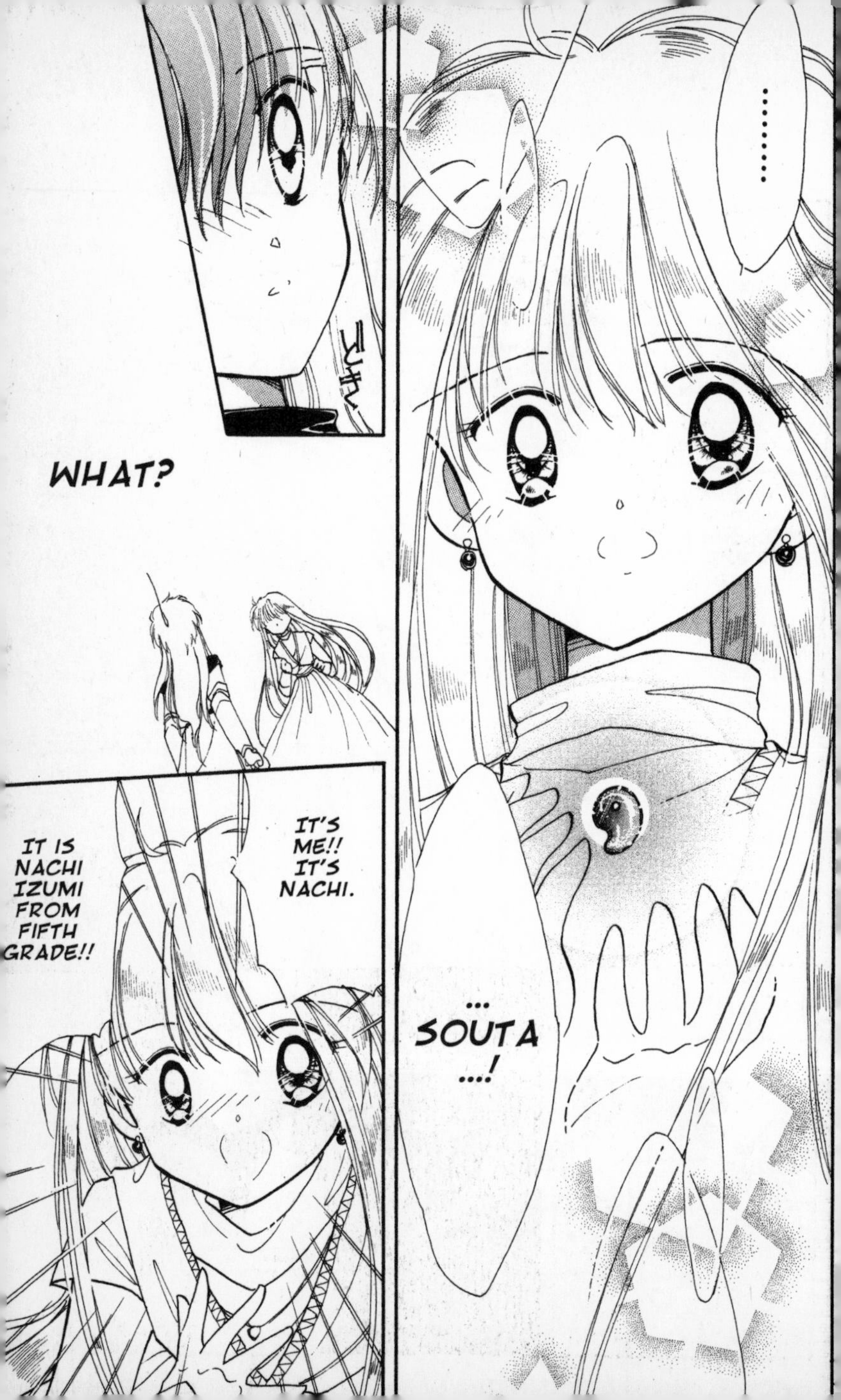
……
... SOUTA ...!
WHAT?
IT'S ME!! IT'S NACHI.
IT IS NACHI IZUMI FROM FIFTH GRADE!!

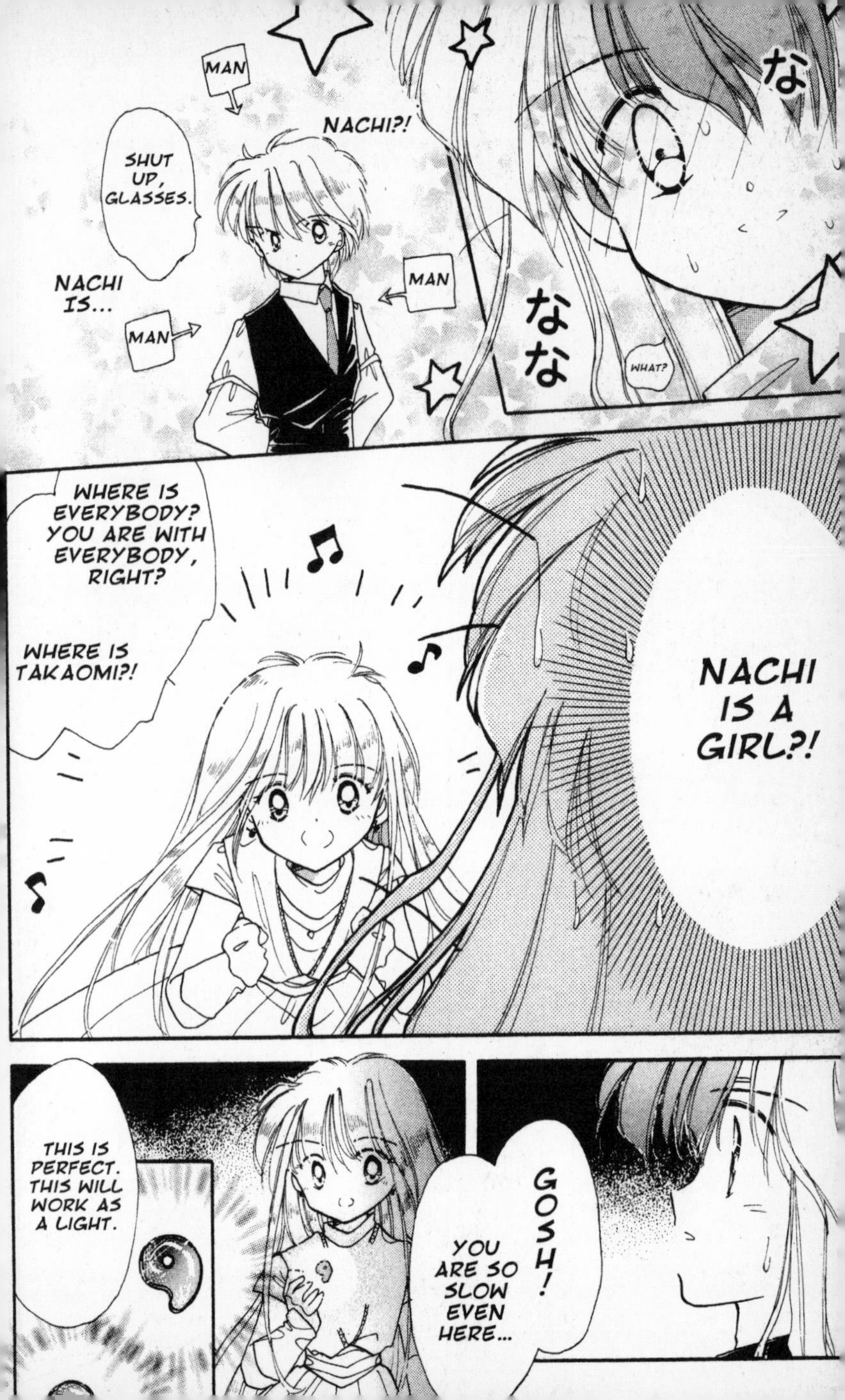
な
なな
WHAT?
NACHI?!
MAN
SHUT UP, GLASSES.
MAN
NACHI IS...
MAN
NACHI IS A GIRL?!
WHERE IS EVERYBODY? YOU ARE WITH EVERYBODY, RIGHT?
WHERE IS TAKAOMI?!
GOSH!
YOU ARE SO SLOW EVEN HERE...
THIS IS PERFECT. THIS WILL WORK AS A LIGHT.

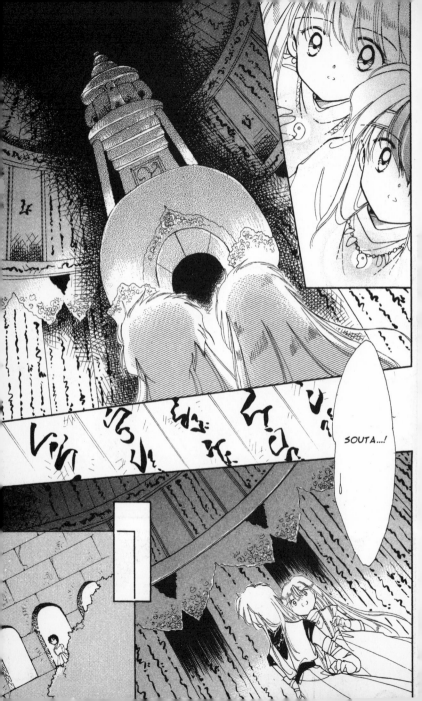

SOUTA...!

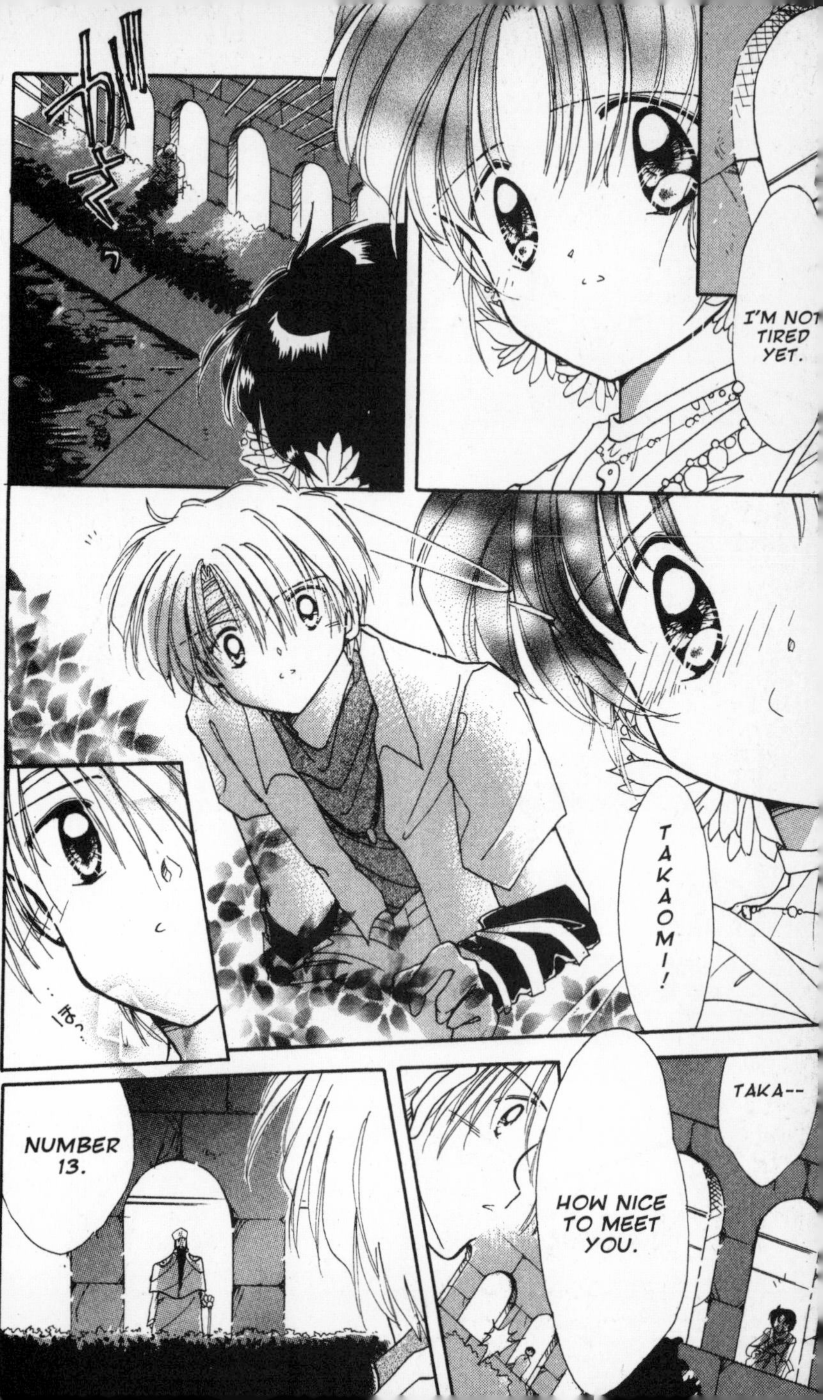
I'M NOT TIRED YET.
TAKAOMI!
ほっ…
TAKA--
HOW NICE TO MEET YOU.
NUMBER 13.

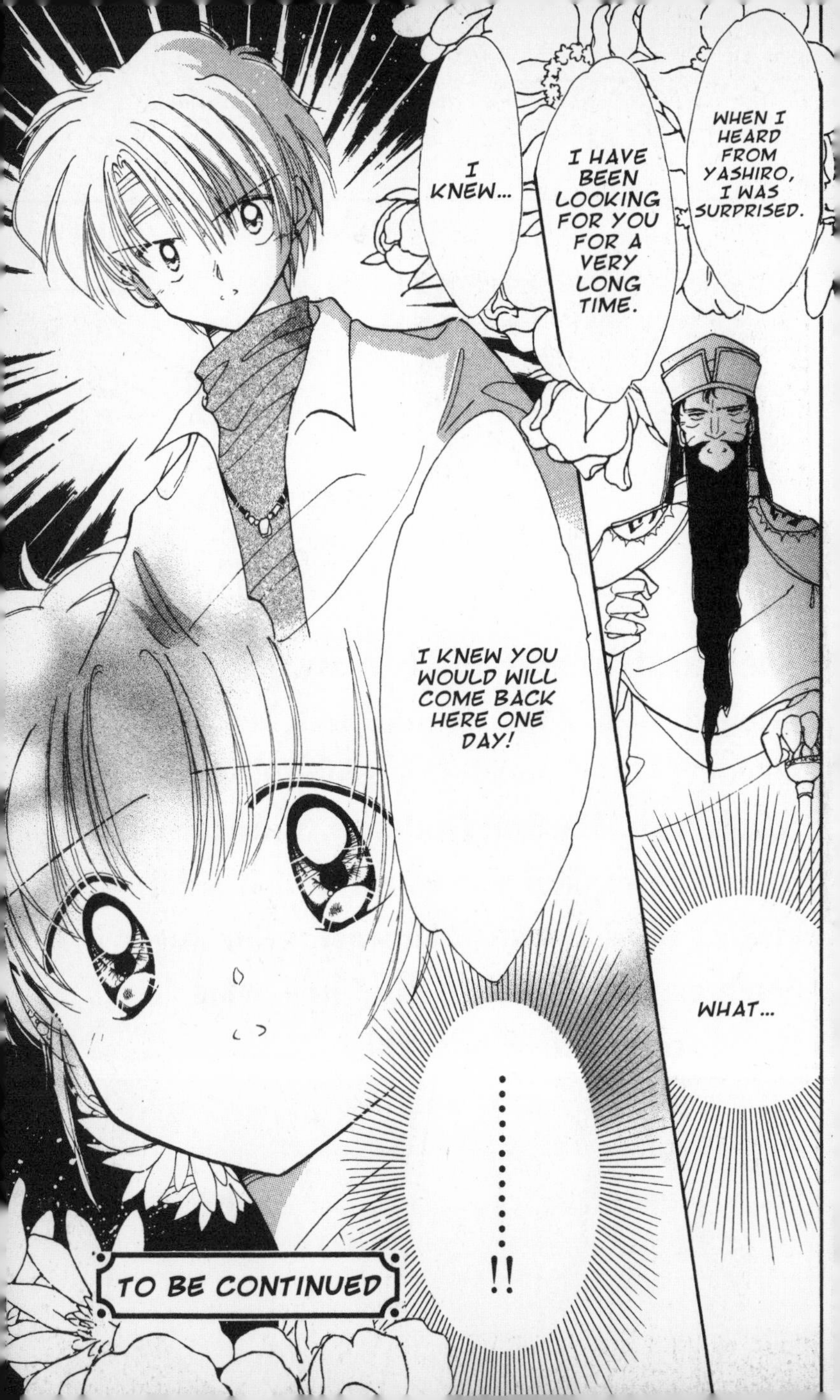
WHEN I HEARD FROM YASHIRO, I WAS SURPRISED.
I HAVE BEEN LOOKING FOR YOU FOR A VERY LONG TIME.
I KNEW...
I KNEW YOU WOULD WILL COME BACK HERE ONE DAY!
WHAT...
......!!
TO BE CONTINUED

In the next volume of

DREAM SAGA

The quest to save the two worlds turns into a tangled web when Yuuki and her companions discover they need the Shinoukyu to get to Amaterasu, the Sun Goddess. Soon they stumble upon the crystal-backworm--and it's throwing a hissing fit at Takaomi! However, this snake in the grass may turn out to hold just what they need to get to the Sun Goddess!

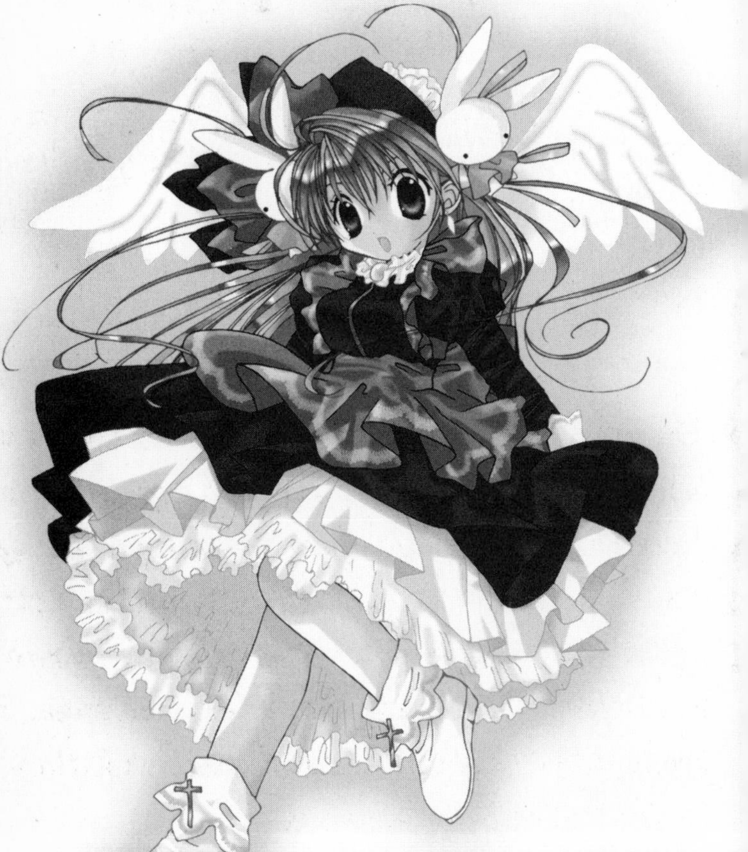

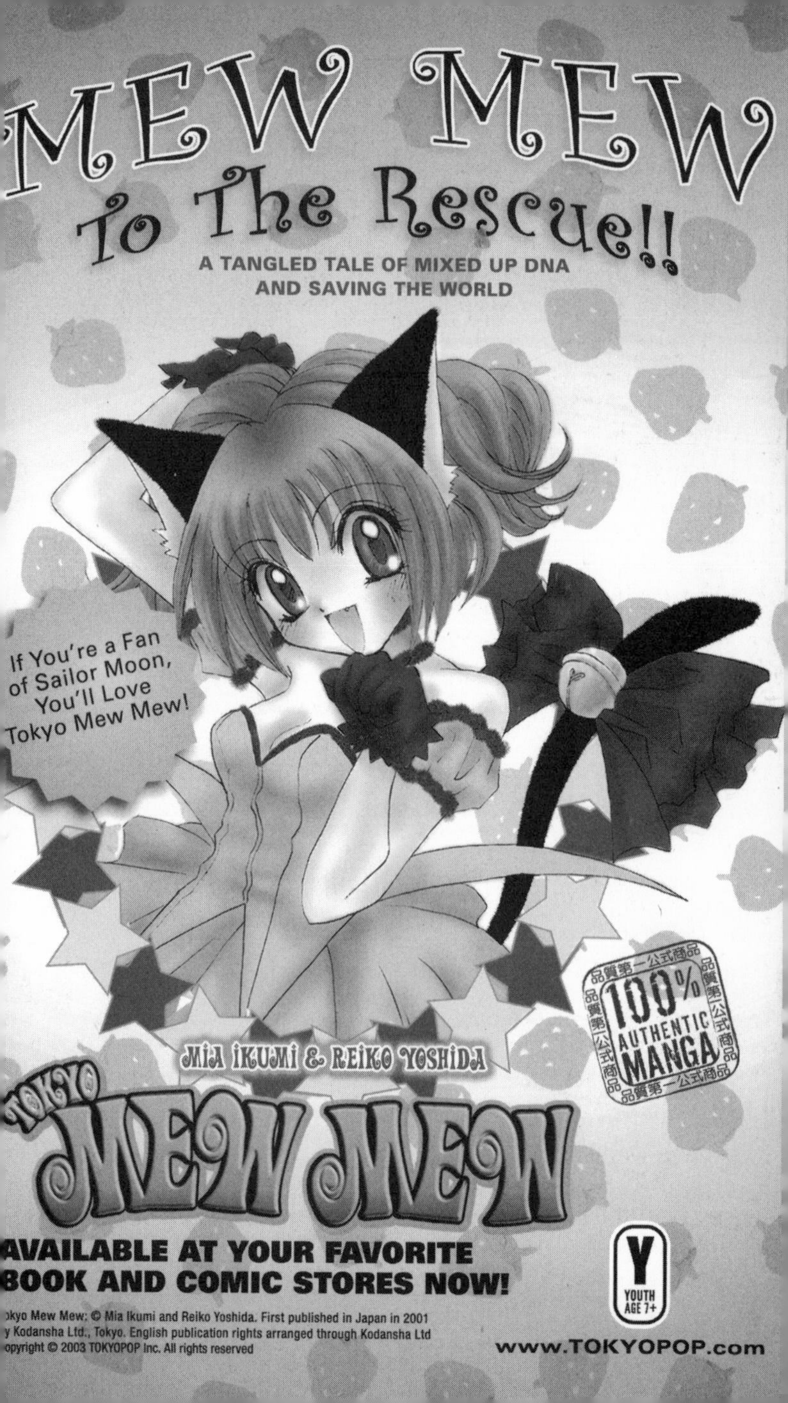
MEW MEW
To The Rescue!!
A TANGLED TALE OF MIXED UP DNA
AND SAVING THE WORLD
If You're a Fan of Sailor Moon, You'll Love Tokyo Mew Mew!
100% AUTHENTIC MANGA
品質第一公式商品
MIA IKUMI & REIKO YOSHIDA
TOKYO MEW MEW
AVAILABLE AT YOUR FAVORITE
BOOK AND COMIC STORES NOW!
Y
YOUTH
AGE 7+
okyo Mew Mew; © Mia Ikumi and Reiko Yoshida. First published in Japan in 2001
y Kodansha Ltd., Tokyo. English publication rights arranged through Kodansha Ltd
opyright © 2003 TOKYOPOP Inc. All rights reserved
www.TOKYOPOP.com

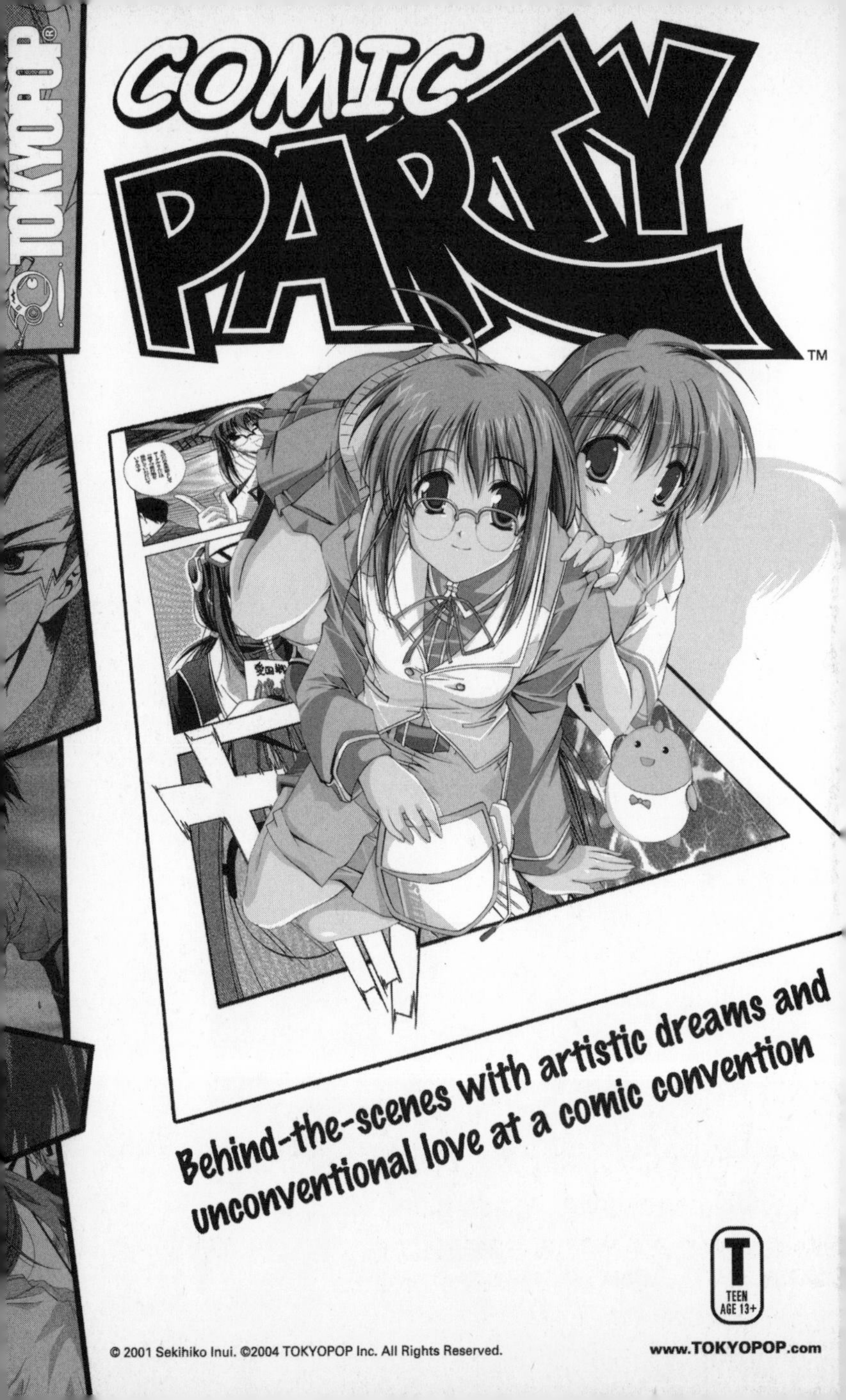
TOKYOPOP®
COMIC PARTY™
Behind-the-scenes with artistic dreams and unconventional love at a comic convention
T TEEN AGE 13+
© 2001 Sekihiko Inui. ©2004 TOKYOPOP Inc. All Rights Reserved.
www.TOKYOPOP.com

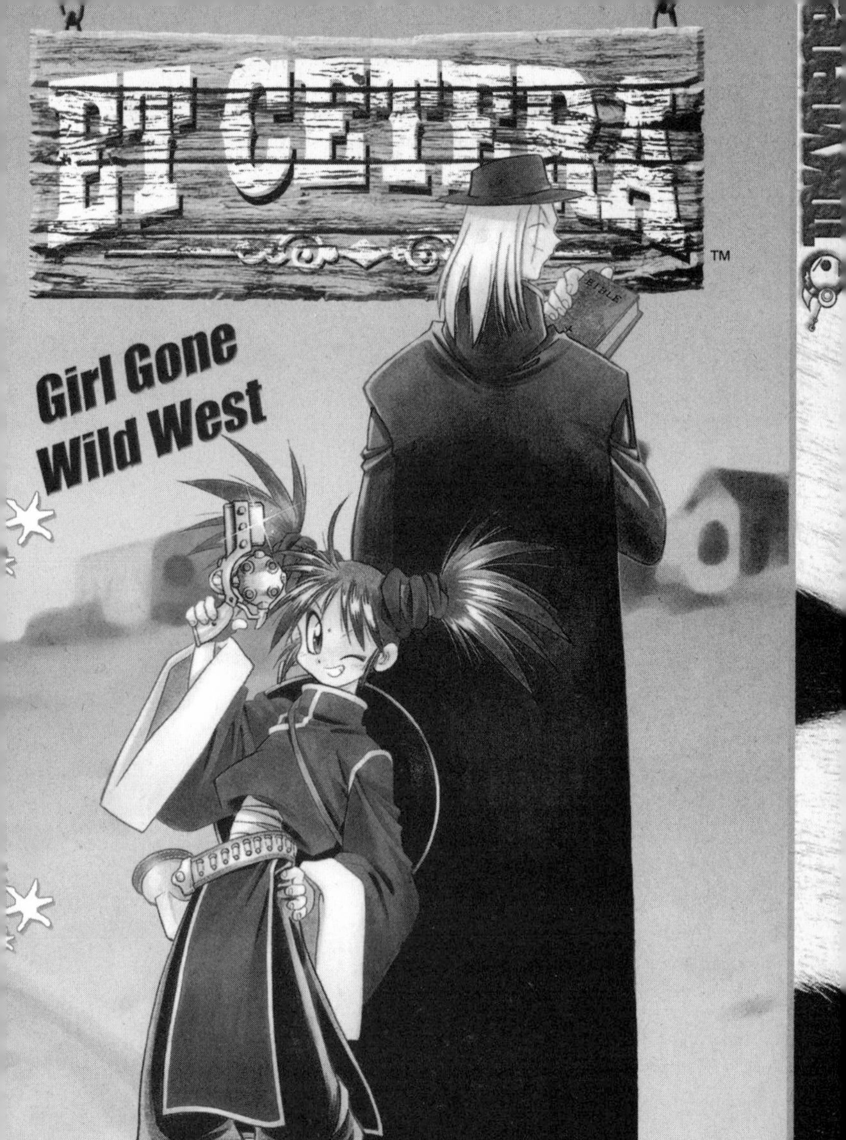
Girl Gone
Wild West
BIBLE
Y
YOUTH
AGE 10+

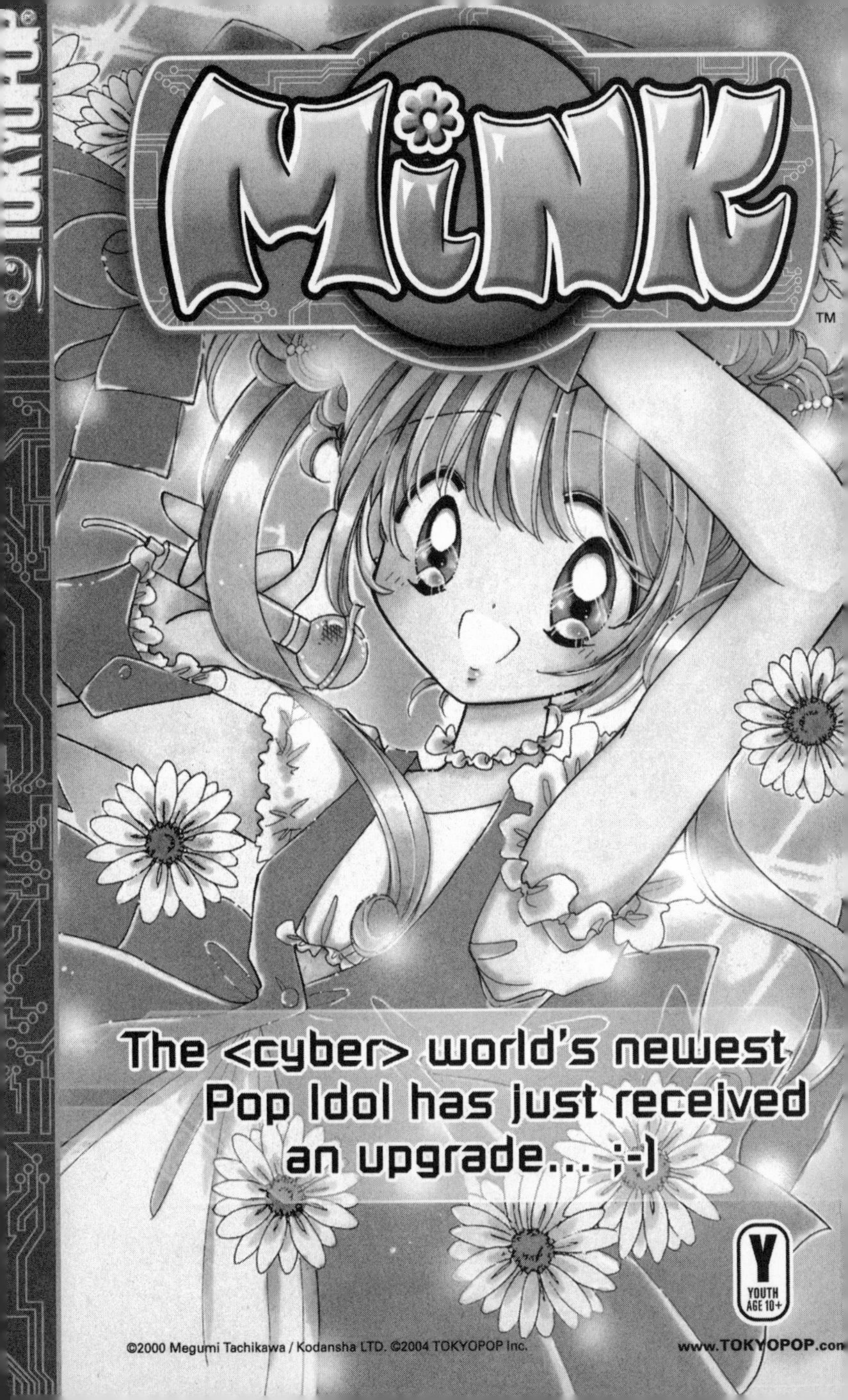
MINK™
The <cyber> world's newest Pop Idol has just received an upgrade... ;-)
Y
YOUTH AGE 10+
©2000 Megumi Tachikawa / Kodansha LTD. ©2004 TOKYOPOP Inc.
www.TOKYOPOP.com

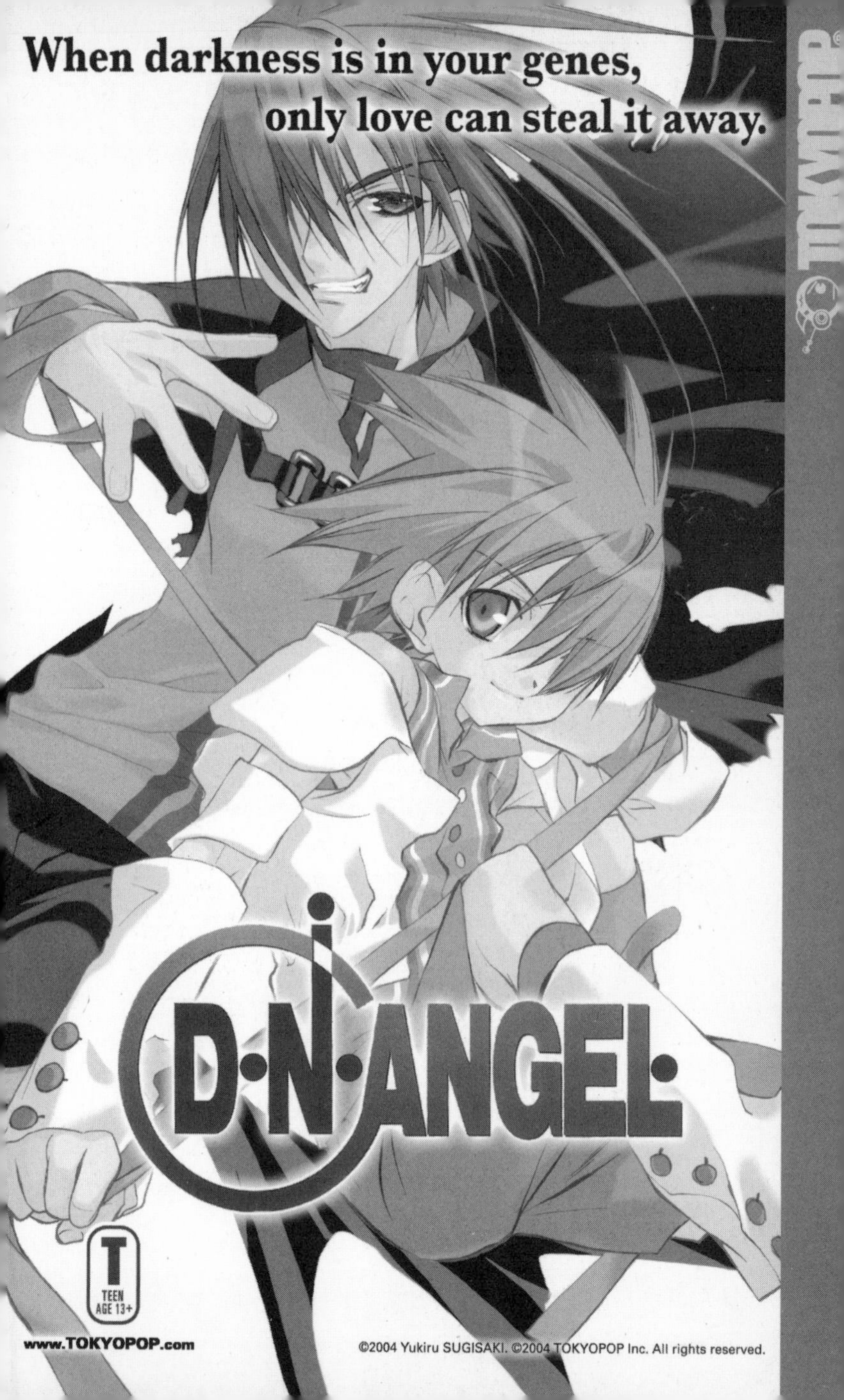
When darkness is in your genes,
only love can steal it away.
TOKYOPOP
D·N·ANGEL
T
TEEN
AGE 13+
www.TOKYOPOP.com
©2004 Yukiru SUGISAKI. ©2004 TOKYOPOP Inc. All rights reserved.

Fruits Basket

Life in the Sohma household can be a real zoo!

ALSO AVAILABLE FROM TOKYOPOP

STOP!

This is the back of the book.
You wouldn't want to spoil a great ending!

This book is printed "manga-style," in the authentic Japanese right-to-left format. Since none of the artwork has been flipped or altered, readers get to experience the story just as the creator intended. You've been asking for it, so TOKYOPOP® delivered: authentic, hot-off-the-press, and far more fun!

DIRECTIONS

If this is your first time reading manga-style, here's a quick guide to help you understand how it works.

It's easy... just start in the top right panel and follow the numbers. Have fun, and look for more 100% authentic manga from TOKYOPOP®!